Formulaic Language: Pushing the Boundaries

ALISON WRAY

OXFORD
UNIVERSITY PRESS

OXFORD
UNIVERSITY PRESS

Great Clarendon Street, Oxford OX2 6DP

Oxford University Press is a department of the University of Oxford.
It furthers the University's objective of excellence in research, scholarship,
and education by publishing worldwide in

Oxford New York

Auckland Cape Town Dar es Salaam Hong Kong Karachi
Kuala Lumpur Madrid Melbourne Mexico City Nairobi
New Delhi Shanghai Taipei Toronto

With offices in

Argentina Austria Brazil Chile Czech Republic France Greece
Guatemala Hungary Italy Japan Poland Portugal Singapore
South Korea Switzerland Thailand Turkey Ukraine Vietnam

OXFORD and OXFORD ENGLISH are registered trade marks of
Oxford University Press in the UK and in certain other countries

© Oxford University Press 2008

ISBN: 978 0 19 442245 1

Printed in China

Contents

Preface and Acknowledgments

My aim in the present book and my previous work has been to assemble specific evidence regarding the nature of formulaic language and to develop theoretical models that can explain it. Part of that endeavour entails evaluating the applicability of an explanation at the extremes of its range, and that is why this book is about boundaries. As the Introduction explains, it is not to be expected that all linguists agree with my conclusions, nor does it matter. What matters is that we continue to extend our exploration until, by degrees, we establish clearer boundaries between what is and is not formulaic.

The book has been in the planning for several years, during which I have talked to many people, engaged in huge amounts of email correspondence, read a lot of books and papers, and listened to a great many conference presentations. Some forums have been particularly valuable in inspiring new ideas, including the 2005 Phraseology conference in Louvain-la-Neuve, the 2007 Formulaic Language Symposium at Milwaukee, and the Cardiff meetings and international postgraduate conferences of the Formulaic Language Research Network. Even though I try to keep notes of conversations, useful quotes and so on, it is certainly possible that I have appropriated others' ideas without realizing it. If I have, I apologize, and trust it will be construed as flattery.

There are many people to thank for their various contributions. I have had inspiring and challenging conversations and/or email exchanges about formulaic language with, amongst others, Ben Bergen, Chris Butler, Georgie Columbus, Ding Yenren, Nick Ellis, Britt Erman, Charles and Lily Wong Fillmore, Tess Fitzpatrick, Lise Fontaine, George Grace, Jeff Holman, Martin Kayman, Kon Kuiper, Camilla Lindholm, Iain McGee, Eugène Mollet, Kazuhiko Namba, Christine Pegg, Ann Peters, Qi Yan, John Schumann, Mike Stubbs, Su Yanling, Paul Tench, Sam Tomblin, Gordon Tucker, Diana van Lancker Sidtis, Arie Verhagen, Ulrich Von Hecker, and Beatrice Warren.

Susan Hunston, Mike Stubbs, and Gordon Tucker read and commented on an early draft of Chapter 3, and Chris Butler, Tom Cobb, and Henry Widdowson provided extensive very helpful comments on the entire manuscript. The final version is much the better for the efforts of these contributors, though any or all of them may, I fear, still take exception to some of the things I say. Benedetta Bassetti, Irina Dahlmann, Sioned Davies, Boyd Davis, Seza Dogruoz, Monika Dóla, Nick Ellis, Tony Fairman, Fanny Forsberg, Pauline Foster, Sylvia Grant, James Hegarty, Jeffrey Holman, Ragnhild Knutsson, Kon Kuiper, Ian MacKenzie, Richard Ogden, Rebecca Shaftman, Norbert

Schmitt, and Alessandra Tanesini all came up with good ideas, sent me information, or answered questions on aspects of their work. With respect to trumpet and bugle calls, I have had much help from experts David Edwards, Major Richard Powell, Crispian Steele-Perkins, and Major Gordon Turner. Graham Rock kindly helped with the preparation of the musical figures. My limited understanding of motor sport flags was patiently augmented by track marshall and long-term Formula One fan, Peter Butcher.

Parts of the empirical research reported in this book were supported by research funds from the Arts and Humanities Research Board/Council, the Nuffield Foundation, and IELTS.

For permission to reproduce material I am grateful to various colleagues with whom I have co-researched and/or co-written: Janet Cowper, Stephen Cox, Tess Fitzpatrick, Kazuhiko Namba, and John Staczek. Thanks also to Mary Goebel Noguchi, Dawn French, Sue Hunter, Sarah Lloyd, Jon Plowman, and various publishers of material already in the public domain for helping me obtain permission to reproduce it. For support in the development of the idea for the book, and the preparation of the manuscript, my sincere thanks to Natasha Forrest, Julia Sallabank, Cristina Whitecross, Maggie Shade, and Henry Widdowson.

Finally, for putting up with me, even when it meant sitting indoors instead of walking outdoors, and for unstinting encouragement, support, and inspiration, huge thanks to Mike Wallace.

Copyright statement

PART ONE
Determining boundaries

1

Introduction

Boundaries

When we express ourselves using language, we encode our ideas and attitudes by combining units of form that are associated with meanings. A dominant view in linguistics has been that lexical units are small, and the combinatory rules quite complex. However, there is increasing evidence that some of the units are larger and contain within them tacit complexity that would otherwise be under the remit of the combinatory rules. These larger units still combine with others, but the overall amount of grammatical activity entailed in expressing a complete message is reduced, and some of it is potentially different in kind, compared with that entailed in expressing the same message using smaller units. Since the smaller units also exist, this account simply proposes a greater flexibility in how language is expressed and understood than was previously assumed. Very few, if any, of the explanatory advantages of the 'small unit' view are lost, while a number of powerful opportunities arise for explaining patterns observed in language, particularly the complete or relative absence of certain configurations that the small unit view predicts to be possible.

'Formulaic language'[1] is a term used by many researchers to refer to the large units of processing—that is, lexical units that are more than one word long. Although it will be demonstrated later that only certain theories can sustain a fundamental distinction between large and small lexical units, for now it will be adequate, and indeed clearer, to adhere to this preliminary characterization. Research into formulaic language has proliferated in recent years, particularly since computer technology has made it possible to search effectively for examples of recurring multiword strings in large corpora—though opinions differ as to the precise relationship between frequency and formulaicity.

Yet there remain mysteries at the heart of the phenomenon: What exactly *is* formulaic language? Why do we have it? How does it arise? How can it help with practical matters like learning another language or communicating when one has a language disorder? In my 2002 book, *Formulaic Language and the Lexicon* (Wray 2002b), I offered possible answers to these and other questions, by locating formulaic language within the larger frame of how we direct our limited language processing capacities towards formulating the messages needed to achieve certain important goals of social interaction. The key proposals developed in that book are recapped in Chapter 2 of this one, as the springboard for new issues that form the focus of the remaining chapters.

This book aims to discover more about the nature and extent of formulaic language by examining a broad range evidence and theory 'at the boundaries'. Furthermore, in the light of the claim that formulaic language is a linguistic solution to a non-linguistic problem—namely our need to promote and protect ourselves in relation to others (Wray 2002b: 101)—it explores ways in which a greater understanding of the scope of formulaic language might inform our engagement with practical challenges in relation to communication.

The unfolding book addresses inherent tensions regarding the identification, definition, and theoretical modelling of formulaicity. Although the Needs Only Analysis model that underpins this book is not truly falsifiable in the Popperian sense, the attempt is made, nevertheless, to examine the extent of its explanatory power by testing the boundaries of its scope. It is at the boundaries that the real test cases are to be found, and grappling with them provides both valuable insights into the robustness of one's existing beliefs, and ground rules for evaluating the place of formulaic language in common and unusual linguistic situations.

At the boundaries

How does one engage at the boundaries? The answer is that one must take risks about what one examines. If one does not, one is not really at the boundaries at all. One must anticipate that at least some of the material one examines is possibly not formulaic—the point is to explore where the borderline is best placed. As in my previous publications, particularly Wray (2002b), my approach in this book is to err on the side of including too much in the first instance, rather than too little, on the assumption that it is better to examine and discard something than to overlook it.

Thus, in this book, the notion of formulaicity is extended to a range of linguistic and non-linguistic phenomena that may, for some, seem too extreme to really be counted as formulaic. They are included because they fall within, or very close to, the boundaries of the theoretical model arising from my 2002b account. The material explored here therefore encompasses not only idioms and common multiword strings with a specific communicative purpose, but also deliberately memorized phrases, extensive oral narratives, performance scripts, and even visual signalling systems. They have in common that a communicative act is effected using one or more internally complex, predetermined units of form. As the various data-based discussions throughout the book will reveal, lengthy memorized texts are evidently internalized as series of smaller chunks, at the boundaries of which variations may occur (see particularly Chapter 20). We might argue the toss, in such cases, about what the formula is: the smaller chunk or the larger script. And that is precisely the point of the exercise—to use a range of evidence and reasoning to come closer to a robust account of the essence of formulaicity.

Formulaic language is investigated here by looking at what happens when language operates beyond its normal scope, where there are unusual constraints on communication that make formulaic language more evident, or where language users choose, or are forced, to favour previously assembled output over something more spontaneous. In many different ways, we are at the boundaries—of language behaviour, of communicative potential, and of linguistic theory—and aim to see what happens when you squeeze a phenomenon until (as we say formulaically) the pips squeak.

Five questions about formulaic language

The impetus of the book is the exploration of five key questions arising from published claims about formulaic language. Each question has one or more dedicated chapters in Part Four of the book, and answers are explored with reference to the theory and data presented in the first three parts.

The first question under consideration is: *Do we use formulaic language by default?* If we do, it means that we attempt first to work with pre-existing multiword forms, and only move to smaller ones if it becomes necessary—very much as Sinclair (1991) proposed with his 'idiom principle' and 'open choice' principle. To what extent are our assumptions about building up utterances using words and rules just a product of our cultural conditioning? Could Biggs' (1998) claim that the Māori language cannot be learnt other than by viewing the phrase as the base component be indicative of alternative ways of viewing what is 'normal'? The question is addressed in Chapter 16, and Chapter 17 develops the theme of a default state for language, by asking the second key question: *What determines the level of formulaicity in language?* The possible origins of the default are considered, along with the dynamics determining when the default is abandoned. The effect of different individuals having different default boundaries is also considered.

The third question, addressed in Chapter 18, is: *How central is formulaic language in natural language learning by humans?* For instance, is formulaic language learning a viable and effective option for adults? Chapter 19 extends the theme by asking the fourth question: *How central should formulaic language be when modelling such learning for computers?* It explores the potential for computers to learn language without having a full set of words and rules.

The fifth and final question is addressed in Chapters 20 and 21: *Does formulaic language constrain what we say and what we think?* The essayist and novelist George Orwell had strong views about the capacity for formulaic language to compromise human creativity: "ready-made phrases ... will construct your sentences for you—even think your thoughts for you ... and at need they will perform the important service of partially concealing your meaning even from yourself" (Orwell 1946: 135). To explore the constraining potential of formulaic language, Chapter 20 looks at what happens when there is a conflict between using formulaic language to achieve something otherwise unachievable, and the limitations of not having a full range of expression. Observations about the choices available during memorization are also explored. Chapter 21 continues the exploration of how formulaic language might constrain us by looking at attempts to use it for social control, before exploring some situations in which formulaicity—albeit not in language—is apparently unavoidable.

The structure of the book

As the above account will have made evident, the book is organized in four parts, providing the contextualization (Part One), theory (Part Two), and evidence (Part Three) necessary for the discussion of the five questions (Part Four). Since much of the evidence derives from the operation of formulaic language when the boundaries with novel expression are pushed to their limits, Part One is concerned with some key theoretical issues regarding the various means by which those boundaries are set and can be identified. Chapter 2 lays out the theoretical starting point, in the form of a summary of some of the main conclusions from my previous book, *Formulaic Language and the Lexicon* (Wray 2002b). There, a comprehensive critical assessment was undertaken, of a broad range of published research reporting various kinds of 'formulaic sequence'—the cover term used for phenomena referred to by many different names, but all evidently in some way potentially 'formulaic'. The review encompassed first and second language acquisition, native speaker discourse, and aphasia. Because the evidence is presented and discussed in such detail in Wray (2002b), the summary position laid out in Chapter 2 is not extensively argued or exemplified. The reader is referred back to Wray (2002b) for a full account of the reasons for arriving at the central claims with which we move forward in this book.

It goes without saying that by making strong initial claims about the nature of formulaic language, the rest of the book is coloured by that particular theoretical stance. Researchers who do not share all the assumptions and views will need to keep in mind the differences between their own model of what formulaic language is and the one used here, when evaluating the validity of the claims subsequently made.

Chapter 3 explores evidence of what happens when formulaicity and novel language are juxtaposed, and includes a commentary on recent claims regarding the processing of idioms. Chapters 4 and 5 then examine the manifestations of formulaic language at the complex boundary between oracy and literacy.

Part Two focuses on key theoretical and empirical issues. Chapter 6 lays out the opportunity for developing an integrated account for formulaic language that encompasses grammatical theory, corpus linguistics, and psycho-social theory. Then, in Chapter 7, selected models from each of these domains are evaluated for their capacity to contribute effectively across the domain boundaries.

Next, the thorny issue of identification is addressed (Chapters 8 and 9). In Wray (2002b) a whole chapter was dedicated to this question, and another to that of definition, but the focus was on the underlying rationale for different potential approaches, and an evaluation of the consequences of adopting them. Here, Chapter 8 engages with the more pragmatic question facing most researchers: What should I do about identification in my own investigation? To this end the advantages and disadvantages of different possible methods are discussed, anchored in an exploration of the options available for definition—for much of the disagreement in the research literature regarding how much formulaic language there is, and what roles it plays, is down to differences in what is included and excluded. Chapter 9 offers an alternative approach to identification that can be used to help justify intuitive judgements about formulaicity and track the uniformity of such judgements over the period of an analysis, and across different judges. Favouring this sort of methodology entails the belief that intuition does, and must, play a role in most approaches to the identification of formulaic language, and that it will often be better to accept that fact and apply some specific guiding criteria to support the approach, than to be so embarrassed about the dangers of subjectivity that the intuitive aspects of the endeavour are concealed and under-acknowledged.

Part Three is markedly different in form and purpose from the others. It presents short accounts of a series of empirical studies that were undertaken by the author, often with specialist collaborators, in order to explore and evaluate the claims made in Wray (2002b). Each study focused on one situation in which formulaicity played a role in communication, and in which that role was made more than usually evident by virtue of 'pushing the boundaries' of normal language use. Little theoretical discussion is offered in the accounts themselves, because Part Four goes on specifically to consider how the studies inform the five key questions listed above. Rather, Part Three can be viewed as a repository of brief factual descriptions of the features of each study, so that, in Part Four, it is not necessary to engage in lengthy digressions to fill in detail when discussing the emergent issues.

Chapter 10 reports how formulaic language was used in a machine translation device in the British Post Office. Chapter 11 looks at how software helps people with cerebral palsy hold conversations by storing turns prepared in advance. Chapters 12 and 13 outline studies of how language learners responded when challenged to memorize prefabricated sentences for later use. In Chapter 14 a court dispute is described: it centred on a formulaic dialect expression that was interpreted literally, turning it into a racial slur.

Chapter 15 examines how, in a television comedy sketch, the impression of naturalness was affected by the fidelity with which the actors adhered to the original script.

Part Four returns to the five questions outlined above, drawing on the contextualization and theory from Parts One and Two, the studies reported in Part Three, and also other lines of evidence, including Harry Potter's spells, flag signals and military bugle calls, language teaching in Papua New Guinea, Aviation English, communication in pre-modern man, cryptic crosswords, actors' attitudes to their script, and the Cultural Revolution in China.

Finally, Chapter 22 reviews the results of 'pushing the boundaries', before demonstrating how an understanding of how formulaic language operates can result in practical applications. The chapter ends with some ideas for future research projects on formulaic language.

Notes

1 'Formulaic language' will be used as the neutral mass (uncountable) noun, while 'formula' is used as the neutral count noun (with the plural 'formulas', other than in quotations where 'formulae' occurs in the original). A new term, 'morpheme equivalent unit' (MEU), is introduced in Chapter 2. It is theory-sensitive, and used to refer to the items in the lexicon of an individual speaker or hearer. 'Formulaic sequence', a term introduced in my earlier work (Wray 1999, 2002b; Wray and Perkins 2000), has a specific definition (see Chapter 8) and is used in that sense only. In practice this means it is used to refer to items observed in text that are inferred to be MEUs for (usually) large groups of individuals in a speech community. Detailed discussion of definitions is provided in Chapter 8.

2
Conceptualizing formulaic language

Introduction

This chapter sets the scene for the exploration of the boundaries of formulaic language. Since boundaries are defined relative to a central ground, the main task is to lay out that ground. First, some observations about the nature of formulaicity are offered, as a means of introducing illustrative examples and demonstrating some of the typical linguistic features associated with it. Next, a theoretically-grounded definition of formulaicity is given. This definition reflects the conclusions drawn from the lengthy evaluation of evidence for various types of formulaic language undertaken in Wray (2002b).

Third, three key conceptual claims about the nature of formulaic language are presented. Each conceptual claim captures a different aspect of the theory developed in Wray (2002b).[1] Inevitably one cannot, in a brief digest, re-present all the arguments and considerations that led to those conclusions, and the interested reader is urged to follow up on the references provided, to see why a particular view was taken. The first claim is that *the mental lexicon is heteromorphic*. This is an observation about how we process formulaic language. The second is that *the content of the lexicon is determined through 'Needs Only Analysis'*, and it relates to how we learn formulaic language. The third claim, that *morpheme equivalent units enable the speaker to manipulate the hearer*, addresses the question of what we use formulaic language for.

Orientation: what is formulaic language?

While most linguists accept that there is such a thing as formulaic language, consensus about what it is exactly is severely limited. Underpinning the notion of formulaic language is the sense that certain words have an especially strong relationship with each other in creating their meaning—usually because only that particular combination, and not synonyms, can be used. For example, if something is beyond consideration we might say it is 'out of the question' but we cannot rephrase the description as '*external to the query'. Theories differ considerably regarding what it means that some words have a particular bond with others. Some accounts, including the one in this book, envision the string of words to have its own separate identity as an entry in the mental lexicon. Others focus on how we might create 'rat runs' in our processing, so that certain formulations are quicker and easier to produce than others with the same meaning. Others still are interested in identifying rules and constraints on them that will generate the formulaic expression. These different theories draw the line between what is formulaic and what is not formulaic in different places.

At the uncontentious end are what are often termed the 'true' idioms—a set of not all that frequent but particularly evocative multiword strings that express an idea metaphorically, such as 'kick the bucket', 'red herring', and 'raining cats and dogs'. It is rare for a theory of language not to give such expressions a special status that pairs the wordstring with a holistic meaning, though even here attempts can be made to see whether parts of the meaning can be mapped onto parts of the form (see 'What goes into the lexicon', below). At the highly contentious other end are collocational associations such as, in academic prose, 'fully developed' and 'highly complex' (Biber, Johansson, Leech, and Conrad 1999: 565). Here, it is not that people doubt that the attraction between the words is particularly strong, but that theories differ as to how one best accounts for that attraction.

Between the two extremes come other types, including expressions that seem entirely detached from normal meanings and/or do not reflect the normal rules of grammar, for example, 'by and large', 'come a cropper'; expressions that are metaphorical but, arguably, are less distant from the literal meaning than idioms, such as 'set one's store by', 'take stock', 'watch one's back', 'take it's/their toll'; expressions in which one or more words have a peculiar meaning, such as 'do someone in'; a wide set of idiomatic turns of phrase, such as 'do let's v'; 'you'd better v'; 'not very well' (in the sense of 'ill'); and—central to some theoretical models but excluded from others—'partly-fixed frames' or 'constructions', complete phrases or clauses partly realized with specific lexical material and partly left open for interchangeable items, for example, 'the end of the N'; 'as a result of NP'; 'the way in which CLAUSE'. These frames are often viewed as carrying their own meaning and pragmatics.

Interacting with the models of language patterning and use are certain assumptions about the 'word' as the fundamental building block of language—the implications of this view are explored in Chapter 5. Seeing the single word as a consistent unit of language, and thus viewing a two-word string as two units joined by a grammatical rule, gives a special status to what, in some cases, is a rather arbitrary result of historical practices. Why, for instance, is 'out of' two units when 'into' is one? Some words, including 'into' and also 'although' and 'cupboard', evidently used to be two words, and it is easy, in retrospect, to imagine that they probably had some properties associated with a single word before they actually became united into one in writing. But unless a pair of words is being written in different ways, a sign of transition (for example, 'in(-)depth', 'what's( )more', 'as( )well', and 'a( ) lot', see Wray 1996), it will obviously be difficult to tell whether any given string of two or more separate words does have the properties associated with formulaicity or not (see Chapter 8).

While some accounts of formulaic language conservatively only attribute formulaicity to material that already displays the tell-tale signs of it—written as a single word or at least hyphenated, pronounced differently as a whole than as a sequence of component parts, or having a meaning that cannot be easily derived from those parts—other models, including the one used in this book, propose that items become formulaic first, and only later begin to develop the tell-tale signs. The implications of this orientation are immense both for the claims one might make about how much of our language is formulaic, and for how we might identify it—for there could be a huge quantity of formulaic material that does not carry any outward sign of being so. Indeed, any string of words might turn out to be formulaic, and it might take a century or more for that fact to become fully evident.

The situation is exacerbated by the need to distinguish between something that is formulaic 'in the language', so to speak, and something that is formulaic for just a particular individual or group; and also to distinguish between what is formulaic for a given speaker and for a given hearer. The notion that the language itself contains formulaic material is inevitable in corpus-driven accounts, where one examines large quantities of text without particular attention to who produced it, and looks for recurrences. If one finds more than a certain number of instances of a particular sequence of words, it is possible to attribute that pattern to 'the language'.

However, within a psycholinguistically driven account there is less value in attributing formulaicity to strings in 'the language', for formulaicity is viewed as the property of a particular string as it is handled by a particular individual. What is formulaic for one person need not be formulaic for another—the reason will become clear as the three claims are discussed below. So a given speaker might produce a word string formulaically, only to have it treated as non-formulaic by the hearer. On the other hand, even an account based on the individual's knowledge will recognize that many word strings are likely to be formulaic for most native speakers—that is what it means to know the same language.

Definition: the morpheme equivalent unit

As the short account above indicates, it is not really possible to say what formulaic language is without adopting a theoretical position of some sort. Yet any theoretical position sidelines others, making it difficult to relate different people's accounts, unless everyone is explicit about what they mean. The solution adopted here is to coin a new term and provide a clear and specific definition for it. The term used will be 'morpheme equivalent unit' (MEU), the definition of which is imbued with the particular theoretical stance laid out in the rest of this chapter. The MEU is defined as:

> a word or word string, whether incomplete or including gaps for inserted variable items, that is processed like a morpheme, that is, without recourse to any form-meaning matching of any sub-parts it may have.

The definition reflects specific claims about the nature and, by implication, provenance of formulaic material in a language—the claims that are presented in the next sections. It is not, therefore, the kind of definition that can really be used to go out and identify examples of formulaic language in real texts, or to find examples suitable for experimental investigations. The relationship between the MEU definition and that of another term used in this book, the 'formulaic sequence' (Wray 2002b: 9), is explored more fully in Chapter 8. A working definition of the terms, sufficient to apply in these earlier chapters, is given in a note in Chapter 1.

Three key conceptual claims about morpheme equivalent units

As noted above, the three key claims presented here summarize features of the model developed in Wray (2002b). It is this model that will provide the context for the interpretations of evidence in the remainder of the book.

The mental lexicon is heteromorphic

The theoretical position taken in this book, on the basis of evidence from multiple sources reviewed extensively in Wray (2002b), is that linguistic material is stored in bundles of different sizes (compare Jackendoff 2002: chapter 6). That is, the mental lexicon contains not only morphemes and words but also many multiword strings, including some that are partly lexicalized frames with slots for variable material, treated as if they were single morphemes—they are MEUs (see definition above).

Not all strings of words, of course, are prefabricated. As linguistic theory has long recognized, what makes human language special is the huge potential it has for novel expression.[2] This potential is only realized because we can both create and understand formulations that we have not encountered before—formulations that, therefore, cannot have been stored in memory in a fully lexicalized form.[3]

What goes into the lexicon

Because not everything can be stored in the lexicon, any model of how language is composed and understood needs to define criteria to determine which items will have their own entry. Separate consideration must be given to what characterizes a lexically stored word string (for example, regarding its meaning, function, form, and so on) and this matter is extensively discussed in

Wray (2002b: chapter 3). The focal issue here is the impact on the philosophy informing a theoretical model, when notice is taken of psychological processes and sociointeractional preferences as well as the basic patterns and the principles underlying them (see Chapter 6). For some theories it is important that one or another feature of the linguistic system be streamlined (i.e. pared of any unnecessary elements). The desirability of streamlining the system is partly a question of explanatory elegance, and partly, perhaps, a product of implicit or explicit assumptions about the constraints under which human language processing operates. For instance, perhaps there are restrictions on how much lexical information we can remember, though, in fact, there is no evidence of this. Other theorists prefer to keep the 'rule system' simple, even at the expense of a streamlined lexicon. That is the position adopted here.

Before the non-streamlined lexical model is explored, it will be helpful to review the main characteristics of the streamlined one. The more that lexical storage is streamlined, the more atomic the lexicon will become. That is, the way to minimize the size of the lexicon is to exclude any items that can be constructed by rule from smaller units. An atomic lexicon will be "like a prison, contain[ing] only the lawless" (Di Sciullo and Williams 1987: 3)—there will be no items in the lexicon that are reducible to smaller semantic units in a somewhat regular way (see Wray 2002b: 265–74 for discussion). An atomic lexicon will still need to admit a few multiword strings, but only those that cannot be generated from smaller parts without a specific rule that has no wider applicability. Examples might include 'by and large', 'very well' (in the sense of 'yes'), 'to boot' (in the sense of 'also'), 'no more' (in the sense of 'dead'), 'at long last' and 'as well', along with—at least for an English speaker with no knowledge of other languages—borrowed expressions such as 'laissez faire' and 'je ne sais quoi'. On the other hand, many word strings could be excluded from an atomic lexicon, even though they carry hallmarks of formulaicity, for example, 'perfect stranger' and 'pack it in' (in the sense of 'stop'). Although these items are non-literal in meaning they are regular in form, and so they can, according to such models, be generated using secondary meanings of the component words, or by employing second-order pragmatic mapping to give a holistic meaning to the composed form. Similarly, word strings with an unusual grammatical pattern, for example, 'believe you me', might be viewed as generated (using a specific rule) rather than holistically stored, because of the transparency of their meaning. Finally, frames containing a gap, for example, 'what say we VERB?' (meaning 'why don't we VERB?'), would be viewed as generated because they admit a potentially very wide range of completions.[4]

The view taken in this book is different, however. It aligns with models that do not require the lexicon to be streamlined (or that do not conceptualize an independent lexicon at all) and that are therefore not constrained to view only irreducible items as core lexis. The inventory of lexical units known by an individual will not only be larger than in an atomic lexicon model, but will also feature some measure of repetition, as words occur both independently and within larger strings. In some models, the motivation for opening up the lexicon to internally complex items is to enable the rule system to be less complex: many rules that affect only a few unusual cases do not need to appear in the grammar if each individual case, or a common lexicalized (or indeed entirely unlexicalized) frame that represents their shared structure is stored as a lexical unit.[5]

Taken to its logical extreme, the more there is stored in the lexicon, the fewer and simpler the rules can be, until, in the end, one would not need any rules at all other than 'find the ready-made expression'. As already noted, this sort of look-up model of language is implausible because of our capacity to generate and understand material we have not encountered before. Yet the plausibility of models at the other extreme, with a lexicon of atomic items and complicated rules, can also be questioned on at least two fronts. Computational linguists have found it remarkably difficult to write rules that can generate all and only the sentences that are grammatical in a language (see Chapter 19), suggesting that either the human mind is very clever indeed, or this approach does not characterize language appropriately. Meanwhile, corpus linguists have shown that the gulf between what grammatical rules predict we might say and what we actually do say is not only large, but rather more principled than was first thought. Although, of course, the remits of different linguistic theories vary, so that they are not necessarily failing when they do not account for a particular aspect of language structure or behaviour, there is scope to speculate about the extent to which a single comprehensive model of language (see Chapter 6) might simultaneously capture what we *could* do, what our intuition defines as *acceptable* (in both grammatical and interactional terms), what we actually do do, as part of a broader account of linguistic competence (Hymes 1972, 1992).

In order to avoid both the extreme positions—that language has no rules and that it has no large units—one might conceptualize a continuum of unit types in the lexicon, ranging from atomic items (i.e. morphemes) to the explicit storage of entire sentences or longer texts. Individual exemplars could be located on that continuum according to their form, meaning, and usage, so as to strike the perfect balance between the human's capacity for creativity with so many structures of language, and an accurate prediction of certain forms that we produce and understand easily.

However, the position taken in this book is that a continuum model is inadequate to account for both creative flexibility and the idiomaticity arising from preferred ways of saying things. That is, it will not be possible to take a particular item or pattern in the language and make a single judgement about whether it should be viewed as generated or stored. Rather, there must be much more fluidity in the model, enabling the same linguistic material to be differently processed at different times. As Langlotz (2006) demonstrates, even idioms—often viewed as the most reliable instance of formulaicity—are subject to systematic semantic and grammatical variation that belies a simple status as invariable lexical units. A convincing account of how idioms can simultaneously be formulaic and open to novelty requires flexibility in relation to how linguistic material is stored and processed (see the discussion of idioms in Chapter 3).

The heteromorphic lexicon model (Wray 2002b) permits multiple part-mappings of the same information in the lexicon. Alongside an entire phrase that is stored whole with its associated meaning and phonological form, subparts (both internally complex in their own right and atomic) may also be stored. Not all possible subcomponents are necessarily so stored, nor are subcomponents necessarily recognizable grammatical constituents, though they may be. The determination of which components are separately stored and, thus, how much flexibility there is for varying the form of the complete string, depends on input evidence and user need (see later section on Needs Only Analysis).

What 'being in the lexicon' means

Different theories characterize the 'lexicon' differently, partly as a function of the level of abstraction at which the theory operates. Traditionally, psycholinguistic models present the lexicon as a 'box' of words in the brain, and although this is essentially a device for conceptualization, the longstanding knowledge that damage to certain areas of the left hemisphere results in disruption to lexical access has underpinned the notion that there are particular areas responsible for storage and others for grammatical configuration. Discussion continues into whether MEUs are stored in and accessed via the left hemisphere, the right hemisphere, or some other brain region (for example, Van Lancker Sidtis and Postman 2006; Wray 2008a).

Meanwhile, in some other theoretical approaches, it does not make any sense to conceptualize a 'store of words' at all. For instance, in Connectionist models, language processing is represented as mimicking neuron activations along synaptic pathways (Onnis, Christiansen, and Chater 2006) that could transcend any local area of storage. Such models considerably narrow the gap between the theoretical representation and the practicalities of computational linguistics, and in some respects they might be viewed as superior to more simplistic and abstracted flow-diagram representations (ibid.: 408). However, there is not such a huge chasm as might at first seem, between neurologically or computationally inspired models and those that represent knowledge in terms of boxes or modules. Modelling language processing always entails some kind of abstraction of an essence of the activity, if it is to be represented in an effective and comprehensible way. A theory that is focused on the sequence of activations will cut the cake in a different way from a theory that is focused on the functions of different stages. Theories in which formulaic word strings are generated in real time under privileged conditions, such as via an automated (proceduralized) route, are in fact not necessarily all that different from those proposing that they are holistically stored and retrieved. All theories must acknowledge that language is generated on line, in the sense that one begins with a thought and transposes that, in real time, into spoken (or written)[6] output. Where the theories can differ is in the steps they identify within that process.

Morpheme equivalent units that are not fully-fixed

As indicated above, the highly efficient and effective integration of formulaicity and novelty during processing may rely on many—indeed most—MEUs being stored not in a fully-fixed form, but as partly-fixed frames. Frames have some fixed lexical material along with slots that permit variation for other material. For example, the frame underlying 'The elephant was as big as big can be' can be represented as 'NP be-TENSE as ADJ$_i$ as ADJ$_i$ can be'. Completing frames requires insertion rules. By inserting different material into the variable slots, numerous versions can be generated with the same pattern, for example, 'A flea is as small as small can be'; 'That tortoise will be as slow as slow can be'.

Some slots permit only a restricted choice of items, while others are very open. There appears to be a continuum of permitted variation, which linguists are only just beginning to identify and characterize. What is 'permitted' is a subset of what is semantically and grammatically possible, and filling a slot in a frame with an item that is not 'permitted' does not necessarily make it either ungrammatical (in the narrow sense of not adhering to formal rules) or nonsensical, just unidiomatic. 'Idiomaticity', in this sense, is a slippery concept, because what is considered 'permissible' depends on the perceptions of speaker and hearer. What is judged unidiomatic from the mouth of a non-native speaker might well be considered witty and inventive from a native speaker. Proficient non-native speakers often complain that when they make jokes that play on words, they are told that they have made a mistake, rather than being applauded for their inventiveness.

The distribution of fixed formulaic sequences and frames in a language is not random. A striking proportion of completely fixed forms take an adverbial role in the grammar, for example, 'as luck would have it'.[7] Sequences that are themselves fairly fixed but are incomplete without additional variable material before and after, tend to form part of a nominal or prepositional group (Butler 1998b: 27). Butler cites London-Lund corpus examples like 'at the end of the'; 'it seems to me that'; and 'and that sort of thing' (p. 25), along with Spanish examples from his own studies, like 'la verdad es que' and 'a la hora de' (ibid.). Most formulaic sequences that fill a verb or verb phrase slot are partly-fixed frames, because the verb component within them must have access to its normal morphological variations, for example, 'get/got/getting cold feet'. Since the verb form is dependent on the subject, the subject slot must also be open, so that the frame for this example is best represented as 'NP get-TENSE cold feet'.

The content of the lexicon is determined through Needs Only Analysis

This is the second of the three claims from Wray (2002b) that are used as the basis of the research reported in this book. Building on an idea from Peters (1983), it is proposed that, within first language acquisition (which continues through an individual's life), a major strategy for learning from input, and indeed the one that operates by default, is Needs Only Analysis (NOA):

> The process of analysis which the [native speaker] child engages in [is] not that of breaking down as much linguistic material as possible into its smallest components. Rather, nothing [is] broken down unless there [is] a specific reason.
> (Wray 2002b: 130)

The conditions under which input remains un(der)analysed are, firstly, that the package of material can be assigned a meaning or function as it stands, and, secondly, there is no evidence of paradigmatic variation within the package. For example, when a native speaker learns the expression 'how do you do?', it can be mapped as a whole onto the meaning/function 'what adults say in the formal situation of meeting someone for the first time, while shaking their hand'. The holistic storage is possible because there is a strong mapping of form to meaning/function, and no examples are encountered of variation in the form directly associated with variation in that meaning/function—there is no 'how does he do?' or 'how don't you do?'. While one may encounter forms that seem to be in paradigm, for example, 'what do you do?' and 'how did you do?', the difference in form cannot be anchored to the difference in meaning, so these expressions are dealt with separately; this arises from letting meaning rather than form drive the process.

In the case of more ordinary language, paradigms of variation will be observed over time, and, in line with Peters (1983), the NOA model proposes that input is checked against existing lexical units, and where variation is identified, some analysis may follow. As an example, consider the case where a child hears 'have you seen daddy's coat?', 'have you seen daddy's phone?', and 'have you seen daddy's other sock?'. The locus of the variation is noted, and segmentation occurs there, but not elsewhere (yet). As a result, the child extrapolates a set of lexical units: (1) 'have you seen daddy's_____ ?', (2) 'phone', (3) 'coat', (4) 'other sock'. The first of these items contains a slot, into which any one of the others can be inserted. The slot represents a level of abstraction that captures all observed variations. The slot will invite at first only limited variation—namely, the items so far observed in it—but gradually may become generalized to permit any similarly behaving item (i.e. the subtype of noun that refers to visible objects), if subsequent observations support that conclusion.

Subsequent input might lead to a further segmentation, whereby 'daddy's' falls into paradigm with 'my', for instance. Ultimately, with such examples, we can assume that the child would develop a flexible representation that permitted a great deal of variability. However, this conservative approach prevents full analysis occurring as the default. Rather, the extent of the analysis is determined by the input evidence, and the conservative extrapolations from it. Evidence from corpus linguistics research clearly shows that collocations are semantically highly sensitive,[8] often in ways that standard constituent analysis cannot capture (see Chapter 7).

The impetus for NOA can be conceptualized in terms of minimizing the speaker's and/or hearer's processing, in that it is preferable to engage in as few operations as possible to express or interpret a message. Fewer operations are required to select a partly-fixed unit and apply one or more lexical insertion rules,[9] than to select individual morphemes and words and assemble them using rules. Corroboration for this view comes from the fact that native speakers overwhelmingly prefer to formulate messages according to patterns that are already common and idiomatic in the language, even though they undoubtedly possess the capability of expressing the same idea in many other ways as well. Another way to conceptualize the motivation for NOA is in terms of the social pressure to speak like others, something that can be achieved by adopting the multiword patterns already in use in the speech community. Wray (2002b) proposes that these two accounts of why NOA prevails are complementary.

In NOA, where no variation is observed, components of a word string will remain united even though a grammatical theory based on constituent structure can identify an opportunity for splitting them. In other words, the constraint on ultimately ending up with full analysis of all multiword strings is that many theoretically possible axes of variation are simply never encountered. The result is that the lexicon will continue to contain multiword strings that could, in principle, be broken down into smaller units, but have not been, because there has never been any need to do so. Add to this the conservatism, mentioned earlier, about drawing general conclusions from limited variation, and the native speaker's knowledge of the language will not only feature lexical units of different sizes, including many partly-fixed frames, but also a huge sensitivity to which items can be put into those frames. This sensitivity may be based on frequency principles, semantic ones, or both. The effect will be that not only fully-fixed but also partly-fixed frames with particular completions will be privileged as idiomatic. That is, sensitivity to idiomaticity is a feature of nativelike knowledge that is largely independent of grammatical knowledge, in that the idiomatic material is a subset of the configurations that the grammar permits or has, in the past, permitted (if we assume MEUs that are now ungrammatical to be the vestiges of previously grammatically regular forms).

Since NOA is not a constraint on analysis, just a determiner of when it occurs, there is never a danger of new configurations not being understood or composed as required. A fundamental feature of the NOA account is that it accommodates the potential for an individual to develop a new insight about how the language works at any time, in response to need. That is, flexibility accretes, in response to input evidence and what the individual wants to say, something which comfortably handles the kind of variation observed in idioms by, for instance, Langlotz (2006).

By moulding language on this basis, native speakers will know what they need to know in order to function within their linguistic environment, while retaining the capacity to cope with novelty as and when it arises. It follows that the language knowledge of different individuals could be vastly different according to the input they are exposed to and the messages they need to express—with the common language of the speech community simply the coincidence of knowledge across individuals, or, indeed, the apparent coincidence, since there might be little evidence in practice of differences in the precise configurations of knowledge between individuals. Thus, there will be differences in comprehension level and in expressive capacity according to education and cultural practices, as research by Chipere (2003) and Dabrowska and Street (2006) suggests.

How NOA operates differently for child native speakers and adult language learners

Needs are dynamic and NOA will trigger different analysis as the needs of an individual change. The outcome of NOA will tend to be similar across a group of people insofar as their needs are broadly equivalent. Children acquiring their first language will have largely similar needs in relation to communication, meeting their physical and emotional agendas and acquiring the language (see Wray 2002b: chapter 6). Furthermore, within a given speech community this will tend to expose them to rather similar input on the whole. The result will be a reasonable level of uniformity in their acquisition of lexical units and therefore in their sense of what sounds idiomatic. Across different speech communities (for example, children acquiring English in the USA, Australia, and Britain), variations in the patterns of input will trigger differences in what is stored in the lexicon and in what are perceived to be permissible variations within slots in frames, resulting in differences between those speakers in what they consider to sound most idiomatic—idiomatic speech thus becomes an index of identity.

Adult foreign and second language learners have different needs (and often substantially different input) from native speaker children. With regard to communication, being adults they have adult life-tasks to fulfil. They also have a range of alternative means for achieving those tasks, which can avoid or minimize communicative interaction (Wray 2002b: chapter 11). As for their learning needs, adults using textbooks and/or attending classes work towards measurements of achievement that are externally set. In addition, the adult mind seems better able than the child's to rationalize patterns explicitly (Grace 1987: 85), something that may be a product not only of how languages are explained in textbooks and classrooms, but also of biological maturity or cultural experience, particularly education and literacy (Wray 2008c)—evidence indicates that naturalistic adult learner language shares some characteristics with adult taught learner language, as well as some with child learner language (see Wray 2002b: chapter 10).

For these reasons, it is hypothesized that adult learners tend overall to analyse input more and to store smaller lexical units (cf. Kjellmer 1991).[10] These then require additional rules to recombine. This proposal offers an explanation for the difficulties that are routinely reported for adult learners in relation to restricting their output to only the idiomatic patterns that they have encountered in input—that is, there is a tendency to express messages in alternative ways, which are meaningful but not nativelike. Such formulations may serve the individual fairly well—indeed they may be preferred in lingua franca situations (Seidlhofer 2004; Wray and Grace 2007) where there are no native speakers to impose the particularities of their variety.

Morpheme equivalent units enable the speaker to manipulate the hearer

Some models assume just one optimal processing choice for any given item or configuration: if there is a lexical entry for a word string, then it will always be accessed, and probably never examined or altered; meanwhile, if there is an entry for the subcomponents of the word string, there is unlikely also to be an entry for the word string itself. However, the heteromorphic lexicon model, by permitting multiple storage, predicts opportunities for choice. The default is to engage in the least processing necessary in order to map the intended idea(s) onto linguistic forms that can be understood effectively by others. The need to communicate effectively, however, means that along with the speaker's own needs or preferences for how an idea is expressed, the needs and expectations of the hearer must also be taken into account.

Taking the hearer into account will generally encourage the speaker to be more formulaic. Just as formulaic material is easier for the speaker to encode, so also, when hearers have a lexical entry for a word string, they will find it easier to decode, compared with something more novel. That is, where a novel word string could be interpreted on the basis of any reasonable meanings arising from the word combination, a formulaic one will often be pre-associated with particular overtones or significance. As a result, a great deal of meaning can be triggered with very little processing and, more importantly, other possible meanings can be downgraded as candidates for interpretation. For instance, a hearer who recognizes the holistic meaning of 'mind how you go' as a valediction, will not engage with a more literal interpretation of it as a command or request to proceed carefully.

Although the speaker's capacity to direct the hearer into formulaic decoding might seem altruistic, in fact it promotes the speaker's own interests. By choosing formulations for which the hearer is likely to have holistic lexical representations, complete with pragmatic and cultural associations, the speaker can exercise control over how the hearer interprets what is said, and minimize the chances of a different interpretation from the intended one. In short, MEUs offer a means for the speaker to influence the thoughts of the hearer, and in this way they can be viewed as one of several solutions to a non-linguistic problem: how to get what you want (Wray 2002b: 100).

Of course, the speaker may not always be sure what sorts of lexical units the hearer knows, particularly if they are not from the same speech community. Speakers may modify their output in various ways to make good the potential gap, including adopting turns of phrase that they believe to be formulaic in the hearer's speech community. It could backfire to use an MEU that the hearer does not know, since it will have to be analysed and it may not mean, literally, what it means formulaically (see Chapter 14). In the case of opaque formulas therefore, including jargon terms used by specialists, the speaker may have to avoid using them if the hearer is to have a chance of understanding the message (see Chapters 17 and 22, and Wray and Grace 2007). At the other extreme, an MEU that is entirely transparent, but just not judged to be part of the hearer's existing vocabulary, might safely be used, even though the hearer has to work harder to unpack it than would be the case if it were, for him or her, a lexical entry in its own right.

Notes

1 A fourth conclusion, that access to the lexicon is distributed across the brain (Wray 2002b: chapter 14), is less central to this book and so is not used as an anchoring conceptual claim here. It is, however, mentioned later, as it becomes relevant in specific discussions.

2 The opposition of 'novel' with 'formulaic' is customarily made in discussions about formulaic language, and it is a useful shorthand here. However, as the three claims described here unfold, it will become clear that the distinction is not sustainable, since it is no less novel to construct an utterance out of multiword lexical units than out of single words or morphemes. Of course, in the former the holistically-retrieved units may well provide runs of familiar configurations, but they are really no different from familiar words—just longer.

3 Some versions of Construction Grammar allow for everything to be lexically stored—see Chapter 7—since constructions can be partly or completely lexically unspecified. The point being made here is that the capacity for novelty must be accounted for somehow. In models that accommodate the existence of grammatical rules, albeit sometimes insertional ones that complete lexically stored frames, novelty is achieved by activating the rules to produce word strings that are not independently stored in the lexicon.

4 It is probably fair to say that the multiword strings most likely to be systematically excluded from an atomic lexicon are those containing a specified verb, for example, 'take the trouble'; 'make one's way'; 'haul over the

coals'; 'see to'. Almost all verbs inside formulaic sequences can be varied morphologically, and where the verb has a wider use than just within that sequence, there is a rationale (within that type of model) for not treating the word string as a lexical unit.

5 See Wray (2002b: 32–3) for a discussion of whether 'Is the Pope a Catholic?' and other such expressions are formulaic and if so, at what level of abstraction.

6 The relationship between speech and writing requires its own discussion. For present purposes, it is simplest to refer only to speech, even though the examples used here may at times map more closely onto what one might find in written language. An extended discussion of how writing might impact on formulaicity can be found in Chapter 5.

7 It would be useful to establish whether this is a feature only of MEUs in English, or whether there is a more general tendency across languages.

8 See, for example, Sinclair (1991: 118) on the absence of 'I' and 'you' from the pronoun set of collocates within four words of 'back'.

9 A lexical insertion rule may, of course, insert a lexical unit that is itself a multiword string. A string so inserted, should it be a partly-fixed frame, will then naturally also attract its own lexical insertion procedure (compare Construction Grammar, described in Chapter 7).

10 This is not to deny Myles' (2004) observation that post-childhood language learners can also learn and use expressions for which they do not have mastery of the internal composition (as Chapters 12 and 13 clearly indicate).

3
Working at the boundaries

Introduction

In Part Three of this book, examples are provided of extreme uses of formulaic language. But in fact one does not have to create extreme situations to see what happens 'at the boundaries'. In the first part of this chapter we examine some instances in everyday language where the relationship between formulaicity and novelty is strained in some way. The second part considers some issues arising from the fact that theorists locate the boundaries in different places.

Conflicts between formulaicity and novelty

A clash of irregular and regular forms

If an individual learns a word string holistically, with a particular meaning or association, it will not matter if it contains material that is at odds with what that individual might produce as a novel configuration. An example might be the expression 'Love thy neighbour', which contains a pronoun from an older version of English. Individuals who are unfamiliar with the archaic pronoun system can still use 'thy' within formulaic strings like this, because no independent mastery of the item is required. But in the example below, a problem arises, as the old form creates a clash in its context of use. 'Love thy neighbour' was used as the title for a song in the 1934 movie 'We're Not Dressing'.[1] The song ends with the lines:

Love thy neighbour,
And you will find your labour
A great deal easier, life will be breezier
If you love thy neighbour.

In the last line, both 'you' and 'thy' occur. The clash is uncomfortable, but the song-writers would have struggled to resolve it, since the 'thy' form is within a formulaic sequence and the 'you' form is not. One option would have been to replace 'love thy neighbour' with the more ordinary (and perhaps less evidently formulaic) 'love your neighbour', but that would affect the entire song, including its title, and the older version was no doubt deliberately selected in order to reinforce the biblical connotations. Alternatively, the writers could have used archaic forms throughout the entire line, or verse, or song—giving 'And thou willst find thy labour' and 'If thou lovest thy neighbour'. Leaving aside the impact on the scansion, this change would have been a very marked departure from the generally modern lyric, and would have enforced upon the listener novel forms that required special attention, where the single formula 'love thy neighbour' does not.

Not all theories would view the use of 'thy' as an instance of irregularity, since the rule for its use is not that difficult to characterize or learn—someone using 'love thy neighbour' could in theory construct it from smaller active units in the lexicon. However, the view taken here is that while, certainly, some people may operate such a rule, one does not need to do so in order to produce and understand that expression. For people who do not, we can see 'love thy neighbour' as containing an irregular form.

The reason for taking this position is that forms like this are strikingly persistent. Native speakers often simply fail to see the many irregularities in languages that the rule-based system and the logic of morphological level semantics ought to reveal. They are overlooked because packages of material, often containing irregular forms, are passed, intact, from one speaker to another, as single lexical units.[2] As a result, language oddities are sustained rather than corrected. For example, native speakers know that in sporting knockout competitions such as the soccer World Cup, progression is from 'the last sixteen', through the 'quarter-finals', to the 'semi-finals'. Patterns exist in English that might permit terms such as 'eighth-finals' and 'half-finals' (to match 'quarter-finals') or 'demi-semi-' and 'hemi-demi-semi-finals' (in line with musical notes). Historical accounts of the provenance of the forms are not an adequate replacement for explaining why languages are not routinely tidied up in such regards.

If native speakers were, as most theories propose, consistently operating with small units of meaning, and rules for combining them, then it should be easier to rationalize such patterns than to perpetuate them.[3] NOA does not deny that such rationalization is *possible*, because, as noted earlier, the availability of small as well as larger units is essential for explaining how we deal with creative language. However, it does maintain that there is a strong bias against dividing multiword units that have a reliable meaning, until there is some specific need to do so. The result is that native speakers can be surprised by the irregularities in their language, having simply accepted them within a multiword package. Having once seen them, they can offer suggestions about regularization (and, indeed, some suggestions may become adopted), but on the whole, the overriding sense is that even though the 'rules' suggest we *should* say x, actually, it is y that sounds right.

Humour

Collisions between formulaic and non-formulaic material can be a source of humour (for example, Kuiper 2007 on the cartoons of Cathy Wilcox). In Figure 3.1, the three jokes all require the reader to see a morpheme equivalent unit (MEU) in a new way: to juxtapose its literal interpretation with its customary idiom interpretation. The jokes are funny because we can map a reliable meaning onto the MEU as a whole, so there is normally no need to look at how its constituents combine to make their own, novel meaning. Jokes invite us to take a second look: they create a need—we need to analyse the MEU if we want to understand the joke.

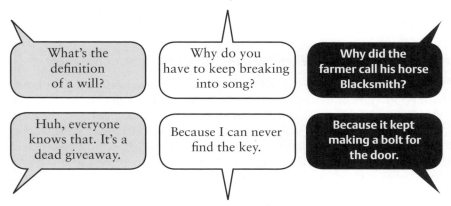

Figure 3.1 *Jokes based on the collision of formulaic and non-formulaic interpretations*

When the impossible becomes possible

How can one connect five consecutive examples of 'and' in a grammatical sentence, or eleven consecutive examples of 'had'? By using formulaic language.

> An innkeeper hired a sign writer to paint a new sign for his establishment. But when he saw the finished product, he was disappointed. 'This won't do,' he said. 'It's too untidy. The spaces between *Pig* and *and* and *and* and *Whistle* are different.'

> A class was set the task of translating a passage from Latin into English. The teacher was particularly interested in checking how the past tenses were handled, and it was in this light that he marked the work. When the translations were handed back, Jones had been given a higher mark than Brown. Jones, where Brown had had *had*, had had *had had*. *Had had* had had the teacher's approval.

These curiosities are possible only because not all instances of the repeated word have the same status in terms of meaning and processing. There is no way to compose a grammatical sentence of English that strings five conjunctions together, or eleven verbs, but it is possible to combine regular usages of these words with identical-looking forms that are in fact noun phrases because they are citations.[4] When you mention a word as a citation or quotation, you enfold it in an extra layer of linguistic wrapping, and that wrapping need not correspond, in terms of grammatical role, to that of the word itself. This is the same process that encloses a formulaic word string in the wrapping of a morpheme, and sometimes, just as here, it takes on a different grammatical identity. For instance, 'how's your father', meaning sexual behaviour, is wrapped as a noun phrase in, for example, 'there was definitely some how's your father going on there'.

When the morpheme equivalent unit constrains expression

The fact that MEUs are, by definition, less subject to variation than novel strings provides other opportunities to observe them 'at the boundaries', for the choice of the formula can offer too little scope for manipulating the form or meaning of the message. For instance, sometimes the scope for expression is too limited for the situation: attempting to pluralize 'too big a piece' gives '*too big a pieces' or '*too big pieces', the latter sounding too much like 'two big pieces' for comfort. Sometimes the need to say something novel may precede a full understanding of how others normally constrain the scope of an MEU, so that it is pushed beyond the bounds of what hearers and readers find idiomatic and comfortable.

Consider the following extract from the diary of 12-year-old Nellie Slater, who, in 1862, described her first sight of the volcanic landscape of Craters of the Moon, Idaho: "We are travelling now through a volcanic country. There's mountains all torn up and it is a very rough desert of a looking place".[5] Her construction 'a very rough desert of a looking place' seems to be a liberal extension of the more constrained MEU 'what sort of a looking x is he/she', where x is normally realized as man, woman, person, etc.[6] The use of the expression to refer to a place rather than a person is not illogical, and may have been common at that time in the US, since the one example that Google provides of 'sort of a looking place' occurs in a letter written in America just one year after Nellie's: "He can tell you what sort of a looking place it is".[7] Similarly Google provides one example of the string 'kind of a looking place', and it dates from just three years after Nellie's entry: "I want you to write what kind of a looking place you are in".[8] On the other hand, there is no easily available evidence that it was usual to extend the form from question ('what kind/sort') to statement, as Nellie has done. Although we can understand exactly what she means, and we can see the rationale for the construction, its unusual, unidiomatic nature indicates that, for us, it pushes at the boundaries of the normal realization of the formula, giving us insights into the nature of those boundaries.

Speech errors

Often the extension of an MEU beyond its normal range occurs in the context of a speech error, though the difference between an error and a deliberately creative change is sometimes in the eye of the beholder. George W. Bush is famous for 'errors' known as 'Bushisms', but often they are attempts to say something that the idiomatic string could not achieve. For instance, when he said: "The power that be, well most of the power that be, sits right here" (Washington, DC, 18 June 2001),[9] he was clearly trying to refer to one person, which 'the powers that be' cannot easily do. Such examples, along with formulaic blends such as 'I don't expect to come up with an answer here and there',[10] 'head over heels in work'; 'something isn't quite seeming right'; 'everybody sit put for a few minutes'; and 'it scared the death out of some of my daughter's friends',[11] are of great importance in modelling the nature of our linguistic knowledge.

Cutting and Bock (1997) showed informants pairs of idioms, and then prompted the production of one of them. By this method they found that idioms with the same syntactic structure were more likely to be blended (for example, 'kick the bucket' and 'meet your maker' resulted in the blend 'kick the maker'). They also found that informants were engaging with both the literal and non-literal meaning (compare the contradictory explanation, earlier, of why formula-based jokes are humorous), and that idioms were responded to identically, whether or not they were semantically transparent. They suggest that their findings "argue against a representation of idioms as noncomponential lexicalized phrases" (p. 57). The rationale for this argument is that if a blend occurs within what is supposed to be a holistically handled word string, it cannot be being holistically handled. This issue is discussed further later in this chapter.

Cutting and Bock would be correct if errors and blends occurred within strings that never varied. If MEUs such as 'the powers that be', 'head over heels in love' and 'scare the life out of' were truly fully-fixed, and stored as such in the lexicon, then on what basis could they be disrupted to create a semantically-motivated error? It would not be anticipated that an MEU could be altered by blending it with another MEU, as with 'scare the death out of' (from 'scare the life out of' and 'scare to death').

However, MEUs are, it seems, rarely quite so fixed and, as Chapter 12 will show, the boundaries either side of a gap for variable material are vulnerable to unintended variation. 'Scare the death out of' is more explicable as an error when it is noted that there is already scope for variation in that locus: 'scare the life/hell/shit out of'. For NOA it is unintentional errors at non-varying loci that are the most difficult to account for (for example, 'Straight as a pancake', Cutting and Bock 1997: 57; 'You just shrug your fingers', said by the author,

2002). Deliberate blends are easy to explain in terms of NOA—they are created in response to a new need: the desire to say something novel or play with words for comic effect. In the same way, the *comprehension* of an unintentional blend created by someone else is achieved by meeting the need for additional processing with a new analysis. In production, though, unintentional blends between multiword lexical units with similar meanings and/or that begin in the same way can only be explained in the same terms as blends between single words—as a product of unwanted multiple activation (see, for instance, Mattys 2006). The problem is that it may not always adequately explain why the changes are semantically apt, rather than nonsensical.

Care needs to be taken, however, because sometimes an example can be construed as unintentional, but actually be deliberate. For instance, an analyst who had not previously encountered the string 'head over heels in work', and who came across it in a context where it could be construed as an error, might be likely to view it as such. Yet Google provides 1690 hits for it.[12] Furthermore, although the British National Corpus has no examples, of the fifteen it has for 'head over heels in', only 11 have 'love' as the completion, the others being 'black', 'the switchback strip of movies', 'lust', and 'roots and treetops'. This suggests that creativity at the boundary between 'in' and 'love' already occurs in the English language, and that the specific expression 'head over heels in work' may be a legitimate new entrant into the lexicon of some people.

How idioms are processed

The short accounts above, about irregularity, humour, and speech errors, directly relate to a long-running discussion in the linguistic, psychological, neurolinguistic, and clinical literature regarding how idioms are processed in the brain. Idioms like 'spill the beans' and 'not NP's cup of tea' are very useful for experiments, because they are evidently formulaic (whatever that means to the given researcher), tend to be well known to native speakers, and have two distinct meanings—a holistic metaphorical meaning and a compositional literal one. For this reason they have been much used to investigate the nature of language processing in both healthy and language-disordered populations. As a baseline, we may take it that native speakers probably *believe* that when they hear an idiom they go straight to the holistic, metaphorical meaning without considering the literal one, other than in situations where the literal one is specifically evoked, as in humour. In other words, when we hear someone say 'I hate his guts' we are not aware of engaging with a literal reading that concerns the unfortunate person's internal organs. When we hear someone say they 'sweated blood' over a piece of work, we do not, we feel, have to consider and discard an image of blood emerging from the speaker's pores in response to effort.

But we do not, of course, have full awareness of how our language processing works, and it is possible that these literal readings are in fact accessed and discarded, below the level of our consciousness. There are few direct ways to arbitrate between the dual-interpretation and single-interpretation alternatives. The humorous effect of having to access both meanings tends to suggest that we normally have only a single interpretation, but in experiments, the dual-interpretation option seems to be supported.

In a classic psycholinguistic experiment, Lackner and Garrett (1972) played ambiguous sentences like 'The spy put out the torch as our signal to attack' (where 'put out' could mean 'displayed' or 'extinguished') into one ear of their informants, while playing a matching unambiguous sentence (for example, 'The spy extinguished the torch in the window') very quietly into the other ear. Although not all ambiguous sentences entail idioms, almost all idioms entail ambiguity, so we can reasonably use this experiment as an indicator of what happens when idioms are processed. They were interested in whether, in normal circumstances, we only decode one possible meaning of a sentence that is ambiguous, and assume that is the correct one unless we encounter evidence to the contrary, at which point we go back and re-analyse it. Again, this hypothesis is consistent with explaining why humour based on ambiguity works. However, their results indicated that "while a subject is listening to an ambiguous sentence and determining its meaning, both its readings are to some extent available to him" (p. 367).

Cutting and Bock (1997) examined something slightly different—whether an idiom is treated holistically or compositionally in processing. If the former, it could still entail that a separate literal meaning was accessed, as Lackner and Garrett propose, but there would nevertheless be an integrity to the holistic form-meaning mapping of the non-literal reading. If idioms were found to be processed compositionally, a more direct mapping would be possible with the literal alternative, including, potentially, decisions about how to interpret individual words. Cutting and Bock showed undergraduate informants two idioms using a 'competition' technique that tends to produce 'speech errors' in the form of blends of the two idioms. They hypothesized that "if idioms are completely lexicalised phrases ... the syntax of an idiom should not play any significant role in the production of blends" (p. 59). However, they found that there was greater blending when idioms had a similar grammatical form than when they had a different form, suggesting that "[i]dioms are not produced as 'frozen phrases' in which the components lose all of their individual word-like properties. Instead, they are syntactically analysed" (p. 63).

In a further experiment they found evidence that the literal meaning of an idiom is available during processing, something that is also not predicted if idioms are holistically stored and accessed. Finally, they compared responses to idioms that were decomposable—in the sense that each word in the idiom could be given its own figurative meaning that contributed to the whole (for example, 'spill the beans', where 'spill' maps onto 'talk about' and 'beans' maps onto 'the secret information')—and idioms that were non-decomposable (for example, 'kick the bucket', where there is no clear indication of how 'kick' or 'bucket' contributes to the meaning of die, even figuratively). They found that decomposability made no difference to the amount of blending, suggesting that non-decomposable idioms are no more frozen than decomposable ones. They conclude, "these experiments suggest that idioms are not produced as 'frozen phrases', devoid of information about their internal syntax and semantics" but rather that "idiom representations are linked to information about the grammatical class of their constituents, about their overall syntactic structures, and about literal meaning" (p. 69).

These two experiments, along with many others producing similar results, seem to indicate that, contrary to the claims made so far in this book, when we encounter an idiom we do not simply make a direct mapping from the holistic form to the non-literal meaning—much more processing, and many more decision points, are involved (see also discussions of the evidence by Gibbs 2007 and Sprenger, Levelt, and Kempen 2006). Evidence from clinical linguistic research appears to concur. There have been a number of studies investigating whether, in various types of clinical population including people with left and right hemisphere damage, autism, and Alzheimer's disease, the literal meaning of an idiom is accessed before, after, or at the same time as, the non-literal meaning (there is a general assumption in these investigations that it *is* accessed). The findings of this research are reported and discussed in Chapter 16. Suffice it here to say that they are a surprise. When people in these different subgroups are observed in non-test conditions, they each appear to have different ease or difficulty with idioms and other formulaic language. But in the tests, all of them tend to choose literal over non-literal readings (Wray 2008a). This clash between what happens in tests and out of them casts some suspicion onto the approaches to testing that are used in clinical investigations and, by extension, also psycholinguistic experiments on normal populations (Wray 1992; Givón 1995).

The heteromorphic lexicon model, based on the principle of NOA, offers a solution to the conundrum of how idioms are processed. Where Cutting and Bock (1997) conclude that their experiments "offer a new kind of evidence for the view that idioms are compositional" (p. 66), according to this model they have evidence only that idioms *can* be compositional. That is, experiments tap into a kind of processing that we can do but do not do in most other circumstances.

Figure 3.2 represents the 'story' of idiom processing from the point of view of this model. Idioms have a historical provenance, in the sense that, at some point in the past we assume, someone coins the idiom by applying a metaphorical meaning to a literal phrase or clause. For instance, we are told by Flavell and Flavell (1992: 113) that 'to have too many irons in the fire' may derive from the literal description of the laundress who keeps too many flat irons heating in the fire, ready to replace the one in use when it has cooled down. The risk in this level of industriousness arises because if the irons are in the fire too long, they will be too hot to use, and could scorch the fabric. Someone, at some point, transferred the image of too many flat irons in a fire to the broader idea of being too busy with different projects to achieve them effectively, and so the idiom was born (Figure 3.2, Section A). Presumably most such coinages do not survive. Those that do, become fixed in the language because the people hearing them are able to recognize the metaphorical meaning. A form-meaning mapping is created in the lexicon, in turn making it easier for the idiom to be recognized in future input and to be used in output. Thus is created a stable circularity (B), in which the idiom is not interrogated in regard to its internal composition—it is not necessary, in other words, to know what sort of irons are being referred to, or indeed even to notice that the expression uses the image of irons and a fire, to understand and use the idiom. This stable component is the central and only consistently operating one.

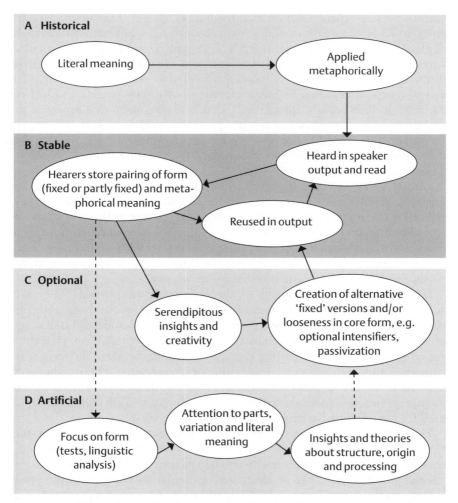

Figure 3.2 The relationship between fixedness and non-fixedness in idioms

There is an optional annexe to the stable loop (C). It is possible for a speaker to contemplate the form of the idiom, and to see creative potential in it. For instance, at some point someone must have thought of making expression 'to cross one's fingers' more emphatic, by adding, with some humour given the relative physical difficulty of the manoeuvre, 'and toes'. The expression 'to cross one's fingers and toes' is now a recognized alternate to the original. Moon (1998) itemizes very many instances where an idiom has more than one form, by virtue of an addition, a deletion—for example, 'a stitch in time (saves nine)', or alternative elements—for example, 'alive and kicking/well' and 'hit the deck/hay/sack'. Other kinds of change might also occur, such as grammatical reorientation, for example, 'x spilled the beans' and 'the beans were spilled by x'. It has been often remarked that some idioms permit such variation while others, such as 'kick the bucket' do not. Explanations often entail convoluted semantic or grammatical constraints, but in this model such explanations are not required directly. It is enough to say that a particular variation sounds odd because it has not been encountered. It follows that if 'the bucket was kicked by x' was encountered in salient contexts (that is, in real usage rather than linguistics textbooks with an asterisk in front of it), it might well become idiomatic.[13] That does not mean that semantic or grammatical constraints could not be invoked to explain why no one has so far successfully coined the passive version of 'kick the bucket', only that the determiner of what people know and consider to be idiomatic is not ultimately a question of rules but of familiarity.

Clearly, variations can only occur by interrogating the holistic form. But as Figure 3.2 shows, once alternatives are created and are used in output, they will enter the stable circle (B). This could occur in one of two ways (and it would be difficult to ascertain which one applied)—a second fixed idiom with a new form, so that there are two rather similar ones with similar meanings; or the editing of the previously fixed form, through NOA, to create a frame permitting the specified variation in the relevant slot.

How, though, are the results of the experiments explained? They are accommodated in the bottom part of the figure (D), as artificial engagements with the form. If you ask people to look at or listen to idioms out of a communicative context and they know they are going to be tested on what they see or hear, it is hardly surprising that they attend to them in a different way from their approach in, say, a conversation or when reading a book. They will become aware of aspects of the form and meaning that they normally would not notice and, in so doing, may well activate different brain regions to those used for communicative language (Wray 1992, 2002b).

However, it is not only in tests that this additional analysis can happen. We can also train ourselves to look at language in a way that is rather independent of how we use it to communicate, even to the extent of being able to ignore normal grammar and read an alternative grammar, as happens with cryptic crossword clues (see Chapter 18). We might then apply our insights back into the mainstream of our language use, by, perhaps, accommodating a gap for variation where most other people do not. It may be noted, in relation to (D) in Figure 3.2 that the same processes are expected to apply more generally to most adult language learners, so that their over-analysis of forms in input, as outlined in Chapter 2, creates a greater scope for variation in form than native speakers have.

If this model is accurate, then there are some significant implications for a number of published investigations of idiom processing. Hillert (2004) used stimuli that he considered to be idioms, such as *Bienenstich*, a type of cake, but literally 'bee sting', and *Eselohren*, the folds on a page that in English make a book 'dog-eared', but literally 'donkey-ears'. This is the equivalent of using English stimuli such as 'dog collar' (as worn by a priest) and 'toad-in-the-hole' (a savoury dish of sausages and pudding). The rationale for viewing such items as idioms, of course, is that their holistic meaning is quite different from their literal one. But these examples must, surely, count as instances where the metaphorical meaning is unlikely to be challenged by a literal reading in normal circumstances. Indeed, we might consider that the literal and non-literal meanings are homophones. Finding, in such experiments, that subjects do have insight into the literal meanings is a compelling indication that an artificial engagement with language is under way.

The question of novelty

Finally, we turn to the question of 'formulaicity' versus 'novelty'. As noted in Chapter 2, note 2, the terms are customarily and conveniently used to distinguish between linguistic material that is retrieved whole from the lexicon and that which is composed from smaller parts by rule. The contrast is particularly clear where one is considering two alternative approaches to formulating the same word string, with different consequences, as with, say, the idiom 'don't let the cat out the bag' and an original sentence used to ask someone not to let your feline pet escape from a fabric holdall. But in most cases, of course, there is no direct comparison to be made, nor is one dealing with anything so invitingly holistic as a true idiom. So our interest here is in the distinction of formulaic versus novel when dealing with whether word strings such as 'What I mean is x' constitute a holistic frame or a from-scratch composition.

Technically, in this model there is no distinction to be made, for everything is a novel composition. The heteromorphic lexicon neutralizes the distinction between holistic and analytic processing.[14] One needs, simply, a set of grammatical rules and a lexicon, as in standard models. The fact that the lexicon is not atomic, and so contains some items with an internal complexity that remains immune from the grammar, means that some rules required in other models are not required here. Meanwhile, the existence of partly-fixed frames means that there must be insertion rules to accommodate appropriate completions.[15] Thus, every time we produce a string of words, whether it entail the combination of morpheme and word-sized units using many rules, or the simple selection of one item from the lexicon, into which, say, a variable item is inserted, we can reasonably say that the output is 'novel'—the units selected are combined at the time of use—it's just that some of those units are quite large.

Nevertheless, it is clear that much of specific interest to our current concerns is lost by collapsing formulaic and non-formulaic language into one type, and it is for this reason that more latitude has been applied in this book to permitting a differentiation that technically does not exist. For practical purposes, therefore, 'novel' is used to refer to output and input that entails small units combined or analysed to create or access meaning, while 'holistic' is used to indicate that such a assembly or analysis has not been required.

Exploring morpheme equivalent units

The remainder of the book uses the observations and claims made in these chapters as the basis for exploration of the phenomenon of formulaic language. It follows that it is taken for granted that:

- the lexicon is able to contain units that are internally complex in form and meaning, including ones that could be broken down according to regular grammatical rules known to exist for the language;
- the unit inventory of the lexicon is determined by the individual's experience of input and how the individual needs to, or has learnt to, handle that input in order to command the language;
- there are communicative advantages to using MEUs, both for the hearer and, more directly, for the speaker.

Notes

1 The song was later adopted as the theme tune for a 1970s British sitcom of the same name. The original song-title has the US spelling 'neighbor', but for the sake of consistency, the British spelling is used throughout here.

2 Indeed, some patterns perhaps only exist at all as artefacts of analysis: "linguists ... have ... come to see that ... structure is not something given in the language, but that it has to be 'analysed out' of the material by the linguist and that if one linguist differs in his analysis from the other it does not follow that either he or the other linguist is wrong" (Bazell 1958: 3).

3 See also Culicover and Jackendoff (2005: 27–8) who propose that it is unnecessary to model as minor modifications of a general rule the child's acquisition of the post-head location of 'enough', 'galore', and 'aplenty' (for example, 'big enough', '*enough big'; 'balloons galore/aplenty', '*galore/*aplenty balloons'). They prefer the parsimonious explanation that 'children hear these words in these positions, so that's where they put them' (p. 28). However, the theroretical context within which their claim is made is different in important regards from the NOA model.

4 Since the entire list of 'hads' can itself be a citation, we can embed it into a new story: Smith knew a slightly different version of this conundrum, that featured only nine 'hads' because he didn't use the past perfect in the story frame. Thus, Jones, where Smith had had 'had *had*, had *had had*. *Had had* had' had had 'had had *had*, had had *had had*. *Had had* had had'. 'had had *had*, had had *had had*. *Had had* had had' had had the citation in Wray's chapter. We now have 36 'hads' in a row. The sentence is logically grammatical, but to all intents and purposes incomprehensible. Furthermore, the sequence of 'had's could itself be subject to citation, so one could make ever longer sentences of this kind. There can be no clearer indication of the way in which linguists find things to do things with language that no normal person would countenance (see Chapter 18).

5 This is part of a longer extract on display at the Craters of the Moon National Monument Visitor Center, Idaho.

6 Based on a Google search (1 October 2006) of the strings 'sort of a looking' and 'kind of a looking'. There are no instances of 'of a looking' in the British National Corpus or the Bank of English.

7 Letter from Private Thomas Winton Fisher, K Company, 51st Virginia Infantry, March 1st, 1863. http://ted.gardner.org/630301tf.htm. Accessed 10 February 2008.

8 Letter to Private James R. Leroy, 2nd Battery, Vermont Light Artillery, from Louise L. Oakes. http://www.vermontcivilwar.org/units/ar/jrl.php. Accessed 10 February 2008.

9 Bushisms like this can be found in many sources, including http://grammar.ccc.commnet.edu/grammar/bush.htm. Accessed 10 February 2008.

10 BBC Radio 4, Today interview, 15 November 2003.

11 These examples are from a corpus collected from US broadcasts by Rebecca Shaftman, to whom I am grateful for permission to quote them.

12 Search done on 1 October 2006.

13 Imagine it were to become the catchphrase in a TV sitcom about an undertaker, for example, 'Hello, John, who's the bucket been kicked by today?'.

14 This observation is not directly made in Wray (2002b), but is implicit.

15 Models like Construction Grammar articulate the grammar-lexicon relationship differently but are not incompatible with the suggestion here—see Chapter 7.

4
Formulaic language and the oral tradition

Introduction

This chapter and the next examine aspects of formulaicity in the relationship between the oral and written mediums. Some of the earliest observations about formulaic language were made in relation to the boundary between oral and written texts—specifically the ways in which writing a text down affects the symbiotic interaction of creativity and repetition observed in oral epics. This chapter reviews key observations about the role of formulaic language in creating and sustaining oral narratives, and the impact of writing down what has previously been memorized. Chapter 5 locates these issues in a more general exploration of the role of autonomy in speech and writing, particularly the question of how the level of formulaicity is appropriately set for effective communication.[1]

Autonomy

Speakers and writers must make fine judgements about what their hearers or readers can bring to the interpretation of their output, if they wish their message to be accurately interpreted. The less that can be taken for granted, the more explicit the text must be and the more autonomous it thus becomes—that is, likely to be interpretable by a range of others. Written texts generally tend to be viewed as more autonomous than spoken ones, though, as we shall see, it is not a simple question of written text being autonomous while spoken is not. Rather, certain kinds of medium open the door to opportunities for autonomy, and in some circumstances high levels of autonomy can become the preferred choice for certain types of text.

Any given output lies on a continuum from less to more explicit, with an explicit text most autonomous; though whether any text can ever be *entirely* autonomous is questionable (Grace 1987: 41ff). Exchanges between a long-term cohabiting couple, for instance, might be so heavily contextualized as to be completely incomprehensible to an outsider, with references to previous conversations or actions (for example, 'so, what did she say?'), or opaque formulaic encodings such as family sayings, quotes from songs they both know, punchlines from a previously-made joke. A visitor to their home would not be assumed to share this cultural knowledge, and would be provided with more explicit input, that took less shared knowledge for granted. The level of explicitness would depend on what the parties judged themselves to share culturally (as determined by age, geographical origin, education, interests, etc). With a total stranger, the level of explicitness might well be negotiated gradually, so that the quantity of formulaically encoded material was honed as commonalities and differences were identified.

The relationship between formulaicity and autonomy in language is, however, more complex than the account so far implies. In the first place, formulaic language is construed in this book as complex lexis. Although lexical material plays a major role in the speaker's positioning of output on the explicitness continuum, there is more to autonomy of text than just lexis. Second, the relationship between linguistic autonomy and the medium of lin- guistic expression—most evidently speech versus writing—is only indirectly expressed in terms of formulaic language.

Therefore, in order to establish just how formulaic language relates to the larger question of shared knowledge, it is necessary to examine how writing impacts on the balance between contextualized and autonomous text. The discussion of these issues begins with an account of how formulaic language has been identified as playing a major role in the specifically oral context of traditional performed epic poetry.

Formulaic language and the oral tradition

The work of Milman Parry (1902–1935) and his student Albert Lord (1912–1991) on formulas in oral epic songs is, for many, the historical anchor point for research into formulaic language. Their analyses of the nature of the Homeric texts, along with their demonstration of how oral poetry was still being composed and performed in Yugoslavia in the first half of the twentieth century, led them to propose that oral texts are obliged, if they are to be performable, always to have certain formulaic features. The examination of their claims, and observations made since, is usefully contextualized by a consideration of our own experience of oral performance texts.

Oral texts

Our literate culture heavily compromises our ability fully to appreciate the nature of a non-literate one, but there are elements of oral culture that we can draw on for insight, most notably our own experience as children using playground rhymes. Rubin (1995) discusses in depth the way that count- ing-out rhymes such as 'Eenie meenie miney mo' reflect the processes of oral transmission (though he also shows that the constraints on such rhymes, being different from those on long poems, result in different patterns of formulaicity, p. 209). We are not surprised to discover that someone of a different age, or from another town, learnt a slightly different version of a rhyme or song, for we recognize that there is no 'definitive' version.[2] Who 'wrote' the original version of 'Eenie meenie'? We do not know, nor is its authorship relevant to its continued usage. How did we learn it? By observation and repetition presumably. Did we learn it faithfully? Possibly not, but as we grew in confidence we no doubt happily pronounced our own version to be 'correct', so that others learnt it from us in good faith.[3] Where would we look for the 'correct' version? Probably nowhere, unless some historical research convinced us that a particular form from the past was the mother form of all the others. What makes such rhymes memorable? Primarily that they have a ritual function that requires their repeated use. Also, features of their structure may help us remember them—rhythm, rhyme, and so on—plus, counter-intuitively perhaps, often the nonsense material within which the important information (if there is any at all) is packed.

Even closer to the experience of the oral epic, perhaps, comes our hearing, and then telling, of fairy stories—though the existence of myriad written versions of the stories renders them less 'pure' as an oral phenomenon. Adults able to resist the temptation to use a book and rather *tell* the stories of *Little Red Riding Hood* and *Cinderella* discover a world of interactive text construction ('and what do you think happened next?') and creative embellishment ('she was wearing a lovely blue gown, and a necklace of sparkling sapphires') that will vary from telling to telling, while the fundamental features of the story continue to be unpeeled in the same order, leading to the same outcome.[4] There are, in short, unwritten rules about how to tell a traditional story, adherence to which will help the listener to discern the difference between the core story, which may not change, and the peripheral features, which may (for an overview of narrative structure theory, see Toolan 2006). There are key linguistic formulations that are obligatory if the story is to have been properly told, such as 'I'll huff and I'll puff and I'll blow your house down'; 'Mirror, mirror on the wall, who is the fairest of them all?'; 'Grandma, what big ____ you have'.

Through such traditions we can at least glimpse the way in which storytellers in non-literate societies could tell and retell their stories in collaboration with their listeners, each performance a different yet equal version of the same thing. Useful comparisons have been made to jazz improvisation (for example, Stevick 1962; H. W. Foster 2004; Silk 2004) where, also, each performance is unique, a presentation of something familiar, but embellished for the day. The patterns of the embellishment are constrained, and often defined to the point of formulaicity by the requirements of the key and rhythm. Yet, as Foster, Silk, and others point out, the performer's projection of on-the-spot creativity is only part of the story, for a great deal of rehearsal, founded on intense familiarity with the material, precedes good quality improvisation.

The nature of formulas in oral texts

Within the context of oral literature, the formula has a particular definition: "In the diction of bardic poetry, the formula can be defined as an expression regularly used, under the same metrical conditions, to express an essential idea" (M. Parry 1928/1971: 13). Characterizing the formula simultaneously in terms of its frequency, form, and function mirrors other general and specific definitions of formulaic language across the research literature (Wray 2002b: chapter 3). The quantity of formulaic material in a text can be difficult to judge, since identifying it depends, in part, on evidence that the same pattern occurs elsewhere in the same text or, preferably, other texts.[5] Nevertheless, Stevick (1962) cites figures arising from scholars' analyses of the Old English works *Cynewulf* (63 per cent formulaic) and Caedmon's *Hymn* (83 per cent formulaic) (p. 383f), going on to observe that the very rarity of works from this period makes it impossible to judge how much of that formulaicity originated with the poet and how much was borrowed from an earlier tradition (p. 385).

Parry's functional definition of the formula is inclusive of a range of forms, from identical repetitions of material, through repetitions with slight changes, to sets of parallel structures all performing the same task but in different, predictable circumstances. The latter could even include grammatical formulations or rhythmical patterns in which no words were in common across exemplars, something which, as MacKenzie (2003) points out, not all commentators have been happy to include within the scope of the 'formula'. However, perhaps the single most striking common formula type in Homer was the noun epithet, a multiword string associated with a particular character in the story—for example, 'brilliant long-suffering Odysseus', 'aged horseman Nestor', 'swift-footed brilliant Achilles', 'cow-eyed queen Hera', and 'old Priam looking like a god' (Rubin 1995: 203). The epithets were repeatedly used when mentioning that character, and rarely if ever used about anyone else. Whallon (1969: 3) notes that Agamemnon is referred to as 'king of men' 47 times, while no one else is referred to as such more than once.[6]

Formulaic material offered advantages to the performer, whose major challenge was to balance his memory limitations, the requirements of the metrical form of the verse, and the content of his story.[7] As Rubin (1995) observes, the recollection of complex oral texts such as epics requires in-built constraints that "serve both to limit choices and to increase the chances of uniquely cuing the target" (p. 176). Cues, which "'activate' and help 'discriminate' the responses that follow", included rhyme, rhythm, stanza structure, and content (pp. 176–7). In this way, formulas provided reliable islands of familiar material.

A second advantage of repeatedly using formulas such as the noun epithets was that they completed the line according to the required metrical pattern (Rubin 1995: 197). Since the characters needed to be mentioned very often in the narrative, it was helpful to have a reliable way to fill up the rest of the line, so that the story itself did not have to be fitted into the remaining syllables (M. Parry 1928/1971: 17). They were, in short, a solution to a practical problem: "the singer's mode of composition is dictated by the demands of performance at high speed, and he depends upon inculcated habit and association of sounds, words, phrases and lines" (Lord 2000: 65). Only by using such formulas could the composer/performer hope to stay within the constraints of the verse form while reeling out his story.

However, preserving the meter could actually compromise the story at times (Rubin 1995: 208). MacKenzie (2003) observes, for instance, that "ships in Homer are regularly referred to as 'swift' even when they are at anchor, drawn up on the beach, or wrecked" (p. 78). This incongruity almost certainly did not matter much, since the audience would recognize the epithets and would not attend to their specific content (M. Parry 1930/1971: 284).[8] In Lord's view, formulas did not enter the poetry already compromised in meaning. Yet it was "certainly possible that a formula that [first] entered the poetry because its acoustic patterns emphasized by repetition a potent word or idea [might subsequently be] kept[,] after the peculiar potency which it symbolised ... was lost" (Lord 2000: 65). In such cases, formulas "began to lose their precision through frequent use. Meaning in them became vestigial, connotative rather than denotative" (ibid.).

A functional explanation for the development and retention of formulaic material in oral literature predicts that, to survive in texts when the functional requirements changed, formulas had to be assigned a new purpose. This is something that seems to have happened very naturally on account of the functional requirements of the audience that naturally operated alongside those of the performer. Whallon (1969) and Brockington (1998) both contend that, their original purpose notwithstanding, noun epithets conveyed significant information to the audience regarding essential features of the character, or those aspects of him or her that were most relevant to that particular story. Formulas also assisted the audience by "increas[ing] the semantic redundancy of the text and thus ... decreas[ing] its indeterminacy, the possibilities of its interpretation. This decrease in indeterminacy ... vouchsafe[d] the conservation of tradition in the production of the 'message' of the text and in its reception" (Bäuml 1984: 35–6). Furthermore, formulas assisted in "directing the participation of the audience in the performance, that is, in the production of the text, for composition and reception meet in the oral performance" (ibid.: 36).

Formulas as a mark of antiquity: solving an ancient mystery

The functions assigned by Parry and Lord to the formulaic material in these epics are very strongly linked to the fact that the performances were presented live to an audience, each one a different improvisation around the traditional theme. As these characteristics would imply, the formulaic features of the oral medium were at least optional—and potentially undesirable—in works that were composed first in writing. Consequently, Parry and Lord argue that the presence in a written text of more than a certain quantity of such formulas is an indication that it began life as an oral work. They reason that since formulas accrete over time (that is, it is unlikely that a single oral performer could invent them all), the oral composition of a highly formulaic work is likely to predate considerably the written version.

Thus arose a debate regarding whether formulaic word strings in ancient and medieval texts could be used as a reliable indication of when and how they were composed. One can never be sure whether the oldest surviving written record of a work marks the date of its creation, or whether there were earlier written versions, now lost. But in addition one cannot be sure how long a text might have existed in oral form before it was ever written down. Interest in these matters first arose in relation to dating the *Iliad* and the *Odyssey*. The earliest written copies were from between 650 and 700 BC, but the works themselves were thought to be up to eight centuries older (MacKenzie 2003: 78). The first century Jewish historian Josephus Flavius doubted that writing existed so early (though in fact he was incorrect—see below), and he supposed that the *Iliad* and the *Odyssey* must have been passed down by word of mouth for many generations. By the early twentieth century, when Parry developed a theory about the provenance of the works, there was still no evidence of writing in Greece at the time of Homer, and unless Homer's dates had been wrongly estimated by several hundred years, ascribing his works to an oral tradition remained the best explanation (Lord 2000: 8–9). Both Parry and Lord considered it inconceivable that the Homeric epics had been composed in writing, for there were clear indications in the style of the work that they 'had origins more mysterious and more complex than later poetic compositions' (A. Parry 1971: p. xi).

By the time it was discovered, in 1952, that Linear B, a script dated to the fourteenth century BC, was a version of Greek (thus confirming that writing was well established at the hypothesized time of Homer), the theory about the role of formulaicity in texts was sufficiently mature for it to be argued that, even though Homer *could* have been literate, his epics were unquestionably oral (Lord 2000: 9). As Bäuml (1984: 31, 33) points out, there is a risk of circularity in first hypothesizing that formulaicity is a mark of orality, and then using formulaicity to *establish* whether a text was an oral composition.[9] He is also less confident than Lord and others, that the methods developed for analysing Homer can be unproblematically extended to more recent, medieval texts such as *Beowulf*, in order to establish whether or not they, too, were first oral. A major part of Bäuml's case relates to how a culture makes the transition from 'oral' to 'literate', and the consequent mechanisms by which even archetypal formulas of the oral tradition might legitimately appear in written compositions. As will become clear below, the transition from oral tradition to written record is considerably complicated by the way in which texts are culturally construed in relation to each other, so that the presence or absence of formulas becomes, arguably, an unreliable measure of the oral or written origin of a work.

The transition to written record

> The art of narrative song was perfected … long before the advent of
> writing … Even its geniuses were not straining at their bonds, longing to
> be freed from its captivity, eager for the liberation by writing. When
> writing was introduced, epic singers … did not realise its 'possibilities'
> and did not rush to avail themselves of it.
> (Lord 2000: 124)

The Yugoslavian data collected by Parry and Lord were significant, and not
only because the oral tradition was directly observable, which made it possible to ask real poets about the processes of learning and performance. They
also provided an opportunity to assess the extent to which the process of transcription might distort a text. This question is important because, of course,
until the invention of audio recording, the oral traditions of past generations
could only be examined through the medium of written records.

Parry and Lord believed that what got written down during the transcription
of an oral poem could not possibly be a true representation of the original, for
a number of reasons. The performer would almost certainly have needed to
break out of performance mode in order to help with the process of transcription, since it would be impossible for the recorder to write down everything
in real time during a performance (Lord 2000: 126). The alternative for the
transcriber would have been to build up a written version gradually, by noting
details over many performances, but such a version could not be viewed as
accurate either, for each performance could be very different from any other.
Thus, it was likely that the transcribed version would be the result of a rather
inauthentic event, in which the performer attempted to present the work

> with no music and no song, nothing to keep him to the regular beat
> except the echo of previous singings and the habit they had formed in his
> mind. Without these accompaniments it was not easy to put the words
> together as he usually did. The tempo of composing the song was differ-
> ent, too. Ordinarily the singer could move forward rapidly from idea to
> idea, from theme to theme. But now he had to stop very often for the
> scribe to write down what he was saying, after every line or even after
> part of a line. This was difficult, because his mind was far ahead.
> (Lord 2000: 124)

Since, also, the role of the audience was integral to the performance, and
indeed constituted an aspect of the very underlying composition, what was
written down could be no more than a static snapshot of a living entity, a
disengaged tableau of a moving scene. Furthermore, it seemed likely to Lord
that the act of transcription was highly dangerous for the future of the oral
work. Once there was a written version of a text, it would become a point
of reference, thus setting in stone something that had previously been fundamentally fluid. Transcription, Lord proposed, was likely to mark the end of

true orality for that work and, in due course, for the tradition in its entirety: 'there was another world, of those who could read and write, of those who came to think of the written text not as the recording of a moment of the tradition but as *the* song. This was to become the difference between the oral way of thought and the written way' (Lord 2000: 125).

Though others contest the extremity of the view (see below), Parry and Lord believed that the techniques of oral and written poetry were so incompatible that no one person could be simultaneously master of both (Lord 2000: 129). As Parry (1930/1971) put it, "Unlike the poet who writes out his lines—or even dictates them—[the oral poet] cannot think without hurry about his next word, nor change what he has made, nor, before going on, read over what he has just written" (p. 270). Formulaicity was a necessity for the oral poet who "[i]n composing ... will do no more than put together for his needs phrases which he has often heard or used himself, and which, grouping themselves in accordance with a fixed pattern of thought, come naturally to make the sentence and the verse" (ibid.). What he gained thereby in fluency he sacrificed in terms of creativity, for "[t]he oral poet expresses only ideas for which he has a fixed means of expression ... he can put his phrases together in an endless number of ways; but still they set bounds and forbid him the search of a style which would be altogether his own" (M. Parry 1930/1971: 270).

Of course, it is not specifically the *action* of writing down a text that determines it to be a written rather than an oral work, any more than reading a written piece aloud would give it all the characteristics of orality. The key difference between a written composition and an oral one lies in the fact that with written composition the audience is not present until after the work is complete, whereas in oral composition/performance the audience is present at, and participates in, the process (Bäuml 1984: 38f). Thus, it is the adoption of new creative practices that makes the real difference. And, over time, even the *potential* for written composition may cast a shadow on the oral tradition, as it becomes "a subculturally distinctive ritual in an illiterate subculture of a literate society" (Bäuml 1984: 39).

In Lord's (2000) view, the composer/performer himself ultimately sounds the death knell for the tradition. Lord describes how an oral performer who learns to read might maintain for a while a mixed repertoire of songs he knew before and new ones that he has learnt from transcribed material. However,

> [w]hen he thinks of the written songs as fixed and tries to learn them word for word, the power of the fixed text and of the technique of memorizing will stunt his ability to compose orally... This is one of the most common ways in which an oral tradition may die; not when writing is introduced, but when published song texts are spread among singers.
> (ibid.: 129–30)

Formulas in written compositions

The interest in dating ancient works on the basis of the presence of formulas (see earlier) is predicated on the assumption that written compositions contain less—or at least different—formulaic material. The functional explanations for the use of formulas support that supposition, insofar as formulas ought to be discarded once they no longer fulfil their original purpose. However, the transition would not be instant, nor the contrast clearly defined. Bäuml (1984) notes that changes in compositional method do not immediately or directly impact on the needs of a listening audience, so that formulaic material serving the interests of the latter must be retained independently of the new opportunities afforded by writing. Davies (1997) suggests, for instance, that

> authors chose to include traditional formulae in their written narratives … not only because they had inherited these techniques from oral tradition, but also because they viewed their texts as performances for a hearing public.
> (p. 123)

The expectations of a listening audience begin, as before, with the requirements inherent in real-time reception, though, as mentioned earlier, listeners may increasingly demand a faithful reproduction of the 'model' that exists in writing.

However, other dynamics also exist, including the possibility of using markers of the old oral style as definers of a 'traditional' form. These various considerations might not only help perpetuate many formulas after they were no longer required for their original reasons, but also demand their deliberate introduction into new written compositions, in order to mark those new works as culturally 'authentic'. Bäuml (1984: 44f) describes the process whereby, as the written medium becomes established in its own right,

> [i]n referring to the oral tradition, the written text fictionalizes it. Since the one is given a role to play within the other, since oral formulae in the garb of writing refer to 'orality' within the written tradition, the oral tradition becomes an implicit fictional 'character' of literacy.
> (p. 43)

On these grounds, Brockington (1998) advises caution when using oral features as an index for the origin of text. They may in fact be "a symptom of the breakdown of the true oral tradition, when such features are deliberately imitated in order to give authenticity—or perhaps more accurately the right flavour—to later material" (p. 136). Thus is created pseudo-orality, in which the inevitable fiction of the narrator is suppressed—that is, the fact that the narrator is not present at the time of the telling, but separate in time and space from the reader, is made less obvious, in a pseudo-authenticity that can come close to parody (Bäuml 1984: 45). Such parody is, arguably, nowadays so inculcated in certain genres of writing for spoken performance that we view it as authentic in its own right. A play script can seem to be a clearer depiction of speech than a true orthographic transcription in which the themes and speaker roles are often much more difficult to identify (see Chapters 15 and 20).

Once the possibility of such complex interactions between oral and written traditions is recognized, it becomes more evident that, as Bäuml (1984) proposes, neither Homer nor the Yugoslavian oral traditions were necessarily all that 'pure'. Both were "product[s] of a culture affected by writing ...[,] products of semi-oral or secondary-oral cultures, in which oracy is surrounded and supported by literacy" (p. 34).[10] This view leads Bäuml to advise caution about comparing this poetry with truly oral traditions such as those found in parts of Africa or Micronesia. It reminds us also that the transition from oral to written culture is a gradual one, and that each can influence the other over a lengthy period. At first, writing may be treated as the less authoritative of the two mediums (see, for instance, Fuller's 2001 discussion of the relative status of written and oral versions of the Vedas). According to Clanchy (1993), as literacy became established in England in the eleventh to thirteenth centuries, it was at first to the "oral wisdom of their elders and remembrancers" that people turned for authoritative information, rather than to the written records. Only by the reign of Edward I (d. 1307) was written evidence starting to be required if a fact was to be established in law (p. 3). However, once writing becomes viewed as the most reliable conduit of information, it will be used in new ways. Expectations will rise about what can be known by an individual and how quickly it can be learnt.[11] Performers might increasingly fear that traditions can only be preserved if they are recorded in writing.

Writing: a cause or symptom of change?

As we have seen, the structure of oral poetry is heavily dependent on formulas for reasons that Parry and Lord identify as fundamental to the oral product. Written texts, in contrast,

> are independent of the performer and subject to the multiple conventions governing the writing and reading of 'literary' texts. They offer the reader a relatively limited measure of semantic redundancy and a correspondingly greater degree of indeterminacy, as well as no possibility of participating in, and thus affecting, their formulation.
> (Bäuml 1984: 36)

For all of these reasons, many of the functions associated with oral texts no longer apply when the text is composed in writing. As a result, the complexities just reviewed notwithstanding, there should be notable differences between the two.

> An *oral* text will yield a predominance of clearly demonstrable formulas, with the bulk of the remainder 'formulaic', and a small number of non-

formulaic expressions. A *literary* text will show a predominance of nonformulaic expressions, with some formulaic expressions, and very few clear formulas.
(Lord 2000: 130)

While Lord's observation is valid within his own definition of the formula, it does not apply so clearly to formulaic sequences more generally, which continue to have a role in written literature. MacKenzie (2003) points out that even though literature composed within a fully-developed literary culture tends to favour originality, so that it is more often viewed as a *source* of formulaic language than a repository for it, written fiction does feature a great deal of formulaic material. It may be there for aesthetic reasons, as a mark of genre, or simply because it is part of the vocabulary of the language. In all events, it remains possible, in written texts as in oral ones, to aim to account for the presence of formulaic language in terms of its functions. Since the needs of a writer and his or her readers are different from those of the oral performer and his or her audience, we should anticipate also that the functions, and hence realizations, of the formulaic sequences will be different.

All the same, as the discussion in this chapter indicates, it would be misleading to make any simple contrast. Parry and Lord's contention was that the introduction of writing actually ultimately destroyed the oral tradition, rather than simply sidelining it. Making available an alternative to formulaic storytelling appeared to change not just the stories but the tellers and their audience. It created a new way of thinking (Olson 1994; Lord 2000: 125). In the next chapter, we explore the role of literacy in shaping our perceptions and in creating the context in which we establish and maintain our repository of formulaic language.

Notes

1 It should be noted that neither chapter directly engages with manifestations of textual difference between speech and writing (for example, Biber 1989, 2000), though key features of studies will be mentioned, as relevant.

2 What is perhaps less obvious but more significant is that the different versions do not more often diversify to the point of becoming unrecognizable as expressions of the same rhyme.

3 See also Wray (2002b: 71, 283) on 'Ibble obble black bobble' and 'How many beans make five?'.

4 See Davies (1996) for one comparative study of story versions.

5 Compare criteria E and H in Chapter 8.

6 Formulas comparable to those in Homer are also found in the Sanskrit epics (Brockington 1998) and in the Welsh Mabinogion tales (Davies 1997, 2007).

7 Taken from the perspective of 'meme' theory (Blackmore 1999), the story survives only if it is memorable. This applies to the audience as well as the performer (Mandler and Johnson 1977: 113).

8 Compare the term 'wild boar' which, in British English at least, does not now entail that the animal is wild. On the contrary, all 'wild boar' in Britain are farmed, unless they escape. In a recent case of animal liberation by activists, radio news discussions about whether the loose animals, living wild, might be dangerous to dog walkers consistently referred to them as 'feral wild boar' to differentiate them from ordinary non-wild wild boar.

9 Though he acknowledges that observing the practices of modern day performers of oral epics did provide Parry and Lord with independent evidence.

10 Stevick (1962) places Old English verse, potentially, into the same ambiguous category (p. 383).

11 For example, the Brahmans in Tamil Nadu observed by Fuller (2001) were not by any means always sufficiently familiar with the traditional texts they were reciting, and were "just winging it" (p. 2). The learning process amongst the priests that Fuller studied entailed a literate approach, in which "verbatim memorization, in significant part, is done from a text to which the student repeatedly returns in order to perfect and test his verbatim mastery" (p. 3). This was supplemented by imitation of the guru's recitation patterns, necessary "to learn how to vocalize the texts with the correct stress, pitch and rhythm" (p. 3).

5
Formulaicity in speech and writing

Introduction

Chapter 4 showed how researchers have construed the effect of literacy on formulaic language in the oral narrative tradition. In this chapter, we explore the proposal that literacy is not the cause, but rather a symptom, of an independently motivated trajectory for autonomy, determined by the extent to which a society engages with outsiders.

Literacy and perceptions of language and the world

How we engage with language

Although a study by Scribner and Cole (1981) denies that it *must* be so (see later), many researchers claim that developing literacy entails cognitive training, including certain reconfigurations of linguistic knowledge, such that "learning to read and write introduces into the system qualitatively new strategies for dealing with oral language, ... [namely] conscious phonological processing, visual formal lexical representation, and all the associations that these strategies allow" (Reis and Castro-Caldas 1997: 445).[1] Interestingly, Reis and Castro-Caldas tend to portray illiteracy as the cause of an abnormal deficit in linguistic ability, even though literacy is a recent innovation in our species. They observe: "the missing of a single skill (grapheme-phoneme association) interferes significantly in the higher development of the language system" (p. 449). In taking this position, they reflect what Grace (2002) terms "culture-centricity",[2] that is, they judge linguistic normality on the basis of a cultural feature that is optional and, in global and historical terms, exceptional (Wray 2008b; see also Chapter 17).

Yet when it comes to the notion of the 'word' it is easier to see how literacy might be viewed as supplying a missing link. There is evidence that until writing is introduced, the precise definition of the 'word' can remain under-specified (Himmelmann 2006: 254)—though, as Himmelmann (2006) notes, it is not that illiterates have no sense at all of what the 'word' is, but rather that there is a fuzzy middle-ground, particularly relating to compounds, particle constructions, and formulaic sequences (p. 255). The requirement to write down language in an alphabetic form forces the issue by demanding word boundaries to be indicated, and this results in a strong saliency for the 'word' in those languages able to define it as a letter string with a gap either side.[3] As Dixon and Aikhenvald (2002) observe, "much that has been written about the word is decidedly eurocentric" (p. 2) and "it appears that only some languages actually have a lexeme with the meaning 'word'" (ibid.). Amongst the languages for which there is dispute about the existence of the word as a reliable category is Chinese (Dixon and Aikhenvald 2002: 3, 32f). While it is clear from their discussion that much hinges on how 'word' is defined—as a phonological, grammatical, or social unit—several studies confirm that Chinese native speakers are unable to match each other's decisions, or replicate their own previous ones, in text segmentation tasks: "[they] identify whole phrases as words and sometimes do not understand instructions asking them to identify 'words'" (Bassetti 2005: 338).

Evidence from semi-literate people in nineteenth century England (Fairman 2000, 2002, 2003, 2006) indicates that even in English the word is not a clearly defined entity for its speakers until they learn the rules. Fairman finds, inter alia, 'be long' (belong), 'shuar ans' (assurance), 'an old stablish fun' (an old established fund), 'a prentice' (apprentice), 'in form' (inform), 'a gree', 'a grid' (agree, agreed), 'con clued' (conclude), 'de stress' (distress), 'so fistient' (sufficient), 'a bay' (obey), 'de terminashon' (determination), 'a nuf' (enough) (Fairman 2006).[4]

Literacy and our world view

Olson (1994) believes that a literate society develops "literate thought" (p. 281), and in this regard, culture-centricity is no doubt inevitable for those who function in a literate society, for "[o]ur modern conception of the world and our modern conception of ourselves are, we may say, by-products of the invention of a world on paper" (ibid.: 282). On the other hand, the traditions and expectations of oracy may, for at least a while, constrain the opportunities afforded by literacy. Bloch (1993) in relation to a village in Madagascar, and Fuller (2001) describing learning practices in India, both note how schooling based around literacy gained a status independent of its effective functions in the local context. Literacy and education were perceived as the gateway to a more secure future, and formulaic learning (i.e. by rote) was favoured as the means for ensuring that information perceived as valuable could be recalled, even if it was not understood and could not be used.

Written text and information

According to Ong (1992), writing "separates the known from the knower ... [as] [t]he objectivity of the text helps impose objectivity on what the text refers to" (p. 307). The effect can be traumatic. Biber (1988: 4) notes how the introduction of written records forced people to confront the possibility that some of the knowledge of past generations was incorrect. Clanchy (1993) believes that the insinuation of literacy into the English way of life in the medieval period was, by virtue of influencing how people thought about themselves and the world, as significant as the invention of printing (p. 1). He describes slow but profound changes to perceptions of knowledge, as written records became viewed as more authoritative than human memory,[5] and as, by the start of the fourteenth century, people in all sections of society became bound by documentation, even if they could not read and write themselves (p. 2). People had to *learn* how to be literate, only slowly understanding how to avoid forgery by the use of seals, signs, and signatures. The use of dates on letters, he suggests, entailed a major change in self-perception, regarding the location of the writer "in the temporal order" (p. 2)—that is, comprehending that the knowledge of the writer is separated by time and events from the knowledge of a later reader.[6]

But is it really literacy that is making the difference, or the schooling by which it is imparted? Scribner and Cole's (1981) study of the Vai in Liberia was able separately to assess each factor, since the Vai's indigenous syllabary was not taught in school, while literacy in English and in Koranic Arabic was. Their conclusion was that it was not literacy, but schooling, that led people to view language and the world in new ways (pp.157, 251).

Formulaicity in language across domains

It will be argued in this section that formulaicity in language is intimately connected with autonomy of expression. By association, then, there is a potential relationship between formulaicity and writing. One aspect of the link regards the 'objectifying' of language, whereby notions of correctness can become detached from usage, so that schooling is required to instil a potentially artificial set of practices (Pawley and Syder 1983a: 559). Thus is created a specialized, somewhat artificial form of language that extends beyond normal acquisition, and requires education to master (Wray 2008b). As such it "has many of the characteristics of learning a second language. It is the product of schooling and book-learning; a fair proportion of native speakers of English never gain a good active facility in [it]" (Pawley and Syder 1983a: 557).[7] Language as an object of analytic examination, rather than as a functional code for communication, has been claimed, in Chapters 2 and 3, to be a determiner of the amount and nature of formulaic material in the lexicon, particularly in adult language learners. Later in this section another line of evidence will be presented for how adult learners, as outsiders, may play a significant role in determining the forms of a language.

Levels of autonomy in speech and writing

According to Pawley and Syder (1983a) there are some clear and consistent differences between speech and writing, which revolve around the role of autonomy (Table 5.1)—though we should not precipitately assume a direct mapping of writing onto autonomous text (see below). These differences, subject perhaps to some negotiation,[8] can serve as a reference point for the ways that formulaicity manifests in the oral versus written domain both in literature and other kinds of text. How autonomy is actually achieved textually is a separate issue, and one indirectly addressed in Biber's work (for example, 1988, 1989).[9]

Although Pawley and Syder's observations imply a stark contrast between the two modes of expression, we have already noted that things are not so simple. There are hybrid varieties of language, which mix features archetypically associated with speech and writing (Biber 1988: 24). Formal lectures and speeches, even if extemporized, can still in many respects resemble written language. Biber, Conrad, and Cortes (2004) found the discourse of classroom teaching to show "a more extensive use of stance lexical bundles and discourse organising bundles than in conversation, while at the same time it [showed] a more extensive use of referential bundles than in academic [written] prose" (p. 399). Meanwhile, emails and text messages can approximate speech in some respects, even though they are written. Indeed, the practice of copying parts of an incoming email message into the reply in order to comment on them creates a kind of intertextuality that mimics conversation even though it takes place with neither the temporal nor spatial proximity needed for a live spoken exchange (Fontaine 2004).

In sum, it can be argued that certain features of written language, including those associated with textual autonomy, are not specifically a product of it. That is, written texts normally have certain characteristics because of the ways in which, culturally, we use written texts. When writing is used to record information for readers who may not share local contextual information, the text must be explicit. But if writer and reader do not need that level of explicitness, it can be dispensed with. The risk of inadequate communication is greatest when the producer and receiver of the text are most distant in time and space. But in so far as similar risks of inadequate comprehension arise in the spoken medium, a speaker, too, might elect to provide cues that create a more autonomous text, even though the hearer is present. It follows that some of the features of a language that are most effectively identified in writing actually might in fact arise independently of it.

A Conversational discourse	B Autonomous discourse
1 Is part of a face-to-face meeting between participants.	1 There is no meeting.
2 What is said at the meeting is the joint creation of all participants.	2 The discourse is a text, created by a composer (or composers) who is (are) separate from the audience.
3 Each message is shaped to fit a particular addressee who is a known quantity.	3 The audience is anonymous. Therefore the text is shaped to be understood by anyone, or by a general class of people.
4 Messages are time-bonded by the constraints of the meeting, together with biological limitations on processing.	4 Composition and reading of the text is free of the time constraints present in face-to-face meetings.
5 Communication is multi-channel. Paralinguistic and kinetic signals, as well as words are employed.	5 Communication is single-channel, using words alone to signal meaning.
6 Observable features of the physical setting may be used to indicate meaning or to interpret signals.	6 The decoder is remote from the addressee; therefore the meaning should be explicit, fully contained in the text.
7 Conversational signals are manipulative as well as informational. Each utterance has personal significance for the addressee, being designed to contribute to an interaction.	7 Messages are impersonal and informational. They convey nothing of the author's unique personality nor do they carry personal significance for the decoder.
8 The discourse does not have a monumental character. It is composed of dynamic elements, which contribute to an interaction and then disappear.	8 The text is a static thing. Once made, it remains, a monument to be examined in isolation as an achievement in itself.

Table 5.1 Pawley and Syder's (1983a) differences between conversational and autonomous discourse (pp. 557–58)

Expressive autonomy in closed and open societies

Evidence from anthropological and linguistic studies of technologically primitive societies suggests that there is a continuum in terms of autonomy in text, according to the social structure of the speech community, and that it corresponds with the level of formulaicity in the language. Thurston (1987, 1989, 1994) models language use within a given community as predominantly either esoteric (inward-facing) or exoteric (outward-facing). Esoterically-oriented communication operates between individuals who know each other and have a single group identity, culture and environment, so that a huge amount of knowledge about daily practices is already shared (Thurston 1989: 556). Communication in such circumstances can take a great deal for granted, reducing the need for explicitness in routine exchanges. One of the features of languages employed for esoteric communication is a high level of formulaicity. Other features, related to formulaicity, are semantic opacity, grammatical irregularity, and phonological and morphological complexity (Laycock 1979; Thurston 1987, 1989, 1994; see also Trudgill 2002).

As Figure 5.1 indicates, implicit encoding simultaneously supports internal social cohesion and creates a barrier to communication with outsiders who do not share the group's knowledge (Thurston 1987; Everett 2005).

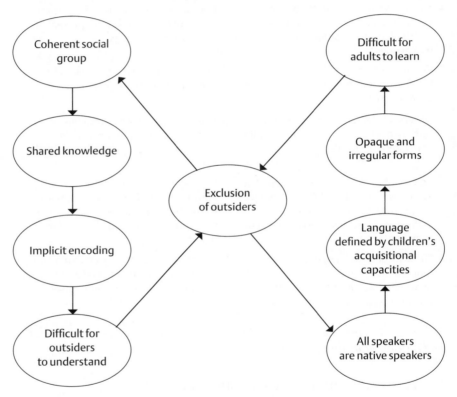

Figure 5.1 The perpetuation of esoteric communication in a closed community

Exoteric communication, on the other hand, is outward-facing, and is suited to interactions with strangers, whether they be unknown individuals in one's own community or members of other groups (Figure 5.2). The larger and more complex a society becomes, the more likely it is to adopt features of exotericity in communication. In such a society, it is not possible to assume

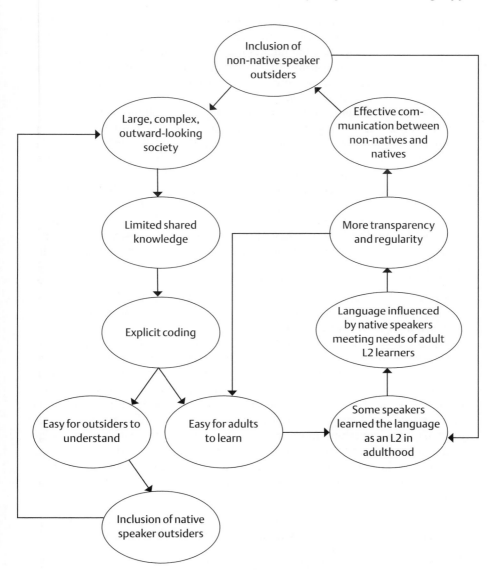

Figure 5.2 The perpetuation of exoteric communication in an outward-looking community

that all addressees share one's knowledge or practices, and so it is necessary to be explicit with regard to reference and structure, so as to reduce the likelihood of misunderstandings. Thus, societies in which an individual regularly needs to interact with strangers and specialists must have available means for keeping communication relatively autonomous—not necessarily as autonomous as writing makes possible, but sufficiently independent of context and previous knowledge for someone to figure out meaning on the basis of general principles. Languages used exoterically will tend to develop and maintain linguistic features that are logical, transparent, phonologically and morphologically simple, and (as a result) learnable by adult incomers (Thurston 1989; Trudgill 1989, 2002).

In principle, the written medium can equally serve either esoteric or exoteric communication, in so far as it is primarily no more than a re-encoding of speech. As always, the efficacy of communication is dependent on the producer's capacity to anticipate the knowledge of the receiver, so that the message is as explicit as necessary to ensure comprehension, yet with the minimum possible processing on the part of the receiver. All the same, in modern (as well as many ancient) cultures, writing has been perceived as a medium offering particular benefits in the service of exoteric communication, not least because the permanency of writing—whereas speech is transient—naturally creates the potential for reception that is spatially and temporally distant from production, with local contextualizing cues no longer available. English, being an internationally prominent language used across many cultures, particularly promotes, for its educated written style, explicitness, clarity, and transparency, though it retains many esoteric features when used between familiar native speakers.

The extensive potential implications of Thurston's proposals about esoteric and exoteric communication are further discussed in Chapter 17. For present purposes, it is sufficient to note that autonomy in linguistic communication is inversely correlated with the perceived cultural knowledge level of the hearer/reader, and that the written medium, while hugely widening the potential gap between speaker/writer and hearer/reader, is essentially just the extreme expression of something more general: the need for producers of language to gauge how much they need to say in order to deliver the desired message effectively. The role of formulaicity in all of this resides in the reverse side of the coin: how *little* can the speaker/writer afford to do and *still* deliver that message effectively?

Conclusion: formulaicity as a measure of autonomy

That there is a desire on the part of the language producer to hit the balance just right between economy and explicitness is predicated on the theoretical position that explicitness is costly in processing terms. Where the speaker anticipates that the hearer has a similar cultural and contextual knowledge base to her own, and possesses a similar lexicon, there will be advantages to using MEUs where possible. They will reduce the amount of processing that must be done by the hearer too—something that is to the speaker's ultimate advantage (Wray 2002b: 99). However, when the speaker has reason to doubt the hearer's level of general or linguistic knowledge, compromises are made in the direction of less formulaicity.

The NOA model predicts that five factors determine the level of formulaicity in a speaker's output: (1) the appropriacy of a formula in expressing *exactly* the desired message; (2) the estimated likelihood of the hearer understanding the formula; (3) the desire on the part of the speaker to signal identity through language; (4) local conditions affecting the processing demands on the speaker and hearer; and (5) the specific desire to express the idea in a novel way. Figure 5.3 unites these considerations with the factors identified in this chapter as likely to reduce the level of formulaicity: the autonomy that is inherent in using the written medium and that arises from operating within a complex, outward-facing society.

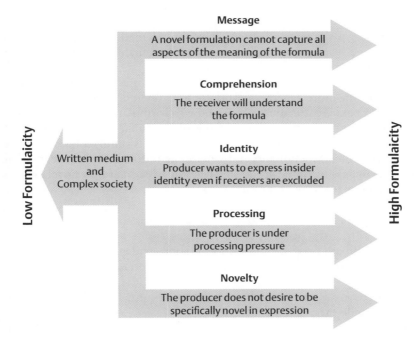

Figure 5.3 Determinants of formulaicity

Where these different factors place contradictory demands on the level of formulaicity, one must dominate. If the speaker's strongest priority is to be novel, then formulaic material will be dispreferred even if other considerations favour it, for it will appear clichéd. Conversely, if the speaker has a strong desire to signal identity with a group that the hearer/reader does not belong to by using an 'in phrase', the price may be that the hearer does not understand what is said.

It has been argued in this chapter that the fundamental differences between spoken and written language are secondary, rather than primary. The medium of expression facilitates, rather than determines, the differences between text types. That is, the written medium has characteristics that alter the needs of the text creator and text receiver and offer different opportunities and constraints when achieving communicative functions. That these emergent features are not *determined* by the fact of writing, only *made more possible* by it, is clear from the variation in levels of autonomy found in texts composed for different purposes. While a public text, certainly, must reflect a wide (though not necessarily all-encompassing) view of what its various readers might be able to understand of its references and allusions, something written for just one other person at one specific time—such as a mobile phone text message, or a note left on the kitchen table—does not need to accommodate more than one reader, or even the same reader on another occasion. Thus the level of autonomy is determined on the basis of when, and by whom, the creator envisages the text to be used. The choices made in relation to form are determined by the perceived needs of the immediate, or spatially, and/or temporally distant, receiver.

Thus, the question of how formulaic sequences appear in a text is simply one aspect of the more general question of how reference is effectively made in texts. Any text creator must choose how to formulate the message in the manner most appropriate to the meeting of the range of actual or future communicative needs. The selection of a MEU unit is simply a lexical choice that has additional functionality if, by mapping onto a complex meaning, it enables the bypassing of the processing necessary for creating a novel expression of the same message or message part.

Notes

1 Indeed, as Biber (1988: 5) notes, there is some evidence that thinking in a literate way *prec*edes the acquisition of literacy and is, in fact, an effective entry to it.

2 See also Olson (1977: 272), Thurston (1989: 559n), Trudgill (1989: 230), and Tomasello (2003: 3–5).

3 In Biber, Johansson, Leech, and Conrad's (1999) corpus survey of English, they "relied on orthographic word units, even though these sometimes rather arbitrarily combine separate words" (p. 990).

4 It is notable that these examples display the insertion of unnecessary word breaks rather than the omission of necessary ones. However, the pattern may be no more than a reflection of the types of words that tend not to be known: long, Latinate ones. Long words are likely to be split. Where Anglo-Saxon words are written, there are instances of conflation and mis-breaks—'taket' (take it), 'a tome' (at home), 'a torll' (at all). Furthermore, Guillaume (1927/1973) offers many examples of conflation in the French of semi-literates—for example, *aidi* (*ai dit*, 'have said'), *cecerai* (*ce serait*, 'this would be'), and *semy* (*c'est mis*, 'it is put').

5 This is now commonplace. In legal contexts, for instance, "the transcript of proceedings … becomes the record of what occurred" (Tiersma 1999:

177), even though there are many reasons why what is written down cannot be more than a pale reflection of the verbal account, which is itself only a partial depiction of the actual event described (Cotterill 2002: 156).

6 There are perhaps parallels here between the learning processes associated with a society becoming literate and those experienced by our own generation in relation to electronic technologies. Graff (1991) suggests that even in societies with high levels of literacy, much of the potential of reading and writing is not tapped because it is not relevant to most people's everyday lives. The same clearly applies in relation to the internet and software.

7 Compare Graff (1991): "In Italy and Hungary ... 40 per cent of the population do not read to any appreciable extent; in France, 53 per cent do not; and in the United States, with low levels of absolute literacy, 'functional' illiteracy is quite high: estimates range up to a full 50 per cent of adults" (p. 2).

8 There are several shortcomings in the Pawley and Syder list (Chris Butler, personal communication). For instance, autonomous discourse, where written (as we assume it usually is) is not 'single-channel' (point 5), since meaning is made using syntactic structures, punctuation, and often typography. Also, written texts actually lie on a cline of autonomy (point 7), since it is certainly possible to include authorial information and direct petitions to particular readers. This reminds us not to read 'autonomous' as 'written' even though there are clearly correspondences between them.

9 For instance, first person pronouns and private verbs—such as 'think', 'feel' (Biber 1988: 105)—featured most often in face-to-face conversation, followed by personal letters and interviews, whereas press reports, academic writing, and official documents had very little (Biber 1989: 11). Biber's claim, substantiated by a multifactor analysis of different text types, is that the contextualized/decontextualized dimension—as he terms the non-autonomous/autonomous one—is just one of many that interact to create a much more intricate range of variational features across texts (Biber 1988: chapter 1).

PART TWO

Locating boundaries

6

Morpheme equivalent units in the bigger picture

Introduction

Overall, much that is written about formulaic language is somewhat atheoretical—or rather, there are often implicit assumptions about theory that are inadequately acknowledged or developed. To take one fairly unequivocal example, formulaic sequences are customarily described as bypassing the normal processes by which language is constructed. The notion of a dichotomy between holistically-accessed and bespoke-generated material offers a valuable starting point for exploring what formulaicity entails. But it requires a solid theoretical justification.

The growing awareness that generative models have often been unhelpfully over-productive and that language falls into repetitive patterns with particular meanings and functions has driven the development of a range of alternative formulations of grammatical knowledge and behaviour that do not exclude formulaic language from the main activity of the grammar, but rather incorporate it as more—even entirely—central. The psycholinguistic notion of large, internally complex units stored in the lexicon has increasingly been captured in both grammatical models and corpus-based investigations (Tomasello 1998). The boundaries between the theoretical models are changing, and it is important frequently to re-evaluate the relationship between claims in one domain and those in the others.

Ultimately, one is looking for a comprehensive model of language that can adequately accommodate the three key facets of formulaic language: its patterns of manifestation, the principles underlying those patterns, and the motivations for its use. The Needs Only Analysis (NOA) model presented in Wray (2002b) and explored further in this book represents an attempt to engage with only one of those three facets, the last. It is an account of the psychological and social reasons why we use formulaic language. Although one central aspect of the psychological explanation entails an account of how lexical storage might work, it is far from a comprehensive cognitive one, and it does not in itself encompass a grammatical model. Nor is there extensive engagement with examples from corpora at the primary level.

So the adequacy of the NOA model must be judged on the extent to which it offers a productive interface with the other two facets. That is, it must meld effectively with at least one account of how formulaic language arises from grammatical principles, and it must comfortably accommodate the evidence from corpus analyses. This chapter and the next examine the extent to which the NOA model can be viewed as a useful contribution to a comprehensive model of language, by exploring the boundaries between grammatical models, patterns discovered in corpora, and models of how our linguistic knowledge is formulated and used.

It is a moving target, and overall there is now sufficient cross-fertilization of approaches for us to aspire to the development of a multifaceted account that brings together our best understandings of language form, knowledge, and behaviour. To that end, it is at the boundaries between the domains that the interesting questions can be asked.

The desiderata for a comprehensive model of language

Three parameters: patterns, their causes, and the principles behind them

We shall assume here the desirability of a usage-driven model[1] of the nature of language (formulaic or otherwise), as the most appropriate way to capture the entirety of the individual's linguistic knowledge and practice. Such a model requires attention to three central parameters:

1 the *patterns of language* that are produced by one or more individuals,
2 a descriptive and predictive account of the *principles underlying the patterns*, and
3 the *causes of those patterns*, that is, what the individual language user does and why.

Some models of the principles (2), particularly those influenced by Chomskyan approaches, deprioritize what is actually said (1) and the social and psychological reasons why things are said in certain ways (3), in order to focus on the hypothesized underlying mental representations of what *can* and *cannot* be said, as evidenced by native speaker intuitions. Other models, however, rather than sidelining linguistic behaviour, pay attention to what, amongst the possible, is also *probable*. The ideal model of language will find a means to accommodate both the human's abstract linguistic knowledge *and* the human's application of it in real communication, and thereby create synergy between accounts of the patterns, their causes and the principles behind them (Givón 1995: xv, 1998: 63–4).[2] Figure 6.1 maps a relationship between the three parameters.

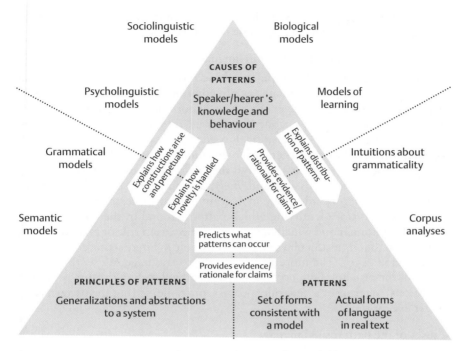

Sociolinguistic models

Biological models

CAUSES OF PATTERNS

Psycholinguistic models

Speaker/hearer's knowledge and behaviour

Models of learning

Grammatical models

Explains how constructions arise and perpetuate

Explains how novelty is handled

Provides evidence/ rationale for claims

Explains distribution of patterns

Intuitions about grammaticality

Semantic models

Predicts what patterns can occur

Provides evidence/ rationale for claims

Corpus analyses

PRINCIPLES OF PATTERNS

Generalizations and abstractions to a system

PATTERNS

Set of forms consistent with a model

Actual forms of language in real text

Figure 6.1 Requirements of a comprehensive theory of language in use

Patterns in language

The patterns of language (bottom right in Figure 6.1) are increasingly discovered by examining large linguistic corpora. Research suggests that "lexical bundles should be regarded as a basic linguistic construct with important functions for the construction of discourse" (Biber, Conrad, and Cortes 2004: 398). Despite a number of notable exceptions, including the *Longman Grammar of Speech and Writing* (Biber, Johansson, Leech, and Conrad 1999) and associated work, there is often an over-representation of written language relative to spoken in corpus studies.[3] This bias to writing somewhat compromises the relationship between the corpus data and accounts of the causes of patterns (top of Figure 6.1), since the forms and structures in speech and writing are not by any means identical.

Overall, the impact of the writing bias on how we conceptualize the principles of patterns (bottom left) is less severe (though there are still considerable issues at that interface, as noted later), because there, too, the written language still tends to predominate, even in cognitive and functional approaches where spontaneous speech is at least recognized as a valid focus of investigation. Corpus evidence of patterns is increasingly used to provide evidence for research into both the causes and the principles of patterns in language, and it acts as an arbiter in assessing the validity of the claims made about how speakers and hearers behave, and how the underlying grammar operates.

Principles underlying the patterns in language

Grammatical (including semantic)[4] models characterize the principles behind the patterns in language, though, as already noted, not all approaches prioritize observed language over the set of hypothesized patterns that native speakers would be able to encode if they needed to, and decode should they encounter them. In fact, all such models need to make predictions about which formulations that have not been observed *could* be observed tomorrow (that is, could turn up in a corpus), though they vary in the extent to which they aim to predict what is possible and *likely*, as opposed to possible yet rather *unlikely*. Explanatory adequacy in a grammatical or semantic model also requires a means of identifying which patterns found in the corpus belong within the grammar and which only occurred because a rule or procedure was violated, so that intuition plays an important role in interpreting corpus data, (Butler 2004: 150). The more dedicated it is to language in use, the more a model of the principles underlying the patterns will seek to capture recurrent 'violations' in terms of a new rule, process, or frame, so that the pattern is no longer exceptional.

Causes of the patterns in language

Language patterns derive from the speaker and are interpreted by the hearer, and there are several angles from which researchers can aim to explain them. Patterns are created when thoughts are matched to abstract linguistic representations, which are then expressed as phonated (or written) forms. These processes are captured in psychological (psycholinguistic or cognitive) models. Clearly, assembling and decoding language entails the use of some sort of grammatical and semantic knowledge, though theoretical models of that knowledge vary in the extent to which they directly aim to represent psycholinguistic processing.

The activities of the human mind must map in some way onto the firing of neurons in the brain, so there are also biological (neurolinguistic) models of how the patterns of language are created and understood (for example, Lamb 1999). Again, there is not always a direct relationship between a psycholinguistic and a neurolinguistic model, though there will be clear points of contact for the two, particularly in the domain of language pathology (for example, after localized brain damage). The choice of one linguistic pattern over another (and the interpretation of a pattern in input as one thing rather than another) is determined by the individual's social awareness and social intent, so that sociolinguistic models also inform our understanding of how the patterns of language are caused. Finally, there must be models of learning, to help account for the accumulation and maintenance of patterns in the individual and in the language itself.

Interactions across boundaries

Each of the three facets of a comprehensive model is exemplified by many approaches, and in the first instance, it is useful to examine how each interacts with each of the others.

The interface between patterns and their causes

One attempt to engage at the boundary of the patterns of text and the causes of those patterns is Hoey's (2005) lexical priming model.[5] In his view, "collocation is fundamentally a psychological concept" (p. 7) and so he goes to the psychological theory of priming to account for collocational patterns in language. Specifically, he proposes,

> As a word is acquired through encounters with it in speech and writing, it becomes cumulatively loaded with the contexts and co-texts with which it is encountered, and our knowledge of it includes the fact that it co-occurs with certain other words in certain kinds of context.
> (ibid.: 8)

Word sequences can also be primed, through a process that he calls 'nesting', in which it is the string as a whole, rather than its component parts, that are primed (ibid.). Nesting, he suggests, offers processing reduction benefits, a view highly compatible with the NOA model. However, he views the priming of word sequences as normally later developed than the priming of single words, and a product of it (i.e. of what in other accounts is termed 'chunking' or 'fusion').

In this crucial regard, Hoey's model of learning and knowledge is substantively different from the one proposed here. In his lexical priming, the word is the fundamental currency of processing (see Chapter 5 for discussion of whether this can hold across all languages), whereas in the NOA model it is not the word, but whichever lexical unit—in many cases the word, but also often larger than the word, or smaller—that constitutes the largest form-meaning mapping so far found adequate to handle the effective manipulation of input and output. These morpheme equivalent units (MEUs) constitute a layer of wrapping that protects the components from analysis under normal circumstances. As a result, words contained within a MEU, although collocational associates in the sense of occurring adjacently in text, are not really 'associates' in his sense at all. Rather, they are sub-parts of a single large unit, much as 'im-' often occurs adjacent to 'possible'. Wray (2002b) suggests that our poor intuitions about collocational patterns are explained if items within the MEU are being excluded from our scrutiny (pp. 276–9).

The interface of the causes of patterns and the principles underlying them

Meanwhile, models of principles of patterns (i.e. grammatical models) can also be usefully informed by accounts of the causes of patterns. For instance, the psychological or social explanation for why a pattern is useful can help to justify treating an attested example as core or peripheral. Perhaps the only reason why pattern *p* is found in a corpus is because it has been recently coined as a deliberate violation of a standard pattern, and adopted for social reasons—as, perhaps, with the sarcastic clause-final negative in 'it's really interesting, not!'. Such sociolinguistic evidence could enable a grammatical model to treat the new 'rule' as an outlier relative to other more long-established formations of the negative. Similarly, neurological investigations of language, along with data from speakers with damage to their linguistic abilities, can help to evaluate the explanatory adequacy of models of the principles of patterns (for example, Walenski and Ullman 2005).

In return, the systematic description of the principles underlying patterns in a language provides a major service for models of the causes. The missing link for causation models is how *new* linguistic patterns will be handled. It is one thing to explain how a set of patterns observed in a corpus is processed and how it is used in social interaction, but quite another to predict, from those models, the fate of a new example. This is because causation models are inevitably post hoc and descriptive—they can explain something once it has happened, but cannot easily predict what will happen next time. A grammatical or semantic theory provides causation models with a basis for defining what else might happen in the future. In other words, robust models of what causes patterns in language need to refer to one or more models of the underlying principles of those patterns, thereby accommodating the potential as well as the actual. This is what differentiates a model of causation from a description of the observed data.

The interface of the patterns and the principles

Finally, models of cause should be able to explain the differences between what is predicted by grammatical or semantic theory (the principles) and what is actually observed in corpora (the patterns) (for example, Barlow 2000; Biber *et al.* 2004). This is achieved by creating a map of the priorities and limitations of humans engaged in real communication, and distinguishing linguistic behaviour from linguistic knowledge. It is probably true to say that, at present, the huge influx of evidence from linguistic corpora, combined with the considerable research activity in areas of speaker/hearer knowledge and behaviour, are combining to place severe pressure on grammatical models to predict less of that which is not actually observed (as well as more of what is).[6] However, unless grammatical and semantic models continue to predict more than is observed there will be no mechanism for explaining human linguistic creativity, our ability to interpret what is new (or error-filled), or how we learn language.

Locating formulaic language in a comprehensive model

Formulaic language can—and must—be viewed from all of the perspectives identified in the outside ring in Figure 6.1: psychological, social, neurological, acquisitional, grammatical, and textual (as revealed in corpora). The models proposed in Wray (2002b) are all located within the top area of the diagram. That is, they address the *causes* of formulaicity in language from the point of view of processing, interaction, brain function, and child and adult language learning.[7]

In order to meet the requirements of a comprehensive model of formulaicity in language, therefore, we must look beyond the domain of the Wray (2002b) models. In Chapter 7, we explore the extent to which existing grammatical theories and descriptions of patterns in corpora are able to complete the picture. To contextualize the discussion, a brief recap is given below of each of the bases for causality (psychological, social, acquisitional, and neurological) outlined in Wray (2002b). A more detailed account was provided in Chapter 2.

Points of reference: causes of formulaic language

The Wray (2002b) model of the psychological causes of formulaic language is predicated on the assumption that there is a premium on working memory capacity, so that it is advantageous during linguistic processing to avoid unnecessary real-time encoding and decoding. MEUs, whether complete or containing gaps for paradigmatic variation, are single lexical units, internally complex both in terms of structure and semantics, but encased in a holistic 'skin' that protects them from being analysed under normal circumstances. Because of their relative resilience to internal examination, MEUs make good mnemonics: a word string is memorized, with more focus on the rhythm and rhyme than the semantics. Later, because it has been faithfully remembered, it can be unwrapped to reveal the information that it was constructed to protect (see Chapter 20). For more on processing as a cause of formulaicity, see Wray (2002b: chapter 4 and *passim*).

The social aspect of the Wray (2002b) model is encapsulated in the proposal that MEUs are a linguistic solution to a non-linguistic problem, namely, the promotion of self (Wray 2002b: 95–100). Formulaic choices will be made on the basis of this single agenda, by means of the drive to manipulate others' actions, knowledge, or emotions to one's own advantage. There is a link between the social and psychological drives to use prefabricated language. MEUs are not only easier for the speaker to encode but also easier for a hearer with similar knowledge to decode. A speaker can, therefore, select MEUs as a means of directing the hearer to certain actions, beliefs, and feelings. Since manipulation extends to controlling how hearers perceive the speaker, formulaicity will feature in greetings, forms of address, and in linguistic markers of social identity, such as 'in phrases'. For more detail, see Wray (2002b: chapter 4).

In the NOA model, the acquisition of MEUs does *not* generally occur, as most models assume, by the gradual accretion of preferred assemblage routes, where word strings are first assembled by rule and later, if frequent enough, processed holistically.[8] Rather, NOA entails minimal engagement with the internal workings of input material, so that the learner is concerned only with mapping *units* onto meanings, without any preference for the structural form of the *unit*. Adult learners apply the same principle of NOA, but because their needs are different, so are the outcomes. For more on first and second language acquisition within the NOA model, see Wray (2002b: chapters 7 and 11).

The neurological component of the Wray (2002b) model distributes access to lexical knowledge around different parts of the brain (Wray 2002b: chapter 14). This idea is not a new one but is developed in new ways, by drawing on evidence from language loss in aphasia. Some of the rather mysterious patterns of language loss and language retention after damage to the 'language areas' of the brain can be explained if linguistic material is indexed to, and can be stimulated by, other brain activity that occurs when that material is used. For instance, brain activity that takes place when recognizing a familiar face might cue the production of a routine greeting. Since the greeting would also be anchored in the 'language areas' of the brain, damage to those areas would create a situation in which the item could not be produced on request (a metalinguistic activity) but nevertheless could be triggered automatically when seeing a familiar person walk past (see, for example, Wray 2008a). For more detail of the model, see Wray (2002b: chapter 13).

This combined account superficially reflects but in fact does not map onto the generative grammarian's aim to model the individual's mental representation of language (as opposed to language as a community phenomenon)—see Culicover and Jackendoff (2005: 10). Certainly, what is theorized is what an individual *knows*, i.e. the mental representation of linguistic knowledge from which particular instances of usage and comprehension derive. But this knowledge is contingent on social as well as psychological processes, so that it is not possible to separate out the linguistic knowledge of the individual from the interactional experience from which it is derived and for which it is used (Hymes 1972, 1992). That is, the *shape* of the knowledge (including lexical units and grammatical rules) is determined by what that individual happens to have experienced. Although no theory, of course, denies a role for input in shaping knowledge, many syntactic models view input as the catalyst for, and instantiation of, underlying patterns, rather than necessarily the designer of them.

To the interface

This chapter has provided the springboard for an extensive examination, in Chapter 7, of how various existing approaches to the modelling of language patterns and the principles behind the patterns fit with the Wray (2002b) account of how the patterns are caused.

Notes

1 I use 'usage-driven' so as not to make unnecessary assumptions in relation to the vast array of work now falling under the heading 'usage-based', a term first coined by Langacker (1987)—for example, see Langacker's own account of the term (Langacker 2000) and the discussion in Gonzálvez-García and Butler (2006: 42ff). All the same, it will be evident that the similarity in terms is matched by a similarity in general priorities. See Kemmer and Barlow (2000: pp. viii-xxii) for the main characteristics of usage-based models.

2 Butler (2003: chapter 6) evaluates in depth the explanatory adequacy of different structural-functional models, including how they interface with psycholinguistic theory, and his own desiderata for a comprehensive model. Butler's enterprise is much more sophisticated than what is offered here. I am grateful to him for pointing to some of the most important points of contact between his account and mine.

3 Although there are now substantial corpora of spoken language, including 10 million words in the British National Corpus, written material still considerably outweighs spoken. Furthermore, there remain severe limitations with analysing oral production through written means—not least in relation to how it is best transcribed to capture features not encoded in normal written text.

4 How semantics is located in theory relative to syntax is a matter of debate. See Culicover and Jackendoff (2005: preface and *passim*). In what follows more attention will be paid to grammatical than semantic theory, but this does not imply that the latter is not important. For one illustration of how semantic theory is used within a Cognitive Linguistic framework (and thus is compatible with several accounts examined here), see Feyaerts (2006).

5 Another is Jackendoff's (2002), considered later.

6 For instance, Tao and Meyer (2006) examined the International Corpus of English for examples of gapping. They found 17,629 sentences containing the local coordination that supports gapping, but only 120 instances of it, just 0.7 per cent (p. 136).

7 There is also an evolutionary adjunct (Wray 1998, 2000b, 2002a; Wray and Grace 2007; and Chapters 17 and 21 in this book), and child and adult language learning are separately modelled (Wray 2002b: chapters 7 and 11).

8 There is, however, nothing to prevent some word strings arising in this way. It is what Peters (1983: 82) terms "fusion".

7
Evaluating models at the interface

Introduction

This chapter explores the extent to which the challenge articulated in Chapter 6 can currently be met. That challenge was to locate formulaic language within a comprehensive model of how grammar, use, and psychological and social motivation interact. Not all the models discussed here emanate from researchers who believe formulaic language to be of central importance to a comprehensive account, though more attention is given to the theories that acknowledge its ubiquity and that recognize some sort of significant functional role for it. Naturally, the theories are discussed and evaluated specifically in regard to their actual or potential interaction with theoretical model outlined in Chapter 2 and reiterated at the end of Chapter 6. Other features of each model are necessarily set aside, and this inevitably means that the accounts here are partial in both senses of the word—incomplete as well as heavily inclined towards a particular set of requirements.

The exploration is probably best seen as progressing along a continuum, even though the section headings—*Generative theory*, *Functional grammar*, *Corpus-driven grammar*, and *The cognitive approach*—may imply a clearer division.[1] First, the virtual exclusion of internally complex items from the lexicon in Chomskyan-style generative grammars is recognized as incompatible with the heteromorphic lexicon model. For this reason, more attention is paid to one particular recent generative model, Simpler Syntax (Jackendoff 2002; Culicover and Jackendoff 2005). It has its roots in the Chomskyan tradition but is "markedly at odds" with aspects of it (Culicover and Jackendoff 2005: 3. For a summary of key differences, and a digest of issues arising from the comparison of his model with a number of others, including Cognitive and Construction Grammars, see Jackendoff 2007). Of particular significance to the present discussion is that it is more liberal in relation to the definition of lexical units.

In Systemic Functional Grammar (SFG), language structure is viewed in a fundamentally different way from the generativists, though it is still, technically speaking, a 'generative' model. With reference to work arising from the Cardiff Grammar (one of the versions of SFG), some suggestions are made for how a better interface with the Wray model might be achieved.

After a brief consideration of other functional models, attention is turned to corpus-driven models (though again we must recognize that there are no clear divisions here, for other approaches to modelling, particularly functional ones and cognitive ones, can be, and often are, strongly influenced by corpus data). Hunston and Francis's (2000) Pattern Grammar, a detailed taxonomy of the configurations in the Bank of English, is first considered. The resemblances between Pattern Grammar and Frame Semantics are noted, before we move, finally, to a discussion of Construction Grammar, a set of allied models positioned within the Cognitive Linguistics framework.

The exploration of models is very far from exhaustive and should be viewed only as indicative of the challenge that we face in trying to sew together the different parts of this complex whole.

Generative theory

Two of the key priorities of Chomskyan models of language structure are (a) humans' *use* of language should be kept distinct from the modelling of the underlying system, and (b) entry to the lexicon depends on the absence of a rule that could generate the form. In contrast, morpheme equivalent status in the present model is a matter of how humans' psycholinguistic and sociolinguistic priorities determine the handling of language as it is observed and used. As a result, performance, processing constraints and interactional behaviour are all central to defining the contents of the individual's lexicon, whereas they are essentially irrelevant for Chomskyan models (Walmsley 2006).

The Simpler Syntax model developed in Jackendoff (2002) and Culicover and Jackendoff (2005) is, by their own definition, rooted in mainstream generative grammar, but bears great similarities to various "alternative" generative models (p. 3). It is a comprehensive account of language that aims to reunite linguistic theory with cognitive science (Jackendoff 2002: p. xii), so that "the study of linguistic structure can provide an entrée into the complexities of mind and brain" (ibid.).[2] This broad approach is in some ways, therefore, highly compatible with the focus of the present chapter, since it "leads to a vision of the language faculty that better facilitates the integration of linguistic theory with concerns of processing, acquisition and biological evolution" (Culicover and Jackendoff 2005: p. x).

The principle of Simpler Syntax is to strip away levels of abstraction that have accreted in mainstream generative theory, on the basis that not only will the grammatical descriptions be more elegant but also the grammars they describe will be more learnable, and thus more plausible (Culicover and Jackendoff 2005: 11–12). The lexicon is not viewed as separate from the grammar (Culicover and Jackendoff 2005: 25ff), and the approach is sympathetic to the idea of heteromorphy in the lexicon. Jackendoff (2002) "arrive[s] at the view that lexical (i.e. stored) items are of heterogeneous sizes, from affixes to idioms and more abstract structures" (p. xv, also ibid.: chapter 6). In particular, he highlights memorized material (including "linguistic examples, poems, song lyrics, and plays") as likely to be stored in the lexicon (p. 153). However, in his view, such material is still treated compositionally, for 'memorized texts *are* made up of linguistic units—they are linked phonological, syntactic, and semantic structures that (at least mostly) conform to rules of grammar. Therefore they invoke the language faculty in their production and comprehension' (p. 152f).

One difficulty with interfacing this view with the Wray (2002b) model lies in Jackendoff's liberal position regarding what "conform[s] to the rules of grammar" (see the quote above). Consider the matter of memorizing a poem in another language. While it is certainly useful to have sufficient lexical knowledge to maintain the gist of the meaning, one does not need the ability to handle the grammatical and lexical content in any productive way. Classical singers memorize texts for the operatic, chamber, and religious repertoire in many more languages than they can speak, and in such cases, their performance effectively outstrips their linguistic competence (cf. Wray 2002a: 129ff; Fitzpatrick and Wray 2006). In these cases, there are too few rules of grammar to account for the success of the outcome as a truly generative event—yet it is far from the case that *no* linguistic activity is involved, for form-meaning links are one way to minimize the danger of forgetting one's lines.

The question simply is this: If we accept that, when performing a memorized text in a foreign language singers manage without a full productive command of the structures and forms that they reproduce, what are they doing when they perform in their native language? Might they not also have the option of bypassing the full generative process? The Wray model presents analytic engagement as a continuum, driven by need, and identifies the production of memorized material as a case where there certainly are opportunities for bypassing aspects of linguistic processing, in the interests of paying attention to other things.

Another focus of attention for Simpler Syntax in relation to complex lexical entries is idioms. As already noted, true idioms have to be admitted to even a strictly atomic lexicon, but, as corpus research has demonstrated (for example, Sinclair 1991; Moon 1998), true idioms are just the extreme end of something much more common and much more difficult to account for in a mainstream generative model. Jackendoff states that idioms must not be seen as a "marginal phenomenon", because "there are in fact thousands of [idioms]—probably as many as there are adjectives" (2002: 167). This implies a fairly liberal definition of 'idiom' and, indeed, he includes frames such as 'give NP a piece of PRO$_e$'s mind'.[3] However, he still restricts 'idioms' to word strings with a meaning that does not map onto their form in a regular way. Yet many idioms fall into a mid position, in which the mapping of component words onto meaning can be achieved through metaphorical extrapolation.

See, for instance, Tucker (2007: 957) and Sag, Baldwin, Bond, Copestake, and Flickinger (2002) on the options for modelling 'spill the beans', where 'spill' can be mapped onto 'release' and 'the beans' onto 'the information'. Jackendoff's position implies that there are firm category types for idioms rather than a continuum from full transparency ('have a nice day!') to total absence of transparency ('by and large'; 'all of a sudden').

In similar vein, the Jackendoff and Wray accounts do not align regarding why so few idioms are syntactically irregular. Jackendoff's definition of 'irregularity' is predicated on a separation of syntactic and semantic irregularity, so that it is possible to account for the structure of an idiom as 'regular' even if the component words do not create, semantically, what they should. This is a legitimate position for a model in which there is a separate syntactic level of representation (see below), and it simply entails assigning the whole string a special meaning, independently of its formal structure. In contrast, in cognitive models (see later), structure is an expression of meaning and/or function, and the absence of semantic compositionality invalidates any formal compositionality, relegating it to historical detritus. As a result, more structures will be viewed as 'irregular' in models where meaning is resident in structures, than in those, such as Jackendoff's and Chomsky's, where structure is an intermediate level between form and meaning.[4]

It follows that while some theories end up with a puzzle over why there are so *few* irregular idioms (Jackendoff 2002: 171), the NOA model considers a great many idioms to be irregular, and can explain why they are so. It is because word strings will gradually drift into irregularity over time, by virtue of being lexically stored (see Chapter 3). That is, in direct contradiction to Jackendoff's view (ibid.), NOA proposes that the capacity of free composition to correct irregularities back to regularity is very underused. It is true, certainly, that the predominant effect of this under-analysis seems to be *semantic* drift towards non-transparency rather than *grammatical* fossilization (though it certainly does occur, for example, 'go the whole hog', 'come a cropper', 'sure as eggs is eggs'). However, the relative scarcity of grammatical irregularity in idioms can be accounted for as a function of literacy—an artificial, external catalyst that increases the likelihood of grammatical forms being updated (see Chapter 5).

Simpler Syntax and the NOA model also differ in two other respects. One regards whether a linguistic form should be viewed as permanently located somewhere along the continuum from fully-fixed to fully-variable. In NOA there are *options* for whether a given string is processed as fixed or variable. The second difference involves how constraints on combinations are conceptualized. Culicover and Jackendoff distance themselves from the derivational approach of mainstream generative models, preferring to account for patterns in terms of constraints. However, constraints, conceptually, entail the *potential* for more to happen than is ultimately *permitted* under that constraint—that is, the constraint determines which of a larger set of possibilities is permissible and which is not. In NOA, patterns that do not occur are not being constrained from occurring. Rather, they are failing to occur because the potential for them to occur (even if logical) has not (yet) been identified. In Simpler Syntax a person's language capacity is characterized by licensed structures and by interfaces between parallel (phonological, syntactic and semantic) structures (Culicover and Jackendoff 2005: 18). NOA holds, simply, that the realization of licensing versus constraints will be only partial, with a long-term potential for augmentation. It will, in short, *emerge* in response to need, and many features may, indeed, never explicitly emerge at all. As a result, there may be an *appearance* of rule-based constraints that is actually no more than an artefact of the existence of larger, intact lexical units that have been inherited with an internal structure tucked inside.

Functional grammar

Although various models in the Functional Grammar tradition are "moving inexorably in the direction of greater attention to the cognitive aspects of language" (Butler 2004: 162), one must not over-generalize, and so the focus of the discussion here will be Systemic Functional Grammar (SFG).[5] While not in the vanguard of the developments Butler describes, SFG does aim to create a sound interface with models of the causes of patterns, for "the nature of language is closely related to the demands that we make on it, the functions it has to serve" (Halliday 1970: 141). However, the emphasis is social rather than psychological, since "the individual is construed intersubjectively, through engagement in social acts of meaning ..." so that language is viewed as a "realisation" of culture (Halliday 2006: 445). With so little attention to language processing, SFG might appear not to be a good candidate for achieving the desiderata of the comprehensive model. However, on account of the commitment to discourse evidence, a close affinity between SFG and corpus linguistics has arisen (Butler 2004: 149), and a number of researchers operate at the interface of the two, including Tucker (1996, 2007) and Stubbs (2001).[6] SFG therefore has potential to contribute to the comprehensive model by relating the principles of patterns to the patterns themselves.

An apparently fundamental sticking point, when looking for affinities between SFG and the Wray (2002b) model lies in the fact that in SFG there is no lexicon as such. In SFG, the realization of a lexical item results from making a series of decisions in parallel progressive decision trees that map, ultimately, onto a single possible outcome. However, the absence of a lexicon per se in SFG is not as troublesome as it might seem. The notion of a 'lexicon' is essentially a metaphorical device and the central issue is whether the phenomenon of lexis is compatibly handled, not whether the lexicon is framed as a separate entity or as the outcome of a series of processes.[7]

Nevertheless, the match is not, under current SFG models, an ideal one, for 'phraseological expressions do not simply fall out in the description [of grammatical and lexical organisation] as a consequence of the general principle of lexicogrammatical integration' (Tucker 2007: 953). Overall, functional approaches to grammatical modelling such as SFG do offer scope for accounting more effectively for its vagaries than Chomskyan models customarily can (for example, Tucker 1996, 2007). However, they still strive to reduce complex material to simpler components where possible (Martinet 2006: 678f). Indeed, because a system network operates with decision trees rather than (as in Chomskyan models) structural arrangements determined by abstract rules (Halliday 2006), one could argue that it is potentially *easier* to model one-off configurations as the product of their components, since doing so need not create a wider generative precedent. But this solution is not desirable, because although the pathway resulting in a given realization is unique, "[n]o additional rule type should be required to account for 'idiosyncratic' grammatical, lexical or phraseological phenomena" (Tucker 2007: 960).

As an alternative, Tucker explores potential modifications to the (Cardiff version of) SFG system design,[8] specifically, "the re-working or re-organisation of the relationship between semantic choice and the lexicogrammatical potential for the realisation of semantic choice" (p. 954). Key to Tucker's concerns is the question of how many decision points are required in getting from an idea to a linguistic realization of it, with particular reference to idioms. He illustrates one aspect of the problem (pp. 962–3) by considering how 'get hold of the wrong end of the stick', meaning 'to misunderstand' can be treated as a mental process, when 'get hold of' is normally a material process. Specifically, the difficulty within SFG is how the mental process can be selected for the verb before the participant has been selected.

Tucker proposes that the entire expression be treated as a "multiword verb" so that 'the wrong end of the stick' "is not a participant role-bearing Complement of the verb *get hold of*, but an extension of it" (p. 966), in the same way that 'take account of' and 'make light of' are treated as single verb items rather than a verb and complement. By viewing the entire string as a single choice, there is no decision point between 'get hold of' and 'the wrong end of the stick' when it is selected as a realization of the mental process 'misunderstand', even though there *is* a decision point after 'get hold of' when it is selected as a material process. If 'the wrong end of the stick' happens to be the Goal, then the literal meaning results, not the metaphorical one.[9]

However, most formulaic sequences are *not* fully-fixed. As soon as there is variation (for example, 'pleased/delighted to see/meet you'; 'I haven't the faintest/foggiest/slightest idea'), it is not possible either to treat the string as a single choice, or to preset the choices. It is then much more difficult, without ad hoc rules, to constrain the system to produce only the versions that are acceptable to native speakers and attested in corpora.[10] Tucker concludes that "[p]hraseological expressions lie between [lexical items and grammatical units], in the sense that they involve the prepackaging of lexicogrammatical units" (p. 957). Thus, the challenge appears to be more than just working out where to draw a line between what counts as a single choice and what entails multiple choices (Tucker 2007: 959). It also involves a hybrid condition, in which there are, potentially, multiple choices constrained by a previous single choice. This scenario does not sit well with the basic Hallidayan position, which only admits as single choices multiword strings that have "no need for any intervening level of grammatical systems and structures" (ibid.: 959).

A solution to this problem is offered at the interface of SFG and the Wray (2002b) heteromorphic lexical model. It challenges SFG to make one radical alteration to its design. SFG, like all abstraction models, reflects the concepts and metaphors of its time (Kuhn 1996). Halliday conceptualized his Grammar in terms of procedural linearity on near-Boolean[11] principles—that is, the meaning-to-form mapping takes place according to ordered series of either/ or(/or) decisions that progressively introduce finer and finer distinctions. However, as Tucker shows, this limits the Grammar's capacity to account for the co-occurrence of items in semi-fixed expressions. On the other hand, the new paradigms, particularly Construction Grammar (see below), make use of templates, and SFG might do likewise, by introducing the partly-fixed frame, for example, "NP be-TENSE sorry to keep-TENSE you waiting" (Pawley and Syder 1983b: 210); "harden ONE's heart towards SOMEONE" (Moon 1998: 140).

Introducing partly-fixed frames as single lexical choices into SFG would mean that, at the point when a decision is made about a variable item, subsequent parts of the form were already lexified. Furthermore, the frame as a whole (including subsequent material) could determine the available choices for the variable items. Completing the lexification of a word string would entail 'back-filling' or 'insertion'. SFG appears to have the mechanisms for handling this procedure—the selection of the partly-fixed frame could be effected via the realizational rule 'lexify' and the insertion of the variable material constrained in the same way as for morphological detail to a lexeme. Indeed a partly-fixed frame will look identical to the kind of predicate frame proposed by Butler (1998a: 189) (within Dikkian Functional Grammar), other than that there will be a second lexicalized form in it.[12]

Introducing partly-fixed frames as single lexical choices is fully in tune with Sinclair's (1987, 1991) definition of the idiom principle,[13] though Sinclair's proposal is less psycho-socially motivated. The impact on a grammatical description as a whole is potentially major. Since the effect of permitting partly-fixed frames is to draw in a new, more liberal place the line between what is treated as regular (i.e. undergoes the normal systemic procedures) and what is irregular (i.e. is lexified at an earlier stage), there is a huge potential for simplifying the grammatical description as a whole, by no longer needing to account for the many cases where a formulation is on its gradual way from reflecting the regular patterns of the language to being semi- and then entirely irregular.[14]

However, ultimately, it is counter-intuitive for a Systemic Functional Grammarian to accept as a lexified form something that can be (to some extent) further described. This is, as Tucker points out, where grammatical models and psycholinguistic models tend to part company:

> What I would argue strongly … is that some kind of analysis is needed. The notion of unanalysed wholes may be tenable in terms both of language use and language learning (see Wray and Perkins, 2000) and analytical awareness of the component parts of a fixed phraseological expression is not an essential prerequisite for language development, interpretation or production … There is no reason why learners or speakers should treat [*pleased to meet you*], or its equivalents in other languages (e.g. *enchanté* in French, *piacere* in Italian), as anything more than a prefabricated 'chunk' associated with a clear pragmatic function. Yet from the analyst's perspective, the lexicogrammar of the expression is unexceptional, describable … And, of course, the majority of such expressions are open both to variation … and to word-play …
> (Tucker 2007: 967–68)

In so far as grammatical models are generalized to describe the 'system'—an abstract and autonomous entity derived from, but also different from, the knowledge of the individuals that use it (Stubbs 2007)—Tucker's contention is reasonable.

But it still leaves SFG to struggle with the question of where to draw the line between what to describe and what to set aside as lexically realized. Tucker observes: "Both the variation and word-play potential in respect of a 'fixed' phraseological expression depend on the analysability of the expression"(2007: 968). On the other hand, there are few absolutes here. It is simply not credible to anticipate clear distinctions between what is compositional and what is non-compositional in a language (Wray 2002b: 265–67). Humans have huge creative capacity. Even the most fixed strings, like 'far and wide' can be 'analysed' and played with to create one off variations—for example, 'half-heartedly, we searched for him quite far and not too wide'. While there must be some mechanism that allows such creations to happen, over-formalizing them in the grammar as legitimate choices leads to too wide a set of options, relative to those actually in regular use. Ideally a grammatical model needs a way for structure to be imposed post hoc as well as 'discovered', with awareness accreting over time in response to input.

Corpus-driven models

The role of input is much more evidently central when an account is informed by corpus data, though that does not necessarily lead to a direct link between the evidence of usage (the patterns) and the processing causes of them. Rather, the capacity for corpus-driven models of the principles for the patterns to adequately interface with the NOA model must be specifically explored. Two models, Pattern Grammar and Frame Semantics, are considered here, both focused, in different ways, on how patterns in form relate to patterns in meaning.

First, though, it is useful to consider briefly the contribution that corpus linguistics itself is increasingly making in closing the divide between observations in the data and models of grammar.[15] To take one example, collostructional analysis (Stefanowitsch and Gries 2003) uses corpus devices to "increase the adequacy of grammatical descriptions, and ... to provide data for linguistic theorising and model-building" (p. 210–11). With a strong focus on meaning, collostructional analysis "starts with a particular construction and investigates which lexemes are strongly attracted or repelled by a particular slot in the construction (i.e. occur more frequently or less frequently than expected)" (p. 214). This entails accurately tagging the collocates for gramatical category, not something that can yet be done automatically, so the analysis is very painstaking. The strength of the approach is in its capacity to demonstrate, using corpus data, that grammar is more specific and restricted than the simple rewrite rules of mainstream generative models claim. "If syntactic structures served as meaningless templates waiting for the insertion of lexical material, no significant associations between ... templates and specific verbs would be expected ..." (p. 236). It is these patterns that the two models below, and also Construction Grammar, in the succeeding section, aim to capture.

Pattern grammar

Pattern Grammar (PG) is a product of research on the COBUILD corpus (Hunston and Francis 2000: 32ff) and is a prime example of a corpus-*driven* model (Tognini-Bonelli 2001): it derives from the corpus evidence rather than, as in a corpus-*based* model, the evidence being used to illustrate an independently derived theory or description. In keeping with this bias, PG "avoids abstract grammatical categories" and, through the data, "exploits the connection between phrase and meaning" (Hunston 2006a: 243). It is "a purely descriptive grammar of English" (Hunston 2006a: 243)[16] and is essentially a taxonomy of collocational patterns in text (though it does have explanatory qualities, see later). A key priority for the COBUILD Pattern Grammars for verbs (Francis, Hunston, and Manning 1996) and nouns and adjectives (Francis, Hunston, and Manning 1998) was to draw from the 300-million-word corpus a comprehensive list[17] of the items with a given pattern that occurred there (Hunston and Francis 2000: 32).

Patterns in PG indicate how meaning is associated with a particular phraseological form that is often partially lexicalized. For instance, Hunston and Francis (2000) discuss issues relating to 'v way PREP/ADV'—for example, "he talked his way into the post of chief costume designer" and "so she does not try to lie her way out of trouble"[18] (p. 100f)—and 'v N to-INF'—for example, "I recommend all readers to follow the manufacturer's instructions" (p. 114). It is revealed that the head words (in these cases, verbs) occurring in these configurations fall into semantic groups, which indicates that there is an interaction between the meaning of the verb alone and the frame within which it occurs. PG views the meaning of the frame as taking precedence, so that the way in which the verb component is interpreted depends on the frame. For instance, 'mistake' occurs in two different frames. In 'mistake NP_i for NP_j', it is semantically classified alongside 'exchange' and 'swap'. In 'mistake NP_i as NP_j', it stands alongside 'classify', 'categorize', and 'name' (Susan Hunston, personal communication).

The justification for considering frames to determine the meaning of verbs rather than the reverse is based on what happens with non-canonical examples. To anticipate an example discussed later, 'he barked them back to their places' means that he caused others to move by means of barking at them. The interpretation comes about because a central meaning of 'bark', as an aggressive production of sound, combines with the meaning of the pattern in which it (unusually) occurs. This pattern, 'V NP back to NP', is canonically associated with directed motion (for example, 'he directed/pointed/guided them back to their places') and since 'bark' is interpreted as entailing such motion, it follows that the frame must be determining the meaning.

The semantic centrality of the frame is a highly significant feature of PG,[19] not least in that it transcends Hunston and Francis' modest claim that "a grammar cannot explain it can only generalize" (2000: 260), by providing a means of predicting how future novel exemplars will be interpreted. In this way it meets the desideratum for grammars, identified in Chapter 6, that they should have some predictive power and be able to account for what native speakers judge as being normal as well as grammatical.

PG, like SFG, blurs the distinction between lexis and grammar, but the models also differ in fundamental ways (Hunston 2006b). One difference regards directionality. Hunston and Francis (2000) state,

> although Halliday notes that the lexicogrammar can be described from either end of the continuum, the use of networks does suggest directionality, with lexis downgraded to the end-point of the grammar. Our own description suggests that taking lexis as the starting point leads to a very different kind of grammar.
>
> (p. 251)

This 'different kind of grammar' is inherently fuzzy and lacking in certainties (ibid.: 260), though, arguably, their perception of it in these terms relates to the expectation that there is some underlying fixed state that can be captured. If, rather, the individual user's grammar is considered to emerge from the interaction of our communicative need and our input evidence (as in NOA), then we must expect that the grammar will be different for each person and constantly changing, making it difficult to pin down, when analysing a multi-authored corpus.

Although it is fundamentally aligned with the corpus evidence, PG interfaces less well with explanations of the causes of patterns. That is, there is no attempt within PG to ask why the patterns occur, nor why we interpret new configurations according to the theoretical prediction just described. Nor is there any engagement with how we *learn* the patterns, how we employ patterns effectively to make meaning and achieve functions in relation to others, or how the brain manages patterns. In these regards, the Wray (2002b) models have the potential to contribute, perhaps, to a broader account than PG offers (and indeed aims to offer) on its own.

Frame semantics

The focus of Frame Semantics (FS) is "describing the meanings of independent linguistic entities (words, lexicalized phrases, and a number of special grammatical constructions) by appealing to the kinds of conceptual structures that underlie their meanings and that motivate their use" (Fillmore 2006: 613). As such, and especially as it is expressed through the computational application FrameNet,[20] it has a great deal in common with PG. In FrameNet, corpus data is marked up according to a semantically-driven framework that can then be interrogated to reveal patterns of collocation.

For instance, in the frame report for 'being employed',[21] one example is 'The undocumented foreigners were WORKING *at the organic farm*', where the four italicized words exemplify the semantic category 'place of employment', subcategory 'location'. In the same frame report, the two italicized words in the example 'My dad WORKS *building houses*' exemplify the subtype 'task'. As these illustrations indicate, because the approach is 'message-driven' there is no strong incentive to treat the 'word' as the only unit, so that mark up can easily apply to multiword strings.

Thus, analysis using FrameNet "differs from that of ordinary lexicography in an important way: instead of working with a single word and exploring all of its meanings, it takes a single frame and examines all of the L[exical] Un[its] that evoke that frame" (Fillmore 2006: 616). FrameNet makes some headway towards tagging a corpus for meaning above the lexical level, something that is a goal of research in Natural Language Processing (Fillmore 2006: 620). Semantic tagging has the potential to provide, for the first time, information about how often given meanings are expressed, and what the range of realizations of them is.[22] This is the information that has been missing up to now in corpus-based frequency counts, which can only tell us how often a particular form occurs. Information about how often a form occurs is of little value until we can also establish how often it *could* have occurred, that is, for what proportion of the opportunities to express that meaning, that particular form was the one selected (Wray 2002b: 30–1).[23]

The FrameNet approach is sympathetic to the idea of message tagging because FS recognizes two levels of semantics. What is conveyed within the words themselves is framed within the broader context of the speech event, thus mapping what is said onto what is *meant*. In this way it is possible to begin with the notion that a speaker first intends to *mean* something and then takes steps to select a linguistic realization that will effectively convey that meaning. However, in the absence of a pre-existing message-tagged corpus, in practice FrameNet has to work from form to meaning rather than the reverse, and analyses rely on the identification of representative lexical units (Fillmore 2006: 617). Nevertheless, the approach complements that of PG. Where PG collects similar forms and looks for patterns in meaning, FrameNet assigns meanings to individual exemplars according to a semantic taxonomy and identifies patterns in form.

In sum, both PG and FS successfully relate patterns in language to descriptive (and somewhat predictive) principles, though in a very different way from more formal grammatical models. The interface with the causes of patterns is more implicit than explicit, by virtue of the focus on semantics and function, but both accounts offer considerable potential for an effective link-up with the NOA explanation of causes.

The cognitive approach

There are many models within the domain of Cognitive Linguistics that might be considered in the present context. However, Construction Grammar has been selected from amongst them, as the most potentially fruitful in offering a strong interface with NOA.

Construction Grammar (ConG)[24] "represent[s] a return to a traditional, 'taxonomic' mode of grammatical analysis" (Michaelis 2006: 73) and in this regard, and others, might be viewed as the intricate theoretical companion to the much more descriptively oriented PG. Or, conversely, since ConG was developed first, PG can be seen as providing the systematic evidence that ConG predicts should be found. ConG is predicated on the principles of Cognitive Grammar, which "denies that there is a distinct level of organization that mediates between phonology and semantics" (Taylor 2002: 21). For Goldberg (2006: 3) constructions are both "conventionalized pairings of form and function" (see also Goldberg 2003: 219; Michaelis 2006: 74) and combinations of one or more other constructions,[25] such that "[a]n actual expression or 'construct' typically involves the combination of at least half a dozen different constructions" (Goldberg 2003: 221). Thus, constructions can be morphemes, words, complex words, completely or partially complete idioms, and phrasal or clausal frames of various kinds—for example, the Covariational-Conditional construction 'the xer the yer'; the Ditransitive construction 'SUBJ [V OBJ$_1$ OBJ$_2$]'; the Passive 'SUBJ AUX VP$_{pp}$ (PP$_{by}$)' (Goldberg 2003: 220, 2006: 3). Creativity in language arises from 'the free combination of constructions' (Goldberg 2003: 222) subject to there being no conflicts entailed in that combination (see Goldberg 2006: 1of for an example of how constructions combine).

Syntactic structure, not having its own level of representation, is viewed as *emergent* (Hopper 1998), that is, a direct product of the symbolic mapping of meaning, so that, without recourse to any independent structural constraints, "grammatical categories ... are defined by the regular association of an experienced conceptual content with an experienced linguistic form" (Israel, Johnson, and Brooks 2000: 119). It follows that typological patterns across unrelated languages will not be attributed to innate linguistic principles but to cognitive similarities in how meaning is symbolized in the pursuit of linguistic expression (Croft 2001). As Goldberg (2003) observes, "What is truly remarkable is the degree to which human languages differ from one another, given that all languages need to express roughly the same types of message" (p. 222).

Like PG,[26] ConG attributes meaning to the construction, not just the words, so that "[t]he ditransitive form evokes the notion of transfer or 'giving'" (Goldberg 2003: 221).[27] This contrasts with the approach in projection-based models (including SFG) in which the meaning derives from the verb. If the meaning of 'giving' is attached to the verb 'give', it will follow that the ditransitive structure in which 'give' appears is brought about by the semantic requirement to identify a Goal and a Recipient, and this is, indeed, how things work in SFG. In contrast, bestowing not only the verb but also the construction with meaning makes it possible to explain how we can understand the meaning of 'giving' even when the word 'give' does not appear. Thus, Goldberg (2003)[28] accounts for how we interpret 'Liza guaranteed Zach a book' as entailing an undertaking to give him a book. In such cases meaning is extracted by combining the information from the lexical item with that from the construction. In the same way, we understand 'He barks them back to work'[29] to entail 'he causes them to move by barking' (Michaelis 2006: 75). Some supporting empirical evidence is reported by Bencini and Goldberg (2000), whose experimental subjects used both the meaning of the construction and the meaning of the verb (rather than just the verb) to sort sentences semantically.

ConG accounts for the awkward cases and then extends that account to the regular 'core' ones, rather than, as in mainstream generative models, accounting only for the core, and treating the awkward cases as peripheral (Goldberg 2003: 222).[30] Taking this approach leads Tomasello (2000) to challenge the prevailing assumption that young children possess the syntactic competence of adults. NOA concurs with the view that this 'adult competence' is not what we see in children, yet nevertheless proposes that children and adults approach language in the same way, for adults maintain an item-based conservative approach alongside their ability to generalize—the latter probably partly a natural function of greater exposure, and partly of schooling (see Chapter 5).

As in the NOA model, in ConG there is no need to hypothesize any hardwired 'language faculty', since a language is acquired on the basis of patterns identified in input (Tomasello 2005). In ConG, the only innate capabilities entail being able to recognize constructions and to expect that they carry different meanings (Lee 2001: 76). ConG denies that there is a poverty of stimulus problem (Goldberg 2006: 72), and Goldberg's own empirical studies have contributed to the evidence that the child's input is skewed towards a small number of key form-meaning pairs, such as the verbs 'go', 'put', 'give' (Goldberg 2006: 76ff). She proposes that '[t]he generality of the meanings of these verbs and their highly frequent and early appearance in children's speech suggests that they may aid a child in generalizing patterns from the input' (Goldberg 2006: 78). NOA adds to this standpoint a causal component: language learning entails mapping form onto meaning or function, under the operational constraint of engaging in minimum analytic activity, i.e. to map the largest possible form onto a meaning or function, and to identify subcomponents according to the boundaries between unvarying and varying material.

In ConG, frequency is the key determiner of what is stored, so that "patterns are stored if they are sufficiently frequent, even if they are fully regular instances of other constructions and thus predictable" (Goldberg 2006: 12–13). The conservatism of analysis entailed in NOA is expressed in ConG in terms of a principle whereby "more specific knowledge always pre-empts general knowledge in production *as long as either would satisfy the functional demands of the context equally well*" (Goldberg 2006: 94, original emphasis). Goldberg additionally notes that learning is informed by negative evidence when an individual anticipates that A will be said, but hears instead B, so that the inference is made that A is undesirable (ibid.: 96).

In this way, the NOA model complements the ConG account of how constructions arise, and, particularly, why the mapping of form to meaning or discourse function is sustained at all levels, from morpheme to phrasal pattern. It can be proposed that the stages by which the child arrives at the adult construction (see, for instance, Dabrowska 2000 on interrogatives; Israel *et al.* 2000 on passive participles; Diessel and Tomasello 2001 on finite complement clauses) entail not only *assembly* (Goldberg 2003: 219, Tenet 4) but a severe conservatism in the approach to *un*constructing complex constructions observed in input, so that there is an attempt to impose meaning onto structure that can, as Diessel and Tomasello (2001) and Israel *et al.* (2000) report, result in the appearance of more complexity than is actually present. NOA proposes that input provides, over time, evidence of where mature users do and do not operate paradigmatic variation within an (at first fully, later partially) lexicalized structure. Thus, the process of acquisition is "better described as a movement towards *greater flexibility* than towards more complex structures or greater accuracy" (Dabrowska 2000: 98, original emphasis), with the initial starting point "a loosely organised inventory of item-based constructional islands" (Cameron-Faulkner, Lieven, and Tomasello 2003: 866).[31]

Language change can then be explained as a result of there being, under certain conditions, evidence that is consistent with two different interpretations—see, for instance, Hopper (1998: 159–60) on the separation of 'of' into a new single-member category, and the extended account of grammaticalization offered by Bybee (2003). In other circumstances, there may be nothing to prevent the child from continuing to construe a complex form in an 'immature way', if a dearth of adults prevents exposure to the full range of possibilities. Jespersen (1922) identified "great wars of long duration" and "the great plagues" as possible causes of swift linguistic change, on account of the absence of adult models (XIV, §5: 260). In short, the vagaries of patterns in a language are directly determined by what its users happen to say.[32]

Despite differences in relation to, inter alia, the perceived role of frequency in determining representation (see earlier discussions), there is a strong case for viewing ConG as an appropriate means of modelling the principles of the patterns observed in corpora, consistent with the NOA account of the social and psychological causes of the patterns.

Conclusion

Models of language seem increasingly able to accommodate the vagaries of idiomatic multiword strings, no doubt because corpus linguistic research cannot be ignored and it finds them ubiquitous. It has been argued in this chapter and the previous one that a comprehensive model of where formulaic language fits into the more general picture of language must consider what the patterns of language are, what principles appear to underlie their form and distribution, and how the social and psychological behaviour of speakers and hearers determines our linguistic behaviour.

Within the theoretical approach taken in this book, the aim is to substantiate, through evidence across domains, that "language use has a major impact on language structure" (Bybee and McClelland 2005: 382). Huge opportunities for explaining linguistic data derive from seriously engaging with the position that "language … is indeterminate, constantly under construction, and structured only by emergent patterns that come and go as the forms that carry them are found useful for their speakers" (Hopper 1998: 172).

The Wray (2002b) model of the causes of patterns lies most comfortably with grammatical theories in which meaning is considered to reside in structures as well as words (Hunston and Francis 2000: 25). In this regard, mainstream generative approaches are unattractive in so far as syntactic representation is separate from semantic representation (Tomasello 1998). The Simpler Syntax model makes many helpful concessions to the interface with corpus evidence and models of cause, but does not concede sufficient ground in relation to the question of representational provenance. In PG and ConG, syntactic structures are the by-product of form-meaning mappings (Taylor 2002; Bybee and McClelland 2005), which is more helpful.

Selecting one theoretical approach over another impacts on what one believes can be achieved. Where mainstream generative models, including Simpler Syntax, are predicated on the existence of determining or guiding innate linguistic principles, a logical corollary of the direct-mapping approaches is that "there may not be any truly correct formal characterization, either of any given language or of the common elements of the set of all possible languages" (Bybee and McClelland 2005: 406). That is, PG and ConG offer a more local product, with no expectation that it can be easily and directly applied to another language (see Goldberg 2006: chapter 9 for an account of why languages sometimes share patterns). A language user's approach to understanding and expressing novel formulations comes about "not because speakers possess a syntax divorced from semantics, as in Generative Grammar, but rather because they possess highly general linguistic constructions composed of word categories and abstract schemas that operate on the categorical level" (Tomasello 1998: p. xx). These constructions predict a narrower range of output, and anticipate that it will be relatively difficult to understand a new kind of structure in input, compared with one that has been encountered before, even if the new one does adhere to the principles identified by others as part of Universal Grammar (see, for instance, Dabrowska and Street 2006).

Naturally, opinions on each side of the theoretical divide differ, as to whether the principle of entirely free combination is essential to an account of linguistic knowledge, or constitutes an over-estimation of it (Bybee and McClelland 2005: 403). In order to ensure that cognitive models do not under-represent the language user's capacity to handle novelty, some mechanism must be provided for ensuring that additional inferences can be made as novel material is encountered and as the need to express novel relations arises. This requires only a perpetuation of the fluidity entailed in learning by observation, so that the patterns acquired can be further interrogated if necessary. It is precisely this contingency that the NOA model offers, and in this respect it therefore enjoys a better interface with cognitive approaches to linguistic structure than generative ones.

On the other hand, the requirement articulated by generative grammarians that there must be a mechanism to explain our capacity to judge the grammaticality of formulations at a level of distance from specific examples we have encountered cannot be easily dismissed. Although there is, as noted in Chapter 5, a potential for educated linguists to mistake culturally imposed norms of grammaticality for deep-seated natural ones, nevertheless such judgements have a substance and reliability that needs explaining within a theory of knowledge about language.

It may not be necessary to hypothesize a separate syntactic module for language in order to account for our capacity to push the boundaries of grammaticality in ways that remain principled, even if they stray into the territory of things we would not say even though we could. The NOA model accommodates the desirability of understanding the provenance of our subtle, sometimes even arcane grammaticality judgements with a preference for viewing grammar as an emergent property of language as it is used.

Goldberg has famously claimed that "it's constructions all the way down" (2006: 18), in the sense that "the network of constructions captures our grammatical knowledge of language *in toto*" (ibid.). Grammaticality judgements undertaken on that basis entail knowing constructions that are essentially instantiations of what in generative grammar would be phrase structure rules—that is, it must be possible to extrapolate from the arrangement of particular words whether or not they conform to the pattern of a permitted construction. Within this context, it is possible for the NOA account to straddle both the ConG and the generative conceptualizations by stating that grammatical language entails the combination (whether according to rule or template) of permitted configurations of MEUs (so that they, too, are present 'all the way down'). Since MEUs are of variable internal complexity, it means that the production of a sentence may entail the combination of morphemes and words according to permitted principles, the selection of a fully-fixed multiword string that requires no modification, or various alternatives that mix the two, such as a sentence composed of freely combined morphemes and words but prefaced by a three-word formulaic adverbial, or the selection of a prefabricated expression with gaps in it for verb agreement and, say, a freely selected noun phrase.

In short, the present model proposes that we hold in our lexicon a store of MEUs and have, in the course of language acquisition, figured out the principles by which they combine, to the extent that the principles can then be applied to new examples. The patterns we have observed over the years in our input determine whether a new example, even if grammatical, is judged to conform to the narrower principle of idiomaticity. The more we engage analytically with language, such as we might on account of advanced education in language and literacy, the greater our tolerance for the potential acceptability of formulations that do not pass muster as idiomatic in normal usage—more than that, the greater our chances of actually producing such formulations, so that they gain a genuine idiomaticity of their own, albeit in a restricted register or context (see Chapter 3, Figure 3.2). It follows that the variation observed between individuals in relation to grammaticality judgements and comfortably achieved comprehension (for example, Chipere 2003) arises on the basis of differences engendered by socio-psychological priorities and culturally selective experiences, which draw in different places the boundaries between what is viewed as inside and outside the frame of familiar language.

Notes

1 For example, Culicover and Jackendoff (2005: 3) include Construction Grammar as an "alternative generative grammar", even though, in this account, its Cognitive Linguistic basis is prioritized. Meanwhile, there is a significant interface between their model and the cognitive domain.
2 On the other hand, while acknowledging the "intrinsic importance" of social factors, Jackendoff considers them "relatively remote" from his concerns in modelling language in terms of cognitive structure (2002: 37).
3 The *e* subscript indicates that PRO must coindex with the subject.
4 Simpler Syntax, it must be said, aims to minimize the role of structure in mediating between meaning and form. However, Gonzálvez-García and Butler (2006: 47) challenge Culicover and Jackendoff's claim to have successfully created an effective interface with cognitively-driven models such as Cognitive Grammar.

5 There is an inevitable tension, when attempting a commentary of this kind, between speaking in general terms about a 'tradition' and accurately representing the different realizations of it. SFG has several 'dialects', and it would be inaccurate to imply that they all take the same approach or make the same distinctions in the same way. My main intention is to comment on generic features of SFG, drawing on the views of Halliday as an anchor point, and giving some attention to the Cardiff Grammar. There are also occasional references to other Functional Grammars, which I have tried to make explicit to avoid confusion. I am grateful to Chris Butler for very helpful comments on an earlier version of this section; any remaining infelicities in framing the differences between the various functional models remain despite his interventions, and are entirely my responsibility.

6 In addition, Butler (1998a, 1998b) draws together corpus linguistics and Dikkian Functional Grammar.

7 However, the 'decision trees' in SFG are not intended to model what happens during language processing, but rather are "simply more and more detailed sets of choices in system networks, the total set of choices being realised as a particular lexical item" (Chris Butler, personal communication).

8 The Cardiff Grammar is a version of Systemic Functional Grammar with two central aims. One is to develop "a series of increasingly complex computer models of sentence generation, as part of a wider program for modelling the generation and understanding of texts" (Fawcett 2005: 3). The other is to develop "a genuinely adequate framework for describing texts, for example, for the purposes of language teaching, literary stylistics, and the many other areas where there is a crying need for a genuinely applicable, functionally motivated description of English and other languages" (ibid.).

9 The more one can have separate representations for the idiomatic and literal meanings of word strings, the easier it is to explain Moon's (2006: 232) observation that "corpora provide very little evidence for any actual ambiguity" in their usage.

10 As noted in Chapter 2, there is value in differentiating between the individual having different options and the kind of variation that corpora capture as being in 'the language' by virtue of different, fixed preferences in different individuals. To what extent does any given individual actually select 'faintest', 'slightest', and 'foggiest' with equal favour in the expression 'not have the _____ idea'? While observation of variation will lead to receptive knowledge of potential for variation, it need not ever extend to variation in production. As observed later, a key distinction between the NOA model and SFG (as indeed most if not all grammatical models) is that the former models what an individual might know, whereas the latter tend to model a collective knowledge.

11 Choices are often but not always two-way.

12 For instance, Butler (1998a: 189) proposes a predicate frame *order* $(X_1)_{Ag}$ $(e_i)_{Go}$ $(X_2)_{Rec}$ to capture examples such as 'John ordered Bill to leave the room'. A partly-fixed frame simply has more than one lexicalized item, meaning that the variable information, if it occurs between the two lexicalized items, is *infixed*—this term reminding us that the two lexicalized forms are, in fact, acting as if they were components of a single morpheme.

13 Sinclair (1987: 320) speaks of "semi-preconstructed phrases that constitute single choices, even though they *might be analysable into segments*", not "even though they *derive from analysable segments*" (my emphasis). However, this is really the limit of any specifically psycholinguistic basis for his idiom principle (Chris Butler, personal communication).

14 "Rather than defining the lexicon as a 'prison' which admits and contains complex items that are already lawless, it makes more sense to define it as a 'house of ill repute' which takes them, regular or not, and is liable to corrupt them to lawlessness over time" (Wray 2002b: 267).

15 What follows applies also to the interface with Construction Grammar, considered in a later section.

16 Although PG challenges a number of theoretical assumptions, it replaces them only with some general observations (Hunston and Francis 2000: 259–60).

17 Though not necessarily an exhaustive one (Susan Hunston, personal communication).

18 This construction is also analysed by Fillmore *et al.* (1988), and Verhagen (2003) analyses its Dutch equivalent.

19 It also features in Construction Grammar under the term 'coercion' (Michaelis 2006: 77–8).

20 http://framenet.icsi.berkeley.edu/ Accessed 10.2.08. For an overview of FrameNet, see Fillmore, Johnson, and Petruck (2003). For an account of how FrameNet relates to other recent computational models of the lexicon, and how it informs findings from corpus linguistic research, see Atkins, Rundell, and Sato (2003).

21 http://framenet.icsi.berkeley.edu/index.php?option=com_wrapperandItemid=118andframe=Being_employed. Accessed 10 February 2008.

22 Hunston (2007) has also demonstrated, within the framework of Pattern Grammar, the potential for defining "semantic sequences, i.e. what is often said". On a different tack, Cameron and Deignan (2006) propose the *metaphoreme*, "an [emergent] bundle of stabilising linguistic, semantic, pragmatic, and affective patterns in the use of the word as metaphor, together with its possibilities for variation" (p. 679). This bundle of information captures the semantics of variations on a metaphor and explains the constraints on their realizations.

23 For instance, Skelton and Hobbs (1999), searching a corpus of medical consultation data for discussions of death had to look separately for 'die', 'death', 'if anything happens to me', etc. This requires the analyst to anticipate all the possible expressions of the message.

24 Construction Grammar has a number of variants, proposed by, inter alia, Fillmore, Kay, and Michaelis, Lakoff and Goldberg, Langacker, Croft, and Bergen and Chang. As Gonzálvez-García and Butler (2006) point out in their detailed critical comparison of Functional-Cognitive approaches, there are major differences between these variants, including the extent to which they can be considered cognitive in orientation and, indeed, the definition that they use of the 'construction'. In an unpublished multivariate statistical analysis of the 36 features and 11 models discussed in their 2006 article, Gonzálvez-García and Butler found Fillmore's model to be very clearly separated from Goldberg's and from Croft's, the latter two being close together and also close to Langacker's Cognitive Grammar (Chris Butler, personal communication). Nevertheless, it will be sufficient for the present discussion to assume that the different varieties of Construction Grammar principally arise from attempts to account for different aspects of language using a broadly common set of principles (Benjamin Bergen, personal communication), and that the differences between variants are "fine points of divergence" (Goldberg 2006: 18). Thus, an attempt will be made to talk in reasonable generalities about a single 'Construction Grammar'. The account developed in this section centres on the Fillmore *et al.* and Goldberg models, with some reference also to the principles of Cognitive Grammar (as laid out by Lee 2001; Taylor 2002).

25 For Langacker (1987) they are combinations only.

26 A number of similarities between Pattern Grammar and Construction Grammar have been identified by Stubbs (2006).

27 She later adds that "the goal argument [must] be an animate being, capable of receiving the transferred item" (p. 221), so that 'Liza sent a book to storage' cannot be reformulated as '?Liza sent storage a book'.

28 Culicover and Jackendoff (2005: 34ff) also offer an explanation along these lines.

29 This is a shortened version of Michaelis' example, which was from a Newsweek article in 1997.

30 The same priority is also claimed for Simpler Syntax (Culicover and Jackendoff 2005: 25–6).

31 Cameron-Faulkner *et al.* (2003) also show that the input encountered by the child is skewed towards the reinforcement of certain structures through frequent exposure in the mother's speech, and that much of the input is non-canonical, for example, subjectless or with subject aux/verb inversion (p. 867).

32 "Our speech is a vast collection of hand-me-downs that reaches back in time to the beginnings of language. The aggregation of changes and adjustments that are made to this inheritance on each individual occasion of use results in a constant erosion and replacement of the sediment of usage that is called grammar" (Hopper 1998: 159).

8
Identifying formulaic material in real texts

Why is identification so difficult?

As any researcher of formulaic language knows, there can be major procedural difficulties when it comes to identifying formulaic material in text. This chapter asks why identification is so difficult, and how the problems can be overcome. Addressing the first issue entails a consideration both of the nature of formulaic language and of the purposes for which identification is used in research. The second question is answered with reference to those different purposes, by reviewing some of the approaches that have been taken by other researchers. Then, in Chapter 9, a method for identification is presented, that is compatible with the theoretical model underpinning this book.

Identification and definition

You cannot reliably identify something unless you can define it, and the relationship between definition and identification is almost circular, for "in order to establish a definition, you have to have a reliable set of representative examples, and these must therefore have been identified first" (Wray 2002b: 19). How one escapes from this impasse depends on how important it is for one's purposes to identify all and only formulaic material in a text. If one does not need to identify it *all*, because one is simply looking for some examples, one can stipulate a relatively narrow definition that excludes the material that would otherwise cause problems. Conversely, if it is important to find all of the formulaic material, but it does not matter if, in the process, one also includes a certain amount of material that actually is not formulaic, a very much more inclusive definition can be used, that treats the difficult borderline material as in, rather than out.

As these descriptions imply, the problem with formulaic language is that between the extremes of what is *definitely* formulaic and what is definitely *not* formulaic, there is a sizeable amount of material that may or may not be. The fuzziness in this regard derives partly from practical procedural issues—you know what you are looking for but you are not sure if you have found it—and partly from more fundamental differences of belief among researchers, about what you should be looking for in the first place. These latter differences to some extent map onto the perspectives explored in Chapters 6 and 7. That is, research focused on the patterns in language will tend to define what is formulaic differently from research focused on the principles underlying the patterns, or from that engaged with the causes of the patterns.

Types of definition, and their implications for identification

The four examples below can be used to explore how different definitions operate in relation to identification:

1 The *formulaic sequence* is "a sequence, continuous or discontinuous, of words or other elements, which is, or appears to be, prefabricated: that is, stored and retrieved whole from memory at the time of use, rather than being subject to generation or analysis by the language grammar" (Wray 2002b: 9).

2 The *morpheme equivalent unit (MEU)* is "a word or word string, whether incomplete or including gaps for inserted variable items, that is processed like a morpheme, that is, without recourse to any form-meaning matching of any sub-parts it may have" (Chapter 2 of this book).

3 *Items included in the analysis* were "all occurrences of 3-word sequences which occurred 10 times or more in [the] corpus" (Butler 1997: 66).

4 *Items selected as experimental stimuli* were "formulaic sequences ... from the *Oxford Learner's Dictionary of English Idioms* ... subjected to a frequency analysis based on the British National Corpus ... [and] well-known to the native participants" (Conklin and Schmitt 2008: 80).

What is immediately clear is that some of these definitions offer greater practical scope for identifying exemplars than others, and this aspect of the differences is considered presently. First, though, we shall focus on the relationship between definitions and their research purposes.

Conklin and Schmitt (2008) (definition 4) were undertaking a study to see whether, as various theories predict, formulaic language is processed more quickly than non-formulaic language. In order to conduct the study they needed some examples that were indisputably formulaic. They were therefore wise to choose conservatively, by prioritizing idioms, as "clearly formulaic in nature since they represent idiosyncratic meanings which cannot generally be derived from the sum of the individual words in the string" (p. 80). They used this uncontroversial definition of the idiom to anchor the selection of items from a secondary source. They made the starting assumption that the items listed in the *Oxford Learner's Dictionary of English Idioms* would indeed be idioms in the sense of their own description but from there they exercised further control, by only using examples found to be relatively frequent in the BNC and that at least eight of the ten native speaker participants could correctly complete in a cloze test. This definition of formulaicity was specifically developed for their own study, in order to meet the particular requirements of it.

Butler's definition (definition 3) is also stipulative and particular, since the length and frequency figures were contingent on the size of the corpus he was using and the amount of material he wanted to isolate from it—such stipulations can be normalized to occurrences per million words, but even so, analysts draw the line in different places (Wray 2002b: 28ff).[1] Unlike Conklin and Schmitt, Butler was not trying to find material to use as input for an experiment. Rather, he wanted to identify examples of formulaic material that he could examine for characterizing features. Unless one believes that non-frequent formulaic material is fundamentally different in nature from frequent material, one might as well begin with the frequent examples and develop one's understanding of what formulaic language is like from there (see later discussion of frequency as a basis for identification).

The attraction of a definition like number 3 is that there are computational means for establishing the relative frequency of recurrent word strings.[2] Although Butler is not implying that formulaic language actually *is* the set of strings three or more words long that occur at least ten times, but simply finding a way to identify some examples for analysis, there certainly are corpus linguists for whom a formulaic word string simply *is* a frequent word string. In this view, any other features associated with formulaicity are either a consequence of frequency or are sustained on account of frequency (for example, Bybee 2002).

For those who do not believe frequency to be the primary determiner of formulaicity, however, definitions like number 3 unquestionably risk excluding some material that is also formulaic and that may not share all of the same characteristics as frequent examples. The Needs Only Analysis (NOA) model holds that morpheme equivalent units (MEUs) (definition 2) come about on account of (a) the processing preference not to break input down, and (b) the attempt to manipulate hearers by offering them a direct form-meaning match that minimizes opportunities for an alternative interpretation. While MEUs may *tend* to be frequent, they do not *have* to be (Wray 2002b: 25–31). This brings us, then, to a consideration of definitions 1 and 2. The first job is to differentiate between them. Then they will be compared with definitions 3 and 4.

Clearly, the definition of the *formulaic sequence* (number 1) and that of the MEU (number 2) are inspired by the same overall view of what formulaicity is: they both entail a claim about the way in which the form is stored in the lexicon. However, MEUs constitute a subset of the formulaic sequences (Figure 8.1). Definition 1 is a procedural, stipulative definition employed in Wray (2002b) to justify the use of different types of example during the exploration of the nature of formulaicity. The formulaic sequence, crucially, encompasses any material that *appears to be* prefabricated, not just that which *is*. In effect, the formulaic sequences are the set of examples that we think may be MEUs, before we can be sure just what an MEU looks like. The potential to have examples of formulaic sequences that we ultimately conclude are not MEUs is a helpful way to ensure that the characteristics developed are discriminatory. Specific ways of establishing whether or not a formulaic sequence is an MEU are presented in the second half of this chapter.

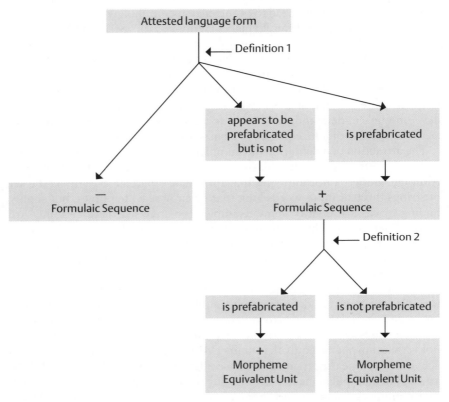

Figure 8.1 The relationship between the formulaic sequence and the MEU

In sum, the definition of the formulaic sequence is one that creates a working space for beginning an analysis. It therefore has certain procedural advantages for researchers who need a broad canvas on which to work—particularly the case when theoretical models are under development or evaluation. The definition of the formulaic sequence can be applied in a more neutral way than that of the MEU, since the latter reflects a specific belief about the nature of the lexicon—that it is heteromorphic. On the other hand, the formulaic sequence itself is not theory-neutral, and so can be used only cautiously where an incompatible theoretical model is preferred, or even under active consideration (for example, that formulaic language is the result of the preferential, speedy combination of frequently associated individual lexical items). This means that even the term 'formulaic sequence' cannot be used in all cases—as the pattern of its appearance in this book, along with that of the neutral term 'formulaic language' (see note 1, Chapter 1), testify.

How definitions apply to examples

Models of the causes of formulaicity such as the NOA model will not furnish the researcher with an easy method of identification.[3] The definition of the morpheme equivalent unit cannot be used directly with natural data—except, possibly, multiword output in types of aphasia that leave the speaker with no remaining capacity to construct novel utterances. Although the formulaic sequence can be used for identification at the general level of items that 'appear to be prefabricated', what appears to be prefabricated needs its own clear definition.

Given that definitions 3 and 4 above are more amenable overall to the practicalities of identification, why should they not be preferred over the more troublesome definitions 1 and 2? The answer lies in the relationship between the definitions and the phenomenon under examination. In a nutshell, there is no value in grasping convenient definitions if they exclude too much of what is actually fundamentally beyond the scope of external identification.

Figure 8.2 Unsorted classes

Figure 8.2 offers an analogy of the challenge inherent in identifying formulaic material in real text. Each of the children in the playground belongs to one of three classes, Class 1, Class 2, or Class 3. Class membership is unequivocal, but cannot be discerned. How could one sort the children out? One might make certain inferences if, for example, one believed the classes to be populated by children of different ages. For instance, one might suppose that the tallest children are most likely to be oldest, and therefore in Class 3, or that the children playing with the most juvenile toys are most likely to be youngest, and therefore in Class 1. However, these external measures are likely to be fallible, since they are only proxies. A child could be both small and in the older age-group. Furthermore, the school might over-rule the general age pattern by placing a very bright younger child in a higher class. And in any case, perhaps the classes are not age-based at all. The problem with attempting to categorize the children is that their actual class membership is only partly signalled by external characteristics, and the bases on which membership is actually determined are not only not evident, but not even fully understood by the onlooker.

Formulaic language can be viewed in the same way. A theoretical model makes a claim about the existence of class memberships—for example, some word strings are formulaic and some are not.[4] The NOA claims, for instance, that, for any given individual, some word strings are stored as single lexical units, and treated as if they were morphemes, while others are not.[5] Although theoretical proposals can be made regarding the way that word strings end up formulaic—for example, the NOA model holds that they have not been broken down any further because they have a reliable form-meaning mapping; conversely, fusion-based accounts claim that the component words are glued together for future convenience in processing—these proposals are still at the abstract level, and there is no direct means to ascertain which category a given word string is in.

With formulaic language the problem is probably entirely intractable—more so than with a playground of children. In both cases one will seek, of course, to develop ever better approaches to the determination of class membership, something that can be achieved both by developing new and more refined theories and by making more observations about the discernible differences between individual children/word strings that might be indicative of their status. But only in the playground can one check, in the end, if one's hunches were correct, for when the play period ends, the children will self-organize into their classes. It will then be possible to make direct observations of the children in each class, and use that to develop more robust predictive methods for future attempts at grouping in the playground. But with formulaic language there is no resolution point, when one's guesses can be finally confirmed or disconfirmed—at least not when class membership is defined in terms of the individual speaker's or hearer's internal knowledge. And this explains why it can seem so attractive to favour other kinds of definition. Definitions 3 and 4 are the equivalent of saying 'I know that only the children in Class 3 are allowed to climb in trees, so I'll just select the children in trees, since I know for sure which class they belong to'. It will identify just the subset of Class 3 children that happen to be playing in trees, but it will reliably exclude all the children who are not in Class 3.

What is important is to resist imposing one's own categorization on all the examples, based on external characteristics rather than a theoretical model. In the playground, this would mean, say, lining the children up and allotting the shortest third to Class 1, the tallest third to Class 3, and the ones in between to Class 2. It would be for theoreticians to make the objection that this categorization had not actually captured the true membership of each class (since, for instance, classes were actually organized on the basis of age, intellectual achievement, or whatever). Such objections represent a clash between theoretical principles and the expediency of using external measures, and they are illustrated by the discussion in chapters 2 and 3 of Wray (2002b), where it is shown that there are inconsistencies between taxonomies based on external characteristics of formulaic sequences and the theoretical claims made about them by the same researchers.

The point of exploring these issues is not to suggest that nothing can be done about the identification of formulaic material in text, but rather to show that all decisions are contingent and, in one way or another, theory sensitive if they are not atheoretical (in which case they will evoke sensitivities in the theoreticians). A researcher's main duty is to adopt a thoughtful and appropriate definition that permits the effective identification of examples suitable for the intended purposes. Doing so entails due consideration of what the research aims to achieve, where it is located in relation to existing theories, and what the consequences are of including and excluding certain sub-classes of material.

Example approaches to identification through definition

Definition and identification in the case studies in this book

As definitions 3 and 4 illustrated, one way to guarantee the reliable identification of examples of formulaic language is by defining what will, in a given analysis, be held to count as formulaic, and then finding examples of that. Although this approach necessarily excludes potentially interesting examples that happen not to fall within the specific definition, there can be benefits for certain kinds of study. The investigations described in Chapters 10 to 15 all aim to examine extreme examples of formulaic sequences 'at the boundaries' and the definitions are specific to the contexts under scrutiny. Although it means anticipating the content of those chapters, it is useful to review here the specific ways in which definition is used there to illuminate aspects of the more general principles underlying formulaicity.

In TESSA (Chapter 10) and TALK (Chapter 11) the word strings defined as formulaic are the ones that have been pre-stored in a computer program.

No other definition is applied (though, of course, it is likely that certain definitional criteria influence the decision to store precisely those items in the computer). The program, for the purposes of the analysis, is considered to mimic the hypothesized storage and processing of the human brain, so that the stored items are viewed as corresponding to MEUs. The focus of interest in these studies is the fate of MEUs and/or of communication using them, when there is little or no scope to modify them in real time.

In the language learning experiments (Chapters 12 and 13), formulaic material is again defined in a particular way that maps onto the MEU: the learners have prepared certain word strings in advance and memorized them, and it is these memorized forms that are viewed as formulaic. The impact of this definitional approach is most clearly seen in Chapter 12, where strings are deemed formulaic not on the basis of their meaning or form, but of their having been presented to the learner specifically *as a unit*. That is, the assumption is made that the learner has not broken down any word strings that were presented whole, and that the beginnings and ends of the word strings as presented constitute boundaries, as do any internal locations where there was paradigmatic variation in the input. Such an assumption is not unreasonable where, as in this case, the learner is a beginner, though, in truth, it is probably naïve to assume that *no* analysis of holistically produced word strings could occur. Chapter 15 also identifies as formulaic material that has been deliberately memorized—this time it is text that has been scripted for theatre and television performance. Scripts are prefabricated in the literal sense, and ostensibly (though, as the discussion shows, not always actually) intended for verbatim repetition.

Chapter 14, in contrast to the others, deals only with a single word string that was at the centre of a court case, and the discussion is precisely focused on whether there is evidence to support its being defined as a MEU for the different people involved.

However, research that does not deal with extreme examples of formulaicity will not usually be able to solve the problem in these local fashions. Nor would it be desirable to, for any bespoke mode of identification of the kind employed in Chapters 10 to 15 necessarily creates a risk that the findings of the study cannot be generalized to any other case. The purpose of such research, of course, is to bring to light generalities that may indeed apply in the less extreme cases where it is not so easy to see what is going on. They are justified, therefore, only in so far as that case can be convincingly made. For research directly on those less extreme cases, the elusiveness of reliable approaches to identification remains a challenge, and yet, for precisely that reason, it is important that the method be both logical and replicable.

Two purposes of identification

Broadly speaking, we can differentiate two practical applications for a robust identification of formulaic sequences in empirical research. One is to analyse output. The other is to prepare input. In the former, a dataset has been gathered, in which MEUs (or some other unit compatible with the theory in use) are believed to exist. A means is required for isolating them so that they can be examined. The conclusions drawn about the quantity and nature of formulaic material in the data will depend on what is included and excluded during identification, and it will be important to acknowledge, perhaps with illustrations lying beyond the definition, how else the analysis might have looked had the lines been drawn in different places.

In the case of input preparation, formulaic material is needed in order to carry out the investigation, so a set of exemplars must be selected, that will be appropriate for their purpose—for example, as stimuli, teaching materials, etc. An infelicitous decision about the definition of the targets cannot easily be modified once the investigation has been carried out, and it is therefore important that the rationale for the identification is clearly and appropriately justified. These two purposes entail different priorities, which will be noted in the course of the following discussion. Most attention will be paid to the first activity—how researchers identify formulaic material in natural data—since this is both the more challenging and the more commonly undertaken activity.

Identifying formulaic sequences in normal language can be rather like trying to find black cats in a dark room: you know they're there but you just can't pick them out from everything else. Key in some approaches to identification is the recognition that "[o]ur speech ... is filled with others' words, varying degrees of otherness or varying degrees of 'our-own-ness' ..." (Bakhtin 1986: 89), so that one is looking for patterns that are common to all speakers (frequency), familiar to oneself (intuition) or, significantly, unfamiliar to oneself (idiosyncratic). Alternatively, assumptions may be made in relation to hypothesized processing, such that formulaic sequences will have different features of presentation (phonology, spelling) or in relation to salience, such that they will have different features of form or meaning.

Frequency

The speed and cleanliness (at least on the surface) of frequency counts make it very attractive to submit one's data to a computer-based analysis. Stubbs (2002), for instance, explores two methodologies for identifying frequent multiword strings in large corpora. The first focuses on collocation, and examines the co-occurrence of content word pairs. The second "identifies frequent co-selections of a content word and an associated grammatical frame" (p. 238). Stubbs' aim in finding a robust method for identification is so that he can analyse the resulting exemplars for semantic and pragmatic features, differences in their distribution across text types, and their role in textual cohesion (ibid.). Identification on the basis of frequency has the potential to exclude material that has the features of the identified exemplars, despite not being frequent. On the other hand, if patterns can be found in the frequent data, there remains the potential subsequently to ascertain whether they can also be detected in less frequent strings. Indeed, even for those who question whether frequency determines formulaicity, it would take a strong case successfully to argue that the frequent examples of formulaic sequences are not a good place to start.

As observed earlier, though, the parameters of identification in frequency-based analyses are a delicate matter, and grossly different results will be obtained, according to the parameters of the count—the length of the string, the number of times it must occur to count as 'frequent', and the flexibility of the search to cope with variations within semi-fixed sequences (Wray 2002b: 28). For example, Adolphs and Durow (2004), investigating whether "the degree of social-cultural integration affects the acquisition of formulaic sequences", isolated and examined the ten most frequent three-word sequences in the transcripts of spoken interviews with L2 learners. But they concede that this approach considerably restricted their reach, relative to the range of formulaic sequences probably present in the data (p. 118).

It is of some importance that frequency is not used simply as an easy solution. Rather, it helps if there is an independently motivated justification for prioritizing frequency, as there is, for instance, in the recent attempt to develop a list of the formulaic sequences that would be most useful for second language learners to focus on in their academic writing (Ellis, Simpson-Vlach, and Maynard 2006).[6]

Phonological indicators of formulaicity

Idiomatic expressions often have their own fixed tonicity, for example,

- 'There's a good girl
- 'What 'of it?
- To be 'at it (Wells 2006: 172)

Elsewhere, Wells observes, "Some instances of a speaker accenting repeated words do not seem to have a logical explanation, and must be regarded as idiomatic. For example, we might complain about a speaker's voice quality or intonation by using the cliché: *It's 'not what he ᵥ said, it's the 'way that he \ said it*. Logically, you would expect contrastive focus on *what* and *way* rather than the repeated focusing on *said*" (p. 179).

Phonology has good potential as a marker of formulaicity in speech, because it may directly reflect the nature of the processing. Making reference to a number of recent studies, Bybee (2006) observes that "high frequency words and phrases undergo phonetic reduction at a faster rate than low and mid frequency sequences" (p. 714; see also Bybee and Scheibman 1999). She continues:

> The explanation for this effect is that the articulatory representation of words and sequences of words is made up of neuromotor routines. When sequences of neuromotor routines are repeated, their execution becomes

more fluent. This increased fluency is the result of representing the repeated sequence at a higher level as a single unit.
(Bybee 2006: 714–15)

She also notes that phonological reduction does not put communicative effectiveness at risk because the hearer can predict the form of a highly frequent item (p. 217). Bybee (2002) suggests that patterns of liaison in French (the pronunciation of a normally silent word-final consonant when followed by vowel-initial word) can be explained according to frequency. The more common a particular pairing is, the more likely the marked form (*with* liaison) is to survive.

Segalowitz and Gatbonton (1995) review evidence showing that repeated practice results in more than just a speeding up of the production: it can make qualitative changes, by restructuring the procedural sequences to involve "fewer, and more informationally encapsulated mechanisms than was the case prior to practice" (p. 139). Most of the research that they refer to relates to fluency in lexical decision tasks and other recognition activities. However, their interest in repeated speaking in a communicative setting (Gatbonton and Segalowitz 1988), reiterated in their (1995) paper, indicates that they consider the effects of practice to extend to spoken output. It follows that the pronunciation of a word string may indicate the level of novelty versus familiarity for that speaker.

If multiword strings can have their own phonological representation that links straight to the holistic meaning (Bybee 2006), one would expect the idiom and non-idiom readings of expressions like 'skating on thin ice' to have different pronunciations, since one has a holistic meaning and the other does not. Van Lancker, Canter, and Terbeek (1981) found this to be so (though only when readers were making an effort to distinguish the two meanings). In the idiom readings, the major lexical words were shorter and there were fewer pauses. The idiom readings also had less marked pitch contours than the literal readings, vowels were closer to neutral, and consonants were more lax. These features are reminiscent of those associated with frequent repetition, as described above, yet the sorts of idioms used in the study (for example, 'rotten to the core', 'keep a stiff upper lip') are not at all frequent (Moon 1998). One could argue that the idiom reading is nevertheless more frequent than the literal one, but it may be that familiarity with the idiom—both our own, and our judgement about how familiar the idiom will be to hearers—is more salient than frequency in explaining why it can have a reduced form.

Perhaps there is greater scope for a reduced form where the word string is known to be formulaic in the speech community, as opposed to just for the individual. Some theoretical models, including the one underpinning this book, distinguish between word strings that an individual has first learnt as a combination of individual words and then reduced to a more fluent form through repetition, and those that the individual learnt as holistic strings from others, complete with their own pre-reduced phonological pattern.

Furthermore, there might be a way of differentiating them in research. The former set, which could include a person's recitation of their address or phone number, would at any point be restorable to the more explicit phonological form from which they derived. The latter, though, might be known only in the reduced form. Since that form would not always differentiate between sounds with similar features (for example, /t/ and /k/ in final position), it could result in problems when trying to write the expression down (see later section on spelling).

Another feature of speech production relevant to research into formulaic sequences is the location of pauses, taken to be a measure of fluency (see Wray 2002b: 35f for a review). Some researchers, including Erman (2007) and Wray (2004; Chapter 12 in this volume), identify the formulaic sequences using other criteria and then see whether pauses occur significantly less often in formulaic than in non-formulaic material. Over time, confidence in the validity of pause location as an indicator of a boundary has increased to the point where pauses are now being used to help identify formulaic sequences (for example, Forsberg 2006; Qi 2006).[7]

Form

What are the formal characteristics of a formulaic sequence? For many researchers, only stretches of more than one word are considered formulaic (for example, Erman and Warren 2000; Wiktorsson 2003).[8] There is clearly sense in attempting to study only multiword strings, since single words have been subject to much research already. However, there are potentially major implications and procedural problems entailed in only looking at two or more words in a string. First, it becomes difficult further down the line fully to address questions about functional similarity between items, if some of them are only one word long and therefore excluded from the analysis, for example, 'hello' versus 'good bye'; 'thanks' versus 'thank you' versus 'thank you very much'. Similarly, there seems little sense in including 'out of' in a study but not 'into'. As these examples suggest, word break locations can be rather arbitrary in some languages. For many native speaker writers, a two-word noun becomes a one-word or hyphenated pre-nominal adjective (for example, 'the effect in the long term' versus 'the long(-)term effect'), and word strings making the transition to single word will display variation in their presentational form, for example, 'no one', 'no-one', 'noone'; 'so called', 'so-called', 'socalled'; 'a lot', 'alot' (Wray 1996). The notion of the MEU neutralizes the difference in status between the formulaic word string, the single word and the morpheme, making it equally relevant to consider them all, insofar as they constitute a reliable mapping of meaning onto a stable form.

Another form criterion recommended by Erman and Warren (2000) and adopted by Wiktorsson (2003) and Forsberg (2006) is that a word string be considered formulaic only if it has a measure of conventionalization, "that is, one member of a prefab cannot be replaced by a synonymous word without causing change of meaning or function and/or idiomaticity" (Erman and Warren 2000: 32). What this approach captures is the characteristic *oddity* of many (some would say most, or all) formulaic sequences; its value in making practical progress in a piece of research is considerable. Nevertheless, it presents a problem, for "restricted exchangeability does not always work, mostly because absolute synonyms can be hard to find" (Fanny Forsberg, personal communication). Furthermore, it potentially creates borderline cases, particularly since it has been shown (for example, Moon 1998) that many so-called 'fixed' idioms actually have many different forms.

It follows that applying the conventionalization criterion, as also the multiword one just discussed, is best justified as a means of reducing the amount of data that one works with. The rationale is that it is reasonable to examine the subset of cases that are most demonstrably formulaic, even if there exist others that are also formulaic, provided one has grounds to believe that there is no fundamental difference between them that could undermine the research.

Idiosyncrasies

Where learner language is the focus, there are additional options for identification. In particular, by using prefabricated material speakers can perform beyond their real level of competence (Wray and Pegg in press). Exceptional length and complexity, and grammatical structures that are more advanced than those found in novel output, are two of the six features used for identification purposes by Myles, Mitchell, and Hooper (1999) in their examination of British secondary school students' knowledge of French. As Myles (2004) points out, identifying formulaicity this way entails having information about what that particular individual knows and doesn't know: "It is therefore important, when wanting to identify unanalysed chunks reliably, to compare them both to the generative competence of individual learners at a given point of interlanguage development, and over the course of this development for this particular learner" (p. 143).

In first language acquisition data—also effective with preschool L2 data (for example, Perera 2001)—Lieven, Pine, and Barnes (1992) identify the "frozen" phrase as a sequence that contains (some) words that do not appear independently of it (p. 295). This is one of a set of identification measures that they use for different types of multiword utterance. Again, assessing whether something is frozen entails having a detailed knowledge of what individuals know at specific points in their development. One problem with this approach is that it will not always pick out as frozen the expressions that are MEUs for the adults too. The approach is founded on the assumption that frozen phrases are temporary in the child's language, and that the parts ultimately enter the general active vocabulary as single words and morphemes. The marker of them having passed into the language is that they are used independently of the expression. Yet common expressions like 'happy birthday' and 'see you later' are no less formulaic for containing words that also combine independently—indeed most of the formulaic sequences in the adult language are of just that kind, and it is part of the child's linguistic journey to acquire them. Although it may be possible to demonstrate that the child *must* have learnt an expression holistically because she does not know the individual words in it, it is not possible to argue that she did *not* learn it holistically if she *does* know the words in it. However, since temporarily frozen phrases are of major significance in first language acquisition, it is arguably not that much of a problem that a few rather obvious formulaic expressions are excluded from the analysis, for they can easily be identified by other means.

Idiosyncrasies can also assist with identification in some other data types. For instance, if one believes that any multiword strings remaining in aphasia must (by virtue of the loss of the capability to assemble novel strings) be MEUs, then it follows that an analysis of aphasic language will reveal some of that person's MEUs. Of course, there is a major danger of circularity in such an approach, but usually, with data from aphasia, independent reasons can be found for believing the items to be formulaic—for example, they are common routines, or known idiosyncrasies of the individual (see Wray 1992, 2002b: chapter 12 for reviews of claims).

Spelling

As noted in Chapter 5, schooling may be responsible for imposing word boundaries within lexical units that have hitherto been processed as single items (and indeed continue to be). If so, spelling could occasionally be used as a means of demonstrating that a word string is a single unit in an individual's lexicon. The acquisition of an MEU in the spoken medium only entails mapping a phonological form onto a meaning. Spelling is normally extrapolated later, using the established conventions for mapping phonemes onto letters. In some cases, there is no way to adjudicate the precise nature of a sound in an expression without recourse to a dictionary. Thus, many native speakers of English are not sure whether 'when the time is right' or 'when the time is ripe' is the correct form of the expression, since the final consonant is normally pronounced in an indeterminate way. Not until they have looked it up and committed the citation form to memory will they have the option of pronouncing the final consonant with its full value.

It is only the formulaic sequences that are shared across individuals that are subject to this kind of underspecification of form. As noted earlier, any MEU that has arisen through the proceduralization of a configuration composed by the individual, such as an address or phone number, will maintain its reliable route back to the original—the individual knows what the full form is. For the same reason, it is only possible to speak of a 'correct' and 'incorrect' form in relation to shared formulaic sequences. When we compose novel material, we choose what we want to say and that makes it correct in its own terms.

Formulaic sequences, though, can have an identity external to, and independent of, our own use of them. Thus it is that we can learn new things about the pronunciation of a word string we already knew, by seeing how it is spelled.

However, it may be inappropriate to assume that the written form inevitably leads to a reliable resolution of the 'correct' versus 'incorrect' dilemma. The evidence in the nineteenth century pauper letters described by Fairman (2000, 2002, 2003, 2006) and discussed in Chapter 5 suggests that the written form is not necessarily an arbiter of disambiguation. Many of the examples suggest that untutored writers operate a chaotic strategy arising from lack of confidence, rather than discover a way to more accurately encode their lexical units. They confront, perhaps, not an opportunity to somehow *correctly* depict the lexical units, but the uncomfortable discovery that writing in words imposes consistency on something fundamentally fluid (cf. Himmelmann 2006).

Intuition

Can the use of intuition to identify formulaic material in texts be justified? Intuition is in the mind of the beholder, of course, and there is justifiable concern that intuitive identifications will not be replicable. However, the case may have been overstated. We should anticipate that formulaic sequences shared across a speech community can be reliably identified by most native speakers, provided they know what they are being asked to look for—that, of course is the nub of the problem, for it brings us back to the question of definition.

Intuitions can come from different sources. Informants' own intuitions can be used to find out what material they believe is formulaic for them—for example, Dóla (in preparation). Data can be independently examined by a set of judges (for example, P. Foster 2001; Van Lancker Sidtis and Rallon 2004), with their consensus view used as definitive for the study. Nevertheless, the single most common application of intuition is by the researcher.

Chenoweth (1995) is very frank about the role of intuition in her analysis of formulaic sequences in student essays. Although she consulted the *BBI Combinatory Dictionary of English* (Benson, Benson, and Ilson 1986) for guidance on collocations, she admits that "referring to it only limited, but did not completely eliminate, my reliance on intuition" (p. 287). Not all researchers are so candid, though it is probably true to say that intuition plays a role in the identification of formulaic sequences in almost all studies, including frequency-based ones. Butterfield and Krishnamurthy (2000) note that decisions made by lexicographers, including those engaging in corpus-based work, must always be guided by professional judgement. Butler (2004) points out that "[t]he important distinction here is between the use of *introspection as data* and the essential utilisation of our intuitions to form hypotheses and analyse data" (p. 150, emphasis added).

Outside corpus research, there can often seem little alternative to the use of intuition to select data, and for many linguists intuition is the legitimate basis of sound research. Koenraad Kuiper (personal communication) reports that his approach, over many years, was to "pencil [...] tentative formulae into cards and look [...] for variant forms in the data". To count as formulaic, Kuiper expected a word string to have "a single discourse function and a lexical core, i.e. a word or set of words around which the formula was built. A variant [of that formula] had to be able to be represented as part of a finite state diagram". Thus his approach used "a blend of native intuition ... and a formal understanding of the kind of structural properties formulaic expressions have". He frequently called on other native speakers to validate decisions.

The combination of personal intuitions and those of others is often used to bolster the credibility of claims about data. Knutsson (2006), comparing native and non-native narratives, first used her own near-native intuition to select likely items from her native speaker dataset. The items were then assessed by native and near-native judges and assessed against four rather more objective criteria: fixedness, frequency, non-compositionality, and syntactic sophistication (pp. 35–6). The efficacy of such an approach depends largely on the purpose of the research. In Knutsson's case, the major requirement was the equal treatment of two datasets in the analysis; it was therefore not imperative to capture all and only the word strings that might by some other criterion be counted as formulaic.

Intuitive judgements are more difficult to justify in studies that aim to count, or discover the essence of, formulaic sequences, since, naturally, the results will be different according to what is included and excluded. A particular case in point is the identification of formulaic sequences in code-switching data (for example, Namba 2008), where the transition from one language to the other will tend to draw the eye to the switched unit, increasingly the likelihood that one feels it to be formulaic in some way. For this reason, Namba is careful to disregard the fact of switching as an *indicator* of formulaicity, while he assesses the plausibility of Backus' (1999) proposal that code-switching is constrained from occurring within MEUs. Were it possible to demonstrate that code-switching does only occur in novel configurations, and not within MEUs, this fact could then be used to assist with identification. However, the situation is complicated by partly-fixed frames, into which variable material—which might be in the other language—can be inserted, and also by the possibility that individuals raised in a code-switching environment may actually acquire MEUs that contain a code-switch (compare 'he has a certain je ne sais quoi').

Although it is clear that intuition must be treated with caution, probably there is no way to escape the need to use it. If so, it may be better to put effort into seeking the best ways of harnessing it effectively, as well as looking for alternatives. In Chapter 9 a procedure is presented that can assist in doing so.

Published lists and corpora

Existing databases, including dictionaries and text books, can be used to find clear, established examples of formulaic sequences. As we saw earlier, this approach is particularly useful when seeking reliable items to use as experimental stimuli. The Schmitt, Dörnyei, Adolphs, and Durow (2004) study, and others in the same project, demonstrate, however, that it is rarely going to be enough to just go to one resource and find exactly the items one needs for a particular investigation. They selected a large set of possible items from reference books, a book on L2 teaching methodology, and the textbooks used by their test subjects (L2 learners), before progressively whittling them down using corpus checks and pre-tests. For example, Spöttl and McCarthy (2004) needed a small set of formulaic sequences for a think-aloud translation task. They selected 20 of the most frequent 100 tokens in the CANCODE corpus and searched the corpus for recurring strings of three or more words containing them. From the resulting list they chose the most frequently occurring strings conveying a complete meaning that was opaque or semi-opaque (p. 196) (for example, 'out of place'; 'there's no way'). In the test, the sequences were presented in a genuine or slightly edited context occurring in the corpus.

Reference resources can be used for other kinds of investigation too. For Moon (1998), whose research entailed establishing how frequent and how fixed 'fixed idioms' were, the question of identification was solved by using the 6,776 idioms listed in an idiom dictionary. Sprenger (2003), engaged in similar research on a Dutch corpus, used 1,102 fixed expressions found by means of a semi-random search in a dictionary (p. 7). As the dictionary was not dedicated to fixed expressions, the items were additionally subjected to semantic and formal criteria before being included in the study (p. 8). Boyd (2004) selected just three phrases: 'the thing is', 'the fact is', and 'the point is', which she then researched extensively in the COBUILD online corpus in order to find out more about their use in real text.

An important question for any researcher to consider before using existing lists to identify formulaic sequences is whether the list has gained authority simply by virtue of being published. As Jones and Haywood (2004) point out, there is little value in rejecting the use of one's own intuitions as too subjective if one instead turns to published lists that are based on other people's intuitions (p. 274). In addition, it needs to be established whether the list was compiled for sufficiently similar reasons to those underpinning the research for which the examples will now be used. For instance, an idiom dictionary may be intended primarily for learners, for those interested in the history of idioms, or as a general reference resource for native speakers, with different decisions made in each case, about what is included. If the research is focused on processing (for example, Underwood, Schmitt, and Galpin 2004), it must be established to what extent the items in a dictionary or textbook might be expected to represent all and only the items hypothesized to be processed in a particular way, or at least a fully representative selection of them.

One of the main attractions of an existing resource is when it provides not just a list of possible items but also information about them that is relevant to the study. Works that use corpus frequency data to furnish information on multiword strings are particularly useful (for example, Biber, Johansson, Leech, and Conrad 1999). As noted earlier, some measure of subjective judgement will still be required. Jones and Haywood (2004), describing how they selected items from Biber *et al.* (1999), observe: "Using the listings of four, five, and six word bundles as source material, we selected a number of bundles of each length, keeping in mind the criteria of usefulness and relevance to the specific language functions we intended to teach" (p. 275).

Frequency lists are useful not only for ensuring that the items are *highly* frequent. Some studies require *low* frequency strings. For instance, Bishop (2004) used only exemplars outside the 2000 frequency band (p. 233). Other research designs may require a careful control of the range of frequencies. McGee (2006), investigating native and non-native speaker intuitions about collocations, needed collocating word pairs that matched very exacting requirements, regarding both their individual and joint frequencies of occurrence. He chose his stimulus items using frequency information from the British National Corpus and search engines on the World Wide Web (i.e. the number of hits).

Mixed criteria

There can be considerable value in combining approaches to identification. Sometimes, doing so may increase the reach of the process, on the basis that most examples will be captured one way or another. Thus, for instance, Forsberg (2006) used 11 criteria, which variously addressed aspects of frequency, phonological and lexical form, usage, meaning, and precociousness relative to normal expectations (it was learner data). The disadvantage of this approach is, as Forsberg notes, that some sort of theoretical account is needed, to explain why a word string that is, say, spoken fluently, but fully transparent in form and meaning, should be equated with another that is irregular in form, or has a strong pragmatic association, etc.

Bespoke designations

Some ways in which the identificational approach can be constrained using thresholds have already been mentioned. Particularly when seeking examples for experimental input, one can go even further, by applying specific constraints to ensure that the items selected possess the characteristics under examination and no others that might confuse the findings.

Bishop (2004), for instance, looked for a particular subset of formulaic sequences for his investigation: strings of two or more words used to express a simple concept, and for which there existed a single word synonym (for example, 'pile up'; 'come in for'). They also had to be unknown to his subjects, so he ran a pre-test to check that they were. Underwood *et al.* (2004) applied four form-based criteria when selecting stimuli for an investigation of eye-movement patterns during the reading of formulaic and non-formulaic word strings. For practical reasons relating to the measuring, it was important that the formulaic strings had certain characteristics: not beginning with several function words, not ending with a function word, being four to eight words long, and predictable from the initial components (Underwood *et al.* 2004: 156).

A risk with specific designations is that the phenomenon under investigation may not be as clear cut as the criteria are, so that what is discovered using the selected items is not representative of anything other than itself, bringing into question the validity of the findings.

To take one example, idioms, although often viewed as the most reliable and definitive type of formulaic sequence, elude precise definition, and their nature becomes more complicated the deeper one delves (Nunberg, Sag, and Wasow 1994). There have been a number of studies in the clinical domain investigating whether, in various types of clinical population including people with left and right hemisphere damage, autism, and Alzheimer's disease, the literal meaning of an idiom is accessed before, after, or at the same time as, the non-literal meaning (see Wray 2008a for a review, and also the discussion in Chapter 11). In such studies, it is taken for granted that the literal meaning *is* accessed at some point, yet this may not always be the case—at least until testing is done (see Chapter 3, Figure 3.2).

Wray (2008a) suggests that in some of these clinical investigations test subjects are being challenged to juxtapose the idiom and literal meanings in a way that is no more than a form of post hoc linguistic game-playing that does not tap into existing knowledge or customary processing.

Conclusion

[D]espite the general consensus on the importance of multi-word units, there is surprisingly little agreement on their defining characteristics, the methodologies to identify them, or even what to call them; and, as a result, there is little agreement across studies on the specific set of multi-word units worthy of description.
(Biber *et al.* 2004: 372)

In this chapter the questions of definition and identification have been problematized, as a demonstration that they are non-trivial concerns for the researcher. Although various solutions used in the research literature have been reviewed, there remains an issue about just how a researcher should proceed, particularly in relation to the use of intuition. In the next chapter a partial solution is offered.

Notes

1 For example, "For the analysis of four-word sequences in the present chapter, we set a minimal cut-off of at least ten times per million words in order for a sequence to be considered a recurrent lexical bundle ... Five and six word lexical bundles are much less common than four-word bundles, and we therefore use a lower cut off for their analysis" (Biber, Johansson, Leech, and Conrad 1999: 990).

2 The complications of variability in common phrases should not be overlooked, however (for example, Stubbs 2002; Tucker 2007). Furthermore, strings identified in this way 'do not usually represent a complete structural unit' (Biber *et al.* 1999: 991).

3 Read and Nation (2004) rightly point out with reference to the definition of the formulaic sequence (Wray 2002b: 9), that there is no very direct way to ascertain whether a given word string has been holistically processed—the same applies to the MEU. However, they are mistaken in interpreting the definition in Wray (2002b: 9) as intended for identification and measurement.

4 Continuum models may hold that there are no firm classes, though in practice they tend to just introduce more classes (Wray 2002b: 62–5).

5 In fact, a word string that is an MEU can also be treated as a sequence of smaller units if the need arises—this flexibility is fundamental to the NOA model.

6 Not that the deliberate introduction of formulaic material for academic writing is unproblematic, as Wray and Pegg (in press) demonstrate in relation to over-formulaic test papers in the IELTS exam.

7 Citation forms will often be demarcated with both slight pauses and a different level of enunciation—usually stronger—than the surrounding material. Thus, making sense of 'the spaces between *pig* and *and* and *and* and *whistle*' (see Chapter 3) is assisted by fuller vowel realizations, stress, and possibly even a glottal stop, on the citation items: *pig* /ənd 'and ənd 'and ənd/ *whistle*. Similarly, *Jones, where* '*Brown* /həd had 'had (.) həd had 'had had (.) 'had had həd had/ *the teacher's approval.*

8 This is not intended to imply that these researchers do not apply other criteria as well.

9
A diagnostic approach to identifying morpheme equivalent units

Introduction

The discussion in Chapter 8 has shown that it is possible to be robust in one's identification of examples of formulaic language if one's definition translates into clear decisions—for example, "a lexical bundle is defined here as a recurring sequence or three or more words" (Biber *et al.* 1999: 990). However, if the true essence of formulaic language lies in how it is *processed*, definitions based on external criteria will probably not capture all the examples (see Chapter 8, Figure 8.2). The definition of the morpheme equivalent unit (MEU), in contrast, captures what is believed to be happening in language processing, but that makes it unhelpful for identification, since it charges us to look for items 'processed like a morpheme' (see Chapter 2). We have no direct means of establishing when that is happening. Yet we do have many potential indicators of it. They cannot be used as *proof*, for it is, in fact, these indicators that have led to the idea of morpheme equivalence (Wray 2002b: 265–69) and we must avoid circularity. On the other hand, there is a way to use the indicators to justify one's belief that a particular word string is an MEU, and that is the method outlined below.

This 'alternative' approach to identification does not claim to achieve the same things as a frequency-based or phonological analysis, and indeed it is not really a *method* for identification at all. Rather, it is a means of demonstrating, through a set of diagnostics, what it is about a particular word string that has led the researcher to believe it to be formulaic. These diagnostics are, therefore, not in conflict with other methods for identification, but rather provide an additional level of information.[1]

Intuition as a tool

Sinclair (1991: 4) observes that "human intuition about language is highly specific and not at all a good guide to what actually happens when the same people actually use the language". Evidently, intuition is not a direct window onto word distribution in text. Although reasons for this discrepancy have been proposed (for example, Wray 2002b: 276), it remains true to say that we have very little understanding of exactly what, in psycholinguistic terms, intuition is reflecting. Yet, despite the well-recognized limitations inherent in subjective judgement, it continues to be crucial to aspects of linguistic analysis. Although we should, of course, continue to develop objective measures of language, ignoring the potential (and indeed actual) role of intuition as a tool is unhelpful. Rather, we should seek new ways of understanding intuition: why intuitive judgements do not always match other evidence (see McGee 2006 for one investigation of this issue); where our intuitions come from; how they emerge developmentally; and the extent to which the intuitions of similar people are the same. Should it be discovered that some or all of our intuitions about language are in fact constructs imposed by, say, our educational experience, then they should be interpreted accordingly (see Chapter 5). In the meantime, it is a question of pragmatism as much as anything—if intuition is going to be a part of how we analyse language, what can we do to ensure that its contribution is clear and open to interrogation?

The diagnostics below aim to make the role of intuition more evident, and to help researchers understand the bases upon which they are making judgements. They can also be used to facilitate comparisons between judges, so that differences in their beliefs about a word string are explicit. In this way, they can serve, to a limited extent, to externally validate what are inherently personal beliefs, making intuition a little more resilient as a tool for investigation.

The criterion-based approach

In formulating criteria for identifying MEUs in datasets, the aim is to enable the researcher to explore why he or she feels that a particular word string has been holistically stored and accessed, by establishing reliable justifications for that intuitive judgement. The 11 criteria reflect observations made across previous research over many years. Between them, they should capture most of the features that are likely to underlie an intuitive judgement. However, they are not intended to be a universal or definitive set. Different data may reveal different features and, of course, different judges may discover different sources of intuition.

Therefore, it is recommended, that, when adopting the diagnostic approach, researchers reflect on whether additional criteria are required for their particular dataset, as well as which of the criteria in the set are not required (some guidance on this is given later). It will be fully appropriate, in reporting the use of this diagnostic approach, to indicate that modifications were made to it, whether for reasons specific to the data or because some more general problem with a criterion was identified.

It should also be noted that these diagnostics are *not* really suitable for 'scoring' the extent of a word string's formulaicity. That is, a word string that has three features is not necessarily more formulaic (or even more likely to be formulaic) than a word string with only one feature. The reasons are: (a) the criteria are in part mutually exclusive, partly not—that is, for some features, having one precludes having others, but for other features having one may actually increase the likelihood of having others. As a result, there can be a clustering of features for some types of word string, while for others there is only the possibility of one feature; (b) the criteria do not all operate at the same level (some relate to form, some to usage, etc.); (c) sometimes the same feature in a word string will be reflected in two criteria; and (d) there are criteria that actually relate to something that is *not* formulaic or not standard about the string, but which nevertheless are indicative of formulaicity at a deeper level.

Validation

The diagnostic criteria were initially tested on a group of eight native English-speaking PhD students and post-doctoral researchers and nine non-native English speakers with high levels of English proficiency studying in doctoral or post-doctoral programmes. They wrote comments on the clarity of the wording and any difficulties in applying the criteria to the examples supplied. In addition, research using the criteria (for example, Foster, in preparation; Namba 2008) has provided feedback on their coverage and efficacy, resulting in some minor adaptations.

Notes on applying the diagnostics effectively

1 The diagnostics are not suitable for deciding *if* a string is an MEU, so the text should *first* be analysed, looking for formulaic sequences (i.e. strings that look as if they may be MEUs). The diagnostics can then be applied to just those strings, to ascertain why they have been judged formulaic. The effectiveness of the judgements and diagnostics can be checked by selecting one or two examples of word strings that are believed not to be formulaic—it would be expected that they will not attract any 'agree' or 'strongly agree' judgements.

2 The diagnostics are grounded in the theoretical position expounded in Wray (2002b) and summarized in Chapter 2 of this book. For those whose research does not fully align with this position, the diagnostics may still be of use, but they must be interpreted with reference to any differences between the researcher's own theoretical position and the present one. For instance, the diagnostics point to word strings that a particular individual uses repeatedly, even if no one else uses them (Criterion E). Other theories may only consider word strings formulaic if they are community-wide. Differences in theoretical position are not a problem, but must be acknowledged if the results of an analysis are to be meaningful.

3 Judgements are made on a five-point scale: 'strongly agree'; 'agree'; 'don't know' or 'not applicable'; 'disagree'; 'strongly disagree'. While 'agree' and

'strongly agree' may be taken as positive evidence of formulaicity, 'disagree' and 'strongly disagree' do not constitute evidence against formulaicity—just the absence of a trait that sometimes indicates it. Therefore, if a word string has a mixture of '(strongly) agrees' and '(strongly) disagrees', the outcome is not contradictory. Rather, it provides rather clear indications about where the evidence of formulaicity lies.

4 Not all of the criteria are applicable to all examples, and there is a guide later to choosing a subset for certain types of data. However, even within those subsets, it should not be expected that an example can necessarily be judged against all the criteria, and 'not applicable' can be selected in such cases.

5 It should not be necessary to speculate beyond the scope of the evidence and of one's confident knowledge. That is, the intention is to reveal the basis of intuitions already made, not to micro-analyse features of the material.

6 Examples containing errors (i.e. in learner or clinical data) need to be handled differently. They should be examined partly on the basis of the attested form in the data, and partly on the basis of the form that was being targeted, where this can be reasonably ascertained. Guidance is given on this.

7 When identifying formulaic sequences in text, and when assessing them against these criteria as potential MEUs, the issue of fixedness must be borne in mind. Most MEUs are not fully-fixed, and capturing the formulaicity of a word string may only be possible if certain details are set aside. These include verb morphology, subjects and objects, and the presence or absence of certain adverbs and adjectives. Thus, the judgements made must be able to recognize that 'Mabel found herself tearing Henry off a very large strip' is a realization of the partly-fixed frame 'NP$_i$ tear-TENSE NP$_j$ off a strip', even though it also features novel material. Since the diagnostic procedure aims to provide the researcher with insights about what has led to identifying a string as formulaic, there is every reason to discuss, as they arise, issues about the boundaries of formulaicity and novelty.

Eleven diagnostic criteria for assessing intuitive judgements about formulaicity

---

A: By my judgement there is something grammatically unusual about this word string.

COMMENTARY

Only a small proportion of MEUs are entirely grammatically irregular (i.e. some idioms), but this criterion is also robust for any word string that the regular grammar of the language cannot easily generate.[2] Wray (2002b: 33) suggests that the ungrammaticality found in some formulaic sequences comes about because the word string is first processed holistically, and then, as a result, is isolated from changes in the language over time, until it stands out as a fossilized remnant of a now defunct rule. Since this process is gradual (because language changes slowly), it follows that there can be subtle shades of grammatical oddity that result from, and therefore indicate, that it is an MEU. For instance, the expression 'holier than thou' contains a pronoun that is no longer productive in English, and 'if I were you' preserves a subjunctive form that many speakers no longer use outside of that phrase.

B: By my judgement, part or all of the word string lacks semantic transparency.

COMMENTARY

In one sense, if you know an expression, it is transparent to you—whatever its composition. However, the spirit of this criterion is the potential for a formulaic word string to mean something as a whole that is different from the combined meaning of its parts, for example, 'by and by' meaning 'soon'; 'beat about the bush' meaning 'prevaricate'. As with grammatical irregularity, semantic opacity may increase over time (Wray 2002b: 266), so we should expect to find examples of word strings that have not yet lost all vestiges of their compositional meaning, but which could no longer be created as novel strings. This includes expressions in which one of the words is found only in that expression, for example, 'run amok'. We can also include under this criterion hyperbole, metaphor, and secondary applications. For instance, 'it's a small world' appears to be a straightforward description, but is used to express surprise at a coincidence. The expression 'very funny!' can convey the very opposite of its literal meaning, indicating that something is annoying to the speaker.

C: By my judgement, this word string is associated with a specific situation and/or register.

COMMENTARY

Some situations strongly attract one or more particular expressions, for example, 'happy birthday' and 'many happy returns' on birthdays, 'congratulations' on 'special' birthdays (18th, 21st, etc.) and other anniversaries. Formulaic expressions are often associated with a particular register, and can signal social relationships, for example, 'your majesty' and 'excuse me, I wonder if you would mind __'. In applying criterion C, we need also to consider creative uses of language, where the expression is deliberately applied out of its customary situation or register. An example would be if a child demanded something and the parent replied, ironically, 'Yes, your majesty'. The fact that the expression is out of context does not reduce its formulaicity. Rather, its formulaicity is what ensures its ironic interpretation. For unintentional misapplication, see Criterion J.[3]

D: By my judgement, the word string as a whole performs a function in communication or discourse other than, or in addition to, conveying the meaning of the words themselves.

COMMENTARY

This criterion homes in on expressions that in some sense 'change the world'. A word string that is routinely employed for a specific act may become so strongly associated with it that using the wrong words weakens or even invalidates the act. Performatives like 'I promise' and 'I now pronounce you man and wife' are clear examples of this type of word string.

E: By my judgement, this precise formulation is the one most commonly used by this speaker/writer when conveying this idea.

COMMENTARY

This criterion is useful in two main situations: firstly, where immature or interlanguage features are observable; secondly, where the speaker has a particular idiosyncratic expression. With regard to the latter, it may well be the case that what appears to the researcher to be an idiosyncratic turn of phrase is, in fact, a standard expression in the speaker's native speech community or family but the researcher is not aware of the fact and so cannot assign '(strongly) agree' to Criterion H (below).[4] Because of the inherent comparison of the speaker's utterance with other utterances that he or she has made, additional data from the same informant should be examined if available. In practice, most data will not be categorizable using this criterion, and 'don't know/not applicable' will be the response.

F: By my judgement, the speaker/writer has accompanied this word string with an action, use of punctuation, or phonological pattern that gives it special status as a unit, and/or the speaker/writer is repeating something just heard or read.

COMMENTARY

The detail of this criterion varies, according to the medium of expression. Inevitably, valuable phonological or visual information may be lost when audio or video material is transcribed, so it would be a good idea to know, at the point of transcription, whether features such the ones noted here are likely to be relevant. The common factor amongst the various manifestations under this criterion is that something extrinsic to the content of the message itself is used to demarcate the word string as special. In the case of an *action* associated directly with a word string, the action anchors the word string as ritually fixed. Examples include symbolic routines performed at key points in religious rituals (genuflecting, making the sign of the cross, ringing a bell), and in superstitious rituals, such as touching wood when saying 'touch wood' meaning 'I hope'. Speakers wishing to distance themselves from someone else's words will sometimes make a 'quotation marks' gesture in the air to indicate that the words are not their own. In written *punctuation*, of course, quotation marks indicate that the quoted passage is fixed, and not open to the writer's own creativity. A range of *phonological patterns* can be used in speech to demarcate a word string. A very clear case is a song extract, where the tune strongly marks the words as being formulaic. Spoken quotations presented as mini-performances may also have noticeable phonological characteristics including a special pitch and tone of voice. When quotations or other word strings (for example, book titles) are embedded into the surrounding text they may surrender their own natural phonological pattern and adopt the intonation appropriate to the part of speech that they now represent. For example, in 'She adopted a do-as-you-would-be-done-by mentality', a full sentence takes the role of an adjective and is likely to have an intonation pattern and rapid delivery that fits its position. A short silence before and after the embedded passage is also common. Overall, phonological demarcation of an MEU may be very subtle, and in normal spoken text we should not expect to find strong phonological indicators unless they are needed to prevent misunderstanding. *Repetition*, to count here, must be local, since there are other criteria that account for the speaker's own use of the expression at other times (E) and others' use of it (H). Here, the focus is on echoing behaviour, including everything from mindless imitation, through quotation and reading aloud, to the appropriate reuse of an expression just encountered.

G: By my judgement, the speaker/writer, or someone else, has marked this word string grammatically or lexically in a way that gives it special status as a unit.

COMMENTARY

Grammatical indications that a word string has morpheme equivalent status for the speaker often come in the form of errors. For instance, a Kuwaiti official interviewed on the radio in December 2002 said, "We hope that Iraq will be free from weapon of mass destructions". For that speaker, 'weapon of mass destruction' was treated so entirely like a single lexical item that it was pluralized at the end instead of internally. In some cases, the speaker's lexical packaging will make it quite clear that the word string is being treated holistically, as with 'I've just learnt the term *pin money*', or 'He was, quote, heavily compromised, unquote'. In a verbal equivalent of ritual action, there are religious practices in which particular words or phrases are always accompanied by a marker (itself formulaic). One such is 'Mohammed, Peace Be Upon Him'. Another, now rather uncommon, was the practice of saying 'God rest his (or her) soul' when mentioning a dead relative or friend. Again, errors are often a good indicator of formulaic word strings: "One word sums up probably the responsibility of any governor, and that one word is 'to be prepared'". This statement, by George W. Bush, suggests that he was processing 'to be prepared' as a single unit. Sometimes it is not the speaker who provides the demarcation. In 'A: What was it Thatcher was called? B: The Iron

Lady', B's response is a specific expression that must take that form if it is to be the correct answer. The demarcation, however, is given by A, who requests the epithet. A particularly useful form of demarcation is when the language changes, as in code-switching and borrowing—it is imperative, however, not to create circularity by claiming both that code-switched material is (likely to be) formulaic and that you can identify something as formulaic *because* it is a code-switched unit (Namba 2008). Certainly in the case of borrowing, it is very likely that the material is formulaic, whether it is a one-off (for example, 'we'd done our *auf wiedersehens* and left by eight o'clock') or a common borrowing into the language (for example, 'it was a case of *chacun à son goût*, I suppose'). In either case, the inserted material may not import all of its original meaning or form (for example, 'They will be tempted to ask, with their grandfathers, where is the use of all this parleyvooing?'),[5] such that it is demarcated, under this criterion, in more than one way.

H: By my judgement, based on direct evidence or my intuition, there is a greater than chance-level probability that the speaker/writer will have encountered this precise formulation before in communication from other people.

COMMENTARY

There is an infinite set of possible grammatical sentences in a language, but not all of them are equally likely to occur. For any given message, there will often be one or more preferred ways of expressing it. The distinctions can be subtle, and are highly sensitive to the norms of the speech community. Where there is evidence in the data that the word string has been used by someone else, the case for agreeing on this criterion will be strengthened. Otherwise, the researcher should draw on his/her own knowledge of the speech variety, or ask members of the speech community for guidance. In the absence of such information, 'don't know/not applicable' should be selected. Nativelike, immature, and non-nativelike forms all can be tested under this criterion. A learner could have picked up an expression from others in the L2 class, or a child could have learnt it from another child. Clearly, in such cases, an accurate judgement relies on evidence regarding the norms of the speakers surrounding the subject, particularly if they themselves do not speak the mature/native variety.

I: By my judgement, although this word string is novel, it is a clear derivation, deliberate or otherwise, of something that can be demonstrated to be formulaic in its own right.

COMMENTARY

This criterion is different from the others, since it relates to expressions that are not themselves formulaic. Someone who says 'I slept like a twig' is clearly making a creative play on 'I slept like a log'. Similarly, if someone sings 'Somewhere over the raincoat' as a joke, it will not be possible to judge the string as formulaic on any of the other criteria since it is evidently novel, yet it will be important not to overlook the formulaic origins of it. Even if one does not know what the allusion is to, it will often be possible to guess that one has been made, and asking around may help uncover the original. It will help to apply the full set of criteria not only to the attested form but also to the underlying original from which it derives, and use the two sets of judgements side by side.

J: By my judgement, this word string is formulaic, but it has been unintentionally applied inappropriately.

COMMENTARY

If a learner, say, uses a formulaic expression inappropriately (for example, 'Excuse me' when a native speaker would say 'I'm sorry'), it will not be possible to assign 'agree' on certain other criteria, because it is not being used in the right way. Here, we can acknowledge that it is formulaic, even though misapplied. It may be useful to apply the full set of criteria both to the item itself and the hypothesized intended one, in order to get the full picture.

K: By my judgement, this word string contains linguistic material that is too sophisticated, or not sophisticated enough, to match the speaker's general grammatical and lexical competence.

COMMENTARY

Since an MEU is learnt as a complete package, the user may not have full command of some or all parts of its internal form. In such cases we can speak of performance outstripping competence. It is possible, for example, for first or second language learners to display, within an MEU, lexical and/or grammatical features that are too advanced relative to their general capabilities in the language. A very clear example is where people learn an expression in a foreign language that they don't speak. Many people in Wales know the drinking expression *iechyd da* 'good health' but have no idea how it is constructed. Meanwhile, people with an acquired language disorder may be able to produce in an MEU linguistic material that is no longer under their creative command. Conversely, an MEU may under-represent the speaker's knowledge. For instance, an MEU that contains a learner error[6] might still be in use long after the speaker's grammar and vocabulary have passed the stage of making that error.

Using the diagnostic criteria

As already noted, not all of the criteria are applicable to all types of output. Furthermore, some of the criteria trigger the parallel evaluation (on all criteria) of the target or original form from which the attested one departs. Guidelines are therefore provided here, about which procedures to follow in which circumstances. As Table 9.1 indicates, Criterion K is normally applicable only to learner data (i.e. L2 and child L1) and data from people with language disorders.

Deviations		A	B	C	D	E	F	G	H	I	J	K*
None		✓	✓	✓	✓	✓	✓	✓	✓	✓		✓
Errors/changes in form	Observed form							✓	✓	✓	✓	✓	✓
	Corrected form	✓	✓	✓	✓	✓				✓	✓		✓
Errors/changes in usage	Observed form	✓	✓	✓	✓	✓	✓	✓	✓	✓	✓	✓
	Appropriate form for context									✓			✓

*K normally applies only to data from learners and those with language disorders

Table 9.1 Application of criteria to different types of data

Examples of the diagnostic criteria in action

In order to demonstrate the criteria in use, some short examples follow here. The first set of examples is from Namba (2008). Namba is examining whether the patterns of Japanese–English code-switching in data from two young children maintain the internal integrity of MEUs. To do that, he uses the diagnostic criteria (including an extra one, L)[7] to establish how likely it is that a given switched unit is formulaic. Examples (1) and (2) in Figure 9.1 illustrate the frame 'it's [Japanese clause]', which the criteria suggest is strongly formulaic. In this construction 'it is' has a non-standard semantic and functional role, acting as a topicalizer meaning, approximately, 'it's a case of'.

---

1 It's *minna*   *waru-ku* *nat-*   *ta*   except for *sono*   *futari*   right?
          everyone bad-INF   become PAST   those   two
      [Everyone became bad except for those two, right?]

2 It's *mizu*   *nai*   you know   *mokusei*   *ni-wa*
          water   doesn't exist   Jupiter   TOP
      [There is no water, you know, on Jupiter]

Figure 9.1 'It's [Japanese Clause]' (from Namba 2008)

Namba's judgements on the criteria are given in Table 9.2, where '(S)A' stands for '(strongly) agree', '(S)D' for '(strongly) disagree' and 'N' for 'not applicable'.

CRITERIA	A Grammatical irregularity	B Semantic opacity	C Situation/register/genre specificity	D Pragmatic function	E Idiolect	F Performance indication	G Grammatical/lexical indication	H Previous encounter	I Derivation	J Inappropriate application	K Mismatch with maturation	L Underlying frame
Judgement	A	SA	N	SA	SA	N	N	A	A	N	N	SA

Table 9.2   Formulaicity in 'it's [Japanese Clause]' (from Namba 2008)

In contrast, when Namba examines the structure 'it was [Japanese clause]' in example (3) (Figure 9.2), he finds no evidence of formulaicity according to the criteria.

---

3 It's really   it was   *tadano*   *jaakuna*   *ishi*   *da-tta*
　　　　　　　　　　　　just　　evil　　will　　COP-PAST
　　　[It was just an evil will]

Figure 9.2   'It was [Japanese Clause]' (from Namba 2008)

In this structure there is no meaning independent of the components 'it' and 'was + clause'. As a result, he allots both the grammatical form (A) and the meaning (B) 'strongly disagree' and is unable to find any opportunity to allocate 'strongly agree' or 'agree' across the other criteria (Table 9.3). He concludes that, according to this method, there is no evidence of the structure being formulaic.

However, when he examines the Japanese element *tadano jaakuna ishi* 'just an evil will', it does appear to be formulaic (Table 9.4).[8] It is an expression used to describe the evil monsters in a super-heroes television programme, and the child is simply copying the words of the superhero character. Namba observes, 'he would never create this phrase as a novel one', justifying the selection of 'strongly agree' on Criterion H. Since the word string has such a specific denotation and connotation, he selects 'agree' for Criterion C. The word *jaaku* is too advanced for the child's current knowledge, leading to 'strongly agree' on K. Thus, even though the word string is both grammatically regular and semantically transparent, there are still grounds for it to be judged as formulaic for the speaker.

	A	B	C	D	E	F	G	H	I	J	K	L
CRITERIA	Grammatical irregularity	Semantic opacity	Situation/register/genre specificity	Pragmatic function	Idiolect	Performance indication	Grammatical/lexical indication	Previous encounter	Derivation	Inappropriate application	Mismatch with maturation	Underlying frame
Judgement	SD	SD	SD	SD	N	N	N	N	N	SD	SD	N

Table 9.3 Formulaicity in 'it was [Japanese Clause]' (from Namba 2008)

The second illustration comes from work in preparation by Camilla Lindholm, who is interested in the use of humour and formulaic language in aphasic talk. The extract in example (4) (Figure 9.3) is in Swedish, with translations given below each line.

	A	B	C	D	E	F	G	H	I	J	K	L
CRITERIA	Grammatical irregularity	Semantic opacity	Situation/register/genre specificity	Pragmatic function	Idiolect	Performance indication	Grammatical/lexical indication	Previous encounter	Derivation	Inappropriate application	Mismatch with maturation	Underlying frame
Judgement	SD	SD	A	N	N	N	N	SA	N	SD	SA	SD

Table 9.4 Formulaicity in 'tadano jaakuna ishi' (from Namba 2008)

(4)	line					
	01	N1	nummer	sju̲tton		
			number	*seventeen*		
	02		(0.6)			
	03	E1	de e	som	sju̲tton också	
			it's	*like*	*seventeen too*	
	04	N1	ja			
			yes			
	05		(0.4)			
	06	E1	[[den da̲r]]			
			that one			
	07	N1	[[bra]]	du hade		
			good	*you got*		
	08		(0.2)			
	09	E1	sjutton också	sätter	vi	di̲t
			'sjutton också'	*put*	*we*	*there*
			[we put 'sjutton också' there]			
	10	N1	jå+å?			
			yes			

Figure 9.3 Playing bingo (extract kindly supplied by Camilla Lindholm)

N1 is a carer, and E1 an elderly patient with language impairments. They are playing bingo. In line 1, N1 calls out the number 17, and the players are supposed to cover the number on their game sheet, if they have it. E1 responds with *de e som sjutton också*, which contains the same form as the word for 'seventeen' but is a blend of two formulaic expressions, *det är som sjutton* ('Good Lord!') and *sjutton också* ('oh darn!'). Lindholm had previously observed other bingo games, and E1 had repeatedly responded with *det är som sjutton (också)* to any number ending in *–(t)ton* ('–teen'). She observes, "This fixed expression is thus to some extent an automatic response triggered by certain numerals. E1 uses it to make jokes. The expression is often accompanied by laughter or uttered with a smile" (Camilla Lindholm, personal communication).

Applying the criteria reveals various indications of formulaicity. It is semantically non-transparent in relation to the context (Criterion B), associated with a particular situation—hearing a number between 13 and 19 in Bingo (Criterion C), and, in expressing humour, it performs a function other than what it directly expresses (Criterion D). He has been heard to say it repeatedly (Criterion E), and it is accompanied by a laugh or smile (Criterion F). It is not grammatically or lexically marked (Criterion G) and will not have been heard from others (Criterion H). However, it is clearly a derivation of two other strings that could be independently judged formulaic (Criterion I). We cannot judge against Criterion J since the string is not one that occurs in the language more widely. As for Criterion K, a full analysis of his linguistic abilities might indeed reveal that aspects of the form of this expression exceed his novel production ability, but that information is not available here.

In line 9 there is further evidence of formulaicity in relation to the word string *sjutton också*. He apparently means to say "we place 'seventeen' there", as he puts his counter on the number. Lindholm comments, "this use of the phrase *sjutton också* (instead of using only the numeral *sjutton*) is ungrammatical". Not only does it evoke agreement on Criteria A and B and, by virtue of his repeated use of it, also Criterion E, but it also clearly adheres to Criterion J, being formulaic in its own right but inappropriately applied here.

These two brief analyses give a flavour of how the criteria can be used to assist the researcher in evaluating the reasons, if any, for believing a word string to be formulaic for that speaker.

Conclusion

As stated earlier, the diagnostic procedure offered here should not be interpreted as an alternative to the various identificational procedures reviewed in Chapter 8: when researching formulaic language, the investigator needs to consider all available approaches in order to maximize the credibility of the analysis. In particular, it must be reiterated that the diagnostics aim to provide the researcher with insights into decisions already made intuitively, not to replace those intuitions. Applying the criteria can be compared to explaining why one considers a particular painting to be a masterpiece. The judgement comes first, and is a personal one. Different people may come to different conclusions. No opinion is wrong, but any opinion can probably be justified on the basis of criteria. For both a painting and a word string, the purpose of criterion-based exploration is not to influence the judgement so much as to shed light on why that judgement has been made. Individuals may well discover, through this process, that they are particularly biased towards viewing one of the criteria as determinant, while others are hardly noticed. The criteria, then, act in the interests of raising researchers' awareness about just what formulaicity can entail, and what they may otherwise unwittingly tend to assume it to entail.

Notes

1 A version of the criteria that follow, including the commentary text, was first published in Wray and Namba (2003). The author is grateful to Kazuhiko Namba and the journal editor, Mary Goebel Noguchi, for permission to reuse material from that paper. In Wray and Namba (2003), the criteria were presented as a means of identifying *formulaic sequences*, but

technically they are a means of establishing whether a formulaic sequence, i.e. a word string that *appears* to be an MEU, actually is an MEU. See Chapter 8, and note 1, Chapter 1, for further explanation of the difference.

2 Of course, the generative capacity of the grammar is viewed differently in different theories. Consequently, a judgement on this criterion reflects the researcher's explicit or implicit beliefs about the relative contribution of grammar and lexicon in cases that contain grammatical oddities such as those illustrated below.

3 Namba (2008), testing these criteria on code-switching data, suggests that 'genre' should be added to the rubric for this criterion.

4 It does not much matter if the 'incorrect' designation is chosen, since these diagnostics only aim to reveal the researcher's intuitions, not the 'truth'. The fact that, in some circumstances, it may be possible to assign '(strongly) agree' on both E and H for the same expression, serves as a reminder that expressions should not be 'scored' for how many '(strongly) agree' judgements they get.

5 Oxford English Dictionary, *parleyvoo* (v). 1881, *Saturday Review*, from French *parlez-vous (Français/Anglais)?* 'do you speak (French/English)?'. Compare also the distress call anglicized as *Mayday* from French *(venez) m'aider* '(come and) help me'.

6 This would come about if the learner constructed the word string when less proficient and then memorized it, or picked it up from another learner.

7 'L: By my judgement, there is an underlying frame and one or more gaps in this word string.' The frame is formulaic and the gaps can be filled with any lexical items. Although the entire set of criteria A to K can, in fact, be used to cover both complete and incomplete MEUs, there is, within the context of Namba's analysis, value in adding this criterion. Its addition illustrates the importance of researchers modifying the criteria to match their needs.

8 The reason for not including *datta* is justified in Namba's accompanying analysis.

PART THREE
Studies at the boundaries

TESSA: a case study in machine translation

Overview

Machine translation demands a pragmatic approach to language processing, and offers opportunities for experimenting with the sorts of units that really contribute to making language look the way it does (see Chapter 19). There is an inherent tension in the design of programs for language-related purposes, between keeping the processing demands down, and retaining flexibility. Although it is theoretically possible to equip a machine translation system with a complete lexicon of all the words in the language, and a complete set of grammatical rules for combining them, it has yet to be done. More importantly, it is, arguably, not really necessary. There is a continuum from the full flexibility that would allow any idea to be expressed, to the complete rigidity of a simple look-up system in which nothing new is computed at all. Between these two there is scope for programs to be designed to maximize efficiency, by only featuring the amount of flexibility that is actually needed. The TESSA system was restricted to one domain, the UK Post Office counter service, making it possible to predetermine the topics and the scope of the messages. In addition, because the discourse of customer-employee transactions is somewhat formulaic, it was reasonable to operate within the bounds of certain structures. A fuller account of TESSA and formulaic language theory can be found in Wray, Cox, Lincoln, and Tryggvason (2004).[1]

The design of the TESSA system

TESSA was an interactive translation system designed for the UK Post Office with the long-term aim of offering multilingual two-directional translation for basic counter transactions. Its instantiation at this early stage,[2] however, was much more limited: one-way translation from spoken English into British Sign Language (BSL), the signs being generated on a video screen using a specially-developed avatar (virtual human) (Cox, Lincoln *et al.* 2002; Cox,

Marshall, and Sáfár 2002; Cox *et al.* 2003). TESSA relied on the assumption that there is a limited range of things that the post office counter clerk needs to say to the customer. 'Need' and 'want' are not the same thing here—human beings, given their full rein of creativity and their desire for social interaction, may *want* to say all sorts of things that TESSA did not accommodate.

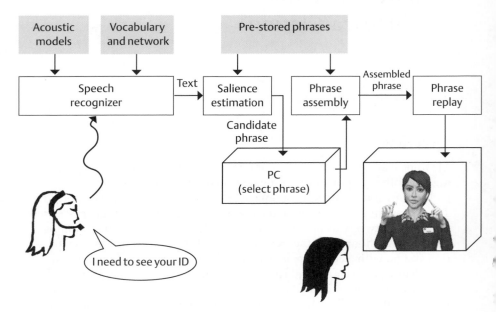

Figure 10.1 The Post Office translation system

Figure 10.1 demonstrates the operation of the system. When the trials of TESSA began, there was advance publicity that the system was being installed in certain post offices, so deaf users would enter expecting to be able to use it. Using speech or gestures, the customer would indicate to a clerk that they wished to use the system. The clerk's activation of the system set in train a series of stages:

1 The clerk spoke into her headset microphone.
2 The automatic speech recognizer selected possible messages from an extensive set of pre-entered targets, and displayed those with the highest probability on a screen.
3 The clerk confirmed the message intended.
4 The whole message, or the message components, were translated into a set of sign generation instructions.
5 The signed translation was generated and displayed on a video screen.

TESSA thus amalgamated three major components, each a computing challenge in its own right: speech recognition, translation, and sign generation.

We are concerned here only with the matching of the recognized speech to the lexicon to facilitate the translation component. For details of the other components, see Cox, Lincoln *et al.* (2002), Cox, Marshall *et al.* (2002), and Cox *et al.* (2003).

The speech recognizer, having performed acoustic matching to the clerk's utterance, would identify the most probable item from amongst those stored in its lexicon. The lexicon was derived from recordings of transactions done in real post offices, and from simulation experiments. The lexicon contained some single words but also a great many word strings (for example, 'your National Insurance number'; 'it to get there tomorrow'). There was no assumption that the counter clerk would formulate a transactional statement in exactly the same way each time. Simulation experiments had generated a number of different expressions of any given sample message (Table 10.1), and TESSA was designed to spot acoustic similarities between pre-entered samples and actual input, in order to make the correct match.

TESSA sample	Paraphrase 1	Paraphrase 2	Paraphrase 3	Paraphrase 4	Paraphrase 5
Where is it going to?	Where are you sending this?	Where will it go to?	Where is the letter going?	Where is the destination?	Where is the item going?
Can you complete another deposit slip please?	You must fill in another deposit slip.	Could you please complete another deposit slip?	Could you complete another deposit slip please?	Could you fill in this deposit slip?	Can you fill another slip in?
Goodbye.	See you later.	Cheerio.	Goodbye.	Thank you, bye bye.	Bye.
Is there anything else?	Do you require anything else?	Is that it?	Can I help you with anything else?	Can I help you with anything else?	Will that be all?
A charge is made for this service.	There is a charge for this service.	You'll be charged for the service.	You will be charged for this service.	You will be charged for this service.	You will have to pay for this service.

Table 10.1 Alternative expressions of phrases used in TESSA, produced in simulation trials

TESSA operated on the principle of semantically-based translation, in which the primary focus is the meaning of the whole message (compare Waibel 1996; Silberman 2000; Matsui *et al.* 2001). As Waibel (1996) observes: "A successful speech translation system ... cannot rely on perfect recognition or perfect syntax. Rather, it must search for a semantically plausible interpretation of the speaker's intent while judiciously ignoring linguistically unimportant words or fragments" (p. 42). Where a full parser would trip up in the attempt even to ascertain which words or fragments were 'linguistically unimportant', semantically brokered message processing takes no account of the form other than as a mechanism for accessing meaning.

There are many different ways of expressing any given message, but the probability approach, applied to the utterance as a whole, is an effective way of gathering them together as versions of the same basic proposition. Most importantly, because the interpretation was based on making the best match, unanticipated variants and speech errors could be accommodated, provided sufficient salient content was identifiable. Of course, because no direct account was being taken of word order, morphology, or other grammatical signals, errors of interpretation could occur. However, they were at least similar to those that would occur in natural human translation if, say, the environment were too noisy for everything to be heard.

The TESSA system contained a corpus of about 500 target phrases, with its own allocated assembly and replay instructions for creating a translation in BSL. Designed to bypass complexity at semantic/structural level, TESSA did not process individual morphemes or words and used only a simple grammar with two basic operations: concatenation (Figure 10.2), and single level insertion. The insertion operation was to accommodate variation in numerical and monetary amounts: the appropriate numbers, as identified in the input, were slotted into a fixed frame, for example, 'That's [@L NTMS] please'.

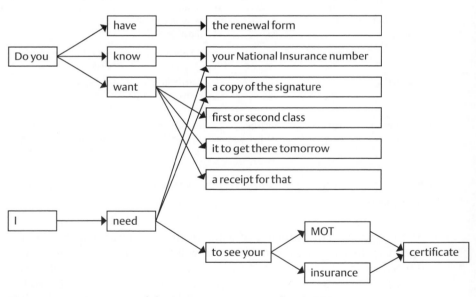

Figure 10.2 A section of the recognition network in TESSA

Thus, TESSA was essentially a somewhat flexible data look-up system, constrained to treat all input as an attempt at one of its target phrases. Whatever the actual form of the input message, once recognized as a version of the target message, it would be mapped on to that target and realized as the same form in BSL. That is, all five example paraphrases of a phrase in Table 10.1 would be translated identically, with no recognition of any subtle differences in emphasis, pragmatics, or idiolect that might account for the speaker's choice of one formulation over another.

Output was based on a database of sign components that had been 'motion-captured' using human models wearing sensors. The movements, stored as representations of a phrase or word, were retrieved and assembled in real time to create the required translation.

TESSA and morpheme equivalent units

The database-matching procedure used in TESSA resembles in some important ways the multiword lexical representation in the Wray (2002b) model. In both cases, the advantage of matching large, internally complex items rather than their components is that it reduces the number of operations needed to proceed from input to, in the case of TESSA, translated output, or, in the case of the human hearer, comprehension. The benefits of this are twofold: less likelihood of error, since there are fewer procedures to go wrong; and faster processing, since there is less to look up and there are fewer rules to apply. On the other hand, there is only limited scope for accommodating flexibility, considerably restricting the capability of the system to handle novel input or subtle expression in output.

However, there is *some* flexibility. In both Wray's model and TESSA there are holistically-managed frames with gaps in, able to take variable material. In this way, even a quite small inventory of fixed strings can be turned into a sizeable set of possible interpretations and outcomes. This halfway house between fixedness and full compositionality renders high dividends in both domains. Many partly-fixed frames admit a very wide range of possible completions—in human language there are constructions like 'no sooner x than y' and 'I have known x for n years'—while even in the narrow world of TESSA the frame 'that's [@L NTMS\ please' has as many completions as there are purchase costs to be paid in the post office. In neither case would it be parsimonious to store every possible version of the completion independently, yet not to store any of the material holistically would be to impose on the system a much greater real-time processing burden than was necessary.

A further aspect of flexibility is seen in TESSA's probability matching, which, while not accommodating any interpretation and expression of the variation, does at least tolerate it, by disregarding non-salient differences between actual input and target phrases. Does this, too, have an equivalent in human language processing? Research into the variation found in ostensibly 'fixed' strings (for example, Tucker 1996) does suggest that word strings may be identified in input on the basis of probability in relation to the occurrence of their most salient components, just as in TESSA. In other words, the individual learns from experience where to expect variation and, through a highly conservative approach to extrapolation, develops a sense of the range that that variation can take. A conservative approach ensures that observation remains the main arbiter of what is permissible. In this way, we can account for why, to use Tucker's (1996) example, the slot in 'I haven't the + RT ODQK@, SHUD idea' is not, in fact, equally likely to attract all superlatives, even if the meaning is appropriate and easy to understand. While 'faintest', 'slightest', and 'foggiest' slip easily into the gap, 'smallest', 'tiniest', and 'vaguest' seem a little less comfortable, and 'weakest', 'roughest', and 'feeblest' seem highly unlikely.[3]

In line with this conservative approach, it may be noted that the possible configurations depicted for TESSA in Figure 10.2 are restricted, relative to what might be deemed possible in a fully generative system. Although 'I need' can link with both 'a copy of your signature' and 'your National Insurance number', the paradigm in that context does not generalize, so that 'Do you know' links only with the second, not the first. Even strings that would make full sense to us, such as 'Do you have a receipt for that' are outlawed, because that message is not one that is needed within the confines of the user context as defined.[4]

The key difference between the Wray (2002b) model and the design of TESSA is that the former includes a mechanism for overriding the holistic processing of multiword strings, by opening them up for further analysis. In humans, *only* storing multiword MEUs would be too restrictive—consider the problem of trying to survive in a foreign country with only the exact entries in a phrasebook (and compare, also, the opportunity for novel real-time construction available in TALK, Chapter 11). TESSA's holistic look-up system is, indeed, too restrictive to deal adequately with the many additional messages that might need to be expressed, from time to time, in post office transactions. However, there might be ways to make up the 'shortfall' in a TESSA-like design, using a more flexible processing system (see Chapter 19).

Notes

1 Some material in this chapter has been adapted from that paper, with the permission of the co-authors.
2 The tiny estimated size of the user population (about 0.1 per cent of Post Office customers) and the then restructuring of the UK Post Office led the Post Office to discontinue research funding for TESSA in 2003. However, the EU has funded research on an enhanced technology (VANESSA) for deaf users since 2004 (Glauert, Elliott, Cox, Tryggvason, and Sheard 2006).
3 That is not to say, of course, that fine-tuned semantics do not play a role in the relative acceptability of collocations—these 'alternatives' are far from being perfect synonyms.
4 Of course, should such a string become necessary, it could be added easily. The point is that combinations are added if needed, rather than all of the possible configurations being available by default.

I I

TALK: a formulaic approach
to supporting communication
in the speech-disabled

Overview

TALK is a software program developed to facilitate conversational fluency in non-speaking individuals, such as people with cerebral palsy. Sylvia, the user studied here, anticipates what she will want to say in a future conversation and types her conversational turns into the TALK database. They can then be accessed during the conversation by clicking on one or more icons, and the utterances are spoken by a voice synthesizer. Although stored material can be edited at the time of use, and novel utterances can be created during the conversation, both activities are slow for the user, and tend to be avoided when possible, in favour of the very fluent alternative of prefabricated turns, even if, from time to time, they do not fully reflect what the speaker wanted to say. TALK can be seen as a natural experiment for investigating the full potential of formulaic sequences to contribute to natural communicational exchange. A more detailed version of this chapter can be found in Wray (2002c).

Introduction

Augmentative communication (AC) systems make 'speech' possible for individuals who have physical difficulties in vocal articulation. Typically, text is entered into a computer and spoken by a voice synthesizer. However, if users enter the material at the time of use, the conversation will often be a very slow and stilted exchange, since the typical user—someone with cerebral palsy, motor neurone disease, or brain damage after a stroke—lacks precise motor control when using a keyboard, mouse, or pointer. Where normal speech rates can be 120 words per minute or more, real-time production AC of this kind characteristically runs at between two and 15 words per minute (Todman, Rankin, and File 1999b: 325). Although ideas can be exchanged, at this speed conversation lacks the spontaneity and freedom characteristic of normal interaction, and can fail to deliver a sense of enjoyment or satisfaction

(Todman and Lewins 1996: 285). To speed up the input, word recognition and predictive selection programs can be used. These anticipate likely completions for words and phrases that have been started, and can be sensitive to the user's personal lexicon and style. However, they only chip at the edges of the problems inherent in producing original text in real time.

Example perspective combinations	Example utterances
You-Why-Future	"Why shouldn't you?" "Why will you do that?"
Me-How-Present	"Just now I use a number of different ways to communicate." "I've been helping John with the TALK system for about four years now."
Me-What-Present	"I generally keep myself busy most of the time." "Eastenders is too depressing for me to watch." "I like all kinds of pizza, but I think my favourite is Hawaiian."

Table 11.1 Example utterances stored and accessed by perspective combination

TALK, developed at Dundee University during the 1990s (for example, Todman, Alm, and Elder 1994; Todman, Elder, Alm, and File 1994; Todman and Lewins 1996; Todman, File, and Grant 1997; Todman *et al.* 1999b; Todman, Rankin, and File 1999a), offers a different approach to the problem of fluency: most of the input is composed in advance. Using TALK, production rates can reach an average of 60 words per minute (Todman *et al.* 1999b: 325), with greater speeds clearly possible.

Example topics	Example utterances
Greet	"Hello, how are you?" "Hi there, it's a long time since I last saw you." "What's your name?" "Hello, I'm Sylvia."
Finish	"Thank you for taking the time to talk to me, I enjoyed our chat very much." "Bye-bye for now. Hope to see you again some time." "Good night." "Cheerio. See you."
Stories	"I went to Vancouver two years ago." "It was for a conference for people who use and work with speech aids." "And John and I did a presentation at the conference." "It went really well."

Table 11.2 Example utterances stored and accessed by topic/function

At first glance, conversations using prefabricated material appear quite unlikely to compare favourably with normal conversations. How could interaction drawing on pre-empted halves of a conversation ever be more than a very blunt tool for genuine information exchange or social engagement? Yet in fact, TALK is very successful as a conversation tool (Todman *et al.* 1999a).

TALK utterances are stored and accessed according to three semantic principles (Tables 11.1–11.3). The first operates on the intersection of three dimensions of perspective: person (me or you); orientation (where, what, how, when, who, or why); and time (past, present; or future) (Todman *et al.* 1999b: 324). Examples are given in Table 11.1 (on p. 138).

Example functions	Example utterances
dunno	"I'm afraid I don't know." "I haven't got a clue."
sorry	"Sorry, go ahead. I interrupted you." "Sorry, I didn't quite catch that." "Sorry but I'm having a bit of trouble here."
hedge	"That's a good question." "Well, I suppose you could say that." "I'll have to think about that."
intrup	"Could I say something there." "Excuse me, may I interrupt there." "I'd like to butt in here."
oops	"I'm sorry about that, it was a mistake." "Sorry for repeating myself there, but my hand slipped." "Sorry, that wasn't what I meant to say there."
wait	"I haven't got an answer in the computer to that just now, so would you please wait until I type out an answer." "Please wait a second while I find the next thing I want to say." "I'll need to edit something here, so please hang on a sec."
agree	"Yes, I suppose so." "Yes, that's very true."
uhhuh	"Right." "Uh-huh." "Yeah yeah."

Table 11.3 Example utterances stored and accessed by interactional function

The second accessing principle is topic/function-based. There is, for instance, a set of options for greeting, another for finishing a conversation, and a large set containing stories (for example, Table 11.2). The story screens often contain extended texts, but Sylvia, the user studied here, tends to split a story across a series of entries, so that there is flexibility about how much is said and when. Some of the effects of this, both deliberate and unintended, are considered later.

The third type of storage and access principle relates to commonly used word strings, such as short interjections. The categories include a set of expressions for 'don't know' ('dunno'), apologizing ('sorry'), hedging ('hedge'), interrupting ('intrup'), requesting time to reply ('wait'), indicating that an incorrect selection has been made ('oops'), agreeing ('agree'), and giving minimal responses ('uhhuh') (Table 11.3).

As the examples for 'wait' in Table 11.3 indicate, the TALK-user also has the option of composing a completely new utterance in real time, or of editing a stored one. Both of these require the entry of individual words, letter by letter and, as noted earlier, this is not only time consuming but liable to error. The user may mistype words, so that they are incomprehensible when synthesized, or inadvertently erase a prepared string instead of forwarding it to the synthesizer. The stakes are high, since the purpose of using TALK is to enable conversation, and if the pauses between utterances are too long the momentum of the exchange is lost.

TALK in action: some observations

Pre-storing material in TALK helps a user like Sylvia conduct fluent conversation by enabling her to produce a turn without much real-time processing. However, she is restricted to only those forms that she has anticipated. Where she does not have appropriate stored material she has several choices: construct her desired turn in real time; access the pre-stored item that is closest and edit it in real time; select a pre-stored item that is not quite what she wanted to say; or avoid replying, by using a pre-stored item stating that she can't answer, or by changing the topic. Adeptness with TALK resides, in part, in working out what to store, so that these choices need to be made as rarely as possible, but it also entails knowing which choices, when they must be made, are likely to achieve the best result.

The 'best result' is not by any means always the communication of the most accurate information. Maintaining the fluency needed for the exchange to continue to be a *conversation* is a high priority, since fluency is the key feature of conversation that cannot be achieved without TALK. Sylvia protects fluency by planning progressions of utterances. A topic might be initiated with a question, and while it is being answered, she is clicking the icons necessary to get her to her own next turn.

Todman *et al.* (1999a, b) report that TALK-users prefer to keep the conversation going with a filler and/or to instigate a topic shift, rather than stop to generate a more accurate response letter by letter. TALK conversations suggest that the user will even compromise on truth and/or grammatical accuracy (relative to the form of the previous utterance) in order to take the turn and sustain fluency. The subjugation of accuracy to fluency is reminiscent of

Tannen's (1984) observation that the drive for rapport and fluency in normal conversation can lead to irrelevance (p. 95) and inaccuracy (p. 76). Even when truth is maintained, a pragmatic leap may be necessary to bridge the gap between the stored form and the message it was intended to convey.

As part of e-correspondence for a project on which she acted as a consultant (reported in Fitzpatrick and Wray 2006; Wray and Fitzpatrick 2008), Sylvia observed:

> If I told you that I went shopping yesterday, you might ask me 'where abouts did you go?' and if I was tired and I didn't feel like going on line to type, I would use one of my stored utterances to say 'I like shopping in Dundee'. And hopefully you would understand me, I went shopping in Dundee.

Maximizing use of the pre-stored material means developing an understanding not only of how conversations operate, so that the predictions about what is likely to be needed are accurate, but also of how language works, so that the formulations stored make a good fit to the context in which they are later used. In Table 11.2, one of the story items is 'And John and I did a presentation at the conference'. In the context of the story, the word 'and' contributes to textual coherence. But it compromises the range of use for the string as an independent item. Similarly, storing 'Did you have a nice weekend, Sian?' precludes using it with any addressee not named Sian. Sylvia became increasingly adept at avoiding this pitfall. She noted:

> your utterances don't need to be too precise. For example: 'I like going there' would do instead of 'I like going to Dundee University'. You can use your utterances for different topics then ... Don't begin an utterance with a conjunctive word like 'and', 'because' or 'but'. I find I can get away without using conjunctive words at the beginning of phrases when I want to join several utterances together. That way I can use the utterances as a single utterance too.

Conclusion

Superficially it is clear that utterances pre-stored in TALK mirror MEUs. The ease with which TALK-users and their speaking partners adapt to the TALK system, and the capacity of TALK to facilitate prolonged exchanges with the fundamental characteristics of conversation, suggest that quite a lot can be done using the highly constrained communicative scope of formulaic language.

In contrast to the TESSA system (Chapter 10), TALK offers the user the opportunity to break away from the holistic, pre-formulated material in order to express more accurately an unanticipated message. Yet the cost of doing so is much higher than in normal conversation. The TALK user is faced with a conflict between the ease of using a restricted range of holistically-stored items, and the need, at times, to say something that is not stored, and which must, therefore, be constructed slowly in real time. The production constraints are such that success in communication can, in effect, be measured in seconds of speech, while failure is measured in seconds of silence. As a result, it becomes interesting to ask just how much pressure effective communication can absorb in the interests of fluency, before it becomes necessary to abandon the formulaic material (see Chapter 20).

12

Formulaic language learning: the beginner

Overview

Beginner learners of a foreign language often target some phrases for memorization, to give the process a kick-start and facilitate basic interaction. But it is rather extreme to rely entirely on memorized material. In the television programme *Welsh in a Week*, however, memorization was the only practical way for participants to meet their end-of-week 'challenge'. On the Monday, participants would be given the challenge of achieving a particular interaction in Welsh by the Friday. The tutorials mostly provided complete phrases and sentences for memorization, though there was some explanation of their form. Of course, there was no expectation of achieving deep or broad knowledge over such a short period, and the programme aimed only to indicate that learning Welsh is fun and worthwhile. Margaret, the participant in this case study, was challenged to present a cookery demonstration to Welsh speakers. The analysis revealed that even though Margaret had correctly memorized the material, under the pressures of performance she introduced a range of typical learner errors, despite being highly motivated to reproduce the targets intact. Her alterations, as also her hesitations, occurred significantly more often at the boundaries between memorized units than within them, and were particularly prevalent at points where her input had provided her with a choice of forms. The study is reported in full in Wray (2004).[1]

Introduction

Investigating the role of formulaicity in language learning is normally difficult. How can you tell what is formulaic in someone's output? If you introduce formulaic sequences, can you be certain they weren't known before? If interlanguage errors occur in what are fixed forms for native speakers (for example, Yorio 1989), how do you distinguish inaccurate learning from an unsuccessful attempt to modify the expression for its context? In this study, there was some opportunity to control for these factors. The entire learning procedure was focused on memorization, and every step of the process was recorded and analysed. The learner was a beginner and so brought very little coherent previous knowledge of the language with her. And the performance situation excluded one of the two major motivations for real time editing—unanticipated input from interlocutors, while retaining the other—high-level anxiety.

The study

The learning context was *Welsh in a Week*, a BAFTA winning television programme broadcast by the Welsh language channel S4C. The data were collected on location with the S4C television crew in 2002. Focused on promoting the use of Welsh in bilingual workplaces, the series used as its participants individuals whose work could be enhanced by the use of Welsh, but who had little or no knowledge of it. Each *Welsh in a Week* programme followed the progress of one learner mastering, in the space of four days (a rather short 'week'), sufficient Welsh to achieve a 'challenge' task.

In preparation for the challenge, the tutor/presenter would give three tutorials in which she introduced the language necessary for achieving the task. The learner had a great deal to learn and practise, before being plunged into the real life situation, all captured on film. The views and feelings of learners were chronicled in interviews, supplemented by video diaries. The learning relied heavily on formulaic material. That is, the phrases and sentences introduced to the learner were presented as holistic units, with no, or only partial, indication of their construction. The material was also very specific. For example, a learner challenged to run a bingo session in a Welsh-medium residential home for the elderly was taught *Oes gynnoch chi gerdyn?* 'Have you got a card?', *Dach chi wedi ennill?* 'Have you won?', and *Gêm arall?* 'Another game?'. A doctor challenged to administer an anaesthetic was provided with *Dach chi wedi bod yn yr ysbyty o'r blaen?* 'Have you been in hospital before?', *Oes gynnoch chi ddannedd gosod?* 'Have you got false teeth?', and *Dw i'n mynd i roi mwgwd ar eich wyneb* 'I'm going to put a mask on your face'.

Margaret, the learner in the study we follow below was challenged to demonstrate to a local Welsh-speaking ladies' group how to prepare two recipes, pork and mushroom casserole and lemon pudding. The demonstration required an uninterrupted scripted monologue, so that Margaret's best strategy was simply to memorize and repeat the linguistic material provided for her. Each of the three tutorials was filmed three times—itself an opportunity for learning—and Margaret was able to take away the materials used, plus supplementary matter, presented on flashcards. It was her responsibility to memorize the material by the next day, fitting her learning around the filming schedule.

The tutor suggested messages that Margaret might need for her challenge, and gave her the appropriate Welsh phrase or sentence, using flashcards. Most flashcards carried multiword strings, ranging in length from two to eleven words, with more than half the input material appeared in strings of four words or more. Long sentences were split into smaller chunks on separate flashcards, showing how they could be built up. These chunks were themselves formulaic—that is, internally complex but presented whole.

Margaret presented her cookery demonstration twice to her live audience. The language she used was not identical across the two events, nor entirely identical to that which she had prepared. Her delivery was fluent (allowing for the natural gaps entailed in cooking something in real time) and evidently entirely comprehensible to the audience, who listened attentively, laughed at her jokes, and even made notes.

Five months after filming (two weeks before the broadcast), Margaret recorded onto audiocassette as much of the material as she could now recall without rehearsal. She also provided a written commentary on her experience and recall. Nine months after filming (four months after the first broadcast of the programme), she was visited by the author who recorded her recalling the material once more, as well as interviewing her.

The data

Material introduced in the tutorials but not used in the challenge is excluded here—we deal only with the various manifestations of the sentences that constituted the 'script' of the cookery demonstration. The script was made up of 63 'items', of which examples are given in Table 12.1. Using the script as a reference point, it was possible to compare the exact forms in which any given item appeared, from its first introduction in a tutorial to the final audio recall nine months after filming.

A typical item would be attempted twice in one tutorial (providing six renderings over the three takes), once in each take of the challenge, and once in each of the two recalls: ten attempts in all. The lowest number of attempts at an item was three, the greatest, 46. High numbers of attempts normally reflected many repetitions in a tutorial, because of difficulty in remembering the sequence, or in pronouncing one or more of the words. Some renderings were simple repetitions of what the tutor said. Others were the result of translation or free recall.

The data were interrogated to establish the extent to which Margaret was able successfully to reproduce the material that she had memorized. The performances will be referred to as Ch1 and Ch2 (for challenge) and the five- and nine-month audio recalls as R+5 and R+9 respectively.

Script	Translation
1 Prynhawn da.	1 Good afternoon.
2 Margaret Owen dw i.	2 I'm Margaret Owen.
3 Mae'n braf eich gweld chi i gyd.	3 It's nice to see you all.
4 Prynhawn 'ma dw i'n mynd i ddangos i chi sut i wneud caserol porc a madarch a pwdin lemon.	4 This afternoon I'm going to show you how to make pork and mushroom casserole and lemon pudding.
5 Yn gyntaf,	5 First,
6 rysait y caserol.	6 the casserole recipe.
7 Bydd angen y cynhwysion yma:	7 You will need these ingredients:
8 Pwys a hanner o borc,	8 A pound and a half of pork,
9 chwe owns neu hanner pwys o fadarch,	9 six ounces or half a pound of mushrooms,
10 dwy owns o fenyn,	10 two ounces of butter,
11 dwy lond llwy fwrdd o flawd,	11 two tablespoonfuls of flour,
...	...
18 Rhowch y menyn yn y badell ffrio.	18 Put the butter in the frying pan.
19 Torrwch y cig yn ddarnau bach.	19 Cut the meat into small pieces.
20 Rhowch y cig a dwy lond llwy fwrdd o flawd mewn cwdyn plastig.	20 Put the meat and two table-spoonfuls of flour into a plastic bag.
21 Siglwch fel hyn.	21 Shake it like this.
22 Rhowch y porc yn y badell ffrio fel hyn.	22 Put the pork into the frying pan like this.
23 Coginiwch y ddwy ochr yn gyflym.	23 Cook quickly on both sides.
...	...
35 Mae'n well 'da fi cig wedi coginio yn dda,	35 I prefer meat well done,
36 felly dw i'n rhoi y caserol mewn ffwrn:	36 so I put the casserole in an oven:
37 ffwrn nwy pedwar,	37 gas mark four,
38 trydan: cant wyth deg.	38 electric: one hundred and eighty.
39 Rhowch yn y caserol.	39 Put it in the casserole [dish].
40 Cogniwch yn araf am dri chwarter awr.	40 Cook it slowly for three quarters of an hour.
41. A dyma un dw i wedi'i baratoi yn gynharach.	41. And here's one I prepared earlier.
...	...
60. Diolch yn fawr iawn am ddod.	60. Thank you very much for coming.
61. Mwynhewch y rysaitau.	61. Enjoy the recipes.
62. Pwy sy eisiau blasu?	62. Who would like to taste?
63. Dewch yma.	63. Come here.

Table 12.1 Example items from the 'Welsh in a Week' script

Analysis

To what extent were memorized strings successfully recalled?

Table 12.2 summarizes the successful delivery of the script items in Ch1, Ch2, R+5, and R+9. Scoring for this calculation was draconian: one mark for an entirely correct recollection, and zero for one or more errors. Errors could be as minor as the loss of an unstressed phoneme or as major as a complete breakdown of the form. However, the entire omission of the item was not counted as an error, and the percentages are based only on those items attempted. Partial omissions are counted as errors.

Ch1	Ch2	R+5	R+9
50/63 (79%)	37/59 (63%)	17/48 (35%)	19/49 (39%)

Table 12.2 Items delivered entirely correctly (of those attempted)

The differences are highly significant (χ^2 = 29.24, df 3, $p < 0.001$). Since R+5 and R+9 were such a long time after the challenge, the low scores are not surprising. However, the significant increase in the number of errors from Ch1 to Ch2 (χ^2 = 4.12, df 1, $p < 0.05$) is less easy to explain, since the two events took place within a few minutes of each other. Watching the film of the two performances, it was evident that, although nervous in both, her first presentation was much more up-beat, and she had a rather better rapport with the audience. Whether because of tiredness, or relief at having the first performance 'in the can', she seemed less engaged second time round, and this may explain her reduced success in recalling the memorized material accurately.

The difference in errors between the less successful challenge (Ch2) and the more successful recall (R+9) is also significant (χ^2 = 6.15, df 1, $p < 0.05$). However, the difference between R+5 and R+9 is not significant (χ^2 = 0.1159, df 1), even though one might have predicted that the accuracy of recall would reduce over the four intervening months. The similarity between them could indicate that the loss of accuracy had already reached a plateau by R+5, with the best-learnt formulas firmly ensconced in memory and the rest already forgotten.

However, another explanation is also possible. The television programme was broadcast soon after R+5. If there was an underlying reduction in accuracy over time, it could have been counterbalanced by the effects of repeatedly watching the video of the programme, as Margaret inevitably did with friends and family. This hypothesis was tested by comparing her performance on the casserole and pudding recipes, since, for reasons of time, the latter was never broadcast. In other words, if Margaret's recall at R+9 was enhanced by her having watched the video several times, this should have improved her recall of the casserole recipe but not the pudding recipe. Table 12.3 summarizes the separate totals for the parts of the script that were broadcast (greeting, casserole recipe, closing) and that were not (lemon pudding).

	Ch1	Ch2	R+5	R+9
Broadcast	35	26	11	12
Not broadcast	15	11	6	7

Table 12.3 Strings delivered entirely correctly in broadcast and unbroadcast parts of the script

While Margaret's recall of the broadcast material was slightly greater at R+9 than at R+5, the same was true for the unbroadcast material. There was no significant change in the accuracy of the broadcast and unbroadcast material between the pre-broadcast recall (R+5) and the post-broadcast recall (R+9) ($\chi^2 = 0.033$, df 1). Thus, it seems that watching the video was not responsible for the retention of accuracy between R+5 and R+9, and that the attrition in her accuracy had indeed reached a plateau by R+5.

These stark figures only reflect the extent to which Margaret was able to reproduce what she had memorized without any error at all, and they hide a considerable amount of information, since no differentiation has been made between error types. Qualitative analyses are therefore presented later. First, however, we explore the location of errors and pauses.

Where were errors and pauses located?

If a word string is processed as a morpheme equivalent unit (MEU), it ought to be relatively resistant to internal dysfluency and inaccuracy (Wray 2002b: 35–7, 219–22). Therefore, we can make the prediction that there would be far fewer pauses and errors *within* MEUs than *between* them. For this analysis, a word string was assumed to be an MEU if Margaret had been introduced to it as a single unit, and had not received any evidence about where or how it might break down. Under this designation, many of the 63 script items were treated as containing two or more MEUs. For instance, three internal boundaries were identified in item 20. One was after *Rhowch* 'put', since nine different instructions in the script began with this word, each with a different form immediately following it. The second and third boundaries enclosed the phrase *dwy lond llwy fwrdd o flawd* 'two tablespoonfuls of flour', since this also appeared separately in the script (item 11). Thus, this script item was viewed as consisting of four MEUs for Margaret: *rhowch; y cig a; dwy lond llwy fwrdd o flawd; mewn cwdyn plastig*. As *y cig a* 'the meat and' and *mewn cwdyn plastig* 'into a plastic bag' clearly indicate, this boundary allocation does not attempt a mapping onto grammatical constituents, and it has no status beyond the individual learner's experience. For these analyses, the data from the four attempts at the script, Ch1, Ch2, R+5, and R+9, were amalgamated; the tutorial data were not included.

Pauses in the delivery of each item on the up to four occasions when it could appear were marked in the transcript. The same procedure was carried out for errors, on a separate transcript. The number of pauses or errors occurring at boundaries between the word strings defined as formulaic was calculated, as was the number occurring at non-boundary locations. Non-boundary pauses/errors could appear either between words or within any word longer than one syllable. There were inevitably many more possible non-boundary places for a pause or error to occur, and so the frequencies of the boundary and non-boundary pauses/errors were calculated as percentages of the respective locations available (amalgamating the many possible locations within a single word to one 'within the word' location). For more detail of the scoring procedure, see Wray (2004: 261).

Using this procedure, it was calculated that there were a total of 245 pauses, distributed across 2,178 possible locations (292 boundary locations, 1,886 non-boundary locations). Pauses occurred at 106/292 (36.3 per cent) possible boundary locations, and at 139/1,886 (7.4 per cent) possible non-boundary locations. In short, fluency within formulaic sequences was considerably greater than fluency between them. This difference is highly significant ($\chi^2 = 211.98$, df 1, $p < 0.001$).

There were a total of 187 errors, distributed across the 2,178 possible locations. Errors occurred at 78/292 (26.7 per cent) possible boundary locations, and 109/1,886 (5.8 per cent) possible non-boundary locations. Thus, errors were considerably more likely to occur at boundaries between formulaic sequences than within the formulaic sequences. This difference, too, is highly significant ($\chi^2 = 39.797$, df 1, $p < 0.001$).

What errors were made?

Too much of a good thing

When a string of words becomes familiar, there is a danger that it will 'run away with you', so that you end up saying something different from what you intended. This seemed to happen for Margaret on a number of occasions. For instance, in Ch1, she began the item *mae'n well 'da fi cig wedi coginio yn dda* 'I prefer meat well done' with *ond* 'but', which is semantically inappropriate. A possible explanation is found in her extensive practice, in Tutorial 1, of the paired formulas *dw i'n hoffi* N_1 'I like N_1' and *ond mae'n well 'da fi* N_2 'but I prefer N_2'. In memorizing the latter, she may have learnt strongly to associate the generic 'prefer' formula with the initial word *ond*, and this interfered when she sought her 'prefer' formula during the challenge.[2] Another instance occurred in Ch2, when, aiming for *dwy lond llwy fwrdd* 'two tablespoonfuls', Margaret said *dwy lond llwy bren* 'two woodenspoonfuls'. Although 'two woodenspoonfuls' is not formulaic in itself, it contains the string *llwy bren* 'wooden spoon' which Margaret had said eight times in Tutorial 2.

Mutations

The key advantage of memorizing linguistic material is that you do not have to know *why* it has the form it has. You just need to remember it. You don't need to make any choices, only use what you have learnt. However, Margaret's mind appeared intent on interfering with this apparently simple business, by editing forms unnecessarily.

The front-mutation system of Welsh is renownedly troublesome for learners. There are three mutations, which apply word-initially, and affect partly overlapping subsets of consonants, changing them to another consonant that contrasts in voicing, nasalization, or aspiration. Even after the learner works out that mutated words need unmutating before they can be found in the dictionary, a major problem persists: the rules governing their occurrence are highly complex. Margaret knew that mutations existed in Welsh and that they were difficult. However, she did not know how they worked or when they applied.

The mutations occurring in the script can be categorized into three types on the basis of how they were introduced in the tutorials. Some were specifically taught. For instance, the tutor used flashcards to demonstrate the soft mutation of *gwneud* □ *wneud* 'make', *coginio* □ *goginio* 'cook', and *dangos* □ *ddangos*[3] 'show' after *dw i'n mynd i* 'I am going to'. The second group were not taught as such, but the existence of the mutated form was evident because the unmutated form had previously been introduced. For example, *menyn* 'butter' was introduced in Tutorial 2 as a separate item of vocabulary. In the script it occurred in both unmutated and mutated form (*fenyn*). The third set occurred *only* as mutations and no mention was made of the fact that they *were* mutated. They included *o flawd* (> *blawd*, 'of flour'), *ar ben* (> *pen*, 'on top of '), and *am bum munud* (> *pum(p)*, 'for five minutes').

	Correct	Incorrect
Specifically taught	56	0
Both forms in use	79	44
Introduced intact	80	1

Table 12.4 Accuracy in reproducing mutated forms (combined data)

Table 12.4 shows that the coexistence of both mutated and unmutated forms within the material was detrimental to accuracy. Furthermore, the inaccuracy increased over time (Table 12.5, where ticks and crosses represent 'correct' and 'incorrect'). The deterioration in accuracy in the 'both used' category was strongly characterized by the replacement of the correct mutated form by the incorrect base form. There were no spurious phonological alterations that might suggest the internalization of an incorrect rule.

	Tutorials		Practice		Ch 1		Ch 2		R + 5		R + 9	
	✓	✗	✓	✗	✓	✗	✓	✗	✓	✗	✓	✗
Specifically taught	31	0	17	0	2	0	2	0	2	0	2	0
Both forms in use	18	4	0	0	19	6	18	7	12	15	12	12
Introduced intact	29	1	4	0	16	0	13	0	8	0	10	0

Table 12.5 Accuracy in reproducing mutated forms (by data type)

These findings suggest that the best way to ensure accuracy with morphological forms beyond one's generative capacity is either repeatedly to practise the sequence in which they occur (as with the tutorial drilling of the specifically taught forms) or to be unaware of their presence. In the former case the learner is, in effect, creating a new formula through 'fusion' (Peters 1983: 82), with the mutation safely tucked inside and made familiar through repetition. In the latter, the formula originally accepted by the learner conceals the mutation. Accuracy is at risk where both the mutated and unmutated forms are in use, and therefore both 'sound right'.

Conclusion

After only very minimal tuition, a virtual beginner in Welsh was able competently to deliver a comprehensible cookery demonstration to native speakers. Furthermore, nine months after filming, she still knew a considerable amount of the material. If, as many have proposed (see Wray 2002b: 191ff for a review), an important function of memorized word strings is as a long term reference resource for the learner—language on tap, so to speak—then she had successfully acquired and maintained that resource, albeit not entirely accurately. Of course, the cookery script was *all* she knew, and so she was no better prepared than before for getting her car fixed by a Welsh-speaking mechanic. Yet, to the extent that our everyday lives do feature a small set of recurring social 'scripts', one can imagine that, armed with a couple of dozen, she might actually be able to pass herself off as linguistically competent quite a lot of the time.

Because Margaret's situation, exceptionally, presented an opportunity for maximum success through memorizing word strings and not altering them, it was possible to examine the extent to which an adult learner is actually able to keep analysis at bay. We have seen that, in the event, Margaret introduced many errors typical of an early stage learner of Welsh, suggesting that she did not have the capability to bypass linguistic analysis, even when it was in her interests to do so.

Notes

1 Material from the original article is reproduced with kind permission of John Benjamins Publishing Company, Amsterdam/Philadelphia. www. benjamins.com

2 Compare Sylvia's comment, in Chapter 11, that it is better not to begin a pre-stored word string with 'but'.

3 <dd> is pronounced in Welsh as /ð/.

13
Formulaic language learning: advanced

Overview

One of the fundamental difficulties with researching how people learn languages is separating out the many interacting variables that operate in realistic conditions of language use. The most scientifically robust way to observe language learning and performance would be to put people into an artificially manipulated situation in which the causes of their behaviour could be tracked and attributed. Yet their use of language would then also be artificial, and may not reflect what they would do in the real world. Typically uncontrolled factors in second language acquisition studies are how motivated each individual was, how relevant they found the material they were taught, and the extent to which they ever really learnt in the first place what they later failed to reproduce. This study aimed to find a middle ground between manipulating variables and enabling a naturalistic performance. It was achieved by having participants memorize a nativelike way of saying something they actually wanted to say, ensuring a high motivation to learn the input, and a direct mapping onto their needs and interests. By tracking their progress while memorizing the material, there was a record of what they had learnt, against which to compare what they were able to produce in the real conversation. The rationale for the design was the success of TALK (see Chapter 11). We wanted to know whether Sylvia's skills with TALK could be transferred to the L2 setting, so that non-native speakers of intermediate to advanced proficiency could make the transition from producing adequate, comprehensible non-native English to sounding nativelike. Full accounts of this work can be found in Fitzpatrick and Wray (2006) and Wray and Fitzpatrick (2008).[1]

Introduction

This project explored the extent to which intermediate to advanced learners can benefit from getting assistance in how to express themselves in a fully nativelike way. The research questions included: Were all participants equally able to memorize and recall nativelike material? What were the limitations on reproducing memorized material in a real conversation? What sorts of conversations were most receptive to the anticipation and effective reproduction of useful material? What sorts of changes tended to be made when memorized material was not perfectly reproduced? Can individual profiles of performance indicate linguistic strengths and weaknesses?

Design

Participants

	Proficiency	Aptitude	Motivation	Other
Ch	High receptive and productive ability	High achiever on all tests	Instrumental	Nervous about talking with natives, reluctant to guess words
Hi	High receptive and productive ability	Moderate aural memory skill, extremely high achiever on other tests	Instrumental	Believed memorizing phrases improves English
Jo	Very poor productive, moderate receptive ability	Moderate aural memory skill, extremely high achiever on other tests	Integrative	Believed memorizing phrases improves English
Lc	Moderate receptive and productive ability	Poor aural memory skill, high sound-symbol sensitivity, moderate achiever on other tests	Instrumental	Only participant to disagree with "I'd like to improve my English so that I can get to know British people better"
Lo	Very poor receptive, and poor productive ability	Poor sound recognition of unfamiliar words, very high sound-symbol sensitivity, moderate to good scores on other tests	Instrumental	Stressed importance of memorizing vocabulary
Sa	High productive, moderate receptive ability	Moderate to high scores on all tests	Instrumental	Did not consider it desirable to speak English like a native. Believed memorizing phrases improves English

Table 13.1 Learner summary profiles

The six participants (mean age 29 years) were female Masters students in health science or development studies at a UK university. Three were Japanese (Ch, Hi, and Sa) and three Chinese (Jo, Lc, and Lo). All participants completed a questionnaire about their language learning history, their daily use of English, their aspirations regarding English language use, and their beliefs about language learning. They took the Lognostics Language Learning Aptitude Test (LLAT) (Meara, Milton, and Lorenzo-Dus 2001), and also completed two vocabulary tests: the Eurocentres Vocabulary Size Test (EVST) of receptive knowledge (Meara and Jones 1988) and Lex30, a test of productive knowledge (Meara and Fitzpatrick 2000; Fitzpatrick and Meara 2004). Both of these tests have been shown to correlate significantly with other measures of proficiency. A summary of the profiles is given in Table 13.1. For full details of the outcomes of the tests, see Fitzpatrick and Wray (2006) and Wray and Fitzpatrick (2008).

Procedure

Each participant worked on a one-to-one basis with the researcher (a native speaker of British English) to identify a conversation or transaction that she anticipated having with a native speaker of English within the next few days. Conversations included: getting a camera film developed at a local store, inviting a classmate over for dinner, asking a lecturer for an extension on an essay, and asking the advice of a vet about how to get hamsters to mate.

Each preparation and performance package was self-contained and took place over seven to ten days. First of all, the participant made an attempt at what she would expect to say during the targeted encounter. This provided a measure of her existing capacity to produce an accurate, nativelike utterance, and ensured that she had ownership of the content. Based on the desired message as articulated by the participant, the researcher offered a colloquial nativelike paraphrase. Normally, around 10–12 such paraphrases were prepared for each planned conversation. They were digitally recorded onto audio CD for the participant to take away and memorize. No written version was provided, and participants were advised not to transcribe the material or make notes.

In their own time, the participants then practised the target utterances, by listening and repeating aloud. After a few days, the researcher and participant met, to check progress and accuracy in the memorization and to address any problems that had arisen. At this meeting, a 'practice performance' of the conversation took place, with the researcher taking the part of the anticipated native speaker interlocutor. Soon after this practice session, the real-life conversation took place. The participant's challenge was to achieve her interactional goals by using, as far as possible, the memorized target utterances. One or two days after the conversation, the researcher interviewed the participant, to get her assessment of its success. Finally, two to three months later, some conversations were revisited, by asking the participant, without warning, to recall as much as possible of the memorized material.

All stages, including the real conversation, were digitally audio-recorded. After the completion of their final cycle, each participant filled in a written questionnaire about the ease, usefulness, and perceived success of the learning experience.

Data

In total the six participants engaged in twenty-one conversation cycles, containing 227 model utterances (10.8 models, on average, per conversation, mean length of a model utterance 10.05 words). The material produced in recall included one or more attempts at a target (in practice and/or real performance, plus delayed recall in some cases). Targets that were never attempted were excluded from the analyses, since it was unclear whether they had been memorized at all, and, if they had, whether they had ever been deemed relevant for use. As a result, the main data consisted of a total of 2,416 memorized words, distributed as in Table 13.2.

	Ch	Hi	Jo	Lc	Lo	Sa
Total words in attempted models	158	731	360	360	151	656

Table 13.2 Profile of dataset

Lc 2:4

I	I'm not quite sure what the teacher expect us to do
MU	I'm not really sure what they want us to include
PP	I'm not sure what the teacher want us to include
RP	I'm not sure what they want us to include
DP	I wanted to know what the teacher expect us to do

Jo 2:7

I	And because the film they got shine ... because this time I ask the matt ... so maybe I will ask how much for the matt
MU	Is a matt finish more expensive than gloss?
PP	And is a matt finish expensive than ... gloss?
RP	And the other question is a matt ... a matt finish more expensive than gloss?
DP	I would like to know how much for gloss one

Figure 13.1 Sample set of target utterance realizations

The data, when transcribed, enabled direct comparisons across the different forms produced, from the initial idea (I), through the model utterance provided by the researcher (MU), to the various performances, in practice (PP), the real situation (RP), and some time later, the 'delayed' performance (DP). Samples are given in Figure 13.1, where Lc is discussing a course assignment with her classmate. Jo is in the chemist's with a film to be developed.

Quantification

Each participant's 'mean propensity to attempt target utterances' was calculated, as *target utterances attempted ÷ target utterances prepared* (Table 13.3). The term 'propensity to attempt ...' better reflects the situation than, say, 'willingness to attempt ...' because a participant who was willing, even eager, to attempt a target utterance, might not always find an opportunity to produce it. An 'attempted target utterance' was one which had been produced partially or completely, with or without native or non-nativelike changes.

	Practice	Real
Ch	0.4	0.5
Hi	0.95	0.66
Jo	1.0	0.93
Lc	0.92	0.7
Lo	0.87	0.52
Sa	0.91	0.51

Table 13.3 Mean propensity to attempt model utterances

A second calculation was of an utterance's 'accuracy/ completeness' (i.e. the closeness of reproduction to the model): *number of words produced with same form and function as in model target utterance ÷ number of words in model target utterance*. The stipulation that a word should have the 'same form and function' was in order to avoid counting words which happened to be identical in form to a target word but which were not an instance of it, for example, 'to' as infinitive marker and 'to' as a preposition. As an illustration, the 'closeness' scores for Lc 2:4 from Figure 13.1 are shown in Figure 13.2.

Lc 2:4			
I	I'm not quite sure what the teacher expect us to do		
MU	I'm not really sure what they want us to include	11 words	
PP	I'm not sure what the teacher want us to include	9 ÷ 11	= .82
RP	I'm not sure what they want us to include	10 ÷ 11	= .91
DP	I wanted to know what the teacher expect us to do	4 ÷ 11	= .36

Figure 13.2 'Closeness' scores for sample data

Analysis

Were all participants equally able to memorize and recall nativelike material?

As Table 13.3 shows, the six participants varied in their propensity to attempt utterances. The accuracy of their recall, calculated as in Figure 13.2, also varied. Individuals who attempted a lot of target utterances in the first conversation were likely to do so in the second (r_s = .943, p < .01), suggesting that it was not the topic or context but the individual's approach to the task that determined the likelihood of attempting recall. On the other hand, no significant correlation was found between the proportion of target utterances attempted in real performance and either the EVST scores (r = −.177, p = .738) or the Lex30 scores (r = −.666, p = .149). This indicates that a person's willingness to attempt a target utterance was not linked to proficiency, at least as measured by EVST/Lex30.

There was a significant correlation (r = .886, p = .019) between the proportion of target utterances attempted at RP by each participant and her score on aural memory, but no correlation with the remaining skills. As regards accuracy, there was no significant correlation between closeness of reproduction and either the EVST score (r = −.392, p = .442) or the Lex30 score (r = −.407, p = .423), nor was closeness of reproduction correlated with any of the aptitude scores including aural memory. One explanation (fully discussed in Wray and Fitzpatrick 2008) may be that the more proficient learners felt more empowered to take risks in the amount of attention paid to what they were memorizing, with the result that they made more errors during recall (see Chapter 20).

What were the limitations on reproducing memorized material in a real conversation?

A paired samples *t*-test revealed a highly significant difference between the proportion of target utterances attempted at PP and the (always lower) number attempted at RP (t = 5.455, p < .0001), indicating that it was more difficult to use the memorized strings in the real conversation. In order to establish whether this was because there was no opportunity to use them, or because when the opportunity arose, the material did not come to mind, two conversations were examined in depth: those in which the difference between practice and real conversation was largest. In both there was unfulfilled opportunity. Sa, in a conversation with a classmate about how her essay preparation was going, used all eleven target utterances at PP, but only four at RP. Yet the conversation provided her with opportunities to use all seven of the unused target utterances. Lo, in one of her conversations, used ten of her eleven target utterances at PP, but only four at RP. Yet the conversation provided opportunities to use four of the seven unused target utterances.

Using the 'closeness' measure described earlier, it was established that the utterances attempted at PP were significantly closer to the target than those attempted at RP ($t = 3.574$, $p < .01$). This means that even when a participant had the capacity and opportunity to use a well-formed word string, and attempted to produce it, changes were often introduced (compare the similar finding in Chapter 12). The post-study comments shed some light on this too. Some participants felt compelled *not* to produce utterances too close to the target. Lo, for example, claimed to make gratuitous changes to the memorized material: 'I just changed some different words but it is the same meaning'. While Lc reported that the use of memorized nativelike sentences helped her think in a more British way, with the result that she was able to communicate more effectively with British people, Da, a participant used in our pilot study, seemed sensitive to how the wordings challenged his cultural/national identity, observing:

> Sometimes I change [the phrases] maybe I think there is a difference between British thinking and Chinese thinking ... We have to do something in my thinking ... actually we ... haven't really changed Chinese thinking to English thinking so sometimes I have to change some words just for me to easy to ... find a good way to express my emotions.

Comments such as these warn us against assumptions that a failure to reproduce an utterance close to the target is simply due to lack of competence or problems with retrieval.

What sorts of conversations were most receptive to the anticipation and effective reproduction of useful material?

No attempt was made to influence the type of conversation that was prepared, because it was important that the participant had free choice. However, it was possible afterwards to categorize the conversations into three unequal groups: informal (where interlocutor was a friend), formal (where the interlocutor was a colleague, tutor, or boss) and unknown (where the interlocutor and participant had never met before).

In the informal and unknown interlocutor conditions, the majority of the prepared utterances were attempted, but in the formal condition, only a little over one quarter were. The distribution was highly significant, $\chi^2 = 22.26$, df $= 2$, $p < 0.01$. As regards closeness to the target, however, while the formal conversations were least close, the differences were not significant. Fitzpatrick and Wray (2006) speculate that formal conversations were treated conservatively, with a low level of risk-taking.

What sorts of changes were made when memorized material was not perfectly reproduced?

A total of 2,416 memorized words contributed to the analysis: the total number of words in the targets that were attempted. The subjects' outputs were categorized according to how they deviated from the targets. Deviations could be nativelike or non-nativelike (judged in terms of the specific utterance in context), and grammatical, lexical, or phrasal (multiword).[2]

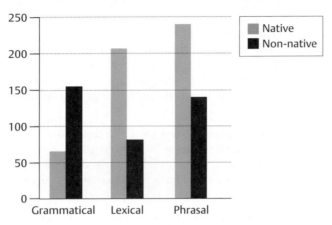

Figure 13.3 Distribution of deviation types

As Figure 13.3 shows, phrase-level deviations were most common (42.6 per cent of the total), and within that category almost two out of three (63.35 per cent) were judged nativelike, that is, changes that a native speaker might make (for example, 'The dissertation title' → 'The title of the dissertation'; 'They usually learn' → 'Usually they learn'). Lexical deviations accounted for one third of the total (32.5 per cent), and of these, 71.8 per cent were nativelike (for example, 'Like this' → 'Just like this'; 'The trouble is' → 'The problem is'). One quarter of the deviations (24.9 per cent) were grammatical, but here seven out of ten changes were non-nativelike (70.5 per cent) (for example, 'A question' → 'A questions'; 'I've got an idea' → 'I've got idea'). Indeed, 41.4 per cent of the total non-nativelike changes were in the grammatical domain.

Amongst grammatical deviations, the three main sources were function words (36.8 per cent), articles (30 per cent), and inflections (19.5 per cent), the latter two highly likely to be changed in a non-native way. This no doubt reflects the fact that, in closed morphological systems, there is usually only one nativelike choice, so that a deviation from it is inevitably non-nativelike. Amongst lexical deviations, 83 per cent of alterations to adjuncts were nativelike, and 57 per cent of those to content words. At the phrasal level, substitutions (47.5 per cent) were the most common form of deviation, with 59.8 per cent of them being nativelike.

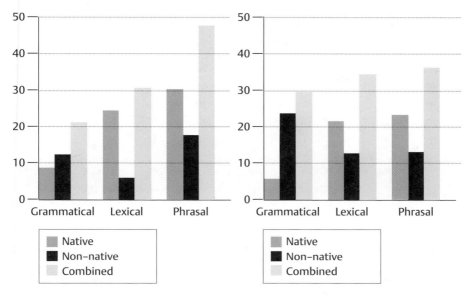

Figure 13.4 Proportions of deviations for Japanese (left) and Chinese (right) subjects

As Figure 13.4 shows, the Japanese subjects made more phrase-level deviations than the Chinese subjects, and grammatical deviations were more likely to be non-nativelike for the Chinese subjects than the Japanese ones. With only three subjects in each group, we cannot draw strong conclusions, of course, but the contrast does at least indicate where future research might focus some attention. Breaking down the grammatical type revealed that the Japanese subjects made very few inflectional deviations (3.9 per cent) compared with the Chinese subjects (33.3 per cent). For Japanese subjects, deviations in function words and articles jointly contributed 82.5 per cent of the grammatical deviations, whereas for the Chinese subjects it was only 53 per cent. However, Japanese subjects' deviations in function words were more likely to be nativelike than non-nativelike, while the reverse was true for Chinese subjects, a contrast that was highly significant ($\chi^2 = 7.87$, df =1, $p < 0.01$), suggesting that Japanese and Chinese learners may have different fundamental susceptibilities in relation to function word accuracy. In contrast, there was no significant difference in the distribution of native and non-native deviations for articles ($\chi^2 = 0.64$).

Can individual profiles of performance indicate linguistic strengths and weaknesses?

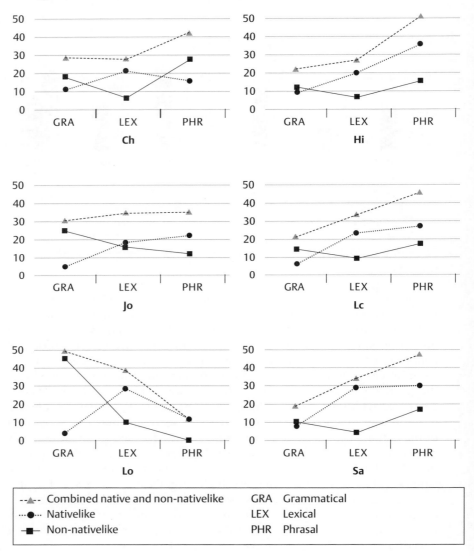

Figure 13.5 Deviation profiles by subject

Figure 13.5 presents profiles of the six subjects by deviation type, showing the native, non-native, and combined distributions. Lo stands out as entirely unlike the others, in having few phrasal deviations and a high proportion of grammatical deviations. Furthermore, almost all of her grammatical deviations were non-nativelike, while all of her phrasal ones were native-like. However, Lo contributed by far the smallest amount of data, with 49 deviations in total, from a target pool of 151 words. Whether the pattern is, therefore, a product of this small amount of data, or whether, conversely, the small quantity of data that Lo produced was the result of weaknesses in her grammatical knowledge or focus, is impossible to say.

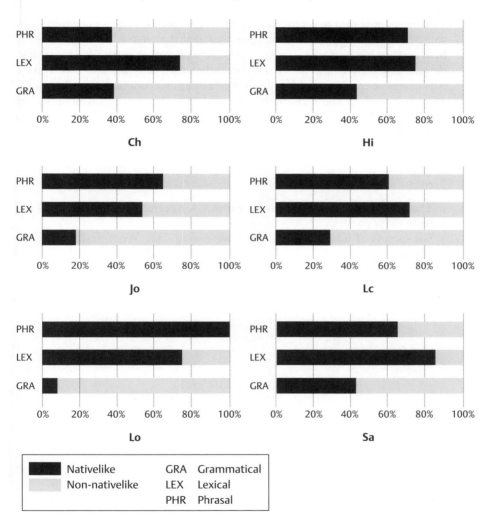

Figure 13.6 Progression towards nativelike choices

The profiles in Figure 13.6 show how far along the pathway from non-native to native each subject had progressed, in relation to grammar, lexis, and phraseology.

Conclusion

The interviews and questionnaires administered to the participants indicated that, in their view, memorization did have the capacity to support them in sounding more nativelike, and that it gave them benefits in terms of confidence and satisfaction as well as experience in using nativelike turns of phrase. However, the results revealed that it was not the most proficient learners that performed best in memorization. Indeed, memorization appeared to be something of a leveller, and this may suggest that it could be particularly beneficial to learners who struggle to shine using other methods of learning, particularly if they have an integrative rather than instrumental motivation. All subjects experienced difficulty it delivering, in a functionally salient situation, as much of the memorized material as they actually knew, and they introduced changes, both deliberately and unintentionally, that were often non-nativelike. The profiles of deviation from the memorized targets revealed differences by L1, by word class, and by function.

Notes

1 The author is grateful to Tess Fitzpatrick for permission to reuse material from these papers.
2 For details of how these decisions were made, see Wray and Fitzpatrick (2008).

14
Meanings of the parts
and meaning of the whole

Overview

Formulaic language rarely brings a case to court, but in the Coonass case it did. The point at issue was whether the term 'coonass', taken as offensive by one party, could reasonably have not been recognized as potentially offensive by another party. The word is from a particular dialect in the US, and is etymologically and semantically unrelated to its apparent internal components 'coon' and 'ass'. But people not familiar with the term would be very likely to attempt to draw out its meaning by examining its composition, particularly if it was written as two words, 'Coon Ass', as it was in this case. At the heart of the discussion in the original paper by Wray and Staczek (2005)[1] is the question of what goes on when we store and process words. It is proposed that for dialect users who had known the word 'coonass' from childhood, it would be a morpheme equivalent unit (MEU), that is, have a semantic entry that rendered unnecessary any examination of its components. If so, they might fail to notice the presence of offensive subcomponents, in the same way as most people would miss seeing that 'molestation' could be interpreted as the place where small furry animals take the train.

The case

In the mid-1990s, an African-American woman working for the US Department of Energy filed legal action against her employer. She claimed a hostile work environment, in which she had been subjected to racial harassment. The case was heard in the United States District Court for the District of Columbia. The event leading to the action was that, on returning from vacation, she found in her desk drawer a framed certificate with the title 'Temporary Coon Ass Certificate' (Figure 14.1)[2] and her name printed on it. The document was signed by a white Department of Energy employee based at a workshop in east Texas, the site of a recent team visit that the Plaintiff had been unable to attend. The Plaintiff, upon receiving the certificate, "immediately experienced emotions of shock, outrage and fury, and felt the certificate and the statements contained therein constituted a serious racial slur".[3] The Plaintiff sought sanctions against the sender, and alleged that: "the Defendant [i.e. her employer] condoned the hostile environment by failing to discipline the sender or take other remedial action".

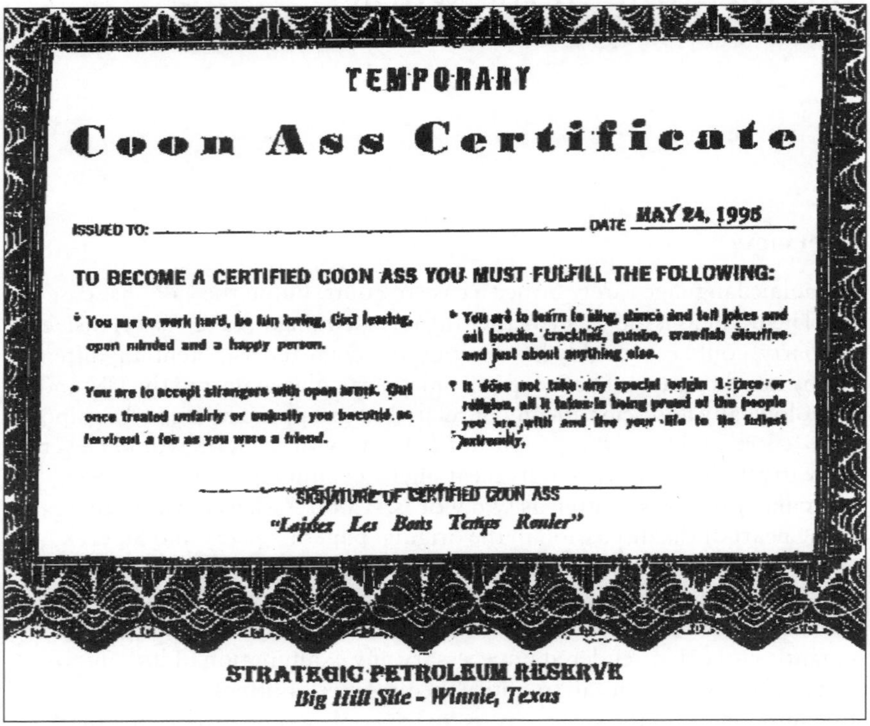

TEMPORARY

Coon Ass Certificate

ISSUED TO: ______ DATE MAY 24, 1995

TO BECOME A CERTIFIED COON ASS YOU MUST FULFILL THE FOLLOWING:

- You are to work hard, be fun loving, God fearing, open minded and a happy person.
- You are to accept strangers with open arms. But once treated unfairly or unjustly you become as fervent a foe as you were a friend.
- You are to learn to sing, dance and tell jokes and eat boudin, cracklins, gumbo, crawfish etouffee and just about anything else.
- It does not take any special origin, race or religion, all it takes is being proud of the people you are with and live your life to its fullest potential.

SIGNATURE OF CERTIFIED COON ASS

"Laissez Les Bons Temps Rouler"

STRATEGIC PETROLEUM RESERVE
Big Hill Site - Winnie, Texas

Figure 14.1 'Temporary Coon Ass' certificate

The court hearings revealed that the sender had issued many of these certificates, after groups of company employees made site visits to his facility. During the visits he would explain the meaning of the term 'coonass' as 'white Cajun', identifying himself as a member of that cultural group. The certificate making each visitor a 'temporary coonass' was thus, he claimed, intended as a gesture of solidarity. When the Plaintiff did not attend the visit as planned, her name mistakenly remained on the list and she received a certificate afterwards. Having missed out on the explanation, she did not interpret the wording as intended.

The Plaintiff was one of two African Americans in that round of certificate distributions. Since the sender would have met the other African-American recipient during the visit, his statement in court, below, is particularly striking:

Q You're familiar with the term 'coon,' aren't you?
A Yes, sir, I am.
Q You understand that that has a racially-derogatory meaning?
A Yes, sir, I do.
Q And you knew that the term 'coon' has a racially-derogative meaning to African Americans at the time that you prepared the certificate that's been marked as Plaintiff's Exhibit Number 1, isn't that true?
A That's correct.
(Trial transcript: cross-examination of Defense witness by Plaintiff's attorney, 21 Aug 1997: 40)

The jury had to decide whether it was possible for someone to know that the word 'coon' was offensive, yet not consider 'coonass' to be:

[T]o determine … whether the Temporary Coon Ass Certificate was racially offensive, you should consider [the sender's] intent to discriminate or not to discriminate against blacks, the subjective effect of the forwarding of the certificate on [the Plaintiff], and the impact it would have had on any reasonable person in [the Plaintiff's] position.
(Trial transcript: summary of the Judge, 25 Aug 1997: 19)

The jury found in favour of the Plaintiff and awarded $120,000 in compensatory damages against the US Department of Energy.

What does 'coonass' *really* mean?

The *Historical Dictionary of American Slang* (1994) (HDAS) and the *Dictionary of American Regional English* (1985) (DARE) both confirm the claim that 'coonass' is a term for Louisiana Cajuns. Cajuns are classically defined as the white descendants of settlers in Acadia, a former French colony of eastern Canada, who were deported by the British, or relocated voluntarily, to the south-western territories, including Louisiana, in the mid-eighteenth century (*American Heritage Dictionary of the English Language* 1992: 9) (AHDEL). 'Coonass' is not, however, a term in general usage. DARE attests that it is confined to the dialects of Louisiana and south-eastern Texas, though it is also known to regional speakers in Mississippi, Arkansas, and Alabama. For many dialect words, the story would end there. But in this case, the following dictionary entries occur in addition to the core definition:

Coonass is still a pejorative for any low-life individual, especially Negroes (DARE).

The term 'coonass' … may have been a racial allusion suggesting a Cajun-black genetic mixture (HDAS).

The combined evidence above suggests that 'coonass' has two meanings, the second alluding to, if not actually referring to, African ancestry. However, the status of the latter entries is questionable, as we shall see presently.

Unequivocal is the offensive meaning of the separate terms 'coon' and 'ass'. A wide range of standard and specialist dictionaries give as one meaning of coon, 'a Negro', and indicate that it is a slang and derogatory term. Its origin is consistently reported as a shortened form of raccoon, itself a word of Algonquian Indian origin. 'Ass' is identified in HDAS as a US version of British 'arse', the buttocks or rump. As such it is considered a 'vulgarism' (HDAS). AHDEL gives the definition "a vain, self-important, silly, or aggressively stupid person", based on the meaning of ass as 'donkey'.

What sort of quality of evidence is obtained from dictionaries though? In the course of questioning, the expert witness for the Defendant made a number of observations regarding the validity of dictionary definitions:

> ... these dictionaries are only as good as the people they're talking to ... These are not definitions. These are recorded testimonies of what people think these things mean.
> (Trial transcript: direct examination of expert witness for the Defense, 22 Aug 1997: 44)

> Those two dictionaries [DARE and HDAS] are based on interviews with people, asking them what regional or slang terms mean to them. The reason for that is because these terms are not—have no standard accepted meaning.
> (Trial transcript: cross-examination of expert witness for the Defense, 22 Aug 1997: 60)

As the observations of this expert witness indicate, care needs to be taken with dictionary entries where there is no evidence of general consensus within a speech community, or where there are grounds for doubting the validity of the statement that the dictionary cites. Specifically with regard to the two attestations, above, that 'coonass' can imply African ancestry, it is possible that the claimed extension of the term to black people is a post hoc rationalization based on folk etymology. In actual fact, the consensus across dictionaries, including both HDAS and DARE, is that 'coonass' has an etymology in which 'coon' does not figure at all, since it is a corruption of the French 'connasse', a vulgarism referring to the female anatomy and used as an insult.

How we make meaning

Language, whether oral or written, exists within a context of use. Both speakers and hearers bring to their understanding of a word or phrase a knowledge founded on a socialization, education, and experience that may be totally or partially shared, or not shared at all. Not living in the dialect area, could the Plaintiff be expected to have known what 'coonass' meant? The expert witness for the Defense thought so:

... it's not unreasonable to think that people—not only people in South
Louisiana and East Texas would be familiar with the term ... People all
over the place know this.
(Trial transcript: cross-examination of expert witness for the Defense by
Plaintiff's attorney, 22 Aug 1997: 49–50)

However, he was himself a south Louisianan of French Acadian descent—that
is, of Cajun ancestry. He originated from, and resided well within, the dialect
area in which the term was in use, and he was highly familiar with it. As a
result, he might have suffered from the same 'blindness' regarding alternative
interpretations of the term as the sender of the certificates claimed to have.

The Plaintiff maintained that, not recognizing 'Coon Ass' as a term in its
own right, she only saw the separate words:

When I pulled [the certificate] out, the first thing I saw was 'coon'. I didn't
see 'temporary'. I didn't see 'ass'. All I could see was 'coon' ... I was
shocked. I was outraged.
(Trial transcript: direct examination of the Plaintiff by Plaintiff's attorney,
20 Aug 1997: 36)

Thus, just as the sender's ethnic identity could have created an exposure to
language that *prevented* him seeing 'coon' in 'Coon Ass', so the Plaintiff's
ethnic identity formed part of the context within which her reading of 'Coon
Ass' caused offence.

In the trial, the expert witness for the Defense was asked whether he viewed
'coonass' as a single word or two words. In reply, he compared it to the
word 'firefly': "*firefly* is not *fire* or *fly*; it's a *firefly*". It's an expression used
together'. In the case of 'firefly' there is, of course, a clear hint as to why it
gained its name, which relates to its component parts. However, internally
complex words and multiword phrases often have an apparent etymology
that is misleading, with subcomponents that do not represent what they seem
to. Thus, the 'ladybird' or 'ladybug' is so-called not because it is female or
resembles a lady, but because it was traditionally a creature of 'Our Lady', the
Virgin Mary (compare German *Marienkäfer*, 'Mary's beetle'). A 'penknife'
is not a knife that is the size or shape of a writing implement, but a knife
originally designed for sharpening quills (pen = 'feather').

What of 'coonass', then? If we set aside the single proposal, discussed
earlier, that the term takes the form it does because it first referred to black
Cajuns, and if we follow instead the more reliable etymology from French,
then 'coonass' is no more made up, historically, of 'coon' and 'ass' than
'season' is made up of 'sea' and 'son'. We must recognize a direct link, within
the dialect area of its use, between a French word for female genitalia and
a consistently applied derogatory term for an immigrant group of French
settlers from Canada, and their descendants. Any association with African
Americans is after the event, and imposed by outsiders.

The Needs Only Analysis (NOA) model (Chapter 2) suggests that people who have been raised in Louisiana or southeast Texas will, having encountered the term 'coonass' and, having accepted without question that it refers to a Cajun, have had no *need* to engage in further analysis of it. In contrast, someone who does not know the word, has an additional 'need', and will therefore engage with more analysis, by breaking down the incomprehensible whole into comprehensible parts, naturally using the word break as the morphological boundary. The result is two words with independent meanings, 'coon' and 'ass'. The decoding that is required by a person encountering 'coonass' for the first time is minimal: no more than the recognition that there are two components, both derogatory, implying that their combination must also be so.

The sender's claim not to have made the connection between 'coon' and 'coonass' makes sense from the perspective of NOA, and would be a case of 'constituent blindness' brought about by the strong and consistent association of a specific meaning with the whole phrase 'coonass', a MEU for that person. More accurately, it would be 'pseudo-constituent blindness', since 'coon' and 'ass' are not historically—or actually for the dialect speakers—constituents of the whole. For such individuals to see 'coon' and 'ass' in 'coonass' can be argued to be unreasonable. On the other hand, it must be noted that the court case was not brought directly against the dialect speaker, but against his employer. Any manager who was not himself from the dialect region in which 'coonass' is used, might reasonably have been expected to spot the danger of this term being let loose on unsuspecting recipients.

Conclusion

Just how a court should handle such a psycholinguistic consideration is a matter for discussion. It could clearly have some bearing on the issue of intent, but one could still argue that however explicable the oversight might be in psycholinguistic terms, it is part of the educational level required of managers or supervisors that they be language-aware in relation to differences between linguistic varieties used, and encountered, in the work place. At the very least, the outcome of this case suggests that individuals in a socially responsible position are expected to appreciate the singularity of their own dialect or slang forms to a sufficient extent that they will refrain from using them with people likely to be unfamiliar with—or to misconstrue—their meaning.

Notes

1 The present account is a shorter version of Wray and Staczek (2005). Permission from John Staczek to rework the paper is gratefully acknowledged.
2 Further discussion of the certificate, including a transcription of the text on it, is given in Chapter 17.

3 Quotations are from court documents. For full references, see Wray and
  Staczek (2005) or the abridged version of the same paper that appears as
  Appendix 1 of Wallace and Wray (2006).

15
Formulaicity and naturalness in a French and Saunders sketch

Overview

The mechanisms by which an actor memorizes and reproduces a lengthy text are arguably different from those entailed in producing a simple idiomatic phrase. However, the fact that a script must be recalled with full accuracy suggests that the actor cannot risk only remembering the gist of the message and creating its expression in real time as a novel configuration— the form-meaning relationship must be robust. It follows that an actor's preparation for performance entails a full internalization of the script— presumably as a reliable sequence of individually memorized turns or parts of turns, along with cues for the recall of the next one. This extreme case of formulaicity is useful to examine, because there is an inherent tension between the need, as part of the performance, to convey spontaneity, and the actual absence of spontaneity when adhering to a script. The many differences in form and provenance of scripted speech compared with spontaneous speech stack the odds against sounding entirely natural. Analysis of *The Extras*, a sketch in the 1994 French and Saunders[1] Christmas Special, reveals a striking contrast between the 'naturalness' of the presentation of the two comedians and that of two guest actors, Richard Briers and Geraldine McEwen. Comparing the transcript of the performance with the written script shows that while Briers and McEwen were largely faithful to the lines they were given, French and Saunders made substantial improvised changes. Discussion of the script and performance of the sketch is contextualized with information from a survey of professional actors, regarding their attitudes toward naturalness and towards the status of a script as a definitive text.[2]

Introduction

Within a second or two of turning on the radio it is normally possible to tell whether one is listening to a scripted drama or an unscripted conversation.

The unavoidable difference between scripted material and normal speech is that the former is not spontaneous. In recent years, experimental attempts have been made to close the gap between natural and scripted speech in performance. Yet, curiously, it seems not to be simply a question of letting the actors say what they like. Directors like Ken Loach and Mike Leigh allow a script to develop out of improvisation by the actors, but the end result is an agreed written version. Spoof fly-on-the-wall documentaries, such as the BBC series *People Like Us* in the 1990s and *The Office* (2001–2003) give the impression of being highly improvised, yet according to writers Ricky Gervais and Stephen Merchant, *The Office* 'was 95 per cent scripted, with some improvisation here and there'.[3] It seems, then, that 'naturalistic' delivery of the kind seen in these productions is achieved despite the material being prefabricated.

Of course, 'naturalistic' performance need not map exactly onto what is truly natural, and arguably *should* not. The audience interprets an acted performance within the frame of recognizing that it is not real. Acting that is intended to be mistaken for reality would cross the boundary into deception, by withholding from the receiver vital information about the fictional nature of the activity.

	Characteristic	Natural spontaneous speech	Scripted speech
1	Content	Spontaneously produced	Pre-determined
2	Speaker's relationship to ideas	Personally generated	Adopted from someone else
3	Form of words	Spontaneously produced	Pre-determined
4	Speaker's relationship to choice of words	Personally generated	Adopted from someone else
5	Role of non-participatory on-lookers	Ignored	Included
6	Features of written language	Unlikely	Somewhat likely

Table 15.1 Differences in provenance and form of natural spontaneous speech and scripted speech

More generally, a number of characteristics present in spontaneous speech are normally absent in acted speech (Table 15.1), though the differences are not absolute. Natural conversations can be pre-planned in terms of content (characteristic 1) (for example, a job interview), they may contain prefabricated forms, including part of previous turns (characteristic 3), and in some circumstances the speakers may 'play to the gallery' of onlookers (characteristic 5). Conversely, the forms of words in a script are not always faithfully adhered to (characteristic 3), though normally this is by mistake:

lapses of memory could result in content being omitted, moved or, in the case of ad-libbing to rescue a problematic situation such as a missed entrance, added. However, changes in content (characteristic 1) are rare and undesirable in scripted material, since there is a story to convey and the components need to be presented in the correct order. In addition, performance material does not usually vary in relation to characteristic 5, since, unlike in normal conversation, it is the onlooking audience, not the speaking characters, that are the target listeners, and the text must be pitched to be comprehensible and contextualized for them.[4]

Despite these differences between spontaneous and scripted speech, it is possible for actors, under some circumstances, to reproduce prefabricated material in a manner that is interpreted as 'natural'. How do they achieve it, and what constraints does prefabrication place upon them?

Naturalness as a goal in acting

In order to discover more about approaches and attitudes to naturalness, a short questionnaire was sent to a small sample of experienced stage, film, and television actors.[5] The responses revealed most of them to believe that cinema and, particularly, television, had led to an increase in linguistic realism. However, several observed that realism could easily conflict with other goals of drama—to entertain and present something striking and interesting rather than ordinary. One actor observed that while drama uses words and actions to *portray* the character's thoughts and feelings, in real life, people often use their words to *disguise* what they really think and feel. Another noted that authors may not always even intend the character to sound natural. A third commented that in historical works, particularly those in verse, the actor needs to transcend naturalness and conform to the rhythms of the scripted speech, which requires practice and often a measure of breath control not usual in natural speech.

All the respondents had techniques for maximizing the naturalness of their delivery. Generally, they entailed becoming highly familiar with the script, so that the prescribed words flowed naturally. Many respondents said that they might ask to make small changes to the script to make it feel more natural, but all acknowledged the right of the author to have the final say. Some playwrights, it was noted, were more amenable to changes than others. Two respondents remarked that it was an insult to playwrights to challenge their wordings, and that actors should be able to deliver *any* line well. Good writing was writing that was easy for actors to deliver. It was universally agreed that once the rehearsals were over, the script of a stage play no longer changed, other than by mistake.

Overall, the impression given by these responses is that 'naturalness' of delivery is a generally desirable goal in most, but not all, circumstances, and that it is achieved through 'ownership' of the linguistic forms. Ownership is attained (a) by participating in the formulation of the lines, as in Mike

Leigh films, (b) by requesting changes to the script to match the actor's own speech patterns better, and/or (c) through familiarization with the lines until the actor can 'feel' them as his/her own (Figure 15.1). It is notable that (a) and (b) entail a measure of shift in features (3) and (4) in Table 15.1. The model in Figure 15.1 can be used as a basis of evaluating the cause of the particular features relating to naturalness and unnaturalness in the comedy sketch *The Extras*.

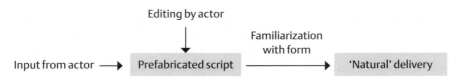

Figure 15.1 The actor's three routes to naturalness in script

The Extras by French and Saunders

The Extras was a seven minute sketch broadcast in the *French and Saunders Christmas Special* 1994. Four actors took part: Dawn French, Jennifer Saunders, and two guests, Richard Briers and Geraldine McEwen, cast to play themselves. In the sketch, French and Saunders play fussy, frivolous female film extras in a science fiction film, in which they have been cast as alien monsters guarding a captured earthling. They are wearing costumes that make them unrecognizable until they take off the head section. They have been sent to the studio canteen for 'early tea' and complain about the unprofessional nature of the production. An assistant enters and tells them that they will not be needed until lunchtime, as they have been over-zealous in their guarding duties, and are to be replaced by other aliens in the film, the Zeronig Pods. They object that the Pods will be hopeless at guarding, having no arms. Briers and McEwen enter, also indignant about the poor quality organization. While McEwen is getting some tea, French and Saunders recognize Briers and, star-struck, go up to talk to him. He is politely dismissive. McEwen returns and is also recognized. Briers and McEwen continue to complain to each other about how badly they are being treated given their status as stars, while French and Saunders admire them from afar. The assistant returns and calls for the Zeronig Pods. Briers and McEwen are helped into Pod costumes, which completely disguise them. French and Saunders are indignant—but not about the lowly roles of their heroes. Pods should not be doing the guarding: they have no arms.

Naturalness in *The Extras*

The presentation styles of Briers and McEwen, on the one hand, and French and Saunders, on the other hand, are strikingly different in the sketch. Broadly speaking, the former two tend to deliver a clearly enunciated line, wait for the laugh, then deliver the next line. In contrast, French and Saunders engage in a chattering style, with many false starts, simultaneous talk, and repetitions. In order to establish whether these differences in 'naturalness' were generally perceived, a video of the sketch was played to eighteen native speakers of English in an undergraduate class. They were asked to rate the language of each actor on a five point scale, from '1: definitely unlike natural, spontaneously produced spoken English conversation' through to '5: very much like natural, spontaneously produced spoken English conversation'. The totals give a naturalness score for each actor, out of a possible 90 points (Figure 15.2), and show that the judges overall viewed the guest actors as less natural in their presentation.

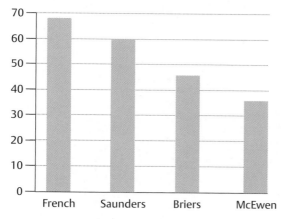

Figure 15.2 'Naturalness' scores for four actors (out of 90)

Symptoms of 'naturalness' and 'unnaturalness'

Briers' and McEwen's delivery was marked by a more declamatory style, something that appeared to be characterized by the intonational patterns. The tonic syllables were categorized as falls, rises, fall-rises, rise-falls, and even (Table 15.2). Figure 15.3 shows that Briers and McEwen used more fall-rises than French and Saunders. There was a significant difference in the pattern distributions of French and Saunders (combined) compared with Briers and McEwen (combined) ($\chi^2 = 12.494$, df = 4, $p < 0.05$).

A comparison of the transcriptions of the speech clearly reveals the differences in delivery (Figures 15.4, 15.5). The speech of French and Saunders has several features reminiscent of natural conversation, that are absent in that of Briers and McEwen. There are 44 incidents of overlapping between French and Saunders, and none between Briers and McEwen. French and Saunders latch their turns while Briers and McEwen leave slight gaps between turns.

French and Saunders' pronunciation features the phonological reduction of unstressed syllables, whereas Briers and McEwen speak all words clearly.

	French (%)	Saunders (%)	Briers (%)	McEwen (%)
Fall	127 (73)	102 (74)	38 (67)	36 (59)
Rise	15 (9)	11 (8)	3 (5)	6 (10)
Fall-rise	17 (10)	14 (10)	12 (21)	15 (25)
Rise-fall	7 (4)	5 (4)	3 (5)	2 (3)
Even	7 (4)	5 (4)	1 (2)	2 (3)
Total	**173**	**137**	**57**	**61**

Table 15.2 Distributions of tonic patterns (percentages in brackets)

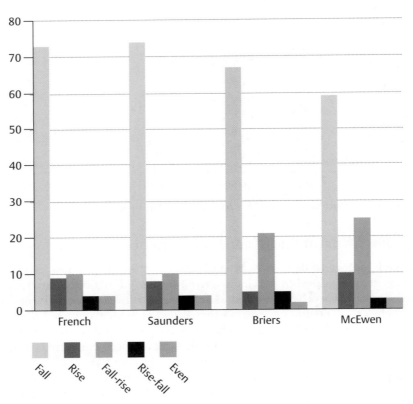

Figure 15.3 Distributions of tonic patterns (percentages)

French and Saunders' speech has false starts, repetition, repairs, and hesitation, while Briers and McEwen's has only a few hesitation features. French and Saunders change tempo, while Briers and McEwen retain a generally even tempo. In addition, French and Saunders continue to speak over audience laughter, increasing the volume accordingly, where Briers and McEwen never overlap their speech with audience laughter, and overall French and Saunders display a much wider range of amplitude, from shouts to whispers, while Briers and McEwen maintain an even moderately loud speech volume.

RB the traffic was appalling (0.5) through hell and high water I get here (0.5) and straight into make-up and a cup of tea (1.0) no breakfast (0.5) which isn't the end of the world for me because I don't eat breakfast
   (*audience laughter*)

RB you see nobody offered (0.5) it's typical (.) still (.) heigh ho (0.5)

GM do you want a coffee (0.5) I'm having to ask you because nobody else seems to have bothered
   (*audience laughter*)

GM not a runner in sight (0.5) I mean I've worked on low budgets before but nothing like this nobody knows what the hell is going on
   (*audience laughter*)

RB you're right (0.5) Mickey Mouse productions (0.5) nobody knows what the h.hell is going on (0.5) .h.h I will have a coffee if you don't mind

---

Figure 15.4 Example of Briers–McEwen dialogue

DF we know who this is (.) over here
JS do we
DF over here [(.)] at two o'clock [(.) at two o'clock
JS   [er]   [two er h. yes
DF no (.) five past two [(.) five past
JS   [oh (.) ye:s
DF do we
JS do we
DF he's very famous
JS o:h
DF does all the big Shakespearean parts
JS yes yes [yes yes yes
DF   [who is it
JS Anthony Andrews is it [(**)] no
DF   [no:] no no no no no (0.5) yes =
JS =yes=
DF =he does a lot of Shakespeare but it's not [him
JS   [look look (.) I'll offer him
   a bourbon (.) and you get a closer look heh heh heh heh
DF right (.) alright (2.0) go on

Figure 15.5 Example of French–Saunders dialogue

Why did French and Saunders sound more natural than Briers and McEwen?

Although the four actors had a different balance of experience on stage, screen, and television, and in comic versus dramatic roles, the most significant difference relevant to this sketch was their relationship with the scripted material. French and Saunders wrote the sketch and Briers and McEwen were invited to participate in it.

Writer-performers have particular privileges in relation to a script when it only involves themselves, as John Bird and John Fortune revealed (personal communication) when asked about their satirical interview sketches (for example, on *Rory Bremner Who Else?*, *Rory Bremner Apparently*, *Bremner, Bird and Fortune*, and *The Long Johns*). In these sketches, an interviewee, 'George Parr', holds a high position in government, industry, or the public services, and in the course of the interview reveals attitudes, assumptions, or incompetencies that resonate with a current political topic. Parr's part can be taken by either actor, while the other takes the role of interviewer. The interviews last about seven minutes and are unscripted and essentially unrehearsed. According to Bird and Fortune, the first time anyone sees the material is when it is performed in front of the live audience in the studio. They prepare by reading around the subject and talking to experts, and then mapping out a general question and answer frame. Fortune remarked: "We don't write a script because then we'd be trying to remember a particular form of phrasing and to do that we'd need to rehearse." Fortune also noted that their kind of improvisation is only possible with someone that you know well and have worked with for many years (in their case over 40): "we know how each others' minds work".

French and Saunders, like Bird and Fortune, have worked together for many years and are accustomed to an improvisation style in their sketches. They also appear to take a similar approach to the development of their sketches. According to Jon Plowman[6] (personal communication), "The [*Extras*] script was developed as much or as little as Dawn and Jennifer [ever] develop their scripts, meaning that although it has a basic shape in rehearsals their bits are not confirmed until the camera script". (The camera script is the script used during production, to coordinate sound, lighting, and camera shots.) Plowman added, however, that "Where a script involves other artists, their bits tend to be more solid from slightly earlier on in order to persuade them to do the sketch in the first place". In other words, Briers and McEwen would have been sent a script from which to learn their lines. In contrast, French and Saunders would not have viewed their own lines in the script as binding at that stage. Nevertheless, Plowman's comments imply that the script would have been finalized for performance at some point.

However, a comparison of the camera script and the transcribed performance reveals that French and Saunders did not adhere to their scripted parts even at that final stage. Lines were rephrased (Figure 15.6), redistributed (Figure 15.7), reallocated (Figure 15.8, 15.9), and augmented (Figure 15.9).

Script

DF That's where the word comes from. It's Greek. She does all the big women's parts

Performance

DF No: no no it comes from the original Greek (.) that's right (.) she's played all the big women's parts her

---

Figure 15.6 Script material rephrased (French)

Script

DF No Richard Briers – Sir Richard Briers. And does film, TV, and great theatre
JS The whole spectrum
DF Of great British acting. Does a lot of Shakespeare. All the greats

---

Performance

DF he's very famous
JS o:h
DF does all the big Shakespearian parts
JS yes yes yes yes yes
      (14 speaking turns omitted)
JS that   [one
DF   [it's   [him
JS   [oh oh ohohohohoh
DF what's (.) o:h he does loads of telly   [and screen and radio
JS   [oh (.) oh the whole spectrum

Figure 15.7 Script material redistributed (French and Saunders)

Script

DF Ridiculous!
JS Yes, ridiculous!
DF This shouldn't happen
JS No
DF I've never been sent for an early tea before

Performance

DF that's ridiculous
JS well that's ridiculous i:nnit
DF ridiculous
JS this shouldn't happen
DF no (.) I've never been sent for an early tea before

Figure 15.8 Turns reallocated (French and Saunders)

Script

DF   Shall we sit here?
         (THEY SIT AND REMOVE HEADS)

JS   That's better I could hardly breathe in there, these are not union conditions. I'm going to tell Vivienne at our next GM

Performance

DF   let's sit down here (.)   [then
JS   [ye:s (.) oh
DF   longing to get this blooming head off
JS   oh
DF   so hot in there
JS   yes
DF   these are not union conditions I hasten to add =
JS   = no (.) I shall be mentioning it to Vivienne at our next GM heh   [heh heh
DF   [ye:s (.) absolutely

Figure 15.9   Turns reallocated and material added (French and Saunders)

Briers and McEwen made far fewer changes, in keeping with the observations made in the survey of actors, described earlier. There were changes of phrasing but they were contained within a functional unit (for example, Figure 15.10). Other changes were restricted to the addition or omission of 'and', 'but', 'you know', 'I see', 'I mean', and 'well'[7] and backchannels.

Script
RB   Well I will have a coffee, that's very kind poppet, but you shouldn't have to

---

Performance
RB   I will have a coffee if you don't mind it's very sweet of you lovey (.) but you shouldn't have to do it

Figure 15.10   Material rephrased (Briers)

Modelling the routes to naturalness in *The Extras*

In terms of the diagram in Figure 15.1, Briers and McEwen had open to them, at most, only two of the routes that enhance naturalness: they could familiarize themselves with the script as laid out and, possibly, request slight changes to it during the rehearsal. They had not participated in the construction of the script (as they might have in a Mike Leigh film). In contrast, French and Saunders, as writers as well as actors, had provided the input for the formulation of the script, and could continue to edit it during rehearsal. As revealed above, however, there is little evidence that they had engaged in careful verbatim familiarization with the form of the script as laid down.

Rather, as Jon Plowman's comments indicate, and in line with the approach taken by Bird and Fortune, they appear to have focused on familiarization with the *content*. As a result, *The Extras* requires a more complicated version of Figure 15.1, as in Figure 15.11.

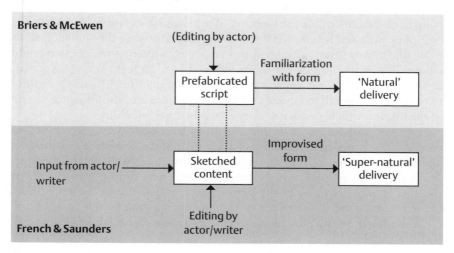

Figure 15.11   Routes to naturalness in The Extras

The risks of 'naturalness'

Classically, the script of a play or sketch is formulaic, in the sense that the form is decided in advance and committed to memory (see Chapter 20). A script has a status, as the product of the writer's creativity, that somewhat protects it from alteration. Yet, in so far as the intention is to represent reality (which is not by any means a given), it is desirable for the text to sound as if it is the spontaneous output of the character at the time of performance. As noted earlier, features characteristic of natural speech but generally absent in scripts will tend to reduce the spontaneity of an actor's scripted presentation. In *The Extras*, the style of Briers and McEwen, on the one hand, and of French and Saunders, on the other hand, contrasts in terms of naturalness, not because the former pair transgress the standard procedures for delivering their text 'naturally', but because French and Saunders are released from some of the constraints on naturalness that are normally imposed by the formulaicity of the script. Specifically, because they are the writers, the ideas have originated with them (characteristic 2, Table 15.1). The form, as written in the script, reflects their speech patterns, collapsing characteristics 3 and 4. In performance, many of those patterns are faithfully reproduced, even though the speakers do not treat the script as a firm reference point and, rather than memorizing and reproducing the script text, improvise around it using their own words (characteristic 4). Because they are not reproducing a written version, there is less likelihood that their words will be influenced by written norms (characteristic 6).

But what of the other two characteristic differences between acted speech and spontaneous speech: the predetermination of content and the need for onlooker inclusion (characteristics 1 and 5)? Departing from the planned content could undermine the integrity of the sketch as a whole. Furthermore, onlooker inclusion is achieved by planning carefully what the audience needs to be told at any given time, so in this regard too, altering the content could have a detrimental effect on the product. It would seem imperative that, however improvised the approach, the content should be sufficiently faithful to what was scripted, to ensure that the story is told and the audience has all of the information necessary to appreciate the final punchline.

However, in this case, something seems to have gone wrong in relation to content. The broadcast omitted a vital element of the story (the information about the Pods taking over as guards), which invalidated the final punchline. It is not possible to tell whether this material was simply missed out, or whether it was delivered in the performance and removed during editing. If the former, then the laughter of the audience as the sketch finishes was not stimulated by the punchline, since they would not have understood it. If the latter, then the studio audience was laughing at a joke from which the subsequent television audience was excluded. Given the often considerable difference in this sketch between the camera script and the performance in terms of what is said and in what order, it is certainly not inconceivable that French and Saunders erroneously omitted a crucial part of the story. However, since the missing sequence involved another character, the assistant, it seems most likely that some version of the content was delivered in the performance, but was subsequently cut. This demonstrates that there is yet one more player in the game: the editor. Editorial decisions are made for many reasons, and the coherence of the story may not always be paramount.

Conclusion

To make a play script sound 'natural', the writer, actors, and editors must all play their part. However, 'naturalness' in a publicly performed dialogue is intrinsically different from 'naturalness' in real conversation. The script's provenance renders it inauthentic in form and content for the actors, who must work hard to gain ownership of it through familiarity. Its representation in the written medium will tend to normalize it towards written forms. The audience of onlookers requires inauthentic detail and contextualization, and a greater degree of directness in the depiction of a character's thoughts and feelings than occurs in normal conversation.

There are various means by which the gaps between natural and scripted performance can be closed, including when the actors, as writers or improvisers, play a part in the formulation of the script; and when the actors, by virtue of being the writers, are licensed to disregard the written script as a reference point[8] and present an improvised performance. But the need for a fixed version evidently extends beyond the practical requirements of production. It is necessary for quality control, to protect the integrity and comprehensibility of the final product. Improvisation is a high risk strategy because it is insufficiently formulaic for its purpose. No matter how much is gained in terms of naturalness of delivery, it is of no value if the audience loses the point.

Notes

1 French and Saunders are a British comedy duo who have worked together on stage and television since the early 1980s. The author is grateful to Dawn French for permission to use the script extracts.

2 This research was first presented at the 1995 conference of the British Association for Applied Linguistics in Southampton: Janet Cowper and Alison Wray. 'How natural can actors sound? A comparison of two acting styles in a French and Saunders sketch'. My thanks to Janet Cowper, who collected and transcribed the data for this study, for permission to reproduce the findings here.

3 http://www.bbc.co.uk/comedy/theoffice/defguide/defguide13.shtml. Accessed 10 February 2008.

4 Usually, in fact, the actors are omniscient in relation to the story in which they are participating, and it might be argued that being so makes it difficult for them to convey the state of mind of their non-omniscient character (and thus to tune in with the non-omniscient audience). In the preparation of the film *Vera Drake*, Mike Leigh withheld from the actors any information about past and future events that their character would not know, so that they could experience, through the character's eyes, the development of the story (http://en.wikipedia.org/wiki/Vera_Drake, accessed 10 February 2008). This experience might make it easier for the actors to convey through their lines the limited knowledge and vision of their character. Nevertheless, the film would be incomprehensible if it were restricted to that vision.

5 In keeping with the undertaking made at the time of the request (1995), comments are not attributed. The following actors participated in the survey: Suzy Aitchison, Peter Alexander, Jane Asher, Harry Fowler, Steve Halliwell, Suzanne Hamilton, Mary Miller, Brian Murphy, Sian Phillips, Andrew Sachs, Tim Pigott-Smith, Angela Pleasance, Kathy Staff, Julie Walters, and Timothy West.

6 Head of Comedy and Light Entertainment, BBC (2005–2007), and producer of the French and Saunders Christmas Special 1994.

7 Compare Chapters 11 and 20, where it is shown that these words are most vulnerable to (the necessity for) editing in prefabricated material.

8 Compare the account, in Chapter 4, of how the written version of an oral text becomes adopted as definitive.

PART FOUR

Examining the boundaries

16

Formulas as the default

Introduction

This chapter addresses the first of the five questions posed in Chapter 1: *Do we use formulaic language by default?* The theoretical framework adopted in this book proposes that multiword morpheme equivalent units (MEUs) will be used where possible—that is, they are the default option. According to Needs Only Analysis (NOA), we break down linguistic material only when we need to in order to access or create new meaning. The individual's aim is to avoid unnecessary processing when assigning meaning to linguistic input forms, and when assigning output forms to meanings. Where a large unit can be associated reliably with a meaning, that form-meaning pairing will be stored and subsequently preferred over one in which a meaning for the whole string is determined by meanings assigned to the components. The evidence supporting this claim is examined in this chapter. The parameters and origin of the default are dealt with in Chapter 17.

Evidence for the default

What would it look like if formulaic language were the default? What sort of mark upon patterns of usage would a preference for formulaic language be expected to have? If formulaic language suffices until an unexpected requirement in the communication of meaning arises, we could reasonably anticipate that some quantity of our everyday language will tend to remain unanalysed. Theorizing such an unevenness of analytic engagement with the language enables us to make a number of testable predictions, including the following, each of which will be considered in this chapter:

- Native speakers may be oblivious to, and tolerant of, irregular forms within units, if those units have not been analysed.
- Native speakers' intuitions about how the language operates will overlook patterns that lie within MEUs.

- Under greater processing pressure, there will be a greater reliance on formulaic language.

Unawareness and tolerance of irregular forms within morpheme equivalent units

In the NOA model, formulaicity is defined, effectively, as the product of the absence of analysis. Wherever a string of words in input is divided under NOA, it must be possible to allocate each sub-part a reliable meaning—such sub-parts will, naturally, thereby become recombinable to a greater or lesser extent. But *within* such sub-parts—irrespective of how long they are—the absence of any need (yet) to break them down into smaller parts entails the absence of assigned meaning to components of the whole in relation to that string, even if, according to some simple linguistic rule, such an assignment is entirely feasible, and indeed the sub-parts of the whole are also stored in the lexicon. If this is so, we should anticipate that native speakers can be easily surprised by the internal composition of word strings that they have never had occasion to break down.

The 'Royal Highness' paradigm

In Britain, there is a part-paradigm of expressions for referring to or addressing royalty, namely, 'Your/His/Her/Their Royal Highness(es)'. Speeches given in the presence of the Queen or a member of the Royal Family begin 'Your Royal Highness'. It is a formula, of course, and a curious one. Why is the Queen her *own* royal highness, rather than that of her people? That is, why it she not addressed as 'My Royal Highness' or 'Our Royal Highness'?[1] And why is she a *Highness* rather than, say, a *Height*? Bizarre though the epithet is, there is a good chance that readers of this paragraph who are native speakers of English will never have noticed how strange the form is, even though they are very familiar with it. Readers who are non-native speakers are rather more likely to have registered the oddity of the expression if they have previously encountered it, for reasons developed in Chapter 18.

Harry Potter and the formulaic spells

J. K. Rowling's *Harry Potter* books feature a great many magical spells, which are almost all identified by the words used to cast them.[2] Avid readers of the series can become extraordinarily knowledgeable about the minutiae of the plots, and might be expected to interrogate any superficially obscure but evidently analysable lexical material, in order fully to command its meaning and use. However, the spells do not appear to instigate such engagement. Few of the incantations themselves (as opposed to the descriptions of them—for example, the Concealment Spell) are transparently English in formation (exceptions include 'Stupefy', which renders someone unconscious). A few are built around an English root (for example, 'Flipendo',[3] which topples something over, 'Orchideous' which turns the wand into a bunch of flowers), or around a Latin or other root that happens also to occur in English (for example, 'Riddikulus', which transforms a Boggart into a form that is humorous to the caster of the spell). Other than such cases, the forms of the spells will not be decodable for a child without a knowledge of Latin (for example, *Rictusempra* > *rictus*, 'gaping mouth', *semper* 'always', which causes uncontrollable laughter), Greek (for example, *Episkey* > *episkeui* 'repair', which heals minor injuries), Aramaic (for example, *Avada Kedavra* > *avada* 'I kill', *kedavra* 'as I speak', which causes instant death), and so on.

An informal investigation with children who were very familiar with the Harry Potter books indicated that they knew the meanings of the names of spells, in the sense that they knew what they did, but they did not know *why* the spells had these names. For instance, when asked what 'Expecto Patronus' meant, children could describe how the spell brings a ghostlike animal that protects the caster, and they could identify Harry Potter's 'Patronus' as a stag. However, even though they therefore had an implicit meaning for 'Patronus', they could not readily identify a meaning for 'Expecto', despite its similarity to English 'expect'. Nor did they have any sense that another spell might be formed using 'Expecto' plus something else. They did rationalize 'Riddikulus' (mentioned earlier) as making something look 'ridiculous'. However, the manner of their reply was consistent with their having thought about it for the first time only when asked the question. That is, it did not seem to have occurred to them that the names of the spells *should* be transparent—they were satisfied with the allocation of a functional meaning to the whole expression, which they then treated as morpheme equivalent (Wray 2002b: 265–9).

Incomplete intuitions, relative to objective evidence

Do native speakers' intuitions about how the language operates overlook patterns that lie within formulas? According to Stubbs (1993: 17), "Native speakers have no reliable intuitions about … statistical tendencies [in lexical distribution]". Sinclair (2004) refers to native speaker intuitions as "elusive and sometimes inconsistent into the bargain" (p. 11), and Hunston (2002) tells us that "Intuition is a poor guide to at least four aspects of language: collocation, frequency, prosody and phraseology" (p. 20). Asking a native speaker what meaning a common word most frequently has can often result in responses that are far removed from the facts. For instance, the 'canonical' meaning of 'take' or 'give', entailing physical action, will tend to be provided, rather than the much more common bleached meaning that these verbs have in multiword verbs such as 'take note of' and 'give way' (see also Sinclair 1991: 112ff on 'back'). It could be that the assignment of meaning to items is not done on a frequency basis, but on a prototype basis. This would allow for the meaning to be centred on a usage that has more significance for how it unifies the other uses, than for the frequency with which it occurs itself. Even if that were so, however, one might anticipate that informants asked not 'what does this word mean?' but, rather, 'what are the most common meanings of this word in usage?' would be able to separate out focal meaning from frequent meaning. They cannot. Hunston's explanation is that "Although a native speaker has experience of very much more language than is contained in even the largest corpus, much of that experience remains hidden from introspection" (Hunston 2002: 20).

Accounting for poor intuitions

NOA, as an account of how we come to know what we do, offers an explanation for why introspecting about language, or using our intuition to make judgements, fails to provide us with the actual facts. However, other explanations are also possible, and two will be briefly examined first.

The first is that, even at its purest and most reliable, intuition is not pure or reliable, but rather created, or at least influenced, by psycholinguistic limitations or cultural factors:

> native-speaker intuitions ... [are] often incorrect, or at least inexact, because each of us has only a partial knowledge of the language, we have prejudices and preferences, our memory is weak, our imagination is powerful (so we can conceive of possible contexts for the most implausible utterances), and we tend to notice unusual words or structures but often overlook ordinary ones.
> (Butterfield and Krishnamurthy 2000: 32–3)

The second explanation is in some ways the very opposite. Perhaps intuition is highly reliable—a mental version of corpus software, counting up the frequencies of different patterns. In this view the reason why intuition and the corpora do not give us the same information is that they are simply measuring different material—that is, our personal experience of language is too far removed from what is found in a constructed corpus. The test of this explanation would be to gather and analyse a personal corpus. If we collected all and only the language that a certain individual had encountered and produced in his or her lifetime so far, that person's intuitions about how language normally operated ought to match the patterns revealed by computer analysis. In fact, most corpus linguists would probably predict that there would still be differences. That is, whatever it is that explains the difference between intuition about how one's language works and how it actually does work is more fundamental than an accident of the corpus sampling.

The third explanation, the one centred on NOA, is that intuition *does* give us a reliable view of something, but it is not the same thing that corpora show us. Rather, there is a particular, partial view of language that intuition is privileged to access, while there are other aspects of language that it cannot see. The explanation is premised on the assumption that when a native speaker is asked a question about how a word works, answering it entails thinking about how that word operates as a free unit. This assumption is, in fact, not really contentious, for the uses to which we put intuition are heavily focused on mastering ways of manipulating words. In the NOA model, since the 'word' is not especially privileged as a unit, we should more properly suggest that intuition accesses information about the distributions of (morpheme equivalent) lexical units—morphemes, words, and word strings.

If centred on how MEUs operate, our intuition would have no direct view of *sub*-lexical units. That is, if you asked someone about the way that 'order' is used, they would be able to access information about how *order* combines with other words to create larger units that are not lexical units in their own right, for example, 'check up on an order', 'put in height order', but they would not be able to 'see' *order* when it is one word within a multiword lexical unit, as in 'in order to'. This is the same principle by which we would see *sing* in 'sing an aria', but not in 'browsing' where, of course, it is not actually a semantic constituent, just coincidentally a form that resembles the word 'sing'. In the same way, *order* in 'in order to' does not really carry the meaning that it has as a separate item, and although historically there is no doubt some explanation for its form, etymology is not part of what we can know about a lexical unit unless we have researched it.

In fact, the differentiation between what we can and cannot 'see' using intuition is not quite so stark, because there are several cultural activities, including literacy and word games, that tend to draw our attention to the internal composition of MEUs (see Chapter 18). These insights are, however, unsystematic and are not required for using the language effectively.

It is important not to overstate the case with regard to morphological compounds, though. It might seem to be predicted, under the NOA account, that our intuition will deprive us of the insight that 'singer' contains the word 'sing'. What the NOA account actually predicts is that our intuition *might* deprive us of that insight: that is, it would be possible to use the words 'sing' and 'singer' accurately without ever registering that they were related in form and meaning. On the other hand, it is, of course, highly likely that we *would* have gained that insight, for we would easily have noticed that there is a productive pattern, 'VERB + er', meaning someone or something that 'VERB–s'. That insight would have been acquired on the basis of observing paradigmatic variation, and would result in our having a separate entry in the lexicon for 'sing' and for '–er'. However, importantly, having these two entries need not remove the entry for 'singer' (though it might—it depends on the remaining salience of the entry in the light of the new information) and the lexicon therefore is modelled as containing a great deal of redundancy (Wray 2002b: 262–68). The conservatism of NOA means that even a rather productive rule such as 'VERB + er' will not be applied to lexical entries for which there has been no evidence that it is a member. So we do not infer that there is a verb '*passenge' on account of the noun 'passenger' even though we have seen 'travel-traveller', 'voyage-voyager', 'trip-tripper', 'ride-rider', 'tour-tourer', and 'visit-visitor'.

The mismatch between intuition and the results of computer searches is, then, consistent with formulaic language being used by default. If lexical units are large unless they have been specifically interrogated, and if, as we suppose here, intuition entails examining the behaviour of lexical units, when a target item is enclosed within a lexical unit that is more than one word long, our intuitive insights will overlook it, while the computer easily finds it. An example is offered by Krishnamurthy (2004), who provides information regarding the most common collocates of the word 'burning' (see Table 16.1) He notes that not all of these collocations seem intuitively likely, including the occurrences of 'London __ burning', 'home__ burning', and 'Paris__burning'. He invites his readers to apply their intuition to think up explanations: perhaps the texts commonly feature material about World War Two; perhaps there are many references to the Great Fire of London of 1666. He notes, also, that the collocation of 'burning' with 'home' seems intuitively less plausible than with, say, 'house'.

He goes on to reveal that 167 of the 177 occurrences of 'London__burning' are in the name of the television programme *London's Burning* (ITV, 1986–2002). All 56 occurrences of 'home__burning' are in the song title 'Keep the Home Fires Burning', and all 31 occurrences of 'Paris__burning' relate to a film and play called *Paris is Burning*. These titles, being associated—as complete forms—with a specific referent in the world, seem not to contribute to the intuitive assessment of how the component words can occur.[4]

	2 words before	1 word before		1 word after	2 words after
	London	wood		desire	fuel
	smell	fires		ambition	hole
Collocates in decreasing order of frequency	home	coal		stove	fuel
	looting	fire		oil	wells
	fire	flag		question	midnight
	fires	cross	**burning**	issue	looting
	week	book		sensation	candle
	smoke	fuel		fossil	
	Paris	eyes		building	
	sun	oil		issues	
	fossil	light		rubber	

Table 16.1 The most common proximate noun collocates of 'burning' (Krishnamurty 2004)

The acquisition of logical forms

A related line of evidence for a default preference for large units, and the application of analysis only according to need, comes from a study of the acquisition of Esperanto (Bergen 2001). According to standard theoretical models, the child's job in first language acquisition is to identify the underlying regularity of the system. The natural linguistic irregularities that the child encounters are therefore taken to be an irritating inconvenience. It follows, within that theoretical view, that should a child's input be totally regular, the process of acquisition would be a smooth one, in which the system was quickly and reliably adopted. However, Bergen found differently.

He gathered data from eight of the estimated 350 children worldwide who are first language speakers of Esperanto, an artificial language that is designed to be entirely regular and transparent. He found that several regular features of the Standard form of Esperanto (SE) were not present in the Native Esperanto (NE) speech of the children, the absence of them rendering the NE system less regular and complete than that of SE. That is, it seems that the children had failed to see certain regular patterns in the input, and had not extrapolated from the evidence they did get, to construct a complete and regular linguistic system.

The shortfalls in their system extended across the domains of grammatical morphology (tense and aspect), lexical morphology, and phonology. They introduced phonologically reduced forms, for instance, which removed morphological information. This information, when present, completed the regular system and, being absent, left gaps in that system. The accusative marker was used in only half of the contexts in which it would appear in SE (p. 586) and even this figure was boosted by the fact that the marker occurred in a common conventionalized greeting—that is, it was the *novel* constructions that were not being given the form.

The data suggest that the children had turned the simple system underlying the input they had received into a much more complex one, by applying only half-rules, and only some of the time. Bergen comments that the depleted tense and aspect system of NE is "startling ... because it seems to contradict bioprogram and other universalist predictions" (p. 580). Bergen's findings are, however, consistent with the default model: the children's extrapolation of patterns was limited to where they had seen variation in the input. Where they had not, they had accepted the largest unvarying unit as a single item, complete with any phonological reduction. Having not analysed the internal components, they could not restore such reductions to their full form.[5]

The default position *in extremis*

The third potential pointer towards formulaic language use being the default option is that it is relied upon to a greater extent as processing demands increase. Here we have to be careful to avoid circularity, since one of the standard ways to identify instances when a speaker is under increased processing pressure—arising from shared attention to different tasks, for instance—is, precisely, to note the increased reliance on formulaic responses. Therefore, it is safer to consider cases in which the processing pressures are inherent rather than transitory, and to explore the extent to which formulaic language represents a *solution* to the constraints rather than simply an expression of them.

Clinical evidence for formulaicity as the default

It is generally accepted that 'there is a limited pool of operational resources available to perform computations, such that processing and storage of linguistic information is degraded when demands exceed available resources' (Weismer 2004: 349). Communication disorders bring with them high demands in relation to the use of language, and therefore default formulaic processing might be expected to contribute to alleviating them. Formulaic sequences are noticeably present in a range of disabilities affecting language, including aphasia, autism, Alzheimer's Disease, and agenesis of the corpus callosum (Wray 2008a). The following sections explore the role that they might be playing.

Autism

Perhaps the condition most archetypically associated with formulaicity is autism, where formulaic sequences occur as part of the more general tendency towards "routines and rituals always ... carried out in precisely the same way" (Paul 2004: 117). An autistic person may have a particular expression for opening conversations, and may talk about the same topics always using the same words (Prizant 1983: 299). In addition, for a proportion of people with autism, judged variously to be between forty and seventy-five per cent (for example, Rutter 1968; Paul 2004), a notable linguistic behaviour is *echolalia*, the repetition of input. In *delayed echolalia* autistic people "repeat snatches of language they have heard earlier, from other people or on TV, radio, and so on" (Paul 2004: 116). *Immediate echolalia* entails "a direct parroting of speech directed to them" (ibid.), though there can also be changes to the form that indicate some awareness of the structure of the language, for example, replying to 'Do you want a drink?' with 'Do I want a drink' (Roberts 1989: 277).

Repeated linguistic behaviour, including echolalia, appears to indicate whereabouts a person is situated on a continuum of severity on the autistic spectrum. The explanation may lie in the use of formulaicity as a means for coping with interaction in an overwhelming and confusing world. There would be, under such an account, a reliance on default processing in order to cope with stressful experiences, with the extent of the behaviour determined by the threshold at which the formulaic/non-formulaic language switch is made. As McEvoy, Loveland, and Landry (1988) put it:

> Autistic children appear to lack many of the strategies for communication and social development present in normal children; consequently, echolalia may be used in situations where normal children would use other skills ... Even those echoes that serve only a turn-taking function ... can help to

maintain social exchange in the face of severe linguistic deficits. Similarly, echolalia may be the only strategy available for responding when a question or statement is beyond the child's comprehension.
(pp. 666–7)

However, as McEvoy *et al.*'s observation indicates, intertwined with the notion that formulaic language provides an easier way to achieve interaction is the idea that there is an underlying linguistic deficit too. Rydell and Mirenda (1991), similarly, propose that formulaic language can act as a filler 'in situations where the cognitive demands exceed the child's linguistic capacity' (p. 135). This indicates that autism entails two potentially distinct problems—the need for repetitive behaviour to make good a shortfall in the capacity to interact and/or cope with incoming information; and reduced linguistic abilities (Wray 2008a). Prizant (1983) proposes that these two may interact, as the person becomes trapped in a gestalt (i.e. holistic) approach to processing,[6] creating a vicious circle:

> A gestalt mode of processing may actually preclude the types of ongoing analysis necessary for subtle listener-sensitive adjustments, resulting in a reliance on familiar routine.
> (p. 303)

If, as Prizant suggests, the situation not only constrains the language, but the language also constrains the capacity to handle the situation,[7] there might be scope to alter the balance from either end, meaning that an individual's default threshold can move, or be moved through intervention. This seems to be so. As regards natural development, echolalia is, for some autistic children, a temporary phase—a step on the route to acquiring a more normal range of language abilities. This may be because repeating input offers them additional chances to process it (Prizant and Duchan 1981: 242). Consequently, for some individuals, the amount of echolalia decreases as general linguistic ability increases (McEvoy *et al.* 1988).

The potential for movement also means that appropriate support will enable individuals to develop a wider range of linguistic responses to situations:

> Through modification and expansion of a child's echolalic utterances in a natural context, a well-trained clinician can help an autistic child develop more effective communication with people and the environment. Success in communication would, therefore, motivate the autistic child to want to learn language, initiate interaction with others, and become an active member of the world around him.
> (Prizant and Duchan 1981: 248)

Accounts of how formulaic language is used by people with autism generally present its use as a *retreat* from the norm. However, if formulaic language represents the default choice for all of us, then autistic people are not doing something different, just doing it in a broader range of situations, because the threshold above which they can escape into more novel expression is partly or completely beyond their reach.

Alzheimer's Disease

Where formulaic language is, for some autistic people, a route *into* language and communication, for people with Alzheimer's Disease it seems to represent the final part of the route *out* of it, being the last coherent language produced. David Snowdon reports that in his longitudinal study of ageing nuns (for example, Snowdon *et al.* 1996; Snowdon 2001, 2003) there were individuals who "could barely articulate a sentence, yet ... managed to answer the priest with appropriate responses" (Snowdon 2001: 22). Such evidence underlines how previous familiarity, a strong functional—even performative—role, and an external trigger are characteristics of formulaic production. In Alzheimer's Disease, formulaic sequences seem to manifest progressively with the deteriorating condition, along with increasing word-finding difficulties, a reduction in focus during story-telling, lower idea density per utterance, and less grammatical complexity (Kemper, Greiner, Marquis, Prenovost, and Mitzner 2001; Orange 2001; Venneri, Forbes-McKay, and Shanks 2005). The fluent production of an MEU could inflate estimates of the remaining command of grammar and lexis, since even a very sophisticated formulation could be retrieved holistically with the same amount of grammatical processing as is required for a single word. It is therefore important to spot formulaic material and ascertain whether it might be morpheme equivalent.[8] Because formulaic sequences often convey functionally effective propositions, a person with Alzheimer's Disease may continue to say appropriate things even when, for other reasons, there is doubt about whether they are really meant. In the extracts in Figure 16.1 (from Brewer 2005: 91–3), Ruth's son (CB) tells her that her husband has died. It is not clear whether her responses have been appositely selected or not.

CB   ... He was my Daddy too, right?
RB   That might be possible

...

CB   I told you yesterday
RB   I didn't hear you

...

CB   ... I just wanted to be sure you knew about it. That's why I'm telling you again. Okay?
RB   Well, who's to blame for it

...

CB   We're going to have a funeral for him Monday
RB   Well, I can't help that either

Figure 16.1   Conversation with a person with Alzheimer's Disease (from Brewer 2005: 91–3)

As in aphasia (below), fillers and little phrases are often used by people with Alzheimer's Disease to replace items that cannot be accessed, or to hold the turn: 'It is as if she were buying a fraction of time to think, retaining the floor as a means of maintaining social connection' (Davis and Bernstein 2005: 67). These items, then, appear to be part of a default level of linguistic operation, which leads to the sometimes rather arbitrary retrieval of whatever can be turned to use.

Aphasia

Even though it was the incidence of formulaic sequences in aphasia that, as early as the seventeenth century, first led clinicians to puzzle about how the human brain processed language (see Benton and Joynt 1960; Van Lancker 1987; Wray 2002b: chapter 12; Van Lancker Sidtis and Postman 2006, for overviews), it is their ubiquity in aphasia that, arguably, presents the greatest explanatory challenge. Formulaic sequences are seen in most types of aphasia, which—given the range of causes and symptoms associated with different aphasias—certainly suggests that they represent a common fall-back option. Nevertheless, it is puzzling that they should, for instance, manifest in both fluent and non-fluent aphasias (though not to an equal extent, Van Lancker Sidtis and Postman 2006). It is possible to construe fluent aphasia as featuring the production of formulaic frames that cannot be appropriately completed because of word-finding difficulties (Wray 2002b: 222ff) while in non-fluent aphasia the capacity to access single lexical units extends to lexical entries that happen to be more than one word long. Certainly, in all cases, the availability of formulaic sequences is most easily explained if they are single lexical units retrieved holistically (i.e. MEUs), since the alternative would be that the damaged grammatical and/or lexical retrieval mechanisms are temporarily reactivated. However, it is also necessary to explain why only a handful of the multiword units previously known to a person tend to remain accessible, rather than all of them, and why, if they are lexical units just like words, they appear to be less affected by the trauma than words are.

A plausible reason why multiword MEUs would be particularly resilient is that they have salient interactional functions for the speaker.[9] Indeed, some people with aphasia deploy them with such skill in conversation that the full extent of the underlying deficit is easy to underestimate (Van Lancker Sidtis 2004). Studies of conversational interaction with and between aphasic people have revealed that formulaic sequences can facilitate a measure of social engagement and integration that formal tests belie the potential for (McElduff and Drummond 1991; Oelschlaeger and Damico 1998).

Wray (2002b: chapter 13) explains the patterns of retention of MEUs[10] by linking discourse function to processing locus, something that could account of the variety of brain areas that have been associated with formulaic sequence production and comprehension in different studies (for example, Van Lancker Sidtis and Postman 2006). She suggests that lexical units with strong functional roles may be accessible from the areas of the brain handling the cognitive activity that customarily triggers their use (in addition to the areas of the left hemisphere that are activated when combining units). A formulaic greeting might be triggered more or less as a reflex when a familiar face is recognized. The same aphasic speaker who aptly produces a phrase in response to a functional stimulus is likely to be quite unable to produce the phrase on request, since the stimulus, in that case, is no longer functional but metalinguistic, requiring access via the damaged 'language' region of the left hemisphere.[11] This 'alternative access' account is distinct from the 'default processing' hypothesis, but far from incompatible with it. It would be because multiword strings are maintained in the lexicon as the default way of expressing their message that it was possible to access them easily without the activity of the standard linguistic processing routes.

Idiom comprehension

One puzzling aspect of patterns observed in clinical linguistic research is that idiom comprehension is very poor in almost all impaired groups, even those with a high productive ability for formulaic sequences. Since idioms are generally viewed as the most clearly identifiable type of formulaic sequence, how might this finding be explained in terms of the default processing model?

Interest in idiom comprehension was for some time particularly focused on individuals with right hemisphere damage. Although most language processing is generally associated with the left hemisphere, right hemisphere damage does have an effect on some aspects of language comprehension and performance (Code 1987), particularly those generally viewed as 'holistic'. Besides difficulties with the comprehension of idioms and metaphors, people with damage to the right hemisphere tend to have disruption to their ability to understand relevance, inference, prosody, and pragmatics, including humour (Chantraine, Joanette, and Ska 1998; Tompkins, Fassbinder, Lehman-Blake, and Baumgaertner 2002; Heath and Blonder 2005; Jung-Beeman 2005). It is now clear that the left and right hemispheres are highly interdependent (Efron 1990; Damasio, Tranel, Grabowski, Adolphs, and Damasio 2004; Poeppel and Hickok 2004), and increasing attention has been paid to agenesis of the corpus callosum, a condition in which the main link between the two hemispheres has not developed properly (Paul, Van Lancker Sidtis, Schieffer, Dietrich, and Brown 2003). On the basis of this evidence, it has been hypothesized that the normal brain synthesizes macro- and micro-interpretations of input. The right hemisphere 'weakly activates large diffuse semantic fields, including information distantly related to the words' while the left hemisphere 'strongly activates small and focused semantic fields' (Jung-Beeman 2005: 514). Natural language comprehension occurs by means of bilateral activity which ensures the integration of the information, so that the specific message is understood within its communicative context (Paul *et al.* 2003: 318).

The corollary of that proposal is that right hemisphere damage would weaken the role of the macro-interpretation, making it more difficult to select the holistic meaning of an idiom over its literal meaning—and this is indeed what is found. However, it should also follow that if the left hemisphere is damaged, it will be the literal interpretation that is difficult to bring into the frame, so that the holistic meaning of an idiom is preferred. And this is not so (Papagno and Genoni 2004; Papagno, Tabossi, Colombo, and Zampetti 2004). A preference for literal interpretations of idioms is also found in agenesis of the corpus callosum (Paul *et al.* 2003; Huber-Okrainec, Blaser, and Dennis 2005), Alzheimer's Disease (Papagno, Lucchelli, Muggia, and Rizzo 2003), and autism (Qualls, Lantz, Pietrzyk, Blood, and Hammer 2004). The first condition, as just noted, affects interhemispheric connectivity. The default model would naturally predict that if a full comparison, or integration, of information was not possible, the default choice would be the holistic one, *not* the componential one. Similarly, we have seen that both Alzheimer's Disease and autism feature a reliance on formulaic sequences. If the default is, as predicted, the holistic choice then, why is it not in the case of idiom identification?

A possible explanation comes from considering the nature of the tasks used to test idiom comprehension.[12] A classic approach is to show the subject four cartoons, three depicting potential interpretations of the idiom, and one distracter. For the stimulus 'he paid an arm and a leg for it', the pictures might include one of a man handing over a large quantity of cash, and another of him handing over bodyparts. Performing well on the text entails understanding the 'game' of language, since, objectively, either of the two pictures just described is potentially appropriate, and preferring the non-literal over the literal is a matter of how one infers the pragmatics of the activity. Furthermore, in the case of those with impaired linguistic comprehension, the task may actually close down processing opportunities that are available to them in normal interaction. The task is inherently decontextualized and metalinguistic—being asked the meaning of an idiom or proverb in a test is a matter of *mention*, which is not the same as *use*. It is plausible that a person who could understand the idiom in a communicative context, when it carried its normal functional load, would not be able to understand it out of that context, where it was an object of linguistic analysis. It may be that the holistic reading is never actually accessed in the test.

In other words, testing may, simply, force subjects away from the default (Wray 1992), into the type of processing that has been made laborious and ineffectual by their impairment. Much as a low level foreign language learner might struggle to decode the individual words of an expression she knows holistically, so the metalinguistic focus on an expression like 'he paid an arm and a leg for it' might result in a paltry outcome that extends no further than recognizing the words for one or two limbs. In such circumstances (i.e. where decoding has resulted in 'arm ... leg') it would not be surprising for the subject to select the picture most consistent with that minimal detail. The inference that the idiom had been taken literally would, in such circumstances, be a major over-interpretation of the subject's response, and the accompanying inference that the idiomatic reading was not available to the subject *at all* might also be inaccurate.

In the light of the myriad evidence that people with aphasia and Alzheimer's Disease perform better in real interaction than they do in formal tests (McElduff and Drummond 1991; Edwards and Knott 1994; Oelschlaeger and Damico 1998; Perkins, Whitworth, and Lesser 1998; Bucks, Singh, Cuerden, and Wilcock 2000; Snowdon 2001; Davis 2005; Davis and Bernstein 2005), it would seem sensible to avoid metalinguistic testing of the type used for idiom comprehension altogether, in favour of observations of language used contextualized in genuine communication. The most effective way to allow individuals to maximize their capacity to apply default level processing (thus, with the minimum additional processing stress) will be to mimic the natural contexts in which the default operates.

Conclusion

Languages like English have a range of ways to express meanings using regular and transparent formulations. Yet native speakers tolerate the retention of irregularity and opacity and—the Esperanto study by Bergen (2001) suggests—introduce it where it does not exist. Native speaker intuition appears blind to many common patterns in language, something that cannot easily be explained if we fully engage with the potential for compositionality that a language like English offers. Language under pressure, as in communication disorders, has been shown commonly to feature the retention of formulaic material when novel compositions are not possible, with interactional function apparently a primary trigger. The various evidence reviewed in this chapter suggests that if the default processing strategy for humans were not to engage in the minimal possible processing capable of matching forms with meanings, languages would not look the way they do.

Notes

1 Third person reference to members of the Royal Family uses the third person possessive, thus 'His Royal Highness the Duke of York', 'Her Royal Highness Princess Anne', and 'Their Royal Highnesses Prince William and Prince Harry'. However, the paradigm is, as noted, incomplete, for the first person is not used, even by Royal Family members themselves for self-reference. It is used creatively, however, for comic effect, as in Thackeray's satire *The Rose and the Ring*, "Is it to be pistols, or swords, Captain?", asks Bulbo. "I'm a pretty good hand with both, and I'll do for Prince Giglio as sure as my name is My Royal Highness Prince Bulbo" (Thackeray, 1855/1964: 66, also 20). Googling the expression 'My Royal Highness' brings up flippant usages by individuals styling themselves as, for instance, 'Imp Queen and World Monarch' (http://impqueen.blogspot.com/), accessed 31 January 2008, but it continues to sound odd to the native speaker.

2 The information given here is drawn in part from the Wikipedia entry, *Spells in Harry Potter*, http://en.wikipedia.org/wiki/Spells_in_Harry_ Potter, and *The Harry Potter Lexicon Encyclopedia of Spells*, http://www. hp-lexicon.org/magic/spells/spells.html, both accessed 31 January 2008.

3 This spell does not appear in any of the books, only in spin-off games and videos.

4 Sinclair (1991: 117), recognizing the capacity for the corpus sample to pull up such proper names, excludes from his analysis of 'back' its collocation with 'anger', which occurs only in the play title *Look Back in Anger*.

5 Bergen's own interpretation of his findings is that the child 'purifies' a language, by figuring out which features of it are superfluous, so that Esperanto is revealed to have more detail than the child needs. The NOA model is simultaneously more extreme and less extreme. It is more extreme because it proposes that the 'superfluousness' is not a genuine and permanent feature of the language per se (though it can be) but rather an illusion created by the limitations of the child's input—future input may reveal that a particular feature is, in fact, important. However, since the patterns of usage for a language are only a subset of what is possible, native speakers will, indeed, acquire and retain a sense that there are things that you *can* say in the language but that you *don't* say. Meanwhile NOA offers a *less* extreme scenario regarding the role of the child in this process. The child is *not* identifying all the moving parts and then figuring out which subset it really needs. Rather, it is identifying only the parts that it has seen move, and will deal with identifying more only when the need to do so arises.

6 See Chapters 20 and 21 for a range of explorations of what happens when one is trapped in formulaicity.

7 Compare Rehbein (1987) who found that Turkish immigrant workers in Germany defined their needs to match the language they could use to achieve them.

8 As noted in Chapters 1, 2, and 8, it is only possible to talk of an MEU in the context of the theoretical framework. Otherwise, one must refer to the outward manifestation of formulaicity, i.e. the formulaic sequence, which is hypothesized to be, but may not be, an MEU.

9 The function view also predicts that, even if as many or more single words were available, it would be the phrases that were most noticeable, since they would be easier to interpret as meaningful when produced as an isolated choice.

10 Though the term 'morpheme equivalent unit' is not used in Wray (2002b).

11 For instance, sentence openers indicating personal stance, such as 'I want', 'You can't', 'I don't', and 'I couldn't' have been observed across different studies of left hemisphere-damaged individuals with severe impairment for novel language production (Van Lancker Sidtis and Postman 2006).

12 A further problem with idiom stimuli in such experiments is described in Chapter 3.

17
Origin and dynamics of formulaic language

Introduction

Continuing the 'default' theme, this chapter examines the question: *What determines the level of formulaicity in language?* Three sub-questions will be used to address this question: *How would the default have come about? Under what circumstances would the default shift?* and *How would different default boundaries between individuals affect their communication?*

How would the default have come about?

Formulaicity and language evolution

Why should humans have developed a default preference for using large lexical units over smaller ones? It has generally been assumed that using formulaic language is a means of relieving processing pressure arising from limitations in short term/working memory[1] capacity (see Wray 2002b: 15–16). The precise nature of these limitations continues to be discussed (Was and Woltz 2007 provide one recent overview). Particularly relevant to the discussions in this chapter is the proposal by Just and Carpenter (1992) that there are individual differences in the amount of working memory available during processing. This would explain why some people are better at handling complex linguistic information than others. Ericsson and Kintsch (1995) suggest that such differences need not be absolute, and that it is possible to augment one's abilities through practice:

> in skilled activities, acquired memory skills allow [the] products [of interim operations] to be stored in long-term memory and kept directly accessible by means of retrieval cues in short-term memory.
> (p. 211)

Chipere (2003) draws on Ericsson and Kintsch's idea to explain differences in the comprehension of complex embedded sentences in native and non-native speakers with different levels of language-focused education (compare Chapter 5 and Wray 2008b).

In fact, it is inherent to conceiving language as having the property of recursion[2] (Hauser, Chomsky, and Fitch 2002), that it will be possible to create sentences that are too difficult to hold in working memory during decoding, even though grammaticality is not breached. Recursion theoretically renders to language the property of discrete infinity,[3] for "[t]here is no longest sentence (any candidate sentence can be trumped by, for example, embedding it in 'Mary thinks that . . .'), and there is no nonarbitrary upper bound to sentence length" (Hauser *et al.* 2002: 1571).

In the light of all this, in asking how formulaic language came into the picture to alleviate processing pressure, it is apposite to establish why humans should ever have come to possess a greater scope for linguistic creativity and expression than can easily be handled by working memory. One explanation commonly offered is that our language capacity evolved quickly—and independently of working memory—so that the latter did not increase its power in tandem. Hauser *et al.* (2002) see recursion as a late and species-specific addition to an underlying system developed over a much longer evolutionary time frame. The decoupling of this final piece in the language jigsaw from everything else helps explain why it seems out of kilter with what we need for effective communication.[4] In fact, it could have emerged not in response to communicative need at all, but as a spandrel (side-product) of other changes (Lightfoot 2000).

Locating the origins of formulaic language in the evolutionary account depends, naturally, on what else is in the story. Taking into account the assumption that the complexities associated with recursion arose late, we can consider two scenarios that between them illustrate the main possibilities.

Formulaic language to the rescue

The first scenario supposes that our pre-modern ancestors initially developed a primitive combinatorial language, much simpler than modern language, and that it did not place over-heavy processing demands upon its users. At that stage, no formulaic language was necessary, since there was no processing strain entailed in encoding and decoding messages. However, at a later point, there was a transition from this protolanguage to full modern human language. It introduced additional complexity and, at the point when working memory could not longer cope, a rescue strategy was needed to minimize the processing demands. This strategy entailed the processing of language in larger chunks.

One model of combinatorial human protolanguage compatible with the first part of this scenario is that of Bickerton (1996, 1998, 2000; Calvin and Bickerton 2000). His protolanguage features proto-nouns and proto-verbs arranged without grammar. Such a protolanguage is powerful in terms of its referential scope, but weak in its expression of the relationships between items. What cannot be encoded grammatically must be inferred pragmatically, placing a major burden on the hearer. For instance, the string 'mammoth run' could mean 'Look, there's a mammoth running', 'Run, there's a mammoth coming', 'Run after that mammoth', 'When you run, you look like a mammoth', etc.—it would be for the hearer to decide which. Bickerton offers a plausible model for the transition from this protolanguage to full human language, one aspect of which is the introduction of recursion (though there are other changes too).

Jackendoff (2002: chapter 8) also offers a combinatorial protolanguage model. Like Bickerton's, it has proto-nouns and proto-verbs, but in addition it has a simple linear grammar, which enables both a differentiation between 'dog bite man' and 'man bite dog' and a measure of semantically-governed hierarchy on the basis of modifiers being adjacent to the item they modify. For him, too, the transition to our full linguistic capacity entails the introduction of Universal Grammar, central to which is recursion.

While neither Bickerton nor Jackendoff seek to accommodate, within their respective protolanguage models, the evolution of formulaic language, both accounts entail a sufficiently simple protolanguage phase for there not to be any need to take refuge in formulaicity at that stage. Therefore we must infer that it would arise after the final transition stage, once there was more pressure on processing.

Thus, in this scenario, formulaic language is a post hoc introduction to language processing, grafted onto the existing system. To put it another way, the lexical units are small first, and only large later. Such an account makes it easy to explain why those under extreme processing pressure should use formulaic language (for example, people with language and communication disorders, see Chapter 16). However, it is less easy to explain other evidence of default processing described in Chapter 16—why we find the juxtaposition of a holistic and componential meaning surprising and humorous, and why our intuition for language patterns seems to overlook the contents of MEUs. These features suggest that we apply a large-unit approach *first*—something that the post hoc story could only accommodate if our entire approach to processing was at some point turned upside down.

Formulaic language first

The second scenario better explains why the default preference for larger rather than smaller lexical units would be found in all language users today—it is a throwback to our evolutionary past. Rather than formulaicity arising late in response to newly-encountered challenges in processing, it was there from the start, predating componential language altogether. This means that when fully modern language appeared, it did so against the backdrop of an existing holistic approach to communication, and the two always worked together to achieve the most effective meaning using the least demanding combination of large and small lexical units available. The combinatory system was able to evolve options that could not be easily supported by working memory, because basic communication was always assured through holistic means. In other words, the new opportunities of the combinatory system could become more extreme because they did not carry the weight of moment by moment communication for survival.

In Wray's (1998, 2000b, 2002a) holistic protolanguage model, communication is achieved using single lexical items with complex meanings, but no combinatorial parts. They are, in other words, MEUs, representing complete propositions. For instance, typical holistic protolanguage form-meaning pairs might be *kaluma* 'sit here' and *tabiku* 'give it to her', the forms being arbitrary and devoid of constituent parts, while the meaning is complex. Such a lexical inventory would render a much less flexible communication system than a combinatorial protolanguage, but one in which propositions could be understood without relying over-heavily on pragmatics. Were there to be a different phonological form for every conceivable idea the system would, of course, be unworkable. So while the lexicon would restrict what could be said (see Chapter 21 for more exploration of this issue), items would also need to apply to enough situations to be remembered. Wray accommodates the latter by hypothesizing that protolanguage items apply to all referents within a given semantic class, for example, female people, edible objects.

Wray envisages the transition from protolanguage to full human language as a progressive fragmentation process, through the instantiation of Needs Only Analysis (NOA). In other words, in this model full human language began to emerge when need drove users to notice, and extract, serendipitous patterns in what had, until that point, been unanalysed form-meaning pairs with complete propositional meanings.

Thus it might be noticed that (by chance) *kaluma* 'sit here' and, say, *demani* 'come here' share both the segment *ma* and a meaning of proximity, making it easy to segment *kaluma* into *kalu* 'sit' and *ma* 'here', and *demani* into *de_ni* 'come' and *ma* 'here'.[5] In order to consolidate that analysis, further examples might be sought, or created through re-orientation and hypercorrection. For instance, if *madiku* meant 'give me that', it might be reconstrued as 'bring that here', giving *ma* 'here' and *diku* 'bring that', the latter itself potentially able to be broken down at a later date.[6] Meanwhile, an occurrence of *na* that was given the same meaning might be 'corrected' to *ma*.

The central difference between the combinatory and holistic protolanguage accounts lies in how they construe the capacity for creative expression at different points in human evolution. A holistic protolanguage would substantially hold back creativity (see Chapter 21), until segmentation provided an explosion of opportunity for combinations, to which recursion could be applied.[7] Indeed, although the two scenario types just described are superficially in opposition, Wray (2002a) and K. Smith (2006) have both noted that they are quite easy to accommodate within a single temporally-sensitive account. It may, indeed, be seen that the holistic protolanguage scenario is different from the combinatorial protolanguage account in only one regard:

the semantic content of lexical units. In the holistic model, a single lexical unit expresses an entire proposition, so there is no need to combine them structurally. Once such units are segmented, they no longer express propositions, and so the need arises to establish ways of combining them. The payoff is a much greater range of propositions that can be expressed, but the cost is the need for combinatory rules which put pressure on processing.

Thus it is possible to tell a single story, of a holistic protolanguage, followed by the development of a combinatorial system alongside it. Wray argues, simply, that if there was a Bickerton-style protolanguage it would be an unstable and shortlived phase, developing very quickly into something in which the onus was removed from the hearer to interpret utterances using pragmatics. Jackendoff's linear grammar model could be that more stable phase, located before the introduction of recursion, and after a long and stable holistic protolanguage phase.

A modern example

It can be difficult to imagine just how recombinable components could emerge from irreducible form-meaning pairs, as described above. One modern example is possibly seen in the recent history of the Māori language (Holman 2007). Referring to expressions like *oho rere te mauri* (an expression signifying shock), *tihei mauri ora* (an expression used to avert evil after a sneeze), *mauri rere* ('panic stricken'), and *mauri tau* ('absence of panic') Holman hypothesizes that until relatively recently 'such phrases were understood in total, without the speakers having to consider what *mauri* meant in isolation' (p. 357).

The anthropologist Elsdon Best "complained ... that many *karakia* [incantations] that he encountered in the mid-1890s were virtually untranslatable, so ancient were the formulations and so encoded the language structures ... Their 'meaning' was contained in their power: it was not simply a question of intelligibility, but of efficacy" (ibid.). Best was more than an observer, however. Holman recounts how he came upon the scene looking for "'meanings' shaped by a post-Enlightenment quest for taxonomies that would order a world of intelligible systems" (p. 358). He first pinned down, and then promulgated amongst Māori speakers, an interpretation of *mauri* as 'life principle, thymos of man'—a reflection of nineteenth century anthropological speculations, rather than traditional Māori perceptions. On this basis, it became possible, post hoc, to assign more 'exact' meanings to the phrases (above), thereby reconstruing for the post-traditional Māori society what their own spiritual vocabulary 'really' signified. In consequence, *Te Matatiki*, a dictionary of new words coined for use in contemporary Māori (Māori Language Commission 1996), offers *mauri moe* 'the unconscious' from Best's definition of *mauri* plus *moe* 'sleep, dream', *mauri ngaro* 'coma' (> *mauri* plus *ngaro* 'absent, disappeared'), *mauri ora* 'awake' (> *mauri* plus *ora* 'well, in health'), and *mauri pōtere* 'subconscious' (> *mauri* plus *pōtere* 'drift about, backwards and forwards') (p. 194).

Continuity

To sum up, one explanation for the origin of default formulaic processing is that it has always been there. According to the holistic protolanguage model, it was the emergence of NOA acting upon lexical units expressing complete propositions that triggered the transition to full modern language. Since the driving force for NOA is *need* triggered by interaction, a plausible catalyst for its emergence would be contact with outsiders (for example, Best engaging with Māori). This possibility is all the more credible in the light of other evidence that contact with outsiders may shift the balance of formulaic to freshly-configured language. The next section explores this evidence.

Shifting the default boundary

In Chapter 5, it was suggested that the balance between formulaic and specially-constructed word strings is not fixed, but rather set according to the amount of contextual and cultural knowledge shared by the speaker and hearer. This idea is now developed in more detail, in order to establish the circumstances under which the default boundary might change.[8]

Idealized scenarios of language use and language change

In line with Thurston (1987, 1989, 1994), the use of language within a small, uniform community is termed 'esoteric'. That is, the community faces inwards and, because there is so much shared knowledge about cultural practices and everyday life, it is possible to speak in jargon, using allusion, metaphor, and inexplicit reference, without communication breaking down. A language used exclusively esoterically is likely only ever to be learnt in infancy by members of the community. As a result, the forms of the language (morphological, phonological, lexical, and grammatical) are filtered only through the tolerant capacity of the infant to acquire complex, irregular material on the basis of NOA, so that the forms perpetuate.[9] The result is that a language used only esoterically will be very difficult for outsider adults to learn, and native speakers, while fully able to manipulate their language within the bounds of its normal range of meanings, may lack the easy capacity to extend that creativity to new the forms—as Mithun (1989: 311), indeed, reports of adult native speakers of Mohawk. A supplementary type of esoteric communication can develop in adulthood within a subgroup of specialists. Newsome (2005), for instance, examines the jargon used by aircraft maintenance engineers. Although, of course, the acquisition of specialist jargon does not occur in childhood, it does, as Newsome found in her study, characteristically entail a long apprenticeship.[10]

If formulaicity operates by default, humans will engage in as little processing as they can, as they attempt to find meaning in what they hear and try to convey their intended meaning through what they say. Naturally, conveying meaning effectively entails developing a sensitivity to what hearers are likely to infer, and, again, the assumption is conservative: that hearers will also try to assign meaning with the least possible processing.

The default (low) level of compositionality that easily supports esoteric communication comes under pressure when communication with outsiders is necessary (Wray and Grace 2007). Outsiders may be speakers of other languages, or speakers of the same language but who are not part of a subcommunity that has its own esoteric code. Outsiders, by definition, do not share the insiders' knowledge and practices, and so less can be taken for granted when referring to entities, actions, values, and so on, that would be easily understood by an insider.[11] Efforts must be made by both parties if there is a desire to communicate effectively (as opposed to maintain social distance). Where both parties share a core language, it may simply be a question of glossing technical terms. Where the outsider is actually learning the language, the combination of the adult learners' errors, based on looking for pattern that is not there (see Chapter 18 and Wray 2002b: chapters 10–11), and the insider's own awareness of where the potential problems lie, may lead to the simplification of complex forms, the regularization of irregular ones, and the augmentation of the lexicon, to match indivisible lexical units with others constructed from transparent parts.

Consistently talking with strangers constitutes 'exoteric'—i.e. outward-facing—communication, and the effect on a language of being drawn into exoteric usage is likely to be long-lasting, even if, subsequently, the language reverts to only esoteric use. Figure 17.1 shows[12] how a language that has only ever been used esoterically supplies the input for the added transparency and compositionality that arises when it is turned to exoteric use (Scenario B). The effects of these changes begin to leak back into the way that the language is used esoterically, leaving it with more compositionality and system than it previously had (Scenario C). These augmentations offer speakers insights into the language that can be used to extend the bounds of creativity, so that a language that adopts, even temporarily, exoteric usage, will be enriched in its capacity to express new ideas.

However, the extent to which these opportunities are exploited will depend on the need to express the new idea, and that in turn will be determined by the activities of the group. Very often, even brief contact with outsiders will cause, or will have been caused by, other social and cultural changes, and it will be those that create and sustain the need to exploit the changes in the language. Urbanization and/or political unification will probably create a permanent need for the flexibility to re-engage exoterically, so that most speakers are diglossic (Kay 1977). The reason is that these changes bring about social stratification, with experts, specialists, and socially and culturally separate subgroups that may use esoteric encoding to demarcate themselves.

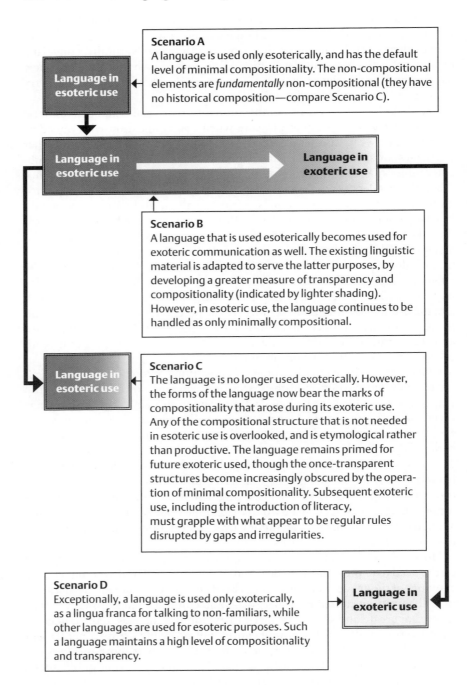

Figure 17.1 A language used esoterically and exoterically

If, after a period of exoteric usage, the language reverts to being used only with, say, relations, friends, and acquaintances, then even with the enhanced opportunities, there will be a reversion to the default level of compositionality. The language will carry evidence of the intervention (Scenario C in Figure 17.1), and the traces of additional compositionality and transparency will make it a little easier than it was in Scenario A to make a transition to exoteric use in the future: there will be more evidence of regular system on which to hang principles of patterns. However, the longer the period of esoteric-only usage, the more unreliable the once regular and transparent forms will become under the influence of the default level of processing. Found only inside certain common formulations, and not used productively, they will not display paradigmatic variation, and, under NOA, it will be the larger formulations that are dealt with, and stored as single lexical units, i.e. MEUs. Over time, what was once regular will drift into irregularity, as described in Chapter 2.

Scenario D presents an alternative progression for a language. It occurs if the language becomes adopted as a lingua franca and is no longer used as the native language of any group. In the absence of any esoteric usage, and any infant acquisition, it will become fully controlled by adults who seek transparency and regularity so that they can maximize its usefulness for communicating with strangers. Here, the default setting of minimal processing is not applied, since it is a foreign code for all speakers. Esperanto, although invented, may be viewed as such a language. No one is a monolingual speaker though there are an estimated 350 people for whom it is one of two or more native languages (Bergen 2001). As noted in Chapter 16, Bergen found 'errors' in the language of such native speakers, suggesting that it is the adults that preserve the regularities of the language, not the children.

Realizations of esoteric and exoteric communication

In our modern world, we should anticipate that there are virtually no languages that match the one in Scenario A. Even the most remote tribes are likely to have had local contacts with outsiders,[13] though it should be noted that contact need not lead to immediate or extensive change if the group is positively resistant to influence (Everett 2005). The main languages of the modern world operate on the basis of a common central 'standard' code that serves exoteric purposes, and numerous overlapping codes that are used to facilitate communication between, and to identify, subgroups. The nature of this standard code is well exemplified by publications like the *Cambridge Advanced Learner's Dictionary* (2005) which aims to "us[e] only words from a list of common words that are easy to understand" (p. viii)—that is, to transform lexis encoded for esoteric communication into a more transparent and explicit form, suitable for exoteric communication. For example, the Dictionary defines 'crankshaft', as "a long metal rod, especially one in a car engine, that helps the engine turn the wheels" (p. 290). The Dictionary is aimed at non-native speakers, but such definitions are equally suitable for native speakers excluded from the esoteric code used by people with specialist technical knowledge.

In sum, the modern world, with its high premium on global communication and on the written word, strongly promotes the mastery of codes that are suitable for exoteric communication. We use them every day as we move in and out of the company of strangers who share different points of contact with us. Yet, once back with those who share our knowledge, we set aside our capacity to apply high levels explicitness in sentences that are composed of transparent parts joined using regular rules, and we revert to the default—the formulaicity inherent in large, often multiword, MEUs.

Different default boundaries and communication

How would communication be affected, if linguistic material fell one side of the formulaic/novel divide for one individual and the other side for another? And how might individuals signal their identity on the basis of choosing, or not choosing, to be formulaic?

Different formulaic knowledge

Esoteric and exoteric reception of 'coonass'

The court case reported in Chapter 14 arose because two individuals spoke different varieties of the same language, with the result that one had a lexical entry for 'coonass' and the other did not. The default level of processing meant that the sender, having a meaning for the word string as a MEU, had no reason to unpack it and notice its apparent composition. In contrast, the receiver, positioned outside the sender's dialect group, treated the phrase as transparent—even though, historically speaking, it is not—and thereby understood it to have a composite meaning, 'coon' plus 'ass'.

Of interest here is how the sender perceived the lexical knowledge of those he gave the certificate to, and how his actions were positioned on the esoteric–exoteric axis. Evidently he did not believe 'coonass' was a word that everyone knew—for he explained it to those who attended his workshop. Yet his gloss of 'coonass' did not amount to breaking it down into its parts. Rather, he was inducting these outsiders into his group by teaching them a holistic jargon form—that is, providing them with a means *not* to have to analyse it into its components. A mark of their new insider status was their capacity appropriately to understand the term 'coonass' on the certificate they received. The certificates were sent as a celebration of the in-group status of the recipients, something that is clear from the wording on them (Figure 14.1). First, the certificate is signed by 'a certified Coon Ass', indicating that the sender is a member of the group. Second, it constitutes a gesture of inclusion, for it welcomes the recipient into membership. Third, the rules for upgrading from 'temporary' to 'certified Coon Ass' status are:

- You are to work hard, be fun loving, God fearing, open minded and a happy person.
- You are to accept strangers with open arms. But once treated unfairly or unjustly you become as fervirent [sic] a foe as you were a friend.
- You are to learn to sing, dance and tell jokes and eat boudin, cracklins, gumbo, crawfish etouffe and just about anything else.
- It does not take any special origin [illegible symbol] race or religion, all it takes is being proud of the people you are with and live your life to its fullest extremity.

The sentiments in the definition of a 'certified Coon Ass' are predominantly positive. Furthermore, membership is marked by additional linguistic material—other dialect words familiar to only the insider. The act of inclusion, albeit humorous, is evident.

It seems, then, that the sender's intention was to shift the boundary for default processing in relation to this word, by introducing it, with its meaning, to people who would otherwise have no alternative but to break it down. By providing a direct form-meaning mapping for them, he was giving them access to the domain of the insider. The court case arose not because someone receiving this initiation complained that there was a *second*, offensive meaning to the term, but because someone who had missed the initiation had no access to the opaque form-meaning relationship, and could only engage with the term as an outsider, looking for meaning in the apparent components.

Legally-binding formulas

When a word string is legally sanctioned, other considerations come into play. Rock (2005, 2007) examines how police officers deliver and explain the 'caution' (the statement and explanation of a detainee's right to silence during questioning). She identifies a number of difficulties arising from a conflict between the extreme formulaicity of the text for the speaker, and the legal requirement to assume that it is a novel text for the hearer. One relates to the tendency to "reel it all off like a robot … because I want to get on with it and I don't relate to what they're listening to" (2005: 84). Overfamiliarity on the part of the speaker can lead to mistakes that might cause legal embarrassment (2007: 157–8).[14] An over-glib presentation of the text also carries the danger that "detainees might miss the caution's warning perlocution, due to its delivery, [especially if] officers … fail to 'say it with meaning'" (2005: 87; see also Rock 2007: 156–8). Most significant to the discussions in this chapter is the awareness of officers that the caution potentially contains language that is jargon-like, i.e. intrinsically incomprehensible to outsiders. Their professional need to communicate results in a major tension, in that they are required to use the legally defined wording—"cautioning is a felicity condition for arrest and detention" (Rock 2007: 156)—yet they also need to be more exoterically-oriented than the wording permits. Rock, examining in depth various attempts to resolve this dilemma by rewriting the caution, notes that officers naturally want to add glosses, but that they have grave concerns about their ability adequately to reformulate the caution without compromising the legality of the speech act.

This situation is unusual, for normally the boundary between esoterically and exoterically-oriented communication is negotiated without an inherent resistance between them. That is, a speaker can usually experiment with the level of formulaic language, using feedback from hearers to modify the amount of explicitness. But with the caution, there is a fixed point—the formal wording—and any explanations must be additional, rather than instead. Since the boundary of shared to unshared knowledge may not be immediately evident, it can mean that the same information must be imparted several times before it is entirely clear that it has been understood. Multiple repetition brings its own dangers, including the loss of novelty and the incorrect inference that each formulation must mean something different (Grice 1975).

Choices about group membership

Rejecting formulaicity to maintain one's identity

If our default preference is to use the largest available lexical units, and doing so automatically signals our membership of groups that also use those units, it follows that a strong desire to exclude oneself from a group might be achieved by rejecting those units in favour of ones appropriate for an outsider. Indications of this were observed in the study of advanced learners of English reported in Chapter 13. Participants joined the study because they wanted to sound more nativelike. However, speaking like a native speaker relocates you in relation to your identity. One subject, Lc, noticed that her sense of identity had shifted, to match the language she had memorized, so that she was thinking in a more British way than before. However, others, including Lo and the pilot subject Da, found that they needed to protect their sense of Chinese identity. They did this by sabotaging the forms they had memorized, i.e. by altering words and endings. Da's explanation, "[I] haven't really changed Chinese thinking to English thinking", reinforces an observation implicit in the discussion, earlier, of Figure 17.1, that outsiders may not necessarily want to become insiders, but rather to create and sustain a new, middle ground that protects enough of their own identity for comfort. If so, we might conjecture that the subjects in the study would have been most comfortable if the linguistic material they were provided with had been fully transparent and regular, as well as being nativelike—that is, a manifestation of an encoding suitable for exoteric communication.

Developing an identity constrained by formulaicity

For Sylvia using TALK (Chapter 11), the collision of expediency in communication and the maintenance of personal identity is differently constrained.

On the one hand, the cost of departing from the default is very great, so that Sylvia is somewhat bound to express her identity with what she happens to have stored. Of course, she is in control of what she puts into and keeps in her computer database, but where she has nothing appropriate available, she is obliged to curtail her self-expression if she is to continue with her low-processing option.

On the other hand, conversation as a vehicle for expressing herself is only possible using TALK, so it is greatly in her interests to find ways of using TALK to support the development of a sustainable identity. This identity cannot be fully 'normal'. It marks her out as someone who is sometimes unable to answer a simple question; sometimes gives a flat and unfeeling reply when an emotionally charged one would be more appropriate; cuts across other people's turns with irrelevant utterances; always wins the turn simply by producing an utterance; tolerates long pauses while she finds what she wants to say; takes long turns to tell a whole story; asks a lot of questions as a means of controlling the topic, and so on. Any of these might be traits that Sylvia dislikes and regrets, but they are aspects of her identity as a conversational partner, enforced by the mode of her communication, itself determined by the limitations of technology. Yet they are really just a more extreme version of the factors that form the conversational identity of anyone else. We all have to find ways of resolving the tensions between ease of processing and the various kinds of accuracy that we desire to express—factual, linguistic, and emotional.

Conclusion

The evidence reviewed in this chapter indicates that we are able to make choices about which lexical units we use—choices that are influenced by our desire to ensure that we communicate effectively, and by our sense of identity. When we encode language we make judgements about which of our MEUs our hearers will be able to find in their own lexicons. In some cases we may deliberately introduce them to a new item in order to create space for a shared identity. Non-native speakers may elect not to use large MEUs that they do have in their lexicon, because they associate them with a group with which they do not fully identify.

Although not discussed so much in this chapter, options also exist for decoding. The plaintiff recipient of the 'coonass' certificate claimed that when she saw the term she only saw 'coon', the most offensive term. However, as shown above, the certificate gave many clues that 'coonass' was a dialect form, and as such, the plaintiff might reasonably have inferred that it needed looking up in a dialect dictionary before offence was taken. That is, as hearers/readers we constantly have to make judgements and choices about what the speaker/writer is most likely to have meant (Grice 1975; Sperber and Wilson 1995). It is on that basis that a native speaker can reject the easy mapping of a form produced by a non-native speaker or a child onto an MEU, in favour of working with the component parts (for example, when hearing 'I received a French letter', meaning 'I received a letter from France'). Similarly, a hearer might choose to treat an MEU as componential rather than acknowledge recognizing a double entendre, so as not to identify with the group of people who know the vulgar meaning. This scope for choice is only possible because we have entries in our lexicon for both large and small lexical units.

Notes

1 'Short term memory' is a general, theory-neutral term, whereas 'working memory' is a term associated with a particular theoretical position, first developed by Baddeley (1986). Although there are therefore differences between them, for the present purpose the two terms can be used interchangeably. For an overview of the hypothesized nature of working memory see, for instance, Wagner, Bunge, and Badre (2004).

2 In recursion, the output of one operation can act as the input for another. The effect is that there is no logical bar on the length and complexity of sentences.

3 However, Pullum, and Scholz (2008) warn against over-interpreting this claim.

4 Pawley and Syder (1983b) observe that clause-embedding is largely eschewed in normal speech, in favour of clause-chaining.

5 It is not intended to imply that segmentation would occur on the basis of a single pair of examples, and the illustration is presented simply for the sake of clarity. The threshold for 'evidence' in a protolanguage is impossible to gauge in the absence of guessing the number of protowords, the range of sounds occurring in them, and the likely meanings of them. See Wray (1998, 2000b, 2002a) for discussion.

6 It is important to emphasize that the starting point really is random phonological strings associated with the complete meanings. There is no underlying, implicit, or subconscious pattern of phonological and semantic sub-parts waiting there for people to find. The amount of chance correspondence you need in order to get things going depends on the frequency of items' occurrence, how tolerant speakers are of counter-examples, and how quickly hypercorrection takes place (so that a counter-example is rationalized to the emerging pattern). Empirical explorations on computer (Kirby 2001, 2002) and in simulation games in my own student seminars suggest that patterns will emerge and can be rationalized.

7 Holding back creativity in this way means that the capacity for recursion in language does not need to have evolved suddenly. It just cannot apply until there are recombinable units.

8 For convenience, the discussion that follows refers to languages as if they were each used by only one group of people. However, it will be clear later

that the same language may exist in more than one state at any one time, according to how different groups are using it.

9 This is not by any means to deny that children acquiring such languages identify components that can be manipulated to express meanings analytically. On the contrary, Mithun (1989), reporting the progress of five children acquiring Mohawk as a first language, shows how they isolated salient components from input and used them productively. However, the logic of the immature system that children come up with during language acquisition does not prevent them from continuing to learn, until they have mastered the adult system, complete with its complexities and irregularities.

10 The same applies to the learning of formulaic military bugle calls, described in Chapter 21.

11 This fact created a tension for Newsome (2005) as she tried, though an outsider, to study the esoteric language of a group of aircraft maintenance engineers: "It was necessary to use enough maintenance language to avoid responses being 'dumbed down' … but not so much that it became obvious that I knew many of the terms (if not yet their meanings) and then receive only half-answers" (p. 62).

12 A different formulation of these scenarios, along with much more detail about how they operate, is given in Wray and Grace (2007).

13 Intermarrying between tribes will, of course, also bring outsiders into a group. However, the incomers may not be powerful in relation to altering the language to meet their needs as learners, and they would influence the forms of the language only if their acquisition of the host language remained incomplete at the point when their children were drawing on their output for their own acquisition. Laycock (1979) reports a rather more proactive approach to tackling inter-group communication: villages customarily exchanging young boys (around ten years old) so that they would become bilingual and thus be able to mediate in disputes (p. 81).

14 However, she also notes the fallacy in the assumption that the text is novel for those hearing it, for detainees have been known to correct police officers who deliver the caution incorrectly (ibid.). The legally-binding presumption that a detainee is unfamiliar with the caution is very conservative. Previous arrests, general street knowledge, or television could all contribute to a pre-existing familiarity with it, though, of course, such knowledge could easily be partial or inaccurate.

18
Formulaic language learning in adults

Introduction

This chapter considers how central formulaic language is in adult foreign and second language learning, and why. Although plenty has been written about the practical and evidential base for formulaicity in learner input and output—see Wray (1999, 2000a, 2002b for reviews)—the theoretical basis for its usefulness remains less thoroughly explored. Explanations are necessarily contingent on whether formulaic language is, for adult learners, an add-on to novel language, or—as claimed here in regard to native speakers—the default, from which novel language represents a deliberate and effortful departure (see Chapters 16 and 17).

Establishing the boundary between formulaic and analytic engagement

In Chapter 2 it was proposed that both children and adults apply the principle of Needs Only Analysis (NOA) to language learning, but that, having very different needs, they engage in different amounts of analysis. It is tempting to see the child's approach as entailing *just the right amount* of analysis, while the adult engages in *too much* analysis, but that view does not take into account the different motivations and requirements of children and adults who approach the challenge of language learning: why they undertake it, and what constitutes a successful outcome. Furthermore, it tends to imply that there is one ideal level of analysis that is effective for developing nativelike knowledge of the language.

Although there is a sense in which that is indeed true—for there seem to be risks entailed in over-analysing language as a learner—things cannot be that simple, for native speakers also continue to analyse the language and can develop very fine-grained knowledge of how linguistic units are composed, and the ways in which they combine. Not only linguists, but also poets, novelists, and other wordsmiths, somehow succeed in making their language elastic, without leaving the zone of nativelike behaviour.

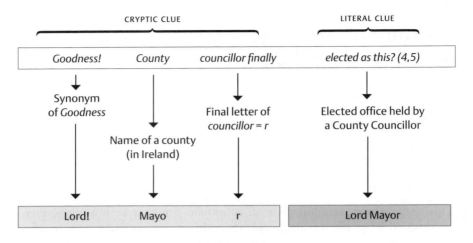

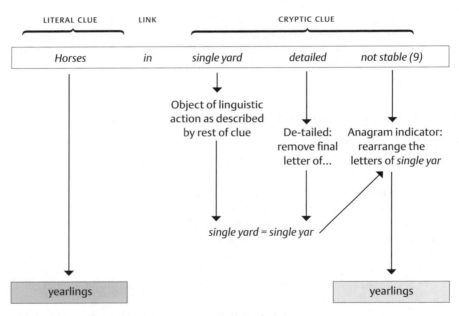

Figure 18.1   Unwrapping cryptic crossword clues

Indeed, even quite arcane linguistic activities that entail gross and bizarre over-analysis are viewed as quintessentially nativelike, albeit not by any means mastered by all native speakers. One such is the pastime of completing cryptic crosswords (and the less common one of creating them). To solve a cryptic crossword clue it is necessary to ignore the normal rules of the language, and look for new ways to break down the linguistic prompt. Figure 18.1 shows how the clue *Goodness! County councillor finally elected as this?* (4,5) is resolved as *Lord Mayor*, and how *Horses in single yard detailed not stable* (9) resolves as *yearlings*.[1] This sort of word play activity indicates that, when the 'need' arises (and completing cryptic crosswords is quite a compulsive hobby), we can analyse language to the point of destruction: we find meaning where there really is none. Thus, the level of analysis that we apply to language is not fixed, and the right amount of analysis to meet one need may be too much or too little appropriately to meet another. What the native speaker has is full control over how much analysis to apply when.

The non-native speaker, to attain nativelike proficiency, needs either to match the native speaker's facility for varying the level of analysis, or else mimic the effect of it by some other means. If, as proposed in Chapter 2 and in Wray (2002b), those who learn another language in the classroom in adolescence or later are bound to identify smaller units and more rules than the native child does, then we have two options for explaining how a subset of such learners do end up effectively nativelike. They either (a) unlearn, or over-write, their knowledge of small units, replacing it with a knowledge of larger ones, or else they (b) find a different route to sounding nativelike.

Deciding between these two possibilities is important, and not just for theories of language acquisition and teaching. Option (b) resembles the assumed means by which computers can be taught to generate nativelike language output. Thus, there are useful dual themes regarding adult language learning and computational modelling (see Chapter 19). We can use the fact that there is no perceived need to turn computers into native speakers, only to *appear* to have done so, as a basis for examining the assumptions underlying second language teaching. The focus, as always, will be the role that morpheme equivalent units (MEUs) might play in narrowing the gap between the performance of the native speaker and of the human (or, in the next chapter, electronic) learner.

Units of language knowledge

Is formulaically-based language learning a viable option for adults? Or is the adult bound, even if the conditions are right, to break down word strings into smaller units?

The circumstances of learning

When children acquire their first language, they learn what to say in a given situation as a part of learning about that situation. In contrast, when adults learn languages, they usually possess from the start an awareness of what they might need to say, because they are mature users of another language. They can anticipate a wide range of potential situations, and, supported by books and teachers and vindicated by the requirements of exercises, tests, and examinations, they will attempt to forearm themselves by stockpiling linguistic information, focusing attention on the level of detail most salient for effective learning in that context (Williams 1999). In anticipation of future situations in which they may use the language, they will aim to learn functional material *before* they need it. Although there is nothing to stop a learner approaching the offline learning of functional language holistically, it may be that unless one learns the word string in an appropriate communicative context, it is not adequately indexed holistically with a meaning.[2] If so, it would be difficult to remember it, unless another strategy were introduced—such as anchoring the form-meaning relationship at the componential level.

The classroom learner's focus on getting good marks may tend to downgrade the value of multiword MEUs in another way too: it will appear safer to produce something novel and transparent (and all being well without errors) over which the learner has full control, than to reproduce a memorized word string for which the learner has, perhaps, only a global sense of meaning and use. Suppose it is not the right expression: how will it be received? An MEU is like a gift purchased pre-wrapped—you pass it on and hope that it is what it was supposed to be. If a speaker chooses the wrong item, it may be difficult for the hearer to repair, particularly if the component parts do not directly add up to the whole. In contrast, an incorrect morphological, grammatical, or even lexical error in a novel construction is usually easy to spot, and to make good.

For the adult learner, the social and psychological stakes in regard to saying the wrong thing are potentially high, so that the options taken will be different from those of the child. If a child says something that is socially or pragmatically inappropriate, precocious, or simply nonsensical, the consequences are rarely dire, and children are accustomed not to dwell on their errors as adults do. The child's freedom to make faux pas in first language acquisition extends sufficiently for it to apply in early second language acquisition too, and it liberates the child to hand over more of those wrapped up packages of language that give the impression of fluency and idiomatic knowledge. Wong Fillmore's (1976, 1979) subjects, Nora (observed from age 5½ to 6½) and Ana (6½ to 7½) both appeared to prioritize having something to say over having something *meaningful* to say. Nora used 'in the high school' as "just nice phrase which she sometimes appended to her sentences. It sometimes meant 'in [kindergarten] class'; at other times, it meant nothing in particular" (1976: 494). Ana did something similar with the phrase 'when I come home'.

Meanwhile, the disadvantages brought by much language learning in adulthood can be exacerbated by well-meaning approaches to teaching that encourage small-item learning. They include the heavy emphasis placed on the word as a unit of learning (see Chapter 5) which will encourage word memorization rather than phrase memorization and which might also extend to the provision of unhelpful information about phonology. For example, papers in the collection by Brown and Kondo-Brown (2006) examine the impact on communication proficiency of the tendency of teachers and learners to focus on fully realized citation pronunciations rather than the reduced phonological forms of connected speech. The dissimilarity between the canonical, isolated form and its integrated counterpart is such that learners "are shocked when they go outside the classroom where they are unable to comprehend what native speakers are saying" (Ito 2006: 17).

One view, implicit in several of the studies in Brown and Kondo-Brown (2006), is that the learner's challenge is to work out how to apply the phonological rules that reduce the full form to the isolated one. However, if the NOA model is correct, then the phonology of a word string in connected speech might not directly derive from the phonology of its parts at all. Learnt independently, with their own form-meaning mappings, there could be separate phonologies for words in isolation and the same words within longer MEUs, and no easy rules from the former to the latter (compare the hazards of transferring spoken words to spelling, discussed in Chapters 5 and 8). In this case, the kind of 'teacher talk' (Cahill 2006: 105) that over-enunciates forms will not lead naturally to a capacity to understand and produce connected speech. Increasing opportunities for genuine uses of formulaic language in communicatively salient contexts presents a challenge for the teacher, and one that, perhaps, fewer rise to than would like (Gatbonton and Segalowitz 2005). However, task-based methods that create opportunities to repeat useful word strings have been found to be effective (Gatbonton and Segalowitz 1988, 2005).

Learning in different situations

But what sort of control do learners really have over their approach to learning? Naturally, it is possible for an individual to make conscious choices about whether to focus on memorizing large or small lexical units, whether to make deliberate efforts to understand and apply grammatical rules, and whether to seek opportunities to use the language in real interactional situations. But to the extent that the motivation for such decisions, as well as the general trajectory of learning, is determined by the situation—including the learner's age and learning opportunity—most of the process will be beyond the effective control of the learner.

The test is to compare the patterns of learning observed across different situations. An obvious place to start is with naturalistic acquisition by adults—particularly through immersion in the L2 community. In such a situation, there will be opportunities for mapping functional language onto its situation through real usage, which should encourage the internalization of some multiword MEUs. However, the adult learner cannot really mimic the child. The child's range of interactive situations is very limited, relative to that of the adult, who may have to speak before there has been sufficient opportunity to observe what others say. There is, nevertheless, some evidence that educated western learners who undergo L2 immersion in the community learn differently—more formulaically—than classroom learners (see Wray 2002b: chapter 10 for a review). The limitations in their learning outcomes may be attributable to expectations on their part about what can be achieved and how, and/or the interaction that they are able to access. Griffiths (2003), exploring the language needs of refugees in the UK in 2001, found that inadequate English language teaching provision was a major hindrance to learning. Meanwhile, ill-conceived assumptions in the host community about what refugees need and who provides it, may create an unhelpful distance between learners and their most valuable asset for input, the native speaker community. As a result, while residing in an existing community of L1 speakers has long been perceived as detrimental to linguistic integration, it has been found that when refugees in the UK are housed in monolingual English communities, they do not necessarily acquire the language any better (Arnot and Pinson 2005: 15).

But suppose the host community is better geared up to support the learning of the incomer. And suppose all parties are unfamiliar with the standard assumptions about language learning that arise from western style education and literacy. How would learning then proceed? A hint is offered by Laycock's (1979) and Thurston's (1987) accounts of language teaching and learning in Papua New Guinea and New Britain. These reports suggest that a formulaic, functional approach to language learning is possible for adults, if the circumstances are right.

Laycock and two polyglot locals arrived in a Papuan village and he made notes as his companions sat by the fire with an elder to learn the language. "Teaching proceeded by means of whole sentences and occasional individual lexical items, either volunteered ... or requested ..." (p. 91). The conversation included, from the 'teacher': "'This is how we say: Give me some areca nut' and 'And this is how we say: Give me some tobacco'"; and from the learners: "'And how do you say: I have no fire?'" (ibid.). Of the errors made, only some were corrected, and by repeating the entire sentence, rather than extracting the component at fault: "No attempt was made to explain any of the morphology ... or even to separate out individual words from sentences, except in the case of important nouns (sago, tobacco, areca nut, betel pepper, fire, water) which were often taught individually" (ibid.). Although Laycock's observations were short-lived, for he and his companions moved on the next morning, he comments: "it seems likely that this method of teaching by whole sentences of potential use—the phrase-book method—is the normal one in Papua New Guinea; my own informants commonly adopted this method during eliciting" (p. 92).

Laycock's suggestion is borne out by independent observations made by Thurston (1987) in New Britain, an island east of the New Guinea mainland:

> The New Britain concept of language instruction is highly systematic in
> that the language taught follows the progression of social use parallel to

the socialisation of the student into the linguistic group. The process begins with the formulae appropriate to the interactional needs of first greeting, leading eventually to the subtle insinuations needed to tease a friend. At all stages, the language taught is governed by its use in actual social situations.

(pp. 72–3)

Although the evidence from Laycock and Thurston is insufficient to draw firm conclusions, it does suggest that the 'phrase-book' approach is one means by which languages without a writing system might be taught to adults who have not been educated in the ways of compositionality for its own sake. Indeed we might conjecture that the reason why teaching was conducted on the basis of complete messages was that, in the absence of a tradition of linguistic analysis for its own sake, propositions seemed more salient as operational units than did individual words or grammatical patterns. Bambi Schiefflin (personal communication),[3] speaking of how the Kaluli of the Papua New Guinean highlands supported their children's language acquisition, notes: "given that [they] had no ideas about dictionaries or grammars, but ideas that language was social, they were teaching sociality".

Making formulaic learning work

If we infer from all of this that formulaic language learning is potentially possible for adults, how effectively might it be incorporated into the mainstream western classroom situation? Although formulaic sequences have been promoted in teaching (see Wray 2000a for a review of three approaches), their perceived—and indeed real—limitations continue to minimize their presence (Kryszewska 2003; Lindstromberg 2003, present two sides of the argument). Formulaic sequences are certainly found in the output of post-childhood learners, but some of them are non-nativelike fused constructions (see Wray 2002b: chapter 10 for a review of studies) and many others are, while technically correct, in some way inappropriately used (for example, De Cock 2004 examines the use of 'of course' in non-native English). Wiktorsson (2003) found that Swedish school and university students learning English tended to use colloquial formulaic sequences more appropriate to speech in their written essays. Conversely, Qi's (2006) Chinese students of English used formulaic sequences in their speech that were more appropriate to writing. These findings indicate the need for learners to encounter a range of different discourse types in order to discover which formulaic sequences are appropriate where.

It is obviously difficult to encounter a broad range of formulaic sequences in genuine functional contexts in a classroom, and direct teaching is necessarily an alternative that must be considered. Although the value of repetition is well-recognized both for word and word string learning (Gatbonton and Segalowitz 1988, 2005; Webb 2007), in western classrooms, there is an

understandable reluctance about encouraging the rote memorization of multiword strings. It is perceived as superficial learning resulting in a performance
capacity that is not necessarily matched by the competence to compose new
strings.

However, studies of how formulaic learning is exploited in China (for
example, Dahlin and Watkins 2000; Kennedy 2002; Zhanrong 2002; Cooper
2004, Ding 2007) have shown that the effectiveness of memorization depends
on its consolidating and/or facilitating, rather than replacing, an understanding of the material (Marton, Dall'Alba, and Tse 1993; Dahlin and Watkins
2000: 67; Cooper 2004: 294). This finding is consistent with the claim of
Nattinger and DeCarrico (1992: 117) that a major value of learning word
strings is to be able to extrapolate new patterns from them. It is important
to differentiate here between word strings that are rich in such potential,
such as ordinary sentences of regular construction that the learner *makes*
formulaic by virtue of memorization, and word strings that are formulaic, or
likely to be, for most native speakers, by virtue of the holistic nature of their
form-meaning mapping. In the former case, the memorized string acts as a
mnemonic for a pattern. The rationale is that one is more likely to produce
novel strings according to the nativelike pattern if one has a memorized
example to refer to, or familiarization with which makes the correct pattern
sound right. But in the latter case, where the formulaicity of the string is a
product of NOA on the part of native speakers, there is a severe risk that the
sequence is not archetypical of the pattern required for novel constructions,
given the natural drift that MEUs undergo relative to the productive lexis and
rules (see Chapter 2).

Halfway between inherently formulaic material and regular sentences that
might be presented as useful exemplars for memorization lie collocations.
It is generally accepted these days that learning isolated items of lexis is of
limited value, and teachers and textbooks often now present new vocabulary
within a collocational or phraseological context—something made possible
by the new generation of corpus-based dictionaries (but see De Cock 2002;
McAlpine and Myles 2003 for reservations about their current scope).

Insofar as collocational pairs have their own holistic mapping (i.e. are
MEUs for the native speaker) we may expect that it will not always be easy
for native speaker teachers to think of the most common collocational pairings for isolated words, when providing examples in class. McGee (2006), in
experiments designed to elicit the most common noun for a given adjective
and vice versa,[4] found that native speaker teachers of English as a foreign
language were quite poor at thinking up the pairings that the British National
Corpus identified as most common. However, they were much more able
correctly to choose the most common pairing from three presented to them.
The explanation offered by the NOA model for these findings is that the
subjects were sensitive to the relative frequency of the different pairings on
display, but that seeing one of the words in isolation did not reliably give
them access to their holistic representation of the pairing. However, contrary

to the suggestion in Chapter 2, that non-native speakers tend to have fewer holistic representations because they learn smaller units, McGee also found that non-native speaker teachers of English (L1 Arabic) performed overall quite similarly to the native speakers. He explores various possible explanations for this levelling, including that the non-native teachers had made the transition to nativelike processing and representation, or, conversely, that the native teachers had, by virtue of their profession, come to think in a non-native way about collocations, and therefore did not perform as differently from non-native teachers as native speakers in other professions would.

In all events, it seems clear that if learning collocations is deemed important, teaching materials need to draw attention to configurations of words—preferably within functionally relevant contexts—in order to supplement the linguistic information that is easily and reliably available to the teacher through intuition.

Limitations of formulaic learning in adulthood

So just how effective is it for an adult to take a formulaic approach to language learning? We saw in Chapter 12 that a beginner learner of Welsh was able to progress, in a period of just four days, from virtually no knowledge, to sufficient productive capacity to deliver a cookery demonstration to a live audience on television. But was it real knowledge? Yes, in that it served its purpose, and yes in that Margaret did understand what she was saying, and did retain quite a lot of the material up to nine months after the learning period. On the other hand, that knowledge was severely limited in two ways. First, only a narrow topic was covered. Second, there was little direct potential for extrapolating to new situations. Although the input did include a number of frames that could be put to new purposes—for example, *Dw i'n mynd i (ddangos i chi (sut i wneud))* ... 'I'm going to (show you (how to make ...))'—Margaret had not been furnished with much additional vocabulary suitable for completing them. Both of these limitations make it difficult to see how Margaret could easily transfer what she had learnt if she wanted to pass the time of day with a neighbour, buy a loaf of bread, or complain about a faulty house repair.

On the other hand, the specific material taught for that television programme was not *intended* to be sufficient to transform a non-speaker of Welsh into a functional speaker, nor could anyone imagine that so little input would be enough to learn a language. A much more interesting question is whether a sizeable series of such inputs, focused on different common interactions, might between them provide a learner with a usable version of the language. That is, what sort of genuinely useful linguistic knowledge might arise, directly and—via the extrapolation of patterns, indirectly—from memorizing, say, *forty* sets of sentences usable in routine situations?

To answer that question, some account must be taken of the potential risks for learners of getting out of their depth with the language. It is a well recognized disadvantage of producing output beyond the scope of your compositional competence that your interlocutors will not realize how little you can understand, and how limited you are in your ability to supplement what you have memorized with new information. In a local bilingual setting, where the most a misunderstanding is likely to do is send you home with the wrong kind of cream cake, and where (as in South Wales) there is always another language (English) to fall back on, more risks might safely be taken in exploring the full potential for formulaic language to offer a bridge to true learning, than in a situation where efficient communication is paramount for, say, the safety of hundreds of people.

The case is well-illustrated by Aviation English. Cushing (1994a, 1994b) graphically demonstrates the imperative for linguistic clarity between pilots and air traffic controllers by chronicling how crashes and near misses have been caused through breakdowns in communication. The International Civil Aviation Organization (ICAO) implemented new language proficiency criteria from 5 March 2008 (Figure 18.2). Although there is provision for using the local language of the ground station where it is known by both parties, the default language, which all operatives must know, is English (International Civil Aviation Organization 2006).

**Holistic descriptors for language proficiency,
International Civil Aviation Organization (2006)**

Proficient speakers shall:

a communicate effectively in voice-only (telephone/radiotelephone) and in face-to-face situations;

b communicate on common, concrete and work-related topics with accuracy and clarity;

c use appropriate communicative strategies to exchange messages and to recognize and resolve misunderstandings (e.g. to check, confirm, or clarify information) in a general or work-related context;

d handle successfully and with relative ease the linguistic challenges presented by a complication or unexpected turn of events that occurs within the context of a routine work situation or communicative task with which they are otherwise familiar; and

e use a dialect or accent which is intelligible to the aeronautical community.

Figure 18.2 Language requirements for pilots and air traffic controllers

The requirements laid out in Figure 18.3 illustrate the tension between formulaicity and creativity that can arise when it is imperative for non-native speakers to communicate effectively. It is evidently accepted that 'rehearsed or formulaic speech' will be an element of the interaction ('Fluency'), but, as Mitsutomi, a language advisor to the ICAO, observes, "it is [not] enough for a pilot to simply learn a list of standard words and repeat the jargon during any given flight" (University of Redlands 2001). Facility with the language, as defined in the ICAO criteria, directly links the ability to use "Basic grammatical structures and sentence patterns ... creatively" and to paraphrase while being prepared for "dealing with an unexpected turn of events".

ICAO Rating Scale for Operational Level 4,
International Civil Aviation Organization (2006)

A speaker will be rated at Operational Level 4 if the following criteria are met:

Pronunciation:
(*Assumes a dialect and/or accent intelligible to the aeronautical community.*)
Pronunciation, stress, rhythm, and intonation are influenced by the first language or regional variation but only sometimes interfere with ease of understanding.

Structure:
(*Relevant grammatical structures and sentence patterns are determined by language functions appropriate to the task.*)
Basic grammatical structures and sentence patterns are used creatively and are usually well controlled. Errors may occur, particularly in unusual or unexpected circumstances, but rarely interfere with meaning.

Vocabulary:
Vocabulary range and accuracy are usually sufficient to communicate effectively on common, concrete, and work-related topics. Can often paraphrase successfully when lacking vocabulary in unusual or unexpected circumstances.

Fluency:
Produces stretches of language at an appropriate tempo. There may be occasional loss of fluency on transition from rehearsed or formulaic speech to spontaneous interaction, but this does not prevent effective communication. Can make limited use of discourse markers or connectors. Fillers are not distracting.

Comprehension:
Comprehension is mostly accurate on common, concrete, and work-related topics when the accent or variety used is sufficiently intelligible for an international community of users. When the speaker is confronted with a linguistic or situational complication or an unexpected turn of events, comprehension may be slower or require clarification strategies.

Interactions:
Responses are usually immediate, appropriate, and informative. Initiates and maintains exchanges even when dealing with an unexpected turn of events. Deals adequately with apparent misunderstandings by checking, confirming, or clarifying.

Figure 18.3 Required proficiency levels for languages used

On the other hand, it is clear that comprehension will be generally enhanced in routine situations if the form of words is predictable, particularly where pronunciation could obscure the delivery and/or where an unfortunate choice of word or structure might introduce ambiguity. Errors, and thus the risk of comprehension, can be reduced by using prefabricated word strings agreed for the task, particularly partly-fixed frames into which key novel information and instructions can be inserted, such as speed, direction, etc.

Yet there is a danger. Reproducing or receiving word strings over which one does not have full mastery creates its own problems. First, the phonological form may become corrupted through repetition without full processing (Wray 2002b: 37f, 76ff). Kuiper (1996) reports how, in auctions and sports commentaries, the fact that speaker and hearer alike can predict the formulaic frames within which the novel information is packaged enables those frames to be spoken indistinctly in the interests of fluency. A proficient hearer can usually unpack and repair a gabbled phrase, but a non-proficient hearer may not be able to do so. Second, as discussed in Chapter 20, there may be unanticipated difficulties for non-native speakers in faithfully learning and reproducing formulaic material, even when there are strong motivations for doing so. That is, learners may take inappropriate risks in relation to their actual capacity to transform memorized information into fully accurate output (Wray and Fitzpatrick 2008).

Opportunities for learning in a new way

What these cases confirm is that true learning does, of course, extend beyond knowing the memorized phrases, and that the extrapolation of patterns will be necessary at some point. However, it is not the noticing of patterns that adult learners find problematic. On the contrary, that is what they tend to do *too* much. The study of the beginner learner of Welsh suggests that, albeit only in low-risk situations, there might be scope for exploring ways of more closely mimicking the Papuan teaching style in an L2 immersion setting. The aim would be to so front-load the learner with functional form-meaning pairings—some genuinely formulaic and thus possibly irregular, others entirely regular in form and meaning—that there were sufficient MEUs to substantially *curtail* the amount of pattern extrapolation normally undertaken by an adult learner. The initial learning would, in this way, contrast greatly with the normal approach, whereby a small number of formulaic word strings is soon swamped by isolated lexis and grammatical rules.

How might such learning progress? Perhaps the facility to deliver a substantial, though still limited, set of effective, functional messages would create a different learning space for the learner within the community. There would be safe topics for effective exchange, based on the learner's memorized strings (compare TESSA, Chapter 10 and TALK, Chapter 11). The unknown—what the interlocutor said back—would be the catalyst for further learning, provided what was said could be adequately matched, through pragmatics, to the existing context. NOA would then operate much more as it does for the child, so that some of the memorized material, along with some of the novel input from interlocutors, was partly segmented to render useful smaller strings—phrases, words, or morphemes—with their own meanings.

Significantly, the construction of novel output by such a learner would be, at first, very primitive, since there would be no independently learnt rules, and since patterns existing in the memorized material would not have been identified unless there was a specific need. As a result, the learner would produce a mixture of the original memorized strings (sometimes not quite appropriately formed for the immediate context—compare the extended usage of *je m'appelle* and *j'habite* in classroom-based French learning found by Myles, Hooper, and Mitchell 1998), segments of those strings, and telegraphic, constructed strings with little morphology or grammar. As a result, the short term outcomes might seem disappointing. However, the NOA approach, evidently so effective for children, might turn out to offer a similarly effective trajectory for the adult over time. The procedure for learning outlined above is similar neither to most classroom learning, where formulaic language is supplemented by a more analytic approach, and where opportunities for genuine functionally motivated usage are relatively sparse, nor to most naturally occurring adult L2 learning, where there is little if any initial input of complete, functionally-indexed nativelike material to kick-start communication. One potential opportunity to test the capacity for learning in this formulaically driven way would be with new immigrants who are not being offered other language learning support. Careful case studies could greatly enhance our understanding of whether, as proposed here, NOA can successfully support effective learning, when the opportunities for, and invitations to, additional analysis that so often accompany adult learning are minimized.

Conclusion

It has been suggested that formulaic language learning is a viable option for adults, provided it is accompanied by understanding, but a distinction has been drawn between the memorization of exemplar word strings that are sufficiently regular to create a basis for pattern extraction, and others—the word strings most likely to be formulaic for native speakers—that are attractive learning targets because of their strong holistic form-function association, but which, for that reason, may well not be a sound basis for pattern extraction. The effectiveness of a formulaic approach in adult language learning has been assessed in relation to the learning situation, with the proposal that NOA does offer scope for a measure of child-like acquisition, but only if the circumstances support it—which, in most adult learning situations, they do not. A specific learning scenario has been outlined, research into which might help shed more light on what the adult learner is and is not able to achieve in relation to formulaic learning.

In the next chapter, parallels are drawn between the typical patterns of adult language learning and those assumed necessary for teaching languages to computers. If it is possible to alter the parameters of adult language learning, it might also be possible to set them differently for computational learning, and a proposal is made for how this might be further explored using the principles of NOA.

Notes

1 The clues come from the *Times* Jumbo crossword, no 621 (14 January 2006) and no 569 (5 March 2005).
2 According to the heteromorphic distributed lexicon model (Wray 2002b: chapter 13), access to a functionally salient item is not only via the language control areas of the brain, but also any area controlling the action or reaction associated with its use. Decontextualized learning may not create such alternative access routes.
3 To George Grace; first cited in Wray and Grace (2007).
4 McGee's interest was not in the kinds of collocation that non-native speakers of lower proficiency might struggle with, such as 'ride a bike' versus 'drive a car' (for example, Nesselhauf 2005), but rather the most common noun collocates following words like 'different', 'full', and the most common adjective collocates preceding words like 'matter' and 'evidence'.

19
Teaching language to computers

Introduction

As a parallel to the consideration, in Chapter 18, of the role that formulaic language plays in adult language learning, this chapter explores the same issues in relation to computers learning human language. Specifically, we shall consider evidence that it is possible to encode as the computer equivalent of a morpheme equivalent unit (MEU) linguistic configurations that, if generated at the time of use, would be unnecessarily wasteful of processing resources.

Of course, there is no reason why what works for humans learning another language should work for a computer, since there is no requirement for computers to process language in the same way as humans. When computers are programmed to handle and/or produce human languages, the aim is only to mimic human linguistic *behaviour*, not necessarily the processes by which that behaviour comes about. However, some of the assumptions underlying many models of L2 learning are the same as those underpinning much computational modelling of language. Most particularly, there is an assumption that all, or almost all, language is novel and needs to be generated from scratch. This assumption seems to have caused extreme difficulties in computational modelling, some of which would be easily overcome by broadening the definition of the lexical unit to accommodate multiword formulaic strings.

The Needs Only Analysis (NOA) model has scope, in addition, to map out a way for computers not only to work with, but also to acquire language, and this possibility is also explored.

What units are most appropriate for natural language processing by computer?

It may seem obvious at first that the most effective approach to developing artificial comprehension and generation of human language will be to teach the computer all the units of the language and how they go together. This view may well be valid. The issue is, what should count as a unit? While it is reasonable to suppose that the best way for a computer to handle 'the red car' is by knowing the three words 'the', 'red', and 'car', and to have a rule for their assembly into a noun phrase, it might be inappropriate to extend this approach to all word strings. It is already accepted that idioms are probably best listed for look-up, and the issue, just as it is for models of human language processing, is where idioms stop and rule-based generation begins. Should 'all of a sudden' be listed whole or should a rule be identified to generate it?

Because words are so easy for a computer to identify, there can be a false barrier in perception between multiword strings and single words. For example, while it might be reasoned that there was value in the computer knowing that 'slowly' is made up of 'slow' and 'ly', this observation would not naturally be extended to dividing 'adoration' into 'adore' and 'ation' or 'pneumatic' into 'pneu' and 'matic'. A native speaker's intuitions will lead to a reasonable separation of active from morbid morphology. Is there a way to extend that practice to multiword strings? We have seen that the holistic storage of word strings is possible but not without consequences. In the cases of both TALK (Chapters 11 and 20) and TESSA (Chapter 10), it was possible to minimize the processing costs by relying very heavily on prefabricated material. The price paid was a lack of flexibility for novel expression.

However, for those engaged specifically in modelling language for natural language processing, including machine translation, flexibility is paramount, so different solutions are needed. It would not be effective or practical simply to list all possible sentences in a language in a large database, given that the aim is to handle a wide, and, ideally, unpredictable range of input and/or output, depending on the application. On the other hand, the peculiar nature of formulaic sequences means that they cannot easily be managed using a purely rule-based generation system either. In short, "M[ulti-] W[ord] E[xpressions] defy naïve attempts to establish a border between grammar and lexicon in terms of the opposition between rule productivity and lexical idiosyncrasy"(Calzolari *et al.* 2002: 1934). Sag, Baldwin, Bond, Copestake, and Flickinger (2002), in similar vein, lay out many of the practical problems inherent in dealing, in the computational context, with multiword expressions, which they accept must be treated independently of their component parts. They comment: "when analyzing semi-fixed expressions, it is important to strike a balance between too weak a mechanism, which will not allow sufficient variability, and too strong a mechanism, which will allow too much" (Sag *et al.* 2002: 9).

The solutions may be different according to the purposes of the endeavour. There are many reasons for developing a means by which computers can handle natural language input and produce natural language output, including the facilitation of both human–human interaction (via translation programs, see below) and human–computer communication. At present, humans must learn to formulate commands to the computer in a mode that is determined by the limitations of what a computer can understand. Being able to give a command in normal language would mean that anyone, without training, could talk to the computer. Thus a Natural Language Interface (NLI) "can allow people to use all the communicative power of language they already possess rather than be forced into an unnatural and limiting mode of communication" (R. W. Smith 2006: 497).[1] A key distinction in the aspirations for Natural Language Processing (NLP) systems is whether they aim to be 'intelligent assistants' that support human users, or decision makers that can replace and extend the range of human capabilities (Jackson and Schilder 2006). Into the latter category falls Machine Translation (MT), particularly where it is designed to facilitate translations between more languages than any single human polyglot could master (see Dorr, Hovy, and Levin 2006; Isabelle and Foster 2006).

The more independently the computer is to work from human intervention, the greater the need for it to handle human language instructions or materials effectively. As already observed, it does not, of course, need to handle language in the same way as humans do, only to mimic the effect. However, mimicking approaches that bypass syntactic parsing or semantic representation are often perceived as no more than expedient shortcuts. They are viewed as fundamentally compromised relative to the representation of knowledge that humans have. It will be argued below that they may in fact be a more accurate model of human processing than more fully-developed parsing models.

The representation of meaning

The question of whether a computer needs to actually understand language in order to process it effectively is almost a philosophical one, since it depends on what 'understanding' is considered to entail. Approaches to NLP and MT demonstrate the fragmentation of the notion of comprehension, as programs are taught, variously, to recognize that one word or phrase in a language can be used interchangeably with, or tends to occur in the same context as, another, and that a word or phrase in language A can be translated into a particular word or phrase in language B. Problems with ambiguity that, because of our pragmatic knowledge, would not tax the human, are resolved by providing the computer with broader, general knowledge or by increasing the amount of reference data that is trawled for statistical patterns of association (Isabelle and Foster 2006).

In addition, there is a sense in which, in MT, the form in the source language *is* the meaning of the form selected in the target language, and vice versa. Where translation proceeds via a more or less neutral intermediate 'pivot' language such as English (see Isabelle and Foster 2006: 410f) or Esperanto (for example, Maxwell, Schubert, and Witkam 1988), or a bespoke semantic representation such as Universal Networking Language (2005) or applications of Wierzbicka's (1996) 'conceptual primitives', there is even more of a sense that the 'meaning' has been captured. Nevertheless, this level of 'knowledge' is merely representation which, complete with the capacity for extrapolation based on prima facie rules or probabilities, permits a limited illusion of 'awareness' of meaning that is very different from the holistic, consolidated knowledge that a human can bring to bear when receiving or producing a text.

The issue of how meaning is represented is central to the question of how NOA might inform approaches to NLP. According to the NOA model, comprehension operates in humans on the basis of extracting general (coarse) meaning using pragmatics and context, and bootstrapping the finer semantic system on patterns gleaned from exposure. Therefore, semantic representation of a kind is a prerequisite for NOA to operate. On the other hand, because it is not refined, it is certainly not (indeed fundamentally not) about assigning meaning to individual units to derive meaning, but, on the contrary, locating the linguistic event broadly in a semantic space, as FrameNet[2] for instance does (see Chapter 7). Although FrameNet is being used to assist in the development of lexical representations for natural language processing (for example, Calzolari *et al.* 2002), its true potential may lie less in offering a representational framework for the meaning of multiword expressions, from which new ones can be predicted, than in providing guidance, on the basis of wide-ranging exemplars from corpora, regarding the extent to which potential new ones are likely to be idiomatic.

Most fundamentally, humans, unlike computers, approach both language comprehension and language interpretation on the basis that pragmatics, context, and cotext play a primary role in shaping the interpretation of text. For instance, Calzolari *et al.* (2002) note that, somehow, a computer program must be assisted in not becoming confused about the real world meanings of *piatto di legno* 'wooden dish' and *piatto di pasta* 'pasta dish' even though the forms are directly paradigmatic and therefore could easily be taken as semantically paradigmatic too. The human solves the problem using pragmatics, and, consequently, does not expect to resolve ambiguity without context. World knowledge enables us to infer that 'he served up the dessert on a pasta dish' most probably means that the dish was one designed for serving pasta on. However, humans are also perfectly capable of considering, given the right encouragement, possible world scenarios in which ice cream is served on top of, say, a lasagne or else on an edible plate. It follows that a successful computer simulation of human linguistic knowledge (arguably, in such cases, a requirement for a successful simulation of behaviour) would detect that the sentence is odd and interesting, rather than either being able to decide that one or other reading is definitely correct or conclude that the ambiguity is irresolvable.

Furnishing a computer program with the capacity to use, or simulate the use of, pragmatic knowledge entails either manual intervention by humans, to tell the computer what the input actually means, or else the addition of extralinguistic knowledge as part of the information base of the system, along with a means of 'reasoning' in order to extract and apply it (Isabelle and Foster 2006: 411). Much can be achieved by constraining the system to a specific domain of operation (as the TESSA translation system was), because many otherwise confounding interpretations of language can be set aside as irrelevant to the context.

Unit size

As already noted, a key challenge for NLP, including MT, is the size of unit to operate with. Probabilistic models (for example, the IBM models, Isabelle and Foster 2006: 415ff), which calculate the statistical likelihood that a particular word or word string will appear in the context of particular others, generate thousands of unlikely associations as the means for spotting the likely ones. Ways of reducing this redundancy have focused in part on the preferred unit size, something that is clearly highly relevant to the question of what part formulaic language might play. In translation contexts, probability models can be constrained by using phrases rather than words, and the results are considered promising (Isabelle and Foster 2006: 420). An alternative to probability is the intelligent cross-comparison of exemplars. The provision of a bilingual corpus for training and reference enables the computer to look for matches of, first, large units such as complete sentences already attested and, progressively, smaller units. Both 'example-based' translation of this kind and the phrase-level probability-based models, however, continue to suffer a key limitation in terms of grammatical and semantic coherence within and across the sentence. As a result, the specific chunks are convincingly translated, but they do not fit together appropriately (ibid.: 420). The reason seems to be that variation between input and existing exemplars is used to separate out identical from non-identical material, and so one variable item can divide what would have been one long matched string with a gap in it, into three separate strings (for example, ibid.: 414, examples 25–6). Viewing language as likely to be constructed of partly-fixed frames with variable items filling the gaps, as in NOA, might greatly increase the opportunities for capturing these elusive macro-relationships within and across sentences.

Operating effectively with prefabricated multiword strings depends on recognizing not only the patterns that they capture, but also their status as units in their own right. For practical modelling purposes they tend to occupy a position somewhere between what can be dealt with in the lexicon and what can be dealt with by the grammar. Yet Calzolari *et al.* observe that:

> the interpretation of M[ulti] W[ord] E[xpression]s can be done using the same representational devices already available in both lexicons [i.e. of English and Italian] for interpreting regular noun constructions: MWEs and regular noun constructions seem to share and make appeal to the same general principles of semantic constitution of lexical items and their combinatorics …
>
> (Calzolari *et al.* 2002: 1939)

This observation suggests the potential to make further concessions towards the notion that MWEs really are single lexical units, provided one is willing to re-evaluate two standing assumptions. One assumption is that the sorts of variation seen in MWEs are different in kind from those seen in words. The other is that just because there are patterns, there needs to be a rule. Both of these assumptions are necessary within some theoretical frameworks adopted in relation to natural language modelling. However, between them, they in fact lead to such an impasse that "MWEs constitute a key problem that must be resolved in order for linguistically precise N[atural] L[anguage] P[rocessing] to succeed" (Sag *et al.* 2002: 14).

A further assumption made in some NLP research is that the scope for new multiword expressions is essentially limitless: "we are concerned with devices in grammar that allow for the production/analysis of new MWEs rather than learned phrases ... A primary motivation for this approach is to enable the fully or semi-automatic recognition/acquisition of MWE lexicon entries" (Calzolari *et al.* 2002: 1935). By this, Calzolari *et al.* mean that "when representing MWEs in computation lexicons we want to exploit regularities in forming MWEs and their translations to avoid simply listing translation equivalents, as well as to account for 'new' MWEs that follow regular rules of formation" (ibid.: 1939). The aim is not unreasonable, nor are they mistaken in recognizing that there must be a way for a program to both recognize and generate MWEs that have not been specifically listed in the database. However, intrinsic in the formulation of these aims is an assumption that MWEs are fundamentally generative, rather than that they have a somewhat fixed range of nativelike realizations that entail constrained paradigmatic variation within partly-fixed frames. In some cases, that range of realizations is so broad that it does, indeed, constitute an effectively 'free choice'. However, in many other cases—and it is these that are the difficulty for NLP and general linguistic modelling—the range is *not* that broad, and thus arises the so far insoluble challenge of how to constrain it.

It follows that an alternative approach would be to challenge the entire assumption that MWEs automatically carry the potential to generate paradigmatic exemplars, and, instead, to suppose that they do not carry that potential unless it is specifically demonstrated in data that they do—and then only to generalize from a small, specified paradigm outwards on the basis of appropriate additional data. Constraining variation in this way is important not only because it helps prevent the problem of over-generation of forms, but also because it explains the pragmatic effect of marginal over-generation, which is often humorous. For an example that is grammatical and meaningful to sound sufficiently right to be acceptable but sufficiently wrong to cause amusement requires the receiver to be sensitive not only to what is possible, but also what is likely. That kind of sensitivity, it will be argued below, is better *built up* from a more conservative perception than *pared down* from a more liberal one.

Could computers acquire a language like a child?

Humans know what they know about languages because of the way that they learn them. Computers, of course, learn what their programmers tell them to learn, and that is determined by at least three things: what computers are able to learn, what they can learn in the time available, and what the programmers consider it appropriate for them to learn. Given the generally strong emphasis on atomistic linguistic modelling over the past 40 or more years, it is not surprising, perhaps, that it has taken a while for phrase-based approaches to show how much promise they have. The lead on using multiword strings has been taken by those developing specific applications where expediency has required the taking of short cuts that would not be possible, or desirable, for the less domain-specific systems that represent the goal of NLP research. Thus, as noted above, there tends to be a sense that when you work with multiword strings you are postponing an important problem for later in order to make some short term headway. It is this implicit assumption—that phrases will ultimately need to be broken down for a full characterization—that will be challenged here. Consequent on this position is the proposal that computer programs might more closely approximate human linguistic behaviour if they can learn about patterns in a way that is similar to the one characterized as NOA.

The kind of model of language that is needed if computers are to become good linguists is one that:

- has the flexibility to recognize and produce new forms without stepping beyond the bounds of what real language data attests;
- is able to identify semantic, grammatical, and pragmatic oddity as interpretable but marked (for example, for humour, error);
- traces the contours of language patterning as evidenced in data, rather than as predicted by an abstract model;
- accommodates and uses such features of human language as fuzzy meaning, collocational restrictions, and irregularity.

These requirements apply to any aspect of NLP that entails interpretation, free production, or translation.

Current approaches, however, tend to operate *despite* the features characterized above, as if they must be overcome in order to reveal the true order underneath. This assumption should be challenged. Some way needs to be found to make it valuable, or at least not detrimental, to the modelled system, that human languages display a deal of apparently unnecessary complexity, for example, variation in the patterns of conjugation and case agreement, sub-rules, etc. Certainly, these complications make it impossible to identify a single rule that applies to all potential members of a word-class or larger composite structure, but that is only a problem if it is assumed that a rule must be captured because there is the potential for generation. In actual fact, the more variation there is in forms, the less likely it is that most of them have any true generative potential. For instance, English has a number of forms that express the plural, but only one, '–s' (along with some form-predictable varia-tions such as '–es') is productive. The others (for example, '–ren' in 'children', '–i' in 'foci', '–a' in 'criteria', '–im' in 'seraphim') may certainly be *described* using a rule, but a descriptive rule is not necessary for generative purposes. The most a system needs to be able to do is recognize a new example: if the rule is non-productive, the new item can simply be added to the closed list.

Applying NOA to computer language learning

NOA suggests an approach to learning in which a computer is exposed to many multiword form-meaning pairs, and enabled to extrapolate according to evidence of paradigmatic variation. That is, directly in parallel with the processes described in Chapter 2, the primary activity would be to undertake the minimum possible processing to establish a reliable meaning for any given input. As more and more examples were encountered, differentiation would be made between sequences of material (for example, letters in written input) that were the same across exemplars, and points of variation would be located. The material contained between two points of variation would be extracted and attributed its own meaning. This meaning[3] would have to be supplied during the learning phase, which means that an NOA-oriented approach to computer language learning would require a measure of human trainer intervention to constrain and shape the initial development. So much is simply a parallel to the input for first language acquisition. However, over time, the accumulated knowledge would enable the system to become increasingly self-sufficient.

Computer simulations by Kirby (2001, 2002) have revealed that even when input has no initial structure at all and only a holistic meaning, it is possible to derive constituent forms with robust sub-meanings on the basis of chance coincidences in the input forms—as predicted for the emergence of constituents from a holistic protolanguage (Wray 1998, 2000b, 2002a; see Chapter 17). Kirby also found that the analysis did not continue ad infinitum, but rather stopped when all of the variation occurring in the data had been accounted for. Finally, he found that the impetus for breaking input down was the need to extrapolate from too little data (a 'bottleneck'). These simu-lations represent instances of NOA in action computationally for language acquisition.

Corpus-based MT systems already operate a limited version of NOA, insofar as they can identify abstractions such as 'x likes to read y' and associate it with *x aime lire y* (Isabelle and Foster 2006: 415). However, the abstraction seems to be reliant on parsing (ibid.: 414), whereas the principle of NOA is that parsing is post hoc, and potentially never completed.[4] Furthermore, because the designated task is translation, the nature of the extrapolation is different, and directly focused on cross-language equivalence for production.

Although some systems do engage in offline processing (ibid.: 414), the production-driven approach precludes the amassing of a body of extrapolated knowledge on the basis of *comprehension* (or its computer equivalent). That is, extrapolations about similarities between single-language examples are geared towards identifying the best presentation of the same information in another language, rather than generalizing about how the differences in meaning are achieved through differences in form.

In the purest version of an NOA model, the computer would have no grammar, just a lexicon containing units with meanings that range from simply referential of an entity or action, through to complex relations (compare Construction Grammar, as discussed in Chapter 7). A less extreme version would separate out large-unit operations from independent small-unit ones, the latter handling those configurations that are deemed grammatical even though they are not idiomatic. For some tastes, the latter is a more palatable option, for amalgamating holistic and analytic approaches mirrors a longstanding debate about dual systems processing for human language (for example, Sinclair 1991; Wray 1992; Coltheart, Rastle, Perry, Langdon, and Ziegler 2001; Van Lancker Sidtis 2002). However, as noted earlier, the key need is to avoid over-generation, and so rules should be added only parsimoniously, if at all.

The use of trainer input, possibly quite intensive, might seem undesirable for a computational model. However, the cost-benefit ratio depends on the transferability of the outcome. Certainly we might baulk at training individually every system that needed to use a given language, even though doing so would allow the language to be custom-built to match the input (and even though that is what we do with our children). But with a large enough corpus of the language marked up for meaning at the propositional level, it might be possible to evolve a general representation of a human language such as English, applicable to many contexts. If so, the main part of the learning process would be a one-off computational procedure for any given target language. The result would be both a master-version of the linguistic knowledge necessary to recognize and produce all and only the grammatical *and* nativelike strings of that language, and simultaneously a prototype, since in each application, learning could continue, driven by subsequent input. As a result, different instantiations of the same mature model would develop differently as and when exposed to different data.

The fundamental features of a language so-learnt would include some that are counter-intuitive in relation to a grammar-centric view of language.

1 A great many patterns visible to the naked eye would *not* be captured and exploited. Only patterns that were specifically demonstrated to be active, through paradigmatic variation in the data, would be identified as productive. Furthermore, a conservative approach to generalization would ensure that much of the paradigmatic variation remained tied to semantically-related groups (compare Pattern Grammar, Chapter 7) or indeed specific lexical items.

2 The patterns identified might often not map onto classic form-meaning configurations recognized in grammatical models. This is because paradigmatic variation would separate out actively interchanging lexical units, leaving the rest of the form to carry the rest of the meaning. Thus, frames with gaps might comfortably contain items that, in other approaches to analysis, were difficult to assign a meaning or grammatical identity to. In this approach, no such separate meaning or identity is required for such items.

Conclusion

It has been argued that there are opportunities to use the parsimony of formulaic processing in Natural Language Processing contexts, to overcome some persistent problems that seem rooted in the belief that language is fully generative. The problem encountered by the western educated adult language learner, in identifying rules that are too productive relative to what corpora attest and native speakers consider nativelike (Chapter 18), is the same problem encountered by the computer—and this may simply be because the computer is trained by western educated adults.

Of course, there are arguments to be made regarding the assumption that it is even desirable for either the adult learner or the computer to acquire language that is entirely nativelike. But if that is the goal, then a model of how native speakers gain their nativelike competence, and particularly how they acquire and sustain their tolerance for complexity and irregularity and develop their sense of what is *likely* as distinct from what is *possible*, seems a sensible place to start.

Notes

1 Achieving a spoken rather than written interface presents additional challenges (for example, R. W. Smith 2006: 501f) both for comprehension (for example, Juang and Rabiner 2006; Rabiner and Juang 2006) and production (for example, Hirschberg 2006; Nusbaum and Shintel 2006), but these are not directly relevant to the present discussion.

2 http://framenet.icsi.berkeley.edu. Accessed 10 February 2008.

3 As noted earlier in the chapter, just what 'meaning' is in this context depends on what the computer is intended to do. It is assumed here—perhaps rather ambitiously—that meanings could be expressed as logical propositions indexed to world knowledge.

4 In NOA there is no doubt that the 'x' and 'y' in 'x likes to read y' will be allocated a robust grammatical and functional role early on. On the other hand, the 'to' in the same sentence might never be allocated a separate role, since it is immutable in the string 'like to VERB'. NOA entails that the occurrence of 'to' in this string is not even necessarily equated with its occurrence in 'long to VERB' and 'hope to VERB', let alone in other

types of string. While this clearly means that a potential generalization is missed, the major problem for other approaches is *over*-generalization, so this conservativism may be well-placed.

20

Formulaicity under pressure

Introduction

Formulaicity comes at a price. There is a tension between saving processing and avoiding the undesirable consequences of using prefabricated forms. How do users resolve that tension? In this chapter, we examine four of the situations presented in Part Three—those in which formulaic language was a particularly useful and valuable choice, while switching to non-formulaic material was costly in some way: a reduction in proficiency (the beginner learner, Chapter 12), a loss of fluency (the TALK software, Chapter 11), a compromise to fidelity and professionalism (the television sketch, Chapter 15), or the sacrifice of accuracy (the advanced learners, Chapter 13). In such situations it might seem obvious that one would stick to the formulaic material, but the dynamics were different in each case, with different outcomes. At the end of the chapter, one theme of the discussion, the way that verbatim memorization was undertaken in three of the four cases, is used to develop a model of how choices are made, risks taken, and opportunities created, during learning and remembering.

Formulaicity for basic proficiency

Margaret, the beginner learner of Welsh (Chapter 12), memorized word strings in order to succeed in a task that even native speakers would find stressful—giving a cookery demonstration to a live audience in front of television cameras. She took the learning very seriously and was extremely well-prepared for her performance. It was necessary to be so, for she had so little knowledge of the language that if she did not use the material she had memorized she would not be able to say anything much at all.

Despite her best efforts, her output was not fully identical to the nativelike input she had been given and had practised. For instance, she occasionally replaced a word within a memorized string with a Welsh synonym gleaned from another, for example, *toddwch y menyn mewn sosban* 'melt the butter in a saucepan' became *rhowch y menyn mewn padell* 'put the butter in a pan'. In addition she occasionally replaced a Welsh word with its English equivalent, for example, *llwyaid o juice* for *llwyaid o sudd* 'a spoonful of juice'; *salt a phupur* for *halen a phupur* 'salt and pepper', and *ychwanegwch y cream* for *ychwanegwch yr hufen* 'add the cream' (Wray 2004: 265). Such cross-language deviations had no consequence for communication, since Welsh speakers are almost always fluent in English as well.

Nevertheless, despite her occasional departures from the script, it is beyond doubt that Margaret's intention was to reproduce all and only the memorized material. And the constraints of performing so far in excess of her competence were marked. She observed afterwards that there had been one major difference between her Welsh language cookery demonstration and the English language ones she was accustomed to doing. In the latter, she would engage in improvised chat while the ingredients were cooking, but in Welsh she had no way of doing so, and felt entirely tongue-tied. Her prepared material only extended to the specific cooking instructions, and they left her with periods of several minutes of silence while the ingredients were cooking. Had she been able to fill these awkward silences with Welsh language chat, she undoubtedly would have. But she could not. She only had what she had prepared formulaically, and she made no deliberate effort to break out of that constraint.

Formulaicity for fluency

Sylvia, using the TALK software (Chapter 11), also faced a high price if she tried to create new utterances in real time. In her case, she risked losing the effect of real conversation, since real time production would reduce the output rate from around 60 words per minute to two or three. At this slow speed the momentum of conversational exchange is forfeited, and only vital information is exchanged. It was, therefore, very much in Sylvia's interests to operate within the constraints of her stored materials.

Her strategies for doing so began at the input stage, by ensuring that what she stored was in a form that rendered it usable in the maximum number of situations. During use, she would steer the conversation towards the topics she had prepared. And if she was confronted with a situation in which she did not have what she needed, she would either use an item she did have—even if it entailed her saying something that was not quite true or did not quite fit pragmatically—or else she would select a holding message such as 'I haven't thought about that much' or 'That's a good question'. If she was having a series of conversations with someone, she also might offer to answer the question next time (Todman *et al.* 1999b: 338). Only in a few circumstances, often to spell out the name of a person or place, would she ask her interlocutor to be patient while she constructed a reply in real time. For Sylvia there was always genuine choice, and the balance she maintained between formulaic and novel material was determined on the basis of the conflicting desires to share honest information and not to undermine the flow of the exchange. Overall, it is striking to see the extent to which she was able to sustain convincing conversations using almost entirely prefabricated turns.

There were a number of things that prefabricated responses were inadequate for. Backchannel responses (Todman, Alm, and Elder 1994) were a particular problem, because by the time she had selected one, the moment had passed. They also came out too loud or with the wrong intonation. For the same reason, Sylvia was reluctant to use her stored utterance 'That's a shame', because the synthesized voice could not deliver it in a manner that sounded sympathetic. This problem arose on account of current technology, but Sylvia's choice about how to deal with it reflected her need to protect aspects of her identity and personality in the eyes of others.

Formulaicity for fidelity

In some situations, it is important to say exactly the right words, and that means one has to memorize them. For example, through custom and practice some expressions become socially or pragmatically obligatory in particular contexts. At the sharp end are performatives (Austin 1962; Searle 1971), where a ritual act is only achieved if the correct words are spoken (see Wray 2002b: 90f for a brief discussion of performatives as formulaic 'situation manipulators'). Many other expressions (for example, 'Thank you', 'Trick or Treat', 'Amen') make a lesser impact on the state of affairs, but nevertheless possess their own social and pragmatic significance. Another reason for using a specified form is to express deference to the originator of its content. In academic writing, quotations have this status, and must be correctly reproduced.

In acting, fidelity to the script is normally paramount—French and Saunders (Chapter 15) notwithstanding—and it is not considered acceptable to paraphrase the words. The challenge that actors face is to gain thorough familiarity with the text, and thereby to deflect attention from the fact that it is not the spontaneous product of the character they are playing. The artificiality of this activity is twofold: the text is not novel at the time of production, and it is not the product of the speaker's own mind. Where other extreme situations, such as oral epics (Chapter 4), TALK (Chapter 11), and the advanced language learning experiment (Chapter 13) do enable the user/speaker to participate in composition to a greater or lesser extent, the actor can only attempt to feign ownership through familiarity.

The temptation to modify a script must be great at times. Living authors can, of course, be consulted, and, as Chapter 15 showed, actors who are also the writers have particular opportunities for taking liberties. The questionnaire survey reported in Chapter 15 revealed that even when the actor has had no part in the composition of the script, it is not uncommon for changes to be negotiated, particularly in stage works where there is enough rehearsal time for experimentation with alternatives. All the same, actors consistently stated that they deferred to the author. One commented: "Actors should of course stick rigidly to the words of the script; the playwright has chosen those words with care and it's insulting to paraphrase."[1] Wolfe's (1992) advice to authors confirms this impression: "You must remind the actor politely but firmly that there is nothing in his contract that allows him to alter lines, as he does not have script approval ... only international bankable stars such as Michael Caine, Sean Connery, etc. have script approval clauses" (p. 101).

Actors will, inevitably, struggle at times if text is difficult to memorize or reproduce convincingly. But evidently the calibre of actors is determined by their ability to deliver difficult material effectively. Not needing to request changes is thus a mark of professionalism. Not surprisingly, classical works are beyond reproach, so that any problems in memorization and delivery lie with the actor. One actor commented: "With Shakespeare ... any alteration to the words alters the balance of the iambic structure ... with other classical writers if you start paraphrasing what they have written you can find yourself in severe difficulties memory wise".

The actors' perception of the theatrical tradition reflects the changes that Parry and Lord identified as inevitable once literary works are customarily written down (see Chapter 4). The actors expressed deference towards drama as a literary art, and to a traditional elevated language of the theatre which some of them considered debased by the recent market-driven demand for oral realism.

Formulaicity for greater accuracy

In the advanced language learning experiment (Chapter 13) the participants had memorized a nativelike version of what they needed to say. If they could successfully reproduce this material, they would be assured of conveying their desired message effectively, and simultaneously signalling to their native speaker interlocutors that they were proficient speakers, which might encourage a more authentically nativelike response. In other words, the prefabricated material offered an opportunity for the learners to raise their game. The material they had memorized could not meet every contingency, of course, and there were times when they were lost for words, having no suitable prefabricated response. So, what did they do, when they were confronted with a conflict between what they *could* say and what they *wanted* to say? They took a range of courses of action.

One solution was to use a filler, either to hold the turn while a solution was found, or to constitute a turn in its own right. The data contained numerous examples of 'oohhhh' and 'ahhhh', with highly emphasized intonation, which, within their context of use, might be glossed as 'that's very interesting' or 'I don't really understand, but please keep talking'. Another way of alleviating the difficulty of not having prepared quite what they wanted was to create a new utterance. Being intermediate to advanced learners, living and studying in the L2 environment, the participants in this experiment generally did have sufficient linguistic knowledge to create a novel utterance if they preferred, or to edit a memorized one to make it more fit for the immediate purpose. In the real conversations, they engaged in quite a lot of novel construction of output, and also edited the material that they had learnt. Their performance at the rehearsal stage indicated that doing so was not because they didn't know the prefabricated material well enough, for they clearly did.

As noted in Chapter 17, the participants departed from the prepared material not only in order to attain a closer fit with the ideas they wanted to convey, but also because of the impression they wanted to create about themselves. Such alteration tended to introduce interlanguage errors, meaning that they sacrificed accuracy. But accuracy was not—as they pointed out in the interviews—their only consideration. These were real interactions in which it was not in their interests unnecessarily to constrain what they said or how they presented themselves, just in order to say something correctly. Communicative proficiency was a package, only one component of which was nativelike production.

Another option at their disposal was to manipulate the direction of the conversation to match the material they had memorized. However, they were generally less able or willing to do this than Sylvia was with TALK. The ability and preparedness to take control of conversations is presumably determined jointly by personality and circumstances. Without doubt, some participants were more adept at manipulation than others. Lo had prepared an utterance to introduce herself (the MU below), but when she walked into the room, the pragmatics were not quite right. She altered her memorized string in order to make it fit the situation (RP):

MU Hello, my name's Louise, I'm a student here
RP I think I have to introduce myself...my name's Louise, I'm student here

Sa, having prepared for a conversation with her flatmate about a weekend trip to Edinburgh, found that the flatmate had even more recently been to Paris. However, she was able to manipulate the conversation back to Edinburgh, with 'So, this weekend you went to Paris and last weekend you went to Edinburgh, so how did you find it, did you enjoy it?'. She also improvised with: 'So, if you can compare Paris and Edinburgh, which one do you like ...?', commenting afterwards: 'If we naturally continue our conversation we talk about Paris ...', showing that she had very deliberately brought the conversation back to a point where she could use her prepared target utterances.

Risk-taking in memorization

The acted performances in the French and Saunders sketch, and the kinds of extreme language learning undertaken by the Welsh beginner and more advanced learners of English, all entailed attempts to memorize material so that it could be retrieved reliably at a later date. We have seen that various factors can play a role in determining the extent to which the faithful reproduction of such material is achieved. Most actors are focused on exact repetition, though French and Saunders were not. The learners were supposed to be similarly focused, but issues of choice and lack of knowledge intervened, with some deviations deliberately made, others unintentionally.

The nature of the deviations bears closer examination. At the heart of the issue is the amount of risk that an individual is prepared to take in relation to the process of memorization—for the less attention paid to the detail of the text, the less likely it is to be remembered entirely correctly. Different scenarios below examine the cases above in the light of how the level of risk taken interacts with the learning approach or capacity of the individual to affect the output.

Verbatim memorization in acting

Actors develop particular skills for effective memorization in which attention to committing the words to memory is not primary, even though it is vital that the original is exactly reproduced. The approach taken entails engaging semantically with the text, "breaking down scripts into what they call 'beats' (the smallest goal-directed chunks of dialogue" (Noice and Noice 2006: 15). The effect is that "a link is forged between almost every word or phrase and the goal that caused the character to utter it" (ibid.). As later discussion will indicate, it seems unlikely that there *are* actually separate links to most individual words in verbatim memorization, but it is plausible that actors use as their lexical units complete sentences and phrases, along with certain key single words that carry a significant semantic or pragmatic load. In other words, they apply Needs Only Analysis (NOA) to identify the largest form that can be associated with a salient meaning.

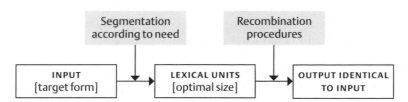

Figure 20.1 Memorization undertaken by a native speaker for verbatim reproduction

Of course, most of the units so-identified would be unlikely to already exist in the individual's lexicon, and those that did would require some kind of additional marking as script items. But once in the lexicon, the units would be available not only for the performance, but for more general use—meaning that actors, in ordinary conversation, might find themselves able to quote apposite phrases from past scripts.

Having divided a text up into memorable parts, reproducing it entails recombining them. Since the lexical units are salient in terms of meaning within the development of the story, the recombination procedures (Figure 20.1) will be mechanisms for remembering what idea needs to be expressed next. Ideally, this will result in a verbatim reproduction of the original. Briers and McEwen presumably prepared for their part in the French and Saunders sketch (Chapter 15) in this way, and indeed a good correspondence was achieved in their performances between the script and the performed version. There were differences, but, a small amount of rephrasing apart (for example, Figure 15.10) they predominantly entailed adjuncts such as 'you know' and 'but'—which may be difficult to anchor exactly as form-meaning pairs.

In sum, an actor, or anyone else, who needs to guarantee the faithful reproduction of a target, cannot afford to take any risks with the amount of attention paid to that target. Not so, however, for memorization in which deviations are permissible.

Taking risks in memorization

Most native speakers, certainly after childhood, rarely if ever need to memorize a text verbatim. However, they might need to become very familiar indeed with the content of a text. We can interpret French and Saunders' improvised performance in this way. They had written a script, but they did not need to internalize the exact forms, only the direction of the story. As seen in Chapter 15, the result was that they exchanged and reordered lines. In addition, they may have omitted a crucial part of the plot—and this indicates that this route to memorization entails a level of risk: the less attention you pay to the 'target' input, the more danger of deviating from it, with some deviations potentially costly.

Outside the realm of acting, we also see instances of risk-tolerant memorization. Someone preparing for an important job interview might rehearse answers to likely questions. In the course of rehearsal, it is likely that some phrases and clauses would become settled in their form, so that they were recalled identically each time. But it would rarely be necessary deliberately to memorize an entire script for such an event, for native speakers will usually have confidence that as long as they can remember the idea they wanted to put across, they can reliably express it in a nativelike way using their normal productive resources.

Figure 20.2 represents the process by which an original input version is internalized sufficiently to enable a meaning-equivalent output. The initial part of the process is the same as for verbatim memorization, but rather than creating new entries in the lexicon that associate the specific form with the salient meaning, existing units can be used when available. New units will only be created when there is no existing unit with the precise meaning—and this is how certain phrases and clauses are recalled verbatim. Because the lexical units are largely the same ones used for the production of everyday output, the generic grammar rules[2] can be used to assemble the messages, resulting in output that is faithful to the meaning of the original but does not necessarily use the same words to express it, and that reflects aspects of the speaker's personal style.

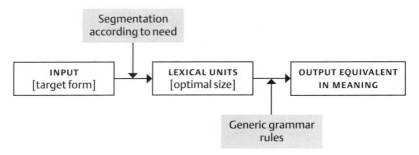

Figure 20.2 Memorization undertaken by a native speaker for non-verbatim reproduction

The risk element lies in the trade-off between saving the effort of creating bespoke lexical units for verbatim reproduction, and being unable to achieve a sufficiently faithful delivery. The less it matters that the original is perfectly reproduced, the more it will be attractive to take risks with the learning.[3]

The calculation of risk by language learners

Suppose a language learner has been charged with memorizing a text—for a class performance of play perhaps, or, as in Chapters 12 and 13, for an experiment in extreme learning. To what extent might that learner dare take risks in order to reduce the effort of memorization, and what would the effects be?

Someone who had absolutely no knowledge of the language, such as Margaret in Chapter 12, or a tourist who just wanted to be able to say 'thank you' to a host, would be obliged to internalize every single formal feature of the prepared material, because, should it be forgotten, there would be no way to reinstate it from general knowledge. At the other extreme, an L2 speaker with nativelike command could, presumably, take risks in just the same way as a native speaker, as outlined above. Learners of intermediate to advanced proficiency like those in Chapter 13 lie between the two.

The process by which they might approach memorization is depicted in Figure 20.3. Like the native speaker they make a judgement about how much specific attention to pay to the input form, and they rely on generic grammar rules to reinstate any detail that has not been learnt. However, because they are not fully proficient, they cannot bring to the situation a nativelike set of lexical units—overall they are likely to have a greater proportion of smaller units than a native speaker would (see Chapter 2). Furthermore, the rules they can apply during utterance assembly are not necessarily the same as those of a native speaker, so that interlanguage errors are likely.

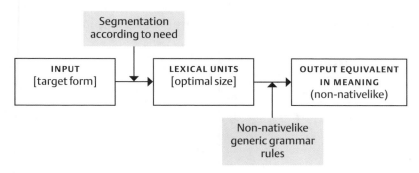

Figure 20.3 Memorization undertaken by a non-native speaker (risk-sensitive)

Risk as an index of proficiency

Since risk-taking in memorization is a nativelike behaviour, the amount of risk that a learner is prepared to take will be correlated with proficiency[4] (Wray and Fitzpatrick 2008). More precisely, individuals' risk-taking reflects not their actual productive knowledge, but rather what they *perceive* their productive knowledge to be—and that is more likely to reflect their *receptive* knowledge. For instance, if a learner sees in a target text the collocation 'take a chance', recognizes it, and knows what it means, confidence in that receptive knowledge could easily prompt an over-estimation of the likelihood of reproducing it reliably. The risk taken might be to only memorize, say, 'VERB chance' or 'VERB NOUN' [*opportunity*] (where 'chance' represents a lexicalized form and *opportunity* only a meaning) rather than the fully lexicalized string. Storing these frames requires one to have the productive ability to complete them appropriately, and if the productive knowledge is inadequate, neither verbatim recall nor a nativelike alternative is guaranteed. This is very much the pattern observed in the deviations made in the advanced learners' study, with, for instance, the omission of plural markers that the learner unquestionably had full command of receptively.

The longitudinal trajectory of the learner is mapped out in Figure 20.4. For as long as proficiency is low, risk-taking will be low (a) and, with all the attention to detail, accuracy will rise in tandem with proficiency (we saw in Chapter 12 that even a beginner cannot be entirely accurate in verbatim memorization, so improvements occur as more is learnt). As noted, risk-taking rises in line with receptive knowledge. Once sufficient risks are being taken for the target material not to be subject to much form-based attention, accuracy will plateau for a while, relative to rising proficiency, for additional risk-taking is undermined by the shortfall between receptive and productive ability—(b) in Figure 20.4. This means that an individual with a higher proficiency level might actually make as many errors in output as one with a lower proficiency level, because the former takes more risks in memorization than the latter. Finally, the proficiency level is high enough for the risk-taking to be vindicated, and accuracy then rises in line with proficiency again.

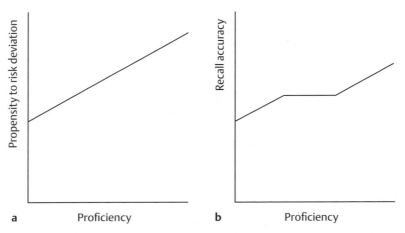

Figure 20.4   Relationship between proficiency and (a) risk-taking and (b) recall accuracy in relation to deviations from the memorized target

This phenomenon offers an interesting opportunity for researchers and teachers. The overall amount of risk is an indication of receptive proficiency. Within that, the proportion of deviations that are non-nativelike is an index of the difference between the learner's receptive and productive knowledge (Wray and Fitzpatrick 2008).

Memorization as a route to success

If errors in memorization arise as a consequence of excessive risk-taking, then a low-risk approach to memorization can disguise the weaknesses of a learner who avoids producing original output. This was, indeed, the purpose of the extreme learning experiments in Chapters 12 and 13. A particular problem arises in proficiency testing if memorization is used as a preparation technique, and ways need to be found to establish the likelihood that an essay or oral presentation contains an inappropriately high proportion of pre-memorized material (Wray and Pegg in press).

However, learners may also seek to memorize text for very positive reasons. Ding (2007) investigated the success of three winners of a national English speaking competition in China. It turned out that they had all attended the same school, in which a teacher required them to imitate recordings of texts by native speakers and be able recite them back without deviation in form, including intonation. By senior level, the texts could be many pages long. Ding notes that memorization did not necessarily build on understanding (see discussion in Chapter 18). Rather, the teacher's rationale seemed to be that competence would be back-filled by virtue of having good exemplars in memory (ibid.: 279). The harsh regime paid dividends, at least for the informants, who found that "what had been memorised became our own language" (Ding 2007: 275). Ding observes, "when they speak English, lines from movies often naturally pop out, making others think of their English as natural and fluent" (ibid.). The process of this learning is mapped out in Figure 20.5. The effort of undertaking verbatim memorization pays off when that output can be recycled by the learner as reliable input for learning. It can be subjected to its own NOA to provide the optimal lexical units and generic grammar rules for a nativelike novel output.

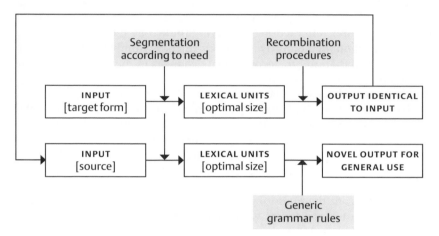

Figure 20.5 Memorization undertaken by a non-native speaker, using low-risk, high fidelity output as input for general learning

Conclusion

Of the learner and user types reviewed in this chapter, the ones most bound to the prefabricated forms they had prepared were those whose professed goal was faithful reproduction—Ding's 'expert' Chinese learners and the actors—and those who needed the prefabricated forms to maintain fluency and proficiency—Sylvia and Margaret.

The former were obliged to surrender of ownership of the words, viewing themselves as agents whose role was simply to re-present the text. The latter two tolerated the absence of free expression. It left Margaret with long silences during her cookery demonstration. Sylvia, able by other means to express her basic thoughts and needs, particularly valued TALK for its social potential, and she was prepared to sacrifice free expression in the interests of maintaining fluency (Alm, Arnott, and Newell 1989; Todman, Lewins, File, Alm, and Elder 1995). Of course, the TALK data were gathered in the lab, and the conversations were not with people whom Sylvia would necessarily have chosen as friends. This might have encouraged Sylvia to prefer the easiest processing route. She noted (see Chapter 11) that if she was tired she would sometimes select a slightly inappropriate prefabricated utterance rather than bother to construct a more accurate one. We might anticipate that outside the lab, where Sylvia's reply to a question could materially affect some aspect of her life, she would be less inclined to select a pre-stored item if it was contrary to what she wanted to say, for here, the conversational flow would be secondary to the content.

Less bound into verbatim memorization were French and Saunders and the advanced learners, the former because it is part of their style to use improvisation methods, and the latter because they were fully focused on using their material in a genuine interaction—conveying the wrong message could have potential impact on their daily lives. Therefore, they would be highly likely to modify prepared material to accommodate changes in the facts, such as the meeting time for a trip to the cinema.

In all the situations, formulaicity and creativity were set in a specific, appropriate balance, and the challenge for the speaker was to maintain the optimal relationship between them. In the next chapter we explore what happens when the constraints of formulaicity are tightened even further.

Notes

1 Comments from the questionnaires are not attributed. For an explanation, and a list of the actors who responded to the survey, see note 5 in Chapter 15.

2 The grammar rules for creating output from items in a heteromorphic lexicon will include rules for stringing together large MEUs such as complete clauses and phrases, and insertion rules for completing partially lexicalized frames.

3 Risk-taking is therefore related to attention and focus.

4 There is another dimension, as Chapter 13 revealed. Learners vary in their confidence level. A nervous learner is more likely to put extra time into memorization, while an over-confident one takes more risks. However, the calculation described below, of the ratio of nativelike to non-native-like deviations means that the actual amount of deviation is secondary. In effect, with fewer deviations per memorized string, one simply needs more data from a nervous learner before one can establish the ratio.

21

Formulaic language, formulaic thought

Introduction

In this chapter we consider further the question: *Does formulaic language constrain what we say and what we think?* Two situation types are reviewed, in which morpheme equivalent units (MEUs), if used, will constrain what can be expressed, or how people behave. The first situation entails the imposition of formulaic language from outside, to prevent the speaker realizing that anything else could be said. In the second, marking the most extreme conditions possible, there is (almost) no escape from formulaicity, and means must be found to make maximum use of the constrained system, and/or tailor what needs to be said to what *can* be said.

Formulaic sequences for social control

In Chapter 20 we saw how the actor, committed to reproducing the playwright's words exactly, is an *agent* in the service of conveying the thoughts and feelings of a fictional character. The shared words do not imply shared beliefs between playwright and character, actor and playwright, or actor and character. This separation is possible because of the understanding of all parties, and of the audience, that what happens on the stage is contained there. Although there may be powerful allusions to the real world, and the playwright may by means of his characters' words and actions deliver his own message, the events and assertions on the stage have full reality only there.

But in other circumstances, people may be encouraged, even forced, to adopt the words of another person as a means of getting them to adopt and proliferate the ideas behind the words. The principle underlying this process is that it is possible to control people's thoughts by controlling what they are able to say. As noted in Chapter 1, George Orwell believed that forms of words had the power to stifle creative thought. Although the vitriol in his 1946 essay was levelled primarily at the obfuscatory language of journalists and politicians, he was also suspicious about the ways in which dictatorships might use and mould language in order to control a population. It is a theme he developed in his novel *Nineteen Eighty-Four* (Orwell 1949), where in Ingsoc—English society under a totalitarian regime—saying the wrong thing is dangerous. In order to avoid being betrayed to the thought police by the relentlessly indoctrinated younger generation, the fearful population learns to speak only the prescribed slogans, until the ideas conveyed in the slogans become their only thoughts.

Aspects of Orwell's fictional world are juxtaposed with the real one in Ji's (2004) account of 'linguistic engineering' during the Cultural Revolution in Maoist China, which she describes as "the great attempt to produce new, revolutionary human beings by enforcing the constant repetition of revolutionary formulae" (p. 317). The aim was to "enforce[e] the habitual use, in relevant contexts, of numerous fixed expressions and standardized scripts that embodied 'correct' attitudes or that had 'correct' propositional content" (p. 4). Formulas, especially slogans and quotations from Mao's writings, were systematically infused into every aspect of daily life, so that "their message would sink into people's brains and guide their behaviour" (p. 5). "If people could be made to speak formulaically and through that learn to think formulaically ... all individuality, all merely personal aspirations would be destroyed" (p. 178).

The mechanism for social control adopted by Mao was to create and sustain conflict between fluid groups designated as pro- or anti-regime. By repeatedly redefining the boundaries of acceptable revolutionary practice he progressively undermined the confidence of individual citizens to judge whether they were (still) on the safe side of the line between conformity and heresy (Ji 2004: 143), until, in the climate of fear created by the possibility of saying the wrong thing, "the safest course ... was to speak and write in Chairman Mao's own words" (p. 155). The verbatim memorization and quotation of Mao's *Little Red Book* became a prestigious indication of commitment to revolutionary ideals, with the result that the inability to quote it suggested counter-revolutionary leanings (p. 151), the personal consequences of which could be dire.

Prescribed formulaic sequences thus became a device for signalling a social identity that it was dangerous not to espouse. However, saying the words entailed more than just a signal: it was intrinsically participatory. Public Criticism Meetings, themselves highly formulaic in structure (Ji, Kuiper, and Shu 1990: 71ff; Ji 2004: 161ff), included obligatory slogan shouting by the audience, so that conformity to the linguistic imperatives became a means of "ensuring that ordinary Chinese were not mere spectators, but active participants in the class struggle ... [who] contributed personally, and usually voluntarily, to the suffering of the accused" (Ji 2004: 169).

In Orwell's world, creative thought was so effectively suppressed through the reformulation of the language that his population is depicted as becoming increasingly passive and suppressed. However, things worked out a little differently in China. For the Revolution to become fully established, individual action was required, and the taking of local initiatives. With citizens so keen to act only in accordance with Mao's words, issues arose regarding how the published words should translate to situations he had not specifically mentioned (Ji 2004: 184). Action required an understanding of the spirit of the words, rather than just their specific content, and, in a context of extreme fear, individuals often doubted their capacity to do this appropriately.

Ji *et al.* (1990) quote an incident reported in Liang and Shapiro (1983), when a group of teenage Red Guards were called upon to write Big Character posters criticizing their teachers:

> ... we suddenly discovered that we didn't know what Capitalism or Revisionism really were. ... we sat in worried silence until my friend Gang Di's older brother, Gang Xian, made a good suggestion. 'Why don't we go down the street and see what other people have written?'
> (Liang and Shapiro 1983: 46, quoted in Ji *et al.* 1990:74)

Meanwhile, where people had more confidence in their ability to unpack and assimilate the content of the official statements, another problem could occur. While the older, educated generation could interpret Mao's words through the traditional culture they had shared with him in pre-Revolutionary times, and through an understanding of how society operated, teenagers with no pre-Maoist experience knew only the words, and had no context in which to interpret them. As a result, inappropriate extrapolations were common, leading to many unsanctioned radical actions by the Red Guards, such as the destruction of ancient temples and the closing of factories (Ji 2004: 158f)—actions that were fundamentally incompatible with the underlying ideals of Maoism. It seems, then, that although prepacking ideas into formulaic sequences was a powerful tool for political oppression in one sense, living out the ideas contained within them required continuing access to novel thought.

Formulaic language as a straitjacket

What would happen to thought and expression if there were no means of avoiding formulaicity at all—that is, if there were no scope for novelty? It seems almost inconceivable that there might be circumstances for modern humans in which there was no escape from holistic form-meaning relationships. But the hypothesized evolutionary protolanguage of our pre-modern ancestors, described in Chapter 17, would be such a case.

The inherent constraints on creativity of a holistic protolanguage

A holistic protolanguage is a straitjacket, in a way that a word-based one, even without rules, is not. It's true that a major challenge to effective communication in the proto-noun, proto-verb based protolanguage that Bickerton (1996, 1998, 2000; Calvin and Bickerton 2000) proposes would be the enormous burden on the hearer to apply context and pragmatics to figure out why the speaker has uttered, say, the word 'tree' or the unpatterned sequence 'tree look'. However, such ambiguity is an invitation to be inventive. The great advantage of applying context and pragmatics to disambiguation is that they are essentially an extension of general knowledge, experience, and common sense, and thereby are rather reliable, both across a community and for the individual over time. There is no need formally to encode information that can be reliably retrieved using general knowledge, and not encoding it leaves the encoded material open to multiple interpretations. As long as hearers expect to *interpret* rather than just *decode* what they hear, speakers have a chance of successfully communicating something new, including something they have invented. Indeed, if anything, the problem with the Bickertonian model is explaining how the protolanguage could have remained stable in its limited form, since speakers and hearers would be trying new things out all the time: inventing new words and, one might imagine, experimenting with associations between them.[1]

It is, in short, the absence of full information that sparks and sustains creativity, since there is a shortfall to make up if you are to know everything you need to know—and making that shortfall up must be achieved by means other than simple observation. Kirby (2002) has demonstrated computationally that learners can only acquire a system if they are subjected to a 'bottleneck', whereby the set of exemplars observed is smaller than the set of exemplars they need to produce for themselves.

In a holistic protolanguage, the door for creative engagement with the communication system is firmly closed. By mapping the entire propositional meaning onto a form of its own, there is no scope for negotiation, and no possibility of novel creations. Certainly a great deal of pragmatics and context will be required in order to learn the meanings of the forms, but no bottleneck effect can be created: if you have not come across the form, you simply don't know it. If speakers invent new forms for new meanings they want to convey, there is no means for others to deduce that meaning from the form. Indeed, inventing a new form will simply be a question of a new coining, rather than building on what already exists.

Thus, a holistic protolanguage tightens around its users, and constrains the development of their communication. Furthermore, the stranglehold on innovation in communication might affect innovation more generally (Wray 2002a). The fixed inventory of messages would be highly efficient for doing the same things one had always done. As Orwell (1949) recognized, the inability to express new ideas has the potential to make it difficult even to think them, or at least to develop the thoughts beyond the superficial level. The result would be major constraints on effecting change and on planning. Interestingly, Mithen (1996) notes that there was virtually no technological innovation for more than a million years after the invention of the hand axe around 1.4 million years ago (pp. 116–23). If there were, indeed, a holistic protolanguage, it might be hypothesized to have coincided with this lengthy hiatus in creativity.

We need not lay this lack of technological progress *directly* at the door of the limitations of protolanguage. However, a holistic protolanguage certainly would support conservatism in a way that a componential language, even of limited scope, would not. Looked at in this way, the inherent stability of a holistic protolanguage matches Mithen's proposal that the early human mind was not 'joined up'—that is, "a cognitive barrier prevented the integration of knowledge" (1996: 131). The absence of novel linguistic expression would conspire with cognitive tunnel vision to impede the making of connections between ideas and the expression of ideas to others. Meanwhile, the existence of a reliable set of holistic expressions with agreed manipulative meanings would reinforce habit and maintain social relationships, supporting the survival of individuals as group members. There was, as Mithen (1996) points out (for example, p. 131), certainly sufficient environmental pressure for innovation to be useful, so we may not attribute its failure to occur to an easy existence. By identifying holistic protolanguage as an impediment to the expression of new ideas, it is easier to explain how early humans could have failed for so long to undergo natural selection for a more integrated intelligence.[2]

However, discussions of human protolanguage are necessarily speculative, and only a limited amount can be learnt from modelling the hypothesized scenario. In order to assess the extent to which a holistic protolanguage might act as a constraint on creative thought, it is useful to look for modern day parallels, to see how similar formal constraints are dealt with.

Modern-day constrained signalling systems

Modern humans use alternative signalling systems when language itself would be ineffective: over long distances, in noisy conditions, and when communicating with a dispersed group. Of course recent technology has enabled linguistic communication to extend its reach, but there are still limits. Flags continue to be used in motor racing for some functions, for instance, even though the audio and visual transmission of messages to the cockpit is also possible. This is because in motor sport, as on the battlefield, where trumpet and bugle calls were used for communication until the introduction of the radio (see below), some messages are immediate and urgent. There is an obligation on the part of the signaller to present them unambiguously to participants who speak many languages, in order to achieve an appropriate and swift response. Pragmatism, then, is normally the source of the decision to utilize a holistic, and thus inherently limited, communication system, instead of the more flexible option, language. Our focus of interest is the extent to which such signalling really is constraining, and what options are taken up for loosening those constraints.

Motor racing flags

In various kinds of motor racing, including Formula One, race officials stand in key positions at the side of the track and use flags to communicate specific information to drivers. While flagging conventions vary from series to series, there are ten flags in Formula One (Figure 21.1), differentiated by colour and design, communicating both factual information and instructions.[3] The glosses for the flags are not single words but complete sentences, indicating that they carry a complete proposition holistically. The scope of this communication is, of course, extremely limited. It serves only the specific requirements of safety and race rules, and no other messages can be conveyed. There is no means, using flags, to inform a driver that his[4] wife has just given birth, nor that his colleague has been injured elsewhere on the track. Furthermore, when a signal is given, the driver is not told *why*, and unless his team chooses to impart that information to him by radio, he must rely on pragmatics and experience to interpret the full meaning of the message. For instance, a red flag simply stops the race. If driving conditions are poor, the driver may infer that it is for that reason. Otherwise, the most likely reason is that a stopped car is causing a dangerous hazard on the track (BBC Sport 2008). From a red flag alone, the driver cannot tell if *both* conditions apply at once—though other flags could be used to give supplementary signals that, together with the red flag, would suggest the level of danger.

As noted earlier, pragmatics is a means of broadening the range of a signal's applicability, by allowing the receiver, as well as the sender, to contribute to the meaning. Thus, although the most common reason for the track being slippery is that there is oil on it (BBC Sport 2008), the red and yellow striped flag is not designated to mean 'there is oil on the track' but 'the track is slippery'. In this way, the flag is available for use in other situations where the track is slippery, and the driver is given the responsibility to infer the reason, should he need to do so.

Several other means exist, by which the limits on the range of signals are alleviated. One is intensification through reduplication: "A single waved yellow flag means slow down, a double waved yellow warns that the driver must be prepared to stop if necessary" (BBC Sport 2008). Another is message modification, by indicating which driver is being addressed. This is done by displaying the car number, and occurs in conjunction with instructions to leave the track (black flag and black flag with orange disc), and with a conduct warning (white and black diagonal halves). A signal's full interpretation may also be contingent on a previous signal. A blue flag gives information to a slower car that a faster one is approaching from behind. However, three showings of the flag transform the warning into an instruction to let the car pass.[5]

In this very tightly constrained signalling system we see how the pragmatism of keeping drivers and officials safe introduces additional subtleties to the interpretation of signals, so that they have sufficient scope to cover all common situations and to handle unusual ones effectively, yet without sacrificing the simplicity and explicitness required for avoiding ambiguity. However, it is also significant that supplementary instructions are drawn up and issued as guidelines for specific series (for example, by the International Motor Sports Association).[6] These guidelines make explicit that procedures tend to differ across regional organizations, thus indicating that one consequence of modern humans applying a limited set of signals to a situation in which a wider range of events can take place than is provided for, is fragmentation into 'dialects' of practice.

Motor racing flags

Chequered flag

The race has ended. Shown first to the winner, and then to every car to cross the line behind them.

Red flag

The race has been stopped, usually because a car is lying in a dangerous position after an accident or because conditions are too poor for racing to be safe.

Yellow flag

Indicates danger ahead and overtaking is prohibited. A single waved yellow flag means slow down, a double waved yellow warns that the driver must be prepared to stop if necessary.

Blue flag

Shown to a driver to indicate that a faster car is behind him and trying to overtake. Shown both to lapped cars and those racing. A lapped car must allow the faster car past after seeing a maximum of three blue flags or risk being penalised. A racing car is under no obligation to move over.

Black flag

Shown with a car number to indicate that the driver must call into the pits immediately, usually because he has broken the rules and will be disqualified.

Red and yellow striped flag

The track is slippery. This usually warns of oil or water on the track.

Green flag

A hazard has been cleared up and the cars can proceed at racing speed.

Black flag with an orange disc

Shown with a car number to indicate that the car has a mechanical problem and the driver must return to his pit immediately.

White and black diagonal halves

Shown with car number to indicate a warning for unsportsmanlike behaviour. A black flag may follow if the driver takes no heed of the warning.

White flag

Warns of a slow-moving vehicle on the track, such as a tow truck or safety car.

Figure 21.1 The basic meanings of motor racing flags (BBC Sport 2008)

Nautical flags

Flags have been used at sea for centuries. As standards, they identify ships, but they are also used to convey other messages. Before there was radio communication they were the most effective way of passing information from ship to ship and ship to shore, but even now they are a valuable supplement, particularly because they are internationally recognized and independent of individual languages. There are 50 international code flags,[7] with others used for ocean racing. Most flags have more than one meaning: they carry a holistic propositional message—for example, 'I am on fire and have dangerous cargo on board. Keep well clear of me' (Figure 21.2) and also an alphabetic or numerical one, so that messages can be spelled out in a language.[8]

Maritime flags

Blue ground with central horizontal white stripe

"I am on fire and have dangerous cargo on board. Keep well clear of me"

White ground with blue cross

"Stop carrying out your intentions and watch for my signals"

Blue ground with white central rectangle, containing central red rectangle

"I require medical assistance"

White ground overlaid with red rectangles in upper left and lower right quandrants

"You are running into danger"

Black ground overlaid with yellow rectangles in upper left and lower right quadrants

"You should stop your vessel instantly"

Blue ground with white transverse cross

"My vessel is stopped and making no way through the water"

Figure 21.2 Example maritime signals

The holistic messages are similar in function to those used in motor racing, namely to inform and instruct. There are signals to indicate that the ship has a diver down, is not manoeuvring well, has a pilot on board, etc. The harbour master can signal instructions to an incoming vessel, and crew on land can also be given signals about returning to ship. Naturally, the set of messages is very limited, and although, in contrast to motor racing and ground battles (see later), reactions to signals are relatively slow, there can also be little opportunity to apply pragmatics, in the absence of other visual cues about a situation.

The supplementary use of flags as codes for letters has the advantage that, in principle, any message can be expressed. On the other hand, the message requires the receiver to be not only familiar with the flags but also to know the language of transmission and be literate in it. It also presents a practical difficulty, since a great deal of space is required for displaying flags. A more efficient form of digitizing language using flags was devized by Captain Sir Home Popham in 1800, and was used by Nelson in 1805 to send his famous message "England expects that every man will do his duty", before the Battle of Trafalgar. The Popham system designated ten signal flags to represent the numbers 0 to 9. In combinations of three they corresponded to words listed alphabetically in the Popham signal book ('England' was coded 253, 'every' 261, and 'will' 958, for instance).[9] However, even this relatively free system constrained Nelson's expressive scope. It was obviously sensible only to convey messages containing words in the signal book. A concession was made in regard to 'duty', which was spelled out using the alphabetic system, but Nelson replaced his preferred 'confides' with 'expects' because the former was not in the book.

The Popham system allowed much greater flexibility in message expression than the holistic flags did, because it provided words that could be combined in many ways. On the other hand, translating the codes would have been a specialized job, and it is unlikely that even a captain could read the messages off the mast without reference to the code book. Much less could the ordinary seaman have read Nelson's message for himself. In other words, part of the price paid for finding solutions to the problem of flexibility can be the exclusion of untrained receivers.

Military trumpet and bugle calls

Nautical signals were sent and received by those in command. Once received, an order would have to be translated into a set of actions to be carried out by the crew, who could be instructed verbally as they were all close by. In contrast, trumpet and bugle calls (as also the drum calls that they replaced) were instructions to the ordinary forces[10] (for example, Figures 21.3, 21.4). They were used operationally in battle until radios were introduced, and in the UK they continued in use in barracks until 1970, when soldiers were given the responsibility of time-keeping using their wristwatches (Powell 2000a: 17).

Figure 21.3 To horse (Hyde 1798)

Figure 21.4 The watering call (Hyde 1798)

Nautical flag signals had the advantage over auditory ones of being permanent, so they could be used like a notice pinned to a gate or message board, for people to read when they happened to look. In contrast, auditory signals, being transitory, had to be received in real time, when transmitted. On the other hand, auditory signals had certain advantages over visual ones. In battle, they could be sent from behind the lines, without requiring the troops to turn around and look for them. They could also be heard in locations where there was no line of vision back to the command post.[11] In camp, signals could reach personnel dispersed over a large area, and a major function of them was to maintain the routines of the day. An account by General Custer's wife Elizabeth of life in a cavalry regiment in the third quarter of the nineteenth century (Custer 1890) gives something of the flavour of how signals operated:

> [The trumpet] was the hourly monitor of the cavalry corps. It told us when to eat, to sleep, to march, and to go to church. Its clear tones reminded us, should there be physical ailments, that we must go to the doctor … We needed timepieces only when absent from garrison or camp. The never tardy sound calling to duty was better than any clock and … we found ourselves saying 'Can it be possible? There's *Stables*, and where has the day gone?'
> (p. v)

Key to the nature of the calls was that they were freestanding and conveyed complete manipulative propositions. For instance, *First Call* awoke the troops, *Mess Call* called the ranks to meals, *To Stable* instructed the cavalry troops to groom and feed their horses, and *Sick Call* commanded all those requiring medical treatment to assemble. Their propositional nature is demonstrated by the English glosses, which are often quite long. Hyde's (1798) handbook of trumpet and bugle signals glosses one of the calls in the Bugle Horn Duty for the Light Infantry (p. 24) as *Turn in the whole and form in a line on the left of the right*. Custer (1890) describes how "by a *Troop* [you must] understand to shoulder your muskets, to advance your pikes, to close your ranks and files to their order, and to troop along with or follow your officer to the place of rendezvous or elsewhere" (p. x).[12]

The calls were non-compositional and essentially arbitrary in form, in that a particular tune was simply assigned a particular meaning. There could be internal repetitions of parts of the tune, but these were to ensure that the transmission could be identified even if not all of it was heard, and they had no semantic value as, say, amplifications. There are a few hints that a call's form could occasionally be iconically inspired, however. For instance, it is reminiscent of the horse's steps that the music for the *Charge* is in two-time and fast, while that for the *Trot* is in three-time and slower. The *Double*, used after another order to indicate that it should be executed 'at the double', i.e. quickly, is played fast. However, it is not at all clear that iconicity was a major component in the construction of calls, nor that a call could be understood on that basis alone. Indeed, too much iconicity might mislead troops into thinking that calls *could* be 'read' in that way, when, in fact, music is not a sufficiently good mimic to be more than a helpful mnemonic. Furthermore, the great advantage of arbitrariness in the signals was that each call could be kept distinctive from others. Any kind of pattern to the representation would have meant that calls with similar meanings sounded similar.

All the same, the troops did have ways of making it easier to remember the calls. Those that were part of the daily routine would no doubt be recognized according the time that they were sounded as much as on the basis of their musical identity. In addition, it was evidently common for strings of words to be associated with the calls, in what Powell (2000a: 17) calls "the cheery doggerel by which soldiers learnt [them]". These words were mnemonics—they imitated the rhythm of the call, thus could be sung along to it, and their meaning was associated with the meaning of the signal. For instance, the *Meal Call* had the words "Oh come to the cookhouse door, boys, come to the cookhouse door", and the *Double* was "Run you buggers, run you buggers, run you buggers, run!" (Powell 2000b: 114). The doggerel tradition is likely to have arisen early on. Custer (1890) observes: "The soldiers, for no one knows how long, have fitted rhymes to the calls … The words of these simple rhymes are just as familiar to military people as the household tales of infancy, and as indelibly impressed on an army child as *Twinkle, twinkle, little star*" (pp. vi–vii).

The enemy has infantry and cavalry

The enemy's cavalry is advancing

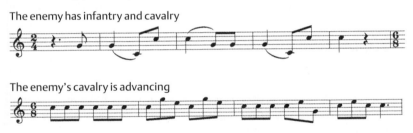

Figure 21.5 Bugle calls from 1805

In battle, the role of the bugler was not only to relay orders, but also often to carry out reconnaissance (David Edwards, personal communication). Since each situation was different, and strategy was dependent on local conditions, there was an inherent risk in using a fixed set of signals, which might easily compromise the instructions and information that could be conveyed. There were, in the prescribed set, some signals with very specific meanings, such as 'the enemy has infantry and cavalry' and 'the enemy's cavalry is advancing' (Figure 21.5).[13] But there had to be a limit on the overall inventory if it were to remain small enough to learn. Unlike on a ship, where the manual could be on hand for reference, these signals needed to be memorized. It was no simple matter to train trumpeters and buglers to play all the different tunes on demand, particularly in the days before most of them were musically literate.

The apprenticeship could be as long as six years (Crispian Steele-Perkins, personal communication). Account also had to be taken of the capacity for the troops to recognize and differentiate the calls accurately. Thus, while pragmatism required the extension of the range of expression, the fact that the signalling units were arbitrary forms associated with meaning also constrained the means by which this could be achieved. The parallels to language are evident, yet only some of the opportunities afforded by linguistic structure were adopted in relation to this holistic system of representation.

Ambiguity

By chance or design, signals often needed to be interpreted somewhat differently according to context. For instance, the appropriate actions on hearing the half hour and quarter hour calls before a parade were different according to which parade was scheduled. Therefore, to respond correctly to these signals, one had to know the parade protocol (Powell 2000b: 115). By the mid-nineteenth century, there was only one call to mean both 'Draw Swords' and 'Return Swords', interpreted according to the current state of the sword.[14] In addition, the routines of the day and customary practice provided a background of meaning against which to interpret non-routine calls. Powell (2000b: 115) notes that "if C[ompany] S[ergeant] M[ajors] were blown, serious matters were afoot". Interpretation was also required in the sense that a call might apply to different people on different days. For instance, calls for those on the duty roster only needed to be obeyed when one had those duties.

Addressee identification

In 1835 Sir Richard Hussey Vivien introduced 'regimental' calls, which could be sounded before another call, to indicate that only that regiment should respond. In the most recent edition of the Ministry of Defence manual (Ministry of Defence 1966) there are 53 pages of brigade and regiment calls, amounting to 174 different signatures.

Concatenation

Individual calls conveyed a complete proposition and could not be broken into constituent units of meaning. All the same, it was possible for them to be assembled into longer strings. Through concatenation it was possible to convey in one macro-call a set of instructions. Figure 21.6 illustrates a single order constructed by stringing together independent calls. Such calls could be argued to bear some resemblance to sentences in language, if we viewed these macro-calls as 'calls' and the component parts as 'constituents'. However, it would be misleading to do so. First, the 'constituents' are complete, freestanding semantic units, and all have the grammatical status of propositions. Therefore, a more appropriate analogy would be that of sentences contributing to a narrative. Second, although the order of the components in the macro-call is fixed, it is because it represents the sequence in which the actions should be carried out, not because it signals relationships between the components.[15] The only possibility of 'grammar' is seen in the use of the signatures at the beginning, if they are construed as creating a frame for the interpretation of what follows; if so, a case could be made for primitive embedding. However, it is probably more accurate to view the signatures as acting semantically rather than grammatically, in defining the participants in the named actions.

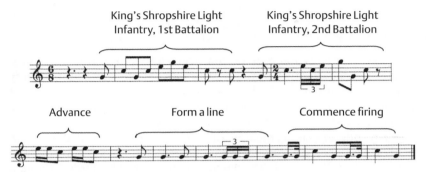

Figure 21.6 An example of a composite call (post 1835)

Dependent calls

Two or three calls did have a slightly different status from the others, in that their own meaning was contingent on what they were applied to. The *Double* command, mentioned earlier, added urgency to a preceding command, and it would therefore not really mean anything if sounded alone. The *As you were* call acted to cancel a previous command. Finally, there was a call used in battle to help deal with complex situations. This call was *Carry out the order*, and it instructed officers to apply the plan that had been agreed upon. There could be several such verbal orders issued in advance, each to be carried out in different circumstances. Thus it would be the context that determined which order was carried out, and the call itself engaged in intertextuality by referring to a previous face-to-face meeting in which tactical decisions were planned for different contingencies.

Structures *not* seen

Other than the examples described above, there is no evidence of grammatical relationships between calls. For instance, it does not seem to have been possible to issue an order to *all* troops *except* a named regiment, or to indicate that *although* the facts signified by call A were true, *nevertheless* so were the facts of call B. There were also no calls that might correspond to partly-fixed frames, where the main message was incomplete until additional information was added, for example, *[named group] go to the [named place]*, and although, as already mentioned, there was an *option* to indicate a named group as the addressee, the default meaning of not naming one was that the order applied to everyone, not no one.

Only in one circumstance is structural embedding seen—when, in the ceremonial version of a call, the routine equivalent is 'quoted' as a theme: "For example, the military call *Call Out the Skirmishers* forms the first phrase of ... the music that we now call *Reveille*" (Crispian Steele-Perkins, personal communication). While these quotations retain their referential meaning in the context of a ceremonial tune, they surrender their illocutionary force as imperatives.

Patterns of constraint in limited signalling systems

We have seen that flags and musical tunes have been, in historically recent times, and in some cases up to the present day, effectively used to convey messages in circumstances where normal spoken or written language is not a practical option. In each case, the specific conditions of use determine the manner in which a basic dilemma is resolved, namely how to express as much as is needed, without making the signalling system too complicated to use. In the highly constrained environment of a motor racing track it is possible to predetermine the full range of essential messages that will be needed, though, as we have seen, there is also a tendency for variations to develop in response to additional needs.

We can use the modern-day examples to speculate about whether a holistic protolanguage would have constrained the actions of its users, as in motor racing and maritime flag signalling, or whether the signals would have been extended and combined, as in military trumpet and bugle signalling. Such a question cannot be answered without first conjecturing what the holistic protolanguage signals meant, when they were used, and how important it was for survival or other reasons that they were effectively conveyed and understood. More precisely, we must also establish the extent to which it is only with language that we, as modern humans, have attained the awareness of new messages that could be expressed if only the signalling permitted it. That is, perhaps the pushing of the creative boundaries in the holistic signalling systems reviewed here simply reflects the fact that they are used by modern humans, who always immediately perceive them as a poor second best to language. If so, holistic protolanguage users were in a very different position, since their signalling system was the most sophisticated available. We are, of course, in the throes of the classic questions raised by Whorf (1956).

These modern examples of extreme formulaicity show that the way to work with a constrained communication system is to accept its limitations. They also show that when the limitations are too great, the solution is not necessarily to break down the fundamental nature of the system. Even the modern mind can find a use for holistic signalling that does not entail introducing compositionality. And this may suggest that a holistic protolanguage could be stable for a long time, while the mind evolved to become modern. It also suggests that, if and when a holistic protolanguage did begin to creak at the seams, the first stages in extending meaning might have been the tolerance of ambiguity (including the use of contextualization to resolve it), the concatenation of propositions into macro-messages, and the identification of addressee.

One final observation should be made. The standard assumption in conceptualising a protolanguage is that everyone is both a speaker and a hearer. However, a striking feature of the holistic systems reviewed here is that the producers and receivers are often different populations—or rather, the population of producers is a subset of the population of receivers, since those who signal can also interpret signals but not always vice versa. In some cases (for example, motor racing, maritime signalling), the difference in expertise between productive and receptive knowledge is not great, so that it would not take much additional training to turn a receiver into a producer. In other cases, particularly trumpet and bugle signalling, the production is so specialized that being a receiver would be far from sufficient to make an easy transition to producer. Meanwhile, where the signalling is codified language, as with the Popham code for naval flags, there seem to arise two classes of receiver. Members of the ship's company might have had some limited ability to read flags off the mast, but official interpretations would be in the hands of specialists who were both producers and receivers. Thus, the evidence here begs the question of whether human protolanguage might have featured a long-term and stable dimorphism, between those who could create and produce signals and those who could only recognize and respond. It is not a question to be answered here, simply one to be raised for future consideration.

Conclusion

This chapter and the previous one have been concerned with whether formulaic signalling could fundamentally constrain its users' expression and thought. Up until now, the two have been rolled together, but now it is useful to separate them. Thus, we can first ask, does formulaic language have the capacity to control thought?

For the modern human, it seems that the answer is probably not. The key reason why formulaic language can be a particularly potent agent of thought control is that a single unit can convey a complete proposition. The more complex and complete the meaning within a lexical unit, the less creativity involved in expressing it. Individual words, however their definition may be regulated, are highly limited in their scope for expression. They must be combined with other words to create meanings, and as soon as that creativity is licensed, the speaker and hearer are empowered to express new thoughts.[16]

However, the China experience indicates that if formulaic sequences are truly to control *thought*, they must be unpacked and assimilated, whether by the speaker, the hearer, or both. A successful inculcation of the ideas enclosed within political (or religious) slogans extends beyond the capacity to reproduce verbatim the original maxims, to the ability faithfully to re-express and expand them. Inevitably, freeing the individual to reformulate the expression of prescribed ideas brings with it the capacity to develop those ideas in new ways, and also potentially to challenge them. Thus, while pre-packing ideas in formulaic sequences can be a powerful tool for political oppression and, certainly, can ensure that speakers only express permitted messages, it is difficult to conceive of them as a means of suppressing novel thought, for as long as novel language is a prerequisite for novel action. On the other hand, it has been suggested that, in the absence of the modern mind and modern language, our ancient ancestors might indeed have been confined by a holistic protolanguage into limited thought that held back their capacity for creative action over many millennia.

However, turning now to the question of whether formulaic language has the potential to constrain our *expression*, the answer is clearly that it does. If the situation requires it, we can experience quite severe limitations on what we say, in the interests of expediency. All of the situations reviewed in this chapter and Chapter 20 have featured some measure of expressional compromise. The limitations are mitigated by means of a pact between producer and receiver, whereby responsibility for some aspects of meaning normally encoded in production is turned over to the receiver, who makes good the shortfall using pragmatics. For instance, actors rely on the fact that the audience understands how the process of scripted performance works, so that the character's speech and actions are not interpreted as those of the performer. The advanced L2 learners entrusted to their hearers the responsibility of repairing their deviant non-native expressions of target messages. The trade was desirable to them because they preferred to act creatively, in order to convey facts accurately and achieve the sociocultural tone that was most comfortable to them. The holistic encoding of messages using flags and bugle or trumpet calls similarly traded expressional range for complicit interpretation based on pragmatics.

It should not be overlooked, however, that constraints on the expressive potential of producers, whether or not there is a knock-on constraint on *their* thought, do potentially hem in the thought, and indeed action, of the receivers. Thus, for instance, a commander in an eighteenth or nineteenth century battle might think of many possible manoeuvres for his troops, but only be able to instigate those for which appropriate signalled instructions existed. His bugler, out on reconnaissance, might see more than he could report back, naturally constraining his commander's understanding of the true situation. In similar vein, TALK-user Sylvia (Chapters 11 and 20) necessarily defined both herself and the content of conversations through the set of prefabricated turns that she relied on. She manipulated her speakers' conversation, and while it would be presumptuous to imply that in doing so she fundamentally constrained their thought, certainly she directed it very forcefully towards those topics that she preferred.

The situations explored in this chapter have, by necessity, been extreme, for it is much more difficult to see how our thought and expression might be affected by formulaicity in our everyday communication. However, the principles are the same: if we have a processing preference for large units, there is an inherent price to be paid in terms of creativity.

Notes

1 Bickerton's explanation for protolanguage not swiftly spiralling into full language is that humans were not yet neurologically equipped for grammar.

2 In a later book, Mithen (2005) directly explores the potential of holistic protolanguage to have characterized the communication of Neanderthals.

3 Light signals are sometimes used in place of flags, and have their own regulations (Fédération Internationale de l'Automobile (FIA) 2007: 6, section 4.2).

4 There are currently no female Formula One drivers.

5 In some racing contexts, the blue flag has a different meaning in practices and races: in the former it is an instruction to give way, while in the latter it is an instruction to permit overtaking at the earliest opportunity (Fédération Internationale de l'Automobile (FIA) 2007: 6, section 4.1.2, d).

6 www.atl-scca.org/Documents %20Word/2006/IMSA %20Communications %20Guidelines %202006.doc. Accessed 10 February 2008.

7 http://www.marinewaypoints.com/learn/flags/flags.shtml. Accessed 10 February 2008.

8 http://en.wikipedia.org/wiki/International_maritime_signal_flags. Accessed 8 February 2008.

9 There were also some shorter combinations for common words.

10 Though the ordinary ranks may have relied on their NCOs or officers to interpret them (David Edwards, personal communication).

11 However, as gunpowder replaced arrows in warfare, it became harder to hear signals, a problem resolved by transferring the medium from the drum to the trumpet and, ultimately, the bugle, which was sufficiently high pitched to cut through gunfire.

12 Audiofiles of bugle calls can be heard at www.fmaalumni.org/bugle_calls. html and http://www.usscouts.org/mb/bugle_calls.html (accessed 10 February 2008), or on the CDs *Sound the Trumpet, Beat the Drum* (available from David Edwards, 5 Holly Ridge, Fenns Lane, West End, Surrey, Guildford, GU24 9QE) and *Bugle Calls for the British Army* (Droit Music, PO Box 2638, Eastbourne, East Sussex, BN20 7HJ).

13 I'm grateful to David Edwards for these examples and also the one in Figure 21.6.

14 Compare, in some varieties of English, the use of 'draw the curtains' for both opening and closing them.

15 It is in contrast, therefore, to Jackendoff's (2002) protolanguage with linear grammar, discussed in Chapter 17, in which word order signifies inter-item relationships.

16 Orwell's (1949) word-based Newspeak suffers from this problem somewhat, in that it could not actually obliterate the potential to express a politically undesirable idea (for example, "Big Brother is ungood").

Orwell suggests, though, that it would be impossible to develop the bland claim into a reasoned point, so that deep objections "could only be entertained in a vague wordless form" (p. 250).

22
Across the boundaries

Introduction

This final chapter takes stock of the effects of 'pushing the boundaries' of formulaic language, and then addresses the question: *So what?* That is, how might our developing understanding of the nature, dynamics, purposes, and provenance of formulaic language inform our approach to communication in practical ways beneficial to society? One particular example is developed in detail, starting with a relatively simple situation and progressively adding layers of complexity, to build an account of the interacting challenges for communication that can occur in residential care homes, with formulaic language variously exacerbating and alleviating the problems. Specific observations are made about the scope for capitalizing on the inherent presence of formulaic language, to support and develop communication potential. Finally, some more general themes are identified for useful future research on formulaic language.

Taking stock at the boundaries

Perhaps one of the most striking consequences of the approach taken in this book is the extent to which even quite evident boundaries between phenomena have often dissolved in the course of discussion. Ten challenges to the boundaries can be enumerated.

1 The morpheme equivalent unit (MEU), introduced in Chapter 2, nullified the boundary between morphemes, words, and prefabricated word strings. All were viewed as single lexical units, subject to the combinatory rules that a language develops to accommodate them.
2 Chapter 3 showed how various boundaries in relation to form and interpretation are assailed when formulaic language is side by side with newly created output.
3 The boundary between speech and writing was examined in Chapters 4 and 5 and it was shown that a key characteristic of that boundary, autonomy,

is actually independently motivated. Furthermore, it is not absolute, but rather operates on a cline, so that the characteristics of speech and writing cannot be neatly divided along the boundary of delivery mode.

4 In Chapters 6 and 7, the boundaries between descriptions, justifications, and explanations for language patterns were explored, and it was argued that there is now very little justification for firmly separating these three facets of the account. The boundaries between linguistic theory and corpus linguistics were shown to be increasingly difficult to define, as new approaches to language description, particularly Pattern Grammar and Construction Grammar, depart from the assumption that what we know about language is fundamentally distinct from what we do with it.

5 In relation to identification (Chapter 8), it was demonstrated that there simply is no way to delineate formulaic language according to one feature, be it form-based, semantic, or functional.

6 In keeping with that conclusion, the diagnostic approach in Chapter 9 specifically warned against making the assumption that one word string can be viewed as *more* formulaic than another on account of it having more identifying features — things are not so simple.

7 In Part Three of the book, the boundaries were again under attack, as different extreme situations were presented, in which the formulaic language used was far from everyday and normal: a finite system computer program (Chapter 10), a computer-based repository of useful utterances (Chapter 11), two bizarre experiences of language learning (Chapters 12 and 13), a legal dispute about the meaning of a dialect term (Chapter 14), and the approaches taken by actors learning a script (Chapter 15).

8 In Chapters 16 and 17, a different kind of boundary was under scrutiny, namely the location of the trip-switch between more and less effortful approaches to language processing — and what its default setting is. It was argued that choices between using a formulaic or newly created expression of a message are contingent on a range of contextual and personal features, so that the boundary moves in response to changing circumstances.

9 That same boundary was explored in relation to language learning in Chapters 18 and 19, with suggestions that the trip-switch might be moved artificially to enable a greater exploitation of the default low-effort option.

10 Finally, in Chapters 20 and 21, the boundary that marks the expressive limitations of formulaic language was considered, by asking questions about what happens when there are conflicts between expressive expediency and expressive range. Formulaic language was set alongside various holistic communication systems — racing and maritime flags, and trumpet and bugle calls — challenging the belief that there is a boundary between different modes of communication that have the same underlying functions and motivations.

This loss of clear boundaries may be uncomfortable for some, but it is a natural consequence of viewing formulaic language as 'a linguistic solution to a non-linguistic problem' (Wray 2002b: 100), namely promoting one's own interests by minimizing processing effort, by conveying one's individual and group identity, and by manipulating others (see Chapter 2). This psycho-social explanation for our use of formulaic language is extremely powerful, because it identifies expediencies in achieving personal goals as the determinants of not only what we do, but also what we know and don't know, how we learn, and what we retain access to under conditions of stress, brain injury, and degeneration. In this way the explanation impacts on theories of language form, meaning, function, and origin. Furthermore, as outlined below, it provides indicators for how we can improve communication in challenging situations.

Formulaic language and the challenges of communication

How formulaic language assists communication

In the course of this book, a number of real-life situations have been explored in which formulaic language has been the solution to a practical problem with communication. A key feature, over and over again, is the acceptance of expediency as a legitimate motivator for finding a solution. For instance, TESSA, the machine translation tool used experimentally in UK post offices in the 1990s (Chapter 10), capitalized on the fact that transactions at the post office are relatively predictable and formulaic. A more sophisticated device could have translated a wider range of messages but the pragmatism underlying the design of TESSA was the recognition that one does not need to anticipate and accommodate every possible situation that might arise. Similarly, the TALK software (Chapter 11) did not seek to turn its user into a fully-functioning speaker, but rather simply to narrow the gap somewhat between that ideal and what was previously possible.

The expediency lesson was transferred to the observations and suggestions put forward in Chapter 19 for improving computer mastery of human language. The proposed system would be heavily constrained, relative to the systems designed to generate all possible sentences from minimal components—but then those systems have not yet proved particularly successful. New, less ambitious approaches may have more potential than has so far been recognized.

More lessons can be learnt, when one ranges more widely across the various claims and findings presented in this book. The potential for theory to contribute to practice is often under-recognized, though, as Lewin (1945) maintained, "nothing is as practical as a good theory" (p. 129). In order to explore the potential for practical applications of our emerging understanding of formulaic language, the next sections develop a fictional scenario, layer by layer, that draws out the various challenges to communication that can build up in a complex situation, and demonstrates opportunities for recognizing when formulaic language is part of the problem in communication, and when it can be part of the solution.

1: An elderly person with an acquired communication disorder

Stage 1 of our scenario examines the dynamics of communication for a person with moderate symptoms of Alzheimer's Disease,[1] living in a residential care home. According to the Alzheimer's Society (2007), "two thirds of care home residents have some form of dementia" (p. iv), and we saw in Chapter 16 that formulaic language features in Alzheimer's Disease (also Davis and Maclagan 2007). This resident has impairments to her comprehension and production of language. She sometimes produces the wrong word, and in comprehension she has difficulties with making semantic connections between words, so that she is unsure, for example, which items on her plate count as 'vegetables'. At the multiword level, problems arise in consequence of her reduced working memory capacity, so it is difficult for her to construct and understand long or complex sentences. She struggles to construct a narrative, and this deprives her of opportunities to express her identity (Moore and Davis 2002).

To support her communication, she relies on a small set of formulaic expressions, but she sometimes uses them inappropriately, which under-mines communication again. In consequence, communication breakdown is common. She is no longer able to undertake intellectually stimulating activities, and operates in a limited set of contexts. The care home is unable to provide her with enough to do. As a result, she often hears and repeats the same routines, which makes what she says rather uninteresting for others. As a consequence of all these factors, her interaction with carers and family has settled into a pattern of routine, phatic exchanges that are superficial, and low in novel content. Overall, her opportunities for interaction are severely limited—"An Alzheimer's Society survey found that the typical person in a home spent only two minutes interacting with staff or other residents over a six hour period of observation, excluding time spent on care tasks" (Alzheimer's Society 2007: p. v).

2: In the care home

Between them, the care home residents have a range of different challenges to deal with, many of them affecting communication. For instance, those with various types of aphasia have their own problems with comprehension and production, including articulatory difficulties arising from facial paraly-sis—these encourage the speaker to use familiar formulaic sequences where possible, in the hope that they will be most easily understood by others. Some have hearing difficulties, and have grown to fear not understanding what is said to them. A solution adopted by some is not to engage in conversations, while others do the opposite and try to monopolize the talk, giving others little opportunity to speak. Such monopolization requires fluency, which can be enhanced through a liberal use of morpheme equivalent units.

The residents have moved from their own homes, and this has considerably reduced the range of opportunities for keeping busy and undertaking a variety of stimulating activities. Many of them have a reduced feeling of self-worth, and they tend to repeat a small set of self-focused expressions and comments that draw attention to them and promote their sense of personal identity. Their reduced autonomy in relation to every day needs such as getting a cup of tea and moving about means they need to manipulate others to meet their needs. This is done using manipulative formulaic sequences, and can give the impression that they are excessively demanding, complain a lot, or are constantly apologizing for being so much trouble.

Communicating with each other, residents have to navigate both their own and their interlocutors' problems, and the easiest solution is to rely on phatic formulaic exchanges which give a superficial impression of social integration but have no depth. Effective communication with staff relies on mutual familiarity with turns of phrase, accent, and so on, and agreed protocols of routine behaviour. However, the turnover of staff is very high (Alzheimer's Society 2007: 37) and there are often newcomers who do not know how things have been done before or how a particular person needs to be addressed if communication is to be effective. It takes a while for residents even to become accustomed to the particular forms of greeting used by new staff. Thus, there is a constant threat to even the minimal level of communication that has been working thus far for an individual resident.

3: Enter the professionals

Care home residents receive attention from a range of medical and other professionals. Those with communication problems may have clinical assessments and/or speech and language therapy. As noted in Chapter 17 (also Wray 1992), individuals who rely on formulaic language in communication can find evaluations and therapy stressful, because increasing their attention to their performance makes them select—or at least seek—smaller lexical units. In the absence of the full range of grammatical capabilities or an effective working memory, these units cannot be combined into sentences. The experience can be so discouraging that it becomes preferable to withdraw from participation. A person with Alzheimer's Disease in a study by Davis and Bernstein (2005) "refused . . . to participate in any interaction where the conversation partner carried notebooks or picture cards or asked content-seeking questions" (p. 60). For such individuals it is important to recognize the value of retaining access to their formulaic resources, and to avoid stressful approaches to assessment—for instance, by favouring observation over testing.

Other professionals become involved despite, rather than because of, the communication difficulties. Residents will naturally present with a wide range of major and minor medical conditions—from cancer to toothache—and issues then arise for the professional about how to approach a range of necessary interactions, such as finding out about symptoms, discussing options and risks, and gaining consent for procedures. These sorts of exchange, though they may be framed somewhat formulaically with hedges and down-toners (Skelton and Hobbs 1999), fundamentally require novel expression. There may not be easy ways to explain issues and options without using complex vocabulary and sentences that exceed the linguistic scope of the addressee. The formulaic responses of people with many communication disorders may make it difficult to ascertain if they have really understood (compare the extract in Chapter 16, Figure 16.1).

Professionals may also bring with them their own communicative challenges. Not all talk easily to patients, and it can be particularly awkward to discuss emotive issues such as serious illness. Many may have little idea how to accommodate their talk when addressing someone with a communication disorder.[2] But in addition, advanced medical training constitutes a classic example of initiation into an esoteric communicative group (see Chapters 5 and 17). A professional discussion between two doctors would be incomprehensible to most outsiders, because it would liberally employ technical jargon and shared-context references that were not known to those outside the professional group. Jargon is a kind of formulaic language, for a word or word string is associated with a complex meaning in a way that would be difficult to work out from its component parts.

Esoterically-oriented communication is very advantageous in minimizing the processing effort of both speaker and hearer, but it ceases to be effective as soon as speaker and hearer have different specific and contextual knowledge and assumptions. It is part of the job of medical professionals to develop effective means of crossing the communication barrier and explain complex technical concepts to patients. Skelton and Hobbs (1999) found no instances of jargon in their corpus of medical consultations. However, they were sampling doctors with particular interest in medical education, who were expected to display good practice (p.109). It remains unclear whether all consultations are so jargon-free.

Evidently, judgements are made by a practitioner regarding the boundary between jargon and common terminology, and they would need to be sensitive to the knowledge base of an elderly care home resident, even leaving aside the added difficulties associated with an acquired communication disorder. Meanwhile, a full understanding of the patient's practical and acceptable options in communication, including the purpose of formulaic sequences, will be necessary before the quality of the interaction can be adequately gauged. For example, a person with a communication disorder may not be in a position to formulate a question, and so may find it less distressing to provide a minimal response that implies understanding.

4: Non-native speaker carers

The final layer of detail regards the quality of the carers' communication skills. According to the Alzheimer's Society (2007), "[c]are staff perceive communication problems as one of the biggest challenges in providing good dementia care" (p. 4); yet it is not yet mandatory for care home staff to be trained (ibid.: vii). However, training is only one part of the challenge, for many of the carers are not even native speakers of English. Care home work has a low status and is poorly paid (Alzheimer's Society 2007: 39), and no qualifications are necessary (ibid.: 57). It is therefore not surprising that work in this sector is attractive to people newly arrived from overseas, who "are well entrenched in the sector" (Keith Dobb, Chairman of the Nottinghamshire Care Association, interviewed in Saleem 2007).

Non-native speakers working in the L2 environment often quickly assimilate a collection of formulaic sequences that can be used to achieve a basic level of communication (Wray 2002b: 172–6), but may then struggle to progress further, finding nativelike formulaic language particularly challenging to understand and produce. It will not be easy for such people to interact with residents who are reliant on producing routine formulaic strings which they may have little capacity to alter or explain. Add to this the difficulties of a non-native pronunciation for residents who are hard of hearing or struggle to hold input in memory long enough to decode it, and the prognosis is not good.

Addressing the complex problem using formulaic language

Recent work in the US by Davis (2006, 2007; Davis, Russell-Pinson and Smith in preparation; Moore and Davis 2002), where similar problems exist, has focused on practical ways to tackle these challenges.

Moore and Davis (2002) describe a process called 'quilting', which native speaker carers and family members can use to support people with Alzheimer's Disease (PADs) in constructing personal narratives about their early lives. In quilting, the carer notices narrative fragments in the speech of the PAD, and remembers them or preserves them in a note book so that they can be used as the building blocks for a later narrative. By using as a prompt a specific turn of phrase from a previous narrative, carers provide PADs with a form-meaning pair that is recognizable as their own and that carries a saliency able to re-evoke a memory recently accessed. Over time, the addition of more and more details enables the narrative to be built up, simultaneously supporting the maintenance of linguistic and cognitive abilities, giving PADs a sense of contentment in expressing aspects of their identity, and furnishing carers with a deeper appreciation of the lives of those they work with. Quilting represents a creative use of fused formulaic sequences—the phrase becomes formulaic through repetition—that builds on, rather than resists, the role of formulaicity as a conduit for communication in the cognitively impaired (Davis and Maclagan 2007).

In a related initiative, Davis (2006, 2007) has been involved in developing training programmes for immigrant care workers that help them learn how to engage in linguistically and culturally appropriate and effective ways with their vulnerable patients, while boosting their own competence in the English language. Again, the method uses formulaic language constructively to bridge a communication gap. For example, there is a 'Caregiver's phrasebook' that introduces a first set of necessary formulaic sequences for greeting and starting conversations.

It is clear that the two approaches developed by Davis could be combined. Once non-native speaker carers have reached a functional level of communicative effectiveness with English, they could begin to apply quilting techniques. In this way, they could enhance the opportunities of those in their care for sharing their personal narratives, while, through the repetition process, rehearsing nativelike fragments of the target language (compare Chapters 12, 13, and 20).

The particular nexus of the communication disabled person, the care home environment, the incoming professional, and the non-native speaker carer is just one of many that must exist in our complex society. It illustrates the challenges of communication faced by many people every day, and indicates ways in which understanding the nature and functions of formulaic language might elucidate practical engagement with those challenges.

Opportunities for future research

It should be evident that there is much more to be understood regarding the role of formulaic language in human communication. Theoretical research is proceeding apace, on many fronts. But many more empirical investigations and studies of practical applications are needed. Of the suggestions offered below, many would be suitable for quite modest research projects such those of a Masters or PhD student.

Adult language learning

- What breadth and depth of language skills could adult learners develop on the basis of learning and using finite sets of formulaic sequences in their appropriate functional contexts? (See Chapters 18 and 20.)
- What sort of language (and how much of it formulaic) can a new immigrant learn directly through the work situation (for example, a newly arrived plumber or nurse)? Is such contextualized learning, in the absence of formal tuition, likely to be adequate? (See discussion in this chapter.)
- Can a language be taught successfully to learners only using translated example sentences, and no explanation, as in the accounts from Papua New Guinea and New Britain? (See Chapter 18.)

Computational linguistics

- Can computers learn idiomatic language through Needs Only Analysis? (See Chapter 19.)
- Is formulaic language equally appropriate for machine translation programs and human-computer communication, given their different parameters of design and use? (See Chapter 19.)

Forensic linguistics

- Are any types of formulaic language sufficiently distinctive to differentiate individual writing styles for authorship identification? (See Chapters 2, 8, and 9.)
- What opportunities and risks arise from formulaicity in police procedures with detainees? (See Chapter 17.)
- How might formulaic language help or hinder a witness when called to recount the same story many times in the course of an investigation and trial?

Performance

- When a text is highly formulaic for the speaker because it is often repeated, but novel for any given hearer (for example, directions to the speaker's house), how does the speaker deliver it, and what features are most likely to be problematic for the hearer?
- What role does formulaic language play in filling hiatuses during public improvisation (for example, speeches, lectures, seminar presentations)?
- How similar is the same story (for example, a fairy story) when told by different people?[3] Is it possible to identify features of a common original text?
- If a story is told by person A to person B, and person B to person C, etc., what determines which formal features of the text recur?
- What stages of proficiency in reproduction does an actor go through, when memorizing a new script? What are the characteristics of the material that turn out to be most difficult to remember? (See Chapters 15 and 20.)
- How do classical singers succeed in memorizing, and performing convincingly, songs in languages they don't speak?

Communication disorders

- How does the deliberate adoption of linguistic routines by carers affect the communication of those with and without linguistic or cognitive impairments? (See this chapter.)
- What is the impact on a person with a linguistic impairment of challenging or accepting the integrity of inappropriate formulaic output as a legitimate expression of an intended message? (See this chapter.)

- What happens to the linguistic formulation of the same story retold at intervals over a period of recovery (for example, from aphasia) or gradual degeneration (for example, due to Alzheimer's Disease)?

Final word

It is the nature of formulaic language to take many forms and to be difficult to define and identify on the basis of its particularities. But in essence it is a simple phenomenon—it is the multiword subset of the set of lexical units. Its relationship with other units of language is therefore also simple. In fact, the notion of formulaic language as such disappears, as it is absorbed into the broader notion of the MEU. Messages are expressed by assembling MEUs. As such, all messages are novel, in the sense that they entail the interaction of combinatory principles (or constructions) and lexical units. Thus, although in the course of this book it has been convenient to contrast formulaic and novel strings, there is really no difference. Simply, in some cases it is more internally complex MEUs that are retrieved from the lexicon, and in other cases less complex ones.

As for what we should understand the role of formulaic language to be, while it may be summarized in terms of a mechanism for the promotion of self (see Chapter 2), the detail of how that role impacts on communication is something that requires our continued engagement with data. There is considerable scope for further research, not only to observe how formulaic language operates in natural situations but also to experiment with interventions, including extreme ones such as those exemplified in this book. Often, it is the bold and exploratory investigations that tell us most about a phenomenon, because they test the boundaries of our definitions and predictions. We do not yet know where all those boundaries are, and, as a result, we do not yet have the full measure of formulaic language.

Notes

1 Symptom details are drawn from Grossman (2004); details about life in a care home come from the report of the Alzheimer's Society (2007).
2 Communication skills are increasingly on the curriculum in medical training, but since such support aims to level what are essentially reflections of personality, it runs the risk of being over mechanistic (Skelton and Hobbs 1999: 108) or too obvious to be helpful (Skelton 2005).
3 Compare, for instance, Webster, Franklin, and Howard (2007) on Cinderella narratives by normal and aphasic speakers.

References

Adolphs, S. and V. Durow. 2004. 'Social-cultural integration and the development of formulaic sequences' in N. Schmitt (ed.), pp.107–26.

Alm, N., J. Arnott, and A. Newell. 1989. 'Discourse analysis and pragmatics in the design of a conversation prosthesis'. *Journal of Medical Engineering and Technology* 13: 10–12.

Alzheimer's Society. 2007. *Home from Home: A Report Highlighting the Opportunities for Improving Standards of Dementia Care in Care Homes.* London: Alzheimer's Society.

American Heritage Dictionary of the English Language. 1992. (3rd edition) Boston, MA: Houghton Mifflin Co.

Arnot, M. and H. Pinson. 2005. *The Education of Asylum-seeker and Refugee Children: Report for the Research Consortium on the Education of Asylum-seeker and Refugee Children.* Cambridge: Faculty of Education.

Atkins, S., M. Rundell, and H. Sato. 2003. 'The contribution of FrameNet to practical lexicography'. *International Journal of Lexicography* 16/3: 333–57.

Austin, J. L. 1962. *How to do Things with Words.* Oxford: Oxford University Press.

Backus, A. 1999. 'Evidence for lexical chunks in insertional codeswitching' in B. Brendemoen, E. Lanza, and E. Ryen (eds.). *Language Encounters Across Time and Space*, (pp. 93–109). Oslo: Novus Press.

Baddeley, A. 1986. *Working Memory.* Oxford: Clarendon Press.

Bakhtin, M. 1986. *Speech Genres and Other Late Essays.* Austin, TX: University of Texas Press.

Barlow, M. 2000. 'Usage, blends and grammar' in M. Barlow and S. Kemmer (eds.). *Usage-based Models of Language*, (pp. 315–45). Stanford, CA: CSLI Publications.

Bassetti, B. 2005. 'Effects of writing systems on second language awareness: Word awareness in English learners of Chinese as a foreign language' in V. Cook and B. Bassetti (eds.). *Second Language Writing Systems*, (pp. 335–56). Clevedon: Multilingual Matters.

Bäuml, F. H. 1984. 'Medieval texts and the two theories of oral-formulaic composition: A proposal for a third theory'. *New Literary History* 16/1: 31–49.

Bazell, C. E. 1958. 'Linguistic typology'. Inaugural lexture, SOAS, 26 February 1958. London: University of London.

BBC Sport. 2008. *Flags Guide.* Available from http://news.bbc.co.uk/sport1/hi/motorsport/formula_one/flags_guide/default. Accessed 10.02.08.

Bencini, G. M. L. and A. E. Goldberg. 2000. 'The contribution of argument structure constructions to sentence meaning'. *Journal of Memory and Language* 43: 640–51.

Benson, M., E. Benson, and R. Ilson. 1986. *The BBI Combinatory Dictionary of English: A Guide to Word Combinations.* Amsterdam: John Benjamins.

Benton, A. L. and R. J. Joynt. 1960. 'Early descriptions of aphasia'. *Archives of Neurology* 3: 109–126/ 205–22.

Bergen, B. K. 2001. 'Nativization processes in L1 Esperanto'. *Journal of Child Language* 28: 575–95.

Biber, D. 1988. *Variation Across Speech and Writing.* Cambridge: Cambridge University Press.

Biber, D. 1989. 'A typology of English texts'. *Linguistics* 27: 3–43.

Biber, D. 2000. 'Investigating language use through corpus-based analyses of association patterns' in M. Barlow and S. Kemmer (eds.). *Usage-based Models of Language*, (pp. 287–313). Stanford, CA: CSLI Publications.

Biber, D., S. Conrad, and V. Cortes. 2004. '"If you look at ..." lexical bundles in university teaching and textbooks'. *Applied Linguistics* 25/3: 371–405.

Biber, D., S. Johansson, G. Leech, and S. Conrad. 1999. *Longman Grammar of Spoken and Written English*. London and New York: Longman.

Bickerton, D. 1996. *Language and Human Behaviour*. London: University of London Press.

Bickerton, D. 1998. 'Catastrophic evolution: The case for a single step from protolanguage to full human language' in J. Hurford, M. Studdert-Kennedy, and C. Knight (eds.). *Approaches to the Evolution of Language*, (pp. 341–58). Cambridge: Cambridge University Press.

Bickerton, D. 2000. 'How protolanguage became language' in C. Knight, M. Studdert-Kennedy, and J. Hurford (eds.). *The Evolutionary Emergence of Language*, (pp. 264–84). Cambridge: Cambridge University Press.

Biggs, B. 1998. *Let's Learn Māori*. Auckland, New Zealand: University of Auckland Press.

Bishop, H. 2004. 'The effect of typographic salience on the look up and comprehension of unknown formulaic sequences' in N. Schmitt (ed.), pp. 227–44.

Blackmore, S. J. 1999. *The Meme Machine*. Oxford: Oxford University Press.

Bloch, M. 1993. 'The uses of schooling and literacy in a Zafimaniry village' in B. Street (ed.). *Readings on Literacy*, (pp. 87–109). Cambridge: Cambridge University Press.

Boyd, E. 2004. '"The thing is ...": A reexamination and reappraisal of such phrases from a lexicogrammatical, discourse analytic and pragmatic perspective'. PhD thesis, University of Wales, Cardiff.

Brewer, J. P. 2005. 'Carousel conversation: Aspects of family roles and topic shift in Alzheimer's talk' in B. H. Davis (ed.). *Alzheimer Talk, Text and Context: Enhancing Communication*, (pp. 87–101). Basingstoke: Palgrave Macmillan.

Brockington, J. 1998. 'Formulaic expression in the Rāmāyana: Evidence for oral composition' in L. Honko, J. Handoo, and J. M. Foley (eds.). *The Epic: Oral and Written*, (pp. 128–38). Mysore: Central Institute of Indian Languages.

Brown, J. D. and K. Kondo-Brown. (eds.). 2006. *Perspectives on Teaching Connected Speech to Second Language Speakers*. Honolulu, HI: University of Hawai'i National Foreign Language Resource Center.

Brown, K. (ed.). 2006. *Encyclopedia of Language and Linguistics* (2nd edition). Oxford: Elsevier.

Bucks, R. S., S. Singh, J. M. Cuerden, and G. K. Wilcock. 2000. 'Analysis of spontaneous, conversational speech in dementia of Alzheimer type: Evaluation of an objective technique for analysing lexical performance'. *Aphasiology* 14/1: 71–91.

Butler, C. S. 1997. 'Repeated word combinations in spoken and written text: Some implications for Functional Grammar' in C. S. Butler, J. H. Connolly, R. A. Gatward, and R. M. Vismans (eds.). *A Fund of Ideas: Recent Developments in Functional Grammar*, (pp. 60–77). Amsterdam: IFOTT.

Butler, C. S. 1998a. 'Enriching the Functional Grammar lexicon' in H. Olbertz, K. Hengeveld, and J. S. García (eds.). *The Structure of the Lexicon in Functional Grammar*, (pp. 171–94). Amsterdam: John Benjamins.

Butler, C. S. 1998b. 'Multi-word lexical phenomena in Functional Grammar'. *Revista Canaria de Estudios Ingleses* 36: 13–36.

Butler, C. S. 2003. *Structure and Function: A Guide to Three Major Structural-Functional Theories. Part 2: From Clause to Discourse and Beyond*. Amsterdam: John Benjamins.

Butler, C. S. 2004. 'Corpus studies and Functional Linguistic theories'. *Functions of Language* 11/2: 147–86.

Butterfield, J. and R. Krishnamurthy. 2000. 'Beyond the dictionary: On-line learning in the classroom'. *TESOL Spain Newsletter* 23: 3–5.

Bybee, J. 2002. 'Phonological evidence for exemplar storage of multiword sequences'. *Studies in Second Language Acquisition* 24/2: 215–21.

Bybee, J. 2003. 'Cognitive processes in grammaticalization' in M. Tomasello (ed.). *The New Psychology of Language, Vol. 2*, (pp. 145–67). Mahwah, NJ: Lawrence Erlbaum.

Bybee, J. 2006. 'From usage to grammar: The mind's response to repetition'. *Language* 82/4: 711–33.

Bybee, J. and J. L. McClelland. 2005. 'Alternatives to the combinatorial paradigm of linguistic theory based on domain general principles of human cognition'. *The Linguistic Review* 22: 381–410.

Bybee, J. and J. Scheibman. 1999. 'The effect of usage on degrees of constituency: The reduction of *don't* in English'. *Linguistics* 37/4: 575–96.

Cahill, R. 2006. 'Teaching reduced interrogative forms to low-level EFL students in Japan' in J. D. Brown and K. Kondo-Brown (eds.), pp. 99–112.

Calvin, W. and D. Bickerton. 2000. *Lingua ex Machina*. Cambridge, MA: MIT Press.

Calzolari, N., C. J. Fillmore, R. Grishman, N. Ide, A. Lenci, C. MacLeod, and A. Zampolli. 2002. 'Towards best practice for multiword expressions in computational lexicons'. *Proceedings of the Third International Conference on Language Resources and Evaluation*, (pp. 1934–40). Las Palmas, Canary Islands: LREC.

Cambridge Advanced Learner's Dictionary. 2005. Cambridge: Cambridge University Press.

Cameron, L. and A. Deignan. 2006. 'The emergence of metaphor in discourse'. *Applied Linguistics* 27/4: 671–90.

Cameron-Faulkner, T., E. Lieven, and M. Tomasello. 2003. 'A construction based analysis of child-directed speech'. *Cognitive Science* 27: 843–73.

Chantraine, Y., Y. Joanette, and B. Ska. 1998. 'Conversational abilities in patients with right hemisphere damage'. *Journal of Neurolinguistics* 11/1–2: 21–32.

Chenoweth, N. A. 1995. 'Formulaicity in essay exam answers'. *Language Sciences* 17/3: 283–97.

Chipere, N. 2003. *Understanding Complex Sentences*. Basingstoke: Palgrave.

Clanchy, M. T. 1993. *From Memory to Written Record: England 1066–1307*. (2nd edition). Oxford: Blackwell.

Code, C. 1987. *Language, Aphasia and the Right Hemisphere*. Chichester: John Wiley.

Coltheart, M., K. Rastle, C. Perry, R. Langdon, and J. Ziegler. 2001. 'DRC: A dual route cascaded model of visual word recognition and reading aloud'. *Psychological Review* 108: 204–56.

Conklin, K. and N. Schmitt. 2008. 'Formulaic sequences: Are they processed more quickly than nonformulaic language by native and nonnative speakers?' *Applied Linguistics* 29/1: 72–89.

Cooper, B. J. 2004. 'The enigma of the Chinese learner'. *Accounting Education* 13/3: 289–310.

Cotterill, J. 2002. '"Just one more time ... ": Aspects of intertextuality in the trials of O.J. Simpson' in J. Cotterill (ed.). *Language in the Legal Process*, (pp. 147–61). Basingstoke: Palgrave Macmillan.

Cox, S., M. Lincoln, J. Tryggvason, M. Nakisa, M. Wells, M. Tutt, and S. Abbott. 2002a. 'TESSA, a system to aid communication with deaf people' in *Proceedings of the Fifth International ASSETS ACM SIGCAPH Conference on Assistive Technologies, Edinburgh*, (pp. 205–12). New York: ACM.

Cox, S., M. Lincoln, J. Tryggvason, M. Nakisa, M. Wells, M. Tutt, and S. Abbott. 2003. 'Development and evaluation of a speech to sign translation system to assist transactions'. *International Journal of Human-Computer Interaction* 16/2: 141–61.

Cox, S., I. Marshall, and É. Sáfár. 2002b. 'What are the difficulties of translating English to sign language?' *The Linguist* 41/1: 6–10.

Croft, W. 2001. *Radical Construction Grammar*. Oxford: Oxford University Press.

Culicover, P. W. and R. Jackendoff. 2005. *Simpler Syntax*. Oxford: Oxford University Press.

Cushing, S. 1994a. *Fatal Words: Communication Clashes and Aircraft Crashes*. Chicago: University of Chicago Press.

Cushing, S. 1994b. 'Plane speaking'. *Verbatim* 21/2: 1–3.

Custer, E. B. 1890. *Following the Guidon*. New York: Harper and Brothers. Republished 1998 by Digital Scanning Inc, Scituate, MA, www.digitalscanning.com.

Cutting, J. C. and J. K. Bock. 1997. 'That's the way the cookie bounces: Syntactic and semantic components of experimentally elicited idiomatic blends'. *Memory & Cognition* 25: 57–71.

Dabrowska, E. 2000. 'From formula to schema: The acquisition of English questions'. *Cognitive Linguistics* 11/1/2: 83–102.

Dabrowska, E. and J. Street. 2006. 'Individual differences in language attainment: Comprehension of passive sentences by native and non-native English speakers'. *Language Sciences* 28: 604–15.

Dahlin, B. and D. Watkins. 2000. 'The role of repetition in the processes of memorising and understanding: A comparison of the views of German and Chinese secondary school students in Hong Kong'. *British Journal of Educational Psychology* 70: 65–84.

Damasio, H., D. Tranel, T. Grabowski, R. Adolphs, and A. Damasio. 2004. 'Neural systems behind word and concept retrieval'. *Cognition* 92/1–2: 179–229.

Davies, S. 1996. 'The reoralization of "The Lady of the Lake"' in H. L. C. Tristram (ed.). *(Re)oralisierung*, (pp. 335–60). Tübingen: Gunter Narr.

Davies, S. 1997. 'Horses in the *Maginogion*' in S. Davies and N. A. Jones (eds.). *The Horse in Celtic Culture: Medieval Welsh Perspectives*, (pp. 121–40). Cardiff: University of Wales Press.

Davies, S. 2007. *Mabinogion*. Oxford: Oxford University Press.

Davis, B. 2005. 'Introduction: Some commonalities' in B. H. Davis (ed.). *Alzheimer Talk, Text and Context: Enhancing Communication*, (pp. xi–xxi). Basingstoke: Palgrave Macmillan.

Davis, B. 2006. *Culturally Competent Materials on Communication and Dementia*. Charlotte: University of North Carolina. http://www.english.uncc.edu/bdavis/AlzAssnYear1report.pdf. Accessed 09.02.08.

Davis, B. 2007. *Culturally Competent Materials on Communication and Dementia: Year Two*. Charlotte: University of North Carolina. http://www.english.uncc.edu/bdavis/AlzGrtRepYr2-DAVISDS.pdf. Accessed 09.02.08.

Davis, B. H. and C. Bernstein. 2005. 'Talking in the here and now: Reference and politeness in Alzheimer conversation' in B. H. Davis (ed.). *Alzheimer Talk, Text and Context: Enhancing Communication*, (pp. 60–86). Basingstoke: Palgrave Macmillan.

Davis, B. H. and M. Maclagan. 2007. 'Formulaicity and fillers in Alzheimer's talk'. Paper presented at the *International Pragmatics Association Conference*, July. Göteborg.

Davis, B. H., L. Russell-Pinson, and M. Smith. (in preparation). 'Collaboration in ESP: Towards a multilingual, multicultural nursing assistant workforce'.

De Cock, S. 2002. 'Pragmatic prefabs in learners' dictionaries' in A. Braash and C. Povlsen (eds.). *Proceedings of the Tenth EURALEX International Congress*, (pp. 417–81). Copenhagen: Center for Sprogteknologi.

De Cock, S. 2004. 'Preferred sequences of words in NS and NNS speech'. *Belgian Journal of English Language and Literatures, New Series* 2: 225–46.

Di Sciullo, A. M. and E. Williams. 1987. *On the Definition of Word*. Cambridge, MA: MIT Press.

Dictionary of American Regional English. 1985. Vol. 1. Cambridge, MA: Belknap Press of Harvard University Press.

Diessel, H. and M. Tomasello. 2001. 'The acquisition of finite complement clauses in English: A corpus-based analysis'. *Cognitive Linguistics* 12/2: 97–141.

Ding, Y. 2007. 'Text memorization and imitation: The practices of successful Chinese learners of English'. *System* 35: 271–80.

Dixon, R. M. W. and A. Y. Aikhenvald. 2002. 'Word: A typological framework' in R. M. W. Dixon and A. Y. Aikhenvald (eds.). Word: *A Cross-linguistic Typology*, (pp. 1–41). Cambridge: Cambridge University Press.

Dóla, M. (in preparation). 'A play on words and rules: Formulaic language in L2 Hungarian'. PhD thesis, University of Pécs, Hungary.

Dorr, E., E. Hovy, and L. Levin. 2006. 'Machine translation: Interlingual methods' in K. Brown (ed.) vol. 7, pp. 383–94.

Edwards, S. and R. Knott. 1994. 'Assessing spontaneous language abilities of aphasic speakers' in D. Graddol and J. Swann (eds.). *Evaluating Language*, (pp. 91–101). Clevedon: Multilingual Matters.

Efron, R. 1990. *The Decline and Fall of Hemispheric Specialization*. Hillsdale, NJ: Lawrence Erlbaum.

Ellis, N., R. Simpson-Vlach, and C. Maynard. 2006. 'The processing of formulas in native and second-language speakers: Psycholinguistic and corpus determinants'. Paper presented at the International Conference on Exploring the Lexis-Grammar Interface, Hanover, Germany.

Ericsson, K. A. and W. Kintsch. 1995. 'Long term memory'. *Psychological Review* 102/2: 211–45.

Erman, B. 2007. 'Cognitive processes as evidence of the idiom principle'. *International Journal of Corpus Linguistics* 12/1: 25–53.

Erman, B. and B. Warren. 2000. 'The idiom principle and the open choice principle'. *Text* 20: 29–62.

Everett, D. 2005. 'Cultural constraints on grammar and cognition in Pirahã'. *Current Anthropology* 46/4: 621–34.

Fairman, T. 2000. 'English pauper letters 1800–34, and the English language' in D. Barton and N. Hall (eds.). *Letter Writing as a Social Practice*, (pp. 63–82). Amsterdam: John Benjamins.

Fairman, T. 2002. '"Riting these fu lines": English overseers' correspondence 1800–1835'. *Verslagen en Mededelingen (Koninklijke Academie voor Nederlandse Taalen Letterkunde)* 3: 557–73.

Fairman, T. 2003. 'Letters of the English labouring classes and the English language, 1800–1834' in M. Dossena and C. Jones (eds.). *Insights into Late Modern English*, (pp. 265–82). Bern: Peter Lang.

Fairman, T. 2006. 'Words in English record office documents in the early 1800s' in M. Kytö, M. Rydén, and E. Smitterberg (eds.). *Nineteenth-century English: Stability and Change*, (pp. 56–88). Cambridge: Cambridge University Press.

Fawcett, R. 2005. *Invitation to Systemic Functional Linguistics: The Cardiff Grammar as an Extension and Simplification of Halliday's Systemic Functional Grammar*. (2nd edition). Cardiff: Cardiff University. Available at: http://www.cf.ac.uk/encap/fontaine/cardiffgrammar/cardiffgrammar.htm. Accessed 10.02.08.

Fédération Internationale de l'Automobile (FIA). 2007. *Appendix H to the International Sporting Code*: http://www.fia.com/resources/documents/1653003624__Appendix_H_a.pdf. Accessed 10.2.08.

Feyaerts, K. 2006. 'Towards a dynamic account of phraseological meaning: Creative variation in headlines and conversational humour'. *International Journal of English Studies* 6/1: 57–84.

Fillmore, C. J. 2006. 'Frame Semantics' in K. Brown (ed.) vol. 4, pp. 613–20.

Fillmore, C. J., C. R. Johnson, and M. Petruck. 2003. 'Background to FrameNet'. *International Journal of Lexicography* 16/3: 235–50.

Fillmore, C. J., P. Kay, and M. C. O'Connor. 1988. 'Regularity and idiomaticity in grammatical constructions: The case of "let alone"'. *Language* 64: 501–38.

Fitzpatrick, T. and P. Meara. 2004. 'Exploring the validity of a test of productive vocabulary'. *Vigo International Journal of Applied Linguistics* 1: 55–74.

Fitzpatrick, T. and A. Wray. 2006. 'Breaking up is not so hard to do: Individual differences in L2 memorization'. *Canadian Modern Language Review* 63/1: 35–57.

Flavell, L. and R. Flavell. 1992. *Dictionary of Idioms and Their Origins*. London: Kyle Cathie.

Fontaine, L. 2004. 'Textual challenges in recursive email texts' in D. Banks (ed.). *Text and Texture*, (pp. 301–28). Paris: L'Harmattan.

Forsberg, F. 2006. 'Le Langage Préfabriqué en Français Parlé L2'. PhD thesis, Department of French, Italian, and Classical Languages, Stockholm University, Stockholm.

Foster, H. W. 2004. 'Jazz musicians and south slavic oral epic bards'. *Oral Tradition* 19/2: 155–76.

Foster, P. 2001. 'Rules and routines: A consideration of their role in the task-based language production of native and non-native speakers' in M. Bygate, P. Skehan, and M. Swain (eds.). *Researching Pedagogic Tasks: Second Language Learning, Teaching and Testing*, (pp. 75–97). London and New York: Longman.

Foster, P. (in preparation). 'Lexical diversity and native-like selection: The bonus of studying abroad'.

Francis, G., S. Hunston, and E. Manning. 1996. *Collins COBUILD Grammar Patterns 1: Verbs*. London: Harper Collins.

Francis, G., S. Hunston, and E. Manning. 1998. *Collins COBUILD Grammar Patterns 2: Nouns and Adjectives*. London: Harper Collins.

Fuller, C. 2001. 'Orality, literacy and memorisation: Priestly education in contemporary South India'. *Modern Asian Studies* 35/1: 1–31.

Gatbonton, E. and N. Segalowitz. 1988. 'Creative automatization: Principles for promoting fluency within a communicative framework'. *TESOL Quarterly* 88: 473–92.

Gatbonton, E. and N. Segalowitz. 2005. 'Rethinking communicative language teaching: A focus on access to fluency'. *The Canadian Modern Language Review* 61/3: 325–53.

Gibbs, R. W. 2007. 'Idioms and formulaic language' in D. Geeraerts and H. Cuyckens (eds.). *The Oxford Handbook of Cognitive Linguistics*, (pp. 697–725). Oxford: Oxford University Press.

Givón, T. 1995. *Functionalism and Grammar*. Amsterdam: John Benjamins.

Givón, T. 1998. 'The functional approach to grammar' in M. Tomasello (ed.). *The New Psychology of Language, Vol 1*, (pp. 41–66). Mahwah, NJ: Lawrence Erlbaum Associates.

Glauert, J. R. W., R. Elliott, S. Cox, J. Tryggvason, and M. Sheard. 2006. 'VANESSA: A system for communication between deaf and hearing people'. *Technology and Disability* 18: 1–10.

Goldberg, A. E. 2003. 'Constructions: A new theoretical approach to language'. *Trends in Cognitive Sciences* 7/5: 219–24.

Goldberg, A. E. 2006. *Constructions at Work*. Oxford: Oxford University Press.

Gonzálvez-García, F. and C. S. Butler. 2006. 'Mapping functional-cognitive space'. *Annual Review of Cognitive Linguistics* 4: 39–95.

Grace, G. W. 1987. *The Linguistic Construction of Reality*. London: Croom Helm.

Grace, G. W. *Collateral Damage from Linguistics? 3: The Role of Culture-centrism*. *Ethnolinguistic Notes* 4, 23. http://www2.hawaii.edu/~grace/elniv23.html. Accessed 10.02.08.

Graff, H. J. 1991. *The Literacy Myth: Cultural Integration and Social Structure in the Nineteenth Century*. New Brunswick: Transaction Publishers.

Grice, H. P. 1975. 'Logic and conversation' in P. Cole and J. L. Morgan (eds.). *Syntax and Semantics 3: Speech Acts*, (pp. 41–58). New York: Academic Press.

Griffiths, D. 2003. *English Language Training for Refugees in London and the Regions*. London: Home Office Online Report 14 March.

Grossman, M. 2004. 'Alzheimer's disease' in R. M. Kent (ed.). *The MIT Encyclopedia of Communication Disorders*, (pp. 240–41). Cambridge, MA: MIT Press.

Guillaume, P. 1927/1973. 'First stages of sentence formation in children's speech' in C. A. Ferguson and D. I. Slobin (eds.). *Studies in Child Language Development*, (pp. 522–41). New York: Holt, Rinehart, and Winston.

Halliday, M. A. K. 1970. 'Language structure and language function' in J. Lyons (ed.). *New Horizons in Linguistics*, (pp. 140–65). Harmondsworth: Penguin.

Halliday, M. A. K. 2006. 'Systemic theory' in K. Brown (ed.) vol. 12, pp. 443–48.

Hauser, M. D., N. Chomsky, and W. T. Fitch. 2002. 'The faculty of language: What is it, who has it, and how did it evolve?' *Science* 298: 1569–79.

Heath, R. L. and L. X. Blonder. 2005. 'Spontaneous humor among right hemisphere stroke survivors'. *Brain and Language* 93: 267–76.

Hillert, D. G. 2004. 'Spared access to idiomatic and literal meanings: A single-case approach'. *Brain and Language* 89: 207–15.

Himmelmann, N. P. 2006. 'The challenges of segmenting spoken language' in J. Gippert, N. P. Himmelmann, and U. Mosel (eds.). *Essentials of Language Documentation*, (pp. 253–74). Berlin: Mouton de Gruyter.

Hirschberg, J. 2006. 'Speech synthesis: Prosody' in K. Brown (ed.) vol. 12, (pp. 49–55).

Historical Dictionary of American Slang. 1994. New York: Random House.

Hoey, M. 2005. *Lexical Priming: A New Theory of Words and Language*. London: Routledge.

Holman, J. P. 2007. 'Best of both worlds: Elsdon Best and the metamorphosis of Māori spirituality. Te painga rawa o ngā ao rua: Te peehi me te putanga kēo te wairua Māori'. PhD thesis, University of Canterbury, Christchurch, New Zealand.

Hopper, P. 1998. 'Emergent grammar' in M. Tomasello (ed.). *The New Psychology of Language, Vol. 1*, (pp. 155–75). Mahwah, NJ: Lawrence Erlbaum.

Huber-Okrainec, J., S. E. Blaser, and **M. Dennis.** 2005. 'Idiom comprehension deficits in relation to corpus callosum agenesis and hypoplasia in children with spina bifida meningomyelocele'. *Brain and Language* 93: 349–68.

Hunston, S. 2002. *Corpora in Applied Linguistics*. Cambridge: Cambridge University Press.

Hunston, S. 2006a. 'Corpus linguistics' in K. Brown (ed.) vol. 3, pp. 234–48.

Hunston, S. 2006b. 'Phraseology and system: A contribution to the debate' in G. Thompson and S. Hunston (eds.). *System and Corpus: Exploring Connections*, (pp. 55–80). London: Equinox.

Hunston, S. 2007. 'Where lexis and grammar meet: Pattern, corpus and phraseology'. Paper presented at the *Formulaic Language Symposium*, University of Wisconsin, Milwaukee.

Hunston, S. and **G. Francis.** 2000. *Pattern Grammar*. Amsterdam: John Benjamins.

Hyde, J. 1798. *A New and Compleat Preceptor for the Trumpet and Bugle Horn*. London: Button & Whitaker.

Hymes, D. 1972. 'On communicative competence' in J. B. Pride and J. Holmes (eds.). *Sociolinguistics*, (pp. 269–93). Harmondsworth: Penguin.

Hymes, D. 1992. 'The concept of communicative competence revisited' in M. Pütz (ed.). *Thirty Years of Linguistic Evolution*, (pp. 31–57). Amsterdam: John Benjamins.

International Civil Aviation Organisation. 2006. *Personnel Licensing, Frequently Asked Questions: Language Proficiency Requirements for Licence Holders*. http://www.icao.int/icao/en/trivia/peltrgFAQ.htm#22. Accessed 10.02.08.

Isabelle, P. and **G. Foster.** 2006. 'Machine translation: Overview' in K. Brown (ed.) vol. 7, pp. 404–22.

Israel, M., C. Johnson, and **P. J. Brooks.** 2000. 'From states to events: The acquisition of English passive participles'. *Cognitive Linguistics* 11/1/2: 103–29.

Ito, Y. 2006. 'The significance of reduced forms in L2 pedagogy' in J. D. Brown and K. Kondo-Brown (eds.), pp. 17–25.

Jackendoff, R. 2002. *Foundations of Language*. Oxford: Oxford University Press.

Jackendoff, R. 2007. 'Linguistics in cognitive science: The state of the art'. *The Linguistic Review* 24/4: 347–401.

Jackson, P. and **F. Schilder.** 2006. 'Natural language processing: Overview' in K. Brown (ed.) vol. 8, pp. 504–18.

Jespersen, O. 1922. *Language—Its Nature Development and Origin*. London: George Allen and Unwin Ltd.

Ji, F. 2004. *Linguistic Engineering: Language and Politics in Mao's China*. Honolulu: University of Hawai'i Press.

Ji, F., K. Kuiper, and **S. Shu.** 1990. 'Language and revolution: Formulae of the Cultural Revolution'. *Language in Society* 19: 61–79.

Jones, M. and **S. Haywood.** 2004. 'Facilitating the acquisition of formulaic sequences' in N. Schmitt (ed.), pp. 269–300.

Juang, B.-H. and **L. R. Rabiner.** 2006. 'Speech recognition, automatic: History' in K. Brown (ed.) vol. 11, pp. 806–19.

Jung-Beeman, M. 2005. 'Bilateral brain processes for comprehending natural language'. *Trends in Cognitive Sciences* 9/11: 512–18.

Just, M. A. and **P. A. Carpenter.** 1992. 'A capacity theory of comprehension: Individual differences in working memory'. *Psychological Review* 99/1: 122–49.

Kay, P. 1977. 'Language evolution and speech style' in B. G. Blount and M. Sanches (eds.). *Sociocultural Dimensions of Language Change*, (pp. 21–33). New York: Academic Press.

Kemmer, S. and **M. Barlow.** 2000. 'An introduction: A usage-based conception of language' in M. Barlow and S. Kemmer (eds.). *Usage-based Models of Language*, (pp. vii–xxviii). Stanford, CA: CSLI Publications.

Kemper, S., L. H. Greiner, J. G. Marquis, K. Prenovost, and **T. L. Mitzner.** 2001. 'Language decline across the life span: Findings from the nun study'. *Psychology and Aging* 16/2: 227–39.

Kennedy, P. 2002. 'Learning cultures and learning styles: Myth-understandings about adult (Hong Kong) Chinese learners'. *International Journal of Lifelong Education* 21/5: 430–45.

Kirby, S. 2001. 'Spontaneous evolution of linguistic structure: An iterated learning model of the emergence of regularity and irregularity'. *IEEE Journal of Evolutionary Computation* 5/2: 102–10.

Kirby, S. 2002. 'Learning, bottlenecks and the evolution of recursive syntax' in T. Briscoe (ed.). *Linguistic Evolution through Language Acquisition: Formal and Computational Models*, (pp. 173–203). Cambridge: Cambridge University Press.

Kjellmer, G. 1991. 'A mint of phrases' in K. Ajmer and B. Altenberg (eds.). *English Corpus Linguistics: Studies in Honour of Jan Svartvik*, (pp. 111–27). London and New York: Longman.

Knutsson, R. 2006. 'Formulaic Language in L1 and L2'. Licentiate dissertation. Department of English, Lund University, Lund.

Krishnamurthy, R. 2004. 'Burning questions, but no burning answers: Collocation and idiomaticity' in G. Lassche (ed.). *KOTESOL 2002 Proceedings: Crossroads: Generational Change in ELT in Asia*, (pp. 207–18). Seoul: KOTESOL.

Kryszewska, H. 2003. 'Why I won't say good-bye to the lexical approach'. *Humanising Language Teaching* 5/2. http://www.hltmag.co.uk/mar03/mart.htm. Accessed 10.2.08.

Kuhn, T. 1996. *The Structure of Scientific Revolutions* (3rd edition). Chicago: University of Chicago Press.

Kuiper, K. 1996. *Smooth Talkers: The Linguistic Performance of Auctioneers and Sportscasters*. Mahwah, NJ: Lawrence Erlbaum.

Kuiper, K. 2007. 'Cathy Wilcox meets the phrasal lexicon: Creative deformation of phrasal lexical items for humorous effect' in J. Munat (ed.). *Lexical Creativity, Texts and Contexts*, (pp. 93–112). Amsterdam: John Benjamins.

Lackner, J. R. and **M. F. Garrett.** 1972. 'Resolving ambiguity: Effects of biasing context in the unattended ear'. *Cognition* 1/4: 359–72.

Lamb, S. 1999. *Pathways of the Brain*. Amsterdam: John Benjamins.

Langacker, R. W. 1987. *Foundations of Cognitive Grammar, Vol 1: Theoretical Prerequisites*. Stanford: Stanford University Press.

Langacker, R. W. 2000. 'A dynamic usage-based model' in M. Barlow and S. Kemmer (eds.). *Usage-based Models of Language*, (pp. 1–63). Stanford, CA: CSLI Publications.

Langlotz, A. 2006. *Idiomatic Creativity: A Cognitive-Linguistic Model of Idiom Representation and Idiom-variation in English*. Amsterdam: John Benjamins.

Laycock, D. 1979. 'Multilingualism: Linguistic boundaries and unsolved problems in Papua New Guinea' in S. A. Wurm (ed.). *New Guinea and Neighboring Areas: A Sociolinguistic Laboratory*, (pp. 81–99). The Hague: Mouton.

Lee, D. 2001. *Cognitive Linguistics: An Introduction*. Oxford: Oxford University Press.

Lewin, K. 1945. 'The Research Center for Group Dynamics at Massachusetts Institute of Technology'. *Sociometry* 8: 126–36.

Liang, H. and **J. Shapiro.** 1983. *Son of the Revolution*. New York: Knopf.

Lieven, E. V. M., J. M. Pine, and H. D. Barnes. 1992. 'Individual differences in early vocabulary development: Redefining the referential-expressive distinction'. *Journal of Child Language* 19: 287–310.

Lightfoot, D. 2000. 'The spandrels of the linguistic genotype' in C. Knight, M. Studdert-Kennedy, and J. Hurford (eds.). *The Evolutionary Emergence of Language*, (pp. 231–47). Cambridge: Cambridge University Press.

Lindstromberg, S. 2003. 'My good-bye to the lexical approach'. *Humanising Language Teaching* 5/2. http://www.hltmag.co.uk/mar03/mart.htm. Accessed 10.2.08.

Lord, A. B. 2000. *The Singer of Tales* (2nd edition). Cambridge, MA: Harvard University Press.

MacKenzie, I. 2003. 'Poetry and formulaic language' in C. Michaux and M. Domincy (eds.). *Linguistic Approaches to Poetry*, (pp. 75–85). Amsterdam: John Benjamins.

Mandler, J. M. and N. S. Johnson. 1977. 'Remembrance of things parsed. Story structure and recall'. *Cognitive Psychology* 9: 111–51.

Māori Language Commission. 1996. *Te Matatiki: Contemporary Māori Words*. Auckland, New Zealand: Oxford University Press.

Martinet, A. 2006. 'Functional Grammar: Martinet' in K. Brown (ed.) vol. 4, pp. 677–82.

Marton, F., G. Dall'Alba, and L. K. Tse. 1993. *The Paradox of the Chinese Learner*. Melbourne: RMIT, Educational Research and Development Unit.

Matsui, K., Y. Wakita, T. Konuma, K. Mizutani, M. Endo, and M. Murata. 2001. 'An experimental multilingual speech translation system' (ed.). *Proceedings of the Perceptive User Interfaces Workshop*, Orlando Florida. http://projectile.is.cs.cmu.edu/research/public/talks/speechTranslation/otherPaper/matsushita.pdf. Accessed 10.02.08.

Mattys, S. L. 2006. 'Speech recognition: Psychology approaches' in K. Brown (ed.) vol. 11, pp. 819–28.

Maxwell, D., K. Schubert, and T. Witkam. (eds.). 1988. *New Directions in Machine Translation: Proceedings of the Distributed Language Translation Conference, 4*. Dordrecht: Foris.

McAlpine, J. and J. Myles. 2003. 'Capturing phraseology in an online dictionary for advanced users of English as a second language: A response to user needs'. *System* 31: 71–84.

McElduff, K. and S. S. Drummond. 1991. 'Communicative functions of automatic speech in non-fluent dysphasia'. *Aphasiology* 5: 265–78.

McEvoy, R. E., K. A. Loveland, and S. H. Landry. 1988. 'The functions of immediate echolalia in autistic children: A developmental perspective'. *Journal of Autism and Developmental Disorders* 18/4: 657–68.

McGee, I. 2006. 'Lexical intuitions and collocation patterns in corpora'. PhD thesis, Centre for Language and Communication Research, Cardiff University.

Meara, P. and T. Fitzpatrick. 2000. 'Lex30: An improved method of assessing productive vocabulary in an L2'. *System* 28/1: 19–30.

Meara, P. and G. Jones. 1988. 'Vocabulary size as a placement indicator' in P. Grunwell (ed.). *Applied Linguistics in Society*, (pp. 80–7). London: CILT.

Meara, P., J. Milton, and N. Lorenzo-Dus. 2001. *Language Aptitude Tests: Lognostics*. Swansea: Express Publishing.

Michaelis, L. A. 2006. 'Construction Grammar' in K. Brown (ed.) vol. 3, pp. 73–84.

Ministry of Defence. 1966. *Trumpet and Bugle Calls for the Army*. London: Her Majesty's Stationery Office.

Mithen, S. 1996. *The Prehistory of the Mind*. London: Thames and Hudson.

Mithen, S. 2005. *The Singing Neanderthals*. London: Weidenfeld and Nicolson.

Mithun, M. 1989. 'The acquisition of polysynthesis'. *Journal of Child Language* 16: 285–312.

Moon, R. 1998. *Fixed Expressions and Idioms in English*. Oxford: Clarendon Press.

Moon, R. 2006. 'Corpus approaches to idiom' in K. Brown (ed.) vol. 3, pp. 230–4.

Moore, L. A. and B. H. Davis. 2002. 'Quilting narrative: Using repetition techniques to help elderly communicators'. *Geriatric Nursing* 23/5: 262–6.

Myles, F. 2004. 'From data to theory: The over-representation of linguistic knowledge in SLA'. *Transactions of the Philological Society* 102/2: 139–68.

Myles, F., R. Hooper, and R. Mitchell. 1998. 'Rote or rule? Exploring the role of formulaic language in classroom foreign language learning'. *Language Learning* 48/3: 323–63.

Myles, F., R. Mitchell, and J. Hooper. 1999. 'Interrogative chunks in French L2: A basis for creative construction?' *Studies in Second Language Acquisition* 21/1: 49–80.

Namba, K. 2008. 'Formulaic language in bilingual children's code-switching'. PhD thesis, Centre for Language and Communication Research, Cardiff University.

Nattinger, J. R. and J. S. DeCarrico. 1992. *Lexical Phrases and Language Teaching*. Oxford: Oxford University Press.

Nesselhauf, N. 2005. *Collocations in a Learner Corpus*. Amsterdam: John Benjamins.

Newsome, G. 2005. 'An estimate of the size of the phrasal E lexicon of aircraft maintenance engineers'. Masters dissertation, Department of Linguistics, University of Canterbury, Christchurch, New Zealand.

Noice, H. and T. Noice. 2006. 'What studies of actors and acting can tell us about memory and cognitive functioning'. *Current Directions in Psychological Science* 15/1: 14–18.

Nunberg, G., I. A. Sag, and T. Wasow. 1994. 'Idioms'. *Language* 70/3: 491–538.

Nusbaum, H. C. and H. Shintel. 2006. 'Speech synthesis' in K. Brown (ed.) vol. 12, pp. 19–31.

Oelschlaeger, M. L. and J. S. Damico. 1998. 'Spontaneous verbal repetition: A social strategy in aphasic conversation'. *Aphasiology* 12/11: 971–88.

Olson, D. R. 1977. 'From utterance to text: The bias of language in speech and writing'. *Harvard Educational Review* 47: 257–81.

Olson, D. R. 1994. *The World on Paper*. Cambridge: Cambridge University Press.

Ong, W. 1992. 'Writing is a technology that restructures thought' in P. Downing, S. D. Lima, and M. Noonan (eds.). *The Linguistics of Literacy*, (pp. 293–319). Amsterdam: John Benjamins.

Onnis, L., M. Christiansen, and N. Chater. 2006. 'Human language processing: Connectionist models' in K. Brown (ed.) vol. 5, pp. 401–9.

Orange, J. B. 2001. 'Family caregivers, communication and Alzheimer's disease' in M. L. Hummert and J. F. Nussbaum (eds.). *Aging, Communication and Health*, (pp. 225–48). Mahwah, NJ: Lawrence Elbaum.

Orwell, G. 1946. 'Politics and the English language'. *Horizon: A Review of Literature and Art* 64/April.

Orwell, G. 1949. *Nineteen Eighty-four*. London: Secker & Warburg/Penguin.

Papagno, C. and A. Genoni. 2004. 'The role of syntactic competence in idiom comprehension: A study on aphasic patients'. *Journal of Neurolinguistics* 17: 371–82.

Papagno, C., F. Lucchelli, S. Muggia, and S. Rizzo. 2003. 'Idiom comprehension in Alzheimer's disease: The role of the central executive'. *Brain* 126: 2419–30.

Papagno, C., P. Tabossi, M. R. Colombo, and P. Zampetti. 2004. 'Idiom comprehension in aphasic patients'. *Brain and Language* 89: 226–34.

Parry, A. 1971. 'Introduction' in A. Parry (ed.). *The Making of Homeric Verse: The Collected Papers of Milman Parry*. (pp. ix–lxii). Oxford: Clarendon Press.

Parry, M. 1928/1971. 'The traditional epithet in Homer' in A. Parry (ed.). *The Making of Homeric Verse: The Collected Papers of Milman Parry*, (pp. 1–190). Oxford: Clarendon Press.

Parry, M. 1930/1971. 'Studies in the epic technique of oral verse-making. I. Homer and the Homeric style' in A. Parry (ed.). *The Making of Homeric Verse: The Collected Papers of Milman Parry*, (pp. 266–324). Oxford: Clarendon Press.

Paul, L. K., D. Van Lancker Sidtis, B. Schieffer, R. Dietrich, and W. S. Brown. 2003. 'Communicative deficits in agenesis of the corpus collosum: Non-literal language and affective prosody'. *Brain and Language* 85: 313–24.

Paul, R. 2004. 'Autism' in R. D. Kent (ed.). *The MIT Handbook of Communication Disorders*, (pp. 115–19). Cambridge, MA: MIT Press.

Pawley, A. and F. H. Syder. 1983a. 'Natural selection in syntax: Notes on adaptive variation and change in vernacular and literary grammar'. *Journal of Pragmatics* 7: 551–79.

Pawley, A. and F. H. Syder. 1983b. 'Two puzzles for linguistic theory: Nativelike selection and nativelike fluency' in J. C. Richards and R. W. Schmidt (eds.). *Language and Communication.*, (pp. 191–226). New York: Longman.

Perera, N. S. 2001. 'The role of prefabricated language in young children's second language acquisition'. *Bilingual Research Journal* 25/3: 327–56.

Perkins, L., A. Whitworth, and R. Lesser. 1998. 'Conversing in dementia: A conversation analytic approach'. *Journal of Neurolinguistics* 11/1–2: 33–53.

Peters, A. M. 1983. *Units of Language Acquisition.* Cambridge: Cambridge University Press.

Poeppel, D. and G. Hickok. 2004. 'Towards a new functional anatomy of language'. *Cognition* 92/1–2: 1–12.

Powell, R. 2000a. 'The bugle's tale (part 1)'. *Band International: Journal of the International Military Music Society* 22/1: 16–17.

Powell, R. 2000b. 'The bugle's tale (part 2)'. *Band International: Journal of the International Military Music Society* 22/3: 114–18.

Prizant, B. M. 1983. 'Language acquisition and communicative behavior in autism: Toward an understanding of the "whole" of it'. *Journal of Speech and Hearing Disorders* 48: 296–307.

Prizant, B. M. and J. F. Duchan. 1981. 'The functions of immediate echolalia in autistic children'. *Journal of Speech and Hearing Disorders* 46/3: 241–49.

Pullum, G. and B. Scholz. 2008. 'Language and the infinitude claim'. http://ling.ed.ac. uk/~gpullum/bcscholz/Infinitude.pdf. Accessed 28.01.08.

Qi, Y. 2006. 'A longitudinal study on the use of formulaic sequences in monologues of Chinese tertiary-level EFL learners'. PhD thesis, Applied Linguistics Program, Nanjing University, Nanjing.

Qualls, C. D., J. M. Lantz, R. M. Pietrzyk, G. W. Blood, and C. S. Hammer. 2004. 'Comprehension of idioms in adolescents with language-based learning disabilities compared to their typically developing peers'. *Journal of Communication Disorders* 37: 295–311.

Rabiner, L. R. and B.-H. Juang. 2006. 'Speech recognition: Statistical methods' in K. Brown (ed.) vol. 12, pp. 1–18.

Read, J. and P. Nation. 2004. 'Measurement of formulaic sequences' in N. Schmitt (ed.), pp. 23–35.

Rehbein, J. 1987. 'Multiple formulae: Aspects of Turkish migrant workers' German in intercultural communication' in K. Knapp, W. Enninger, and A. Knapp-Potthoff (eds.). *Analysing Intercultural Communication*, (pp. 215–48). Berlin: Mouton.

Reis, A. and A. Castro-Caldas. 1997. 'Illiteracy: A cause for biased cognitive development'. *Journal of the International Neurological Society* 3: 444–50.

Roberts, J. M. A. 1989. 'Echolalia and comprehension in autistic children'. *Journal of Autism and Developmental Disorders* 19/2: 271–81.

Rock, F. 2005. '"I've picked some up from a colleague": Language, sharing and communities of practice in an institutional setting' in D. Barton and K. Tusting (eds.). *Beyond Communities of Practice: Language, Power and Social Context*, (pp. 77–104). Cambridge: Cambridge University Press.

Rock, F. 2007. *Communicating Rights: The Language of Arrest and Detention.* Basingstoke: Palgrave Macmillan.

Rubin, D. C. 1995. *Memory in Oral Traditions: The Cognitive Psychology of Epic, Ballads, and Counting-out Rhymes.* New York: Oxford University Press.

Rutter, M. 1968. 'Concepts of autism'. *Journal of Child Psychology and Psychiatry* 9: 1–25.

Rydell, P. J. and P. Mirenda. 1991. 'The effects of two levels of linguistic constraint on echolalia and generative language production in children with autism'. *Journal of Autism and Developmental Disorders* 21/2: 131–57.

Sag, I., T. Baldwin, F. Bond, A. Copestake, and D. Flickinger. 2002. 'Multiword expressions: A pain in the neck for NLP' in A. Gelbukh (ed.). *Computational Linguistics and Intelligent Text Processing: Third International Conference, Mexico City*, (pp. 1–15). Heidelberg/ Berlin: Springer-Verlag.

Saleem, A. 2007. 'New immigration rules to hit care home staff'. News report, 7 August. *Surrey Care Association*.

Schmitt, N., (ed.). 2004. *Formulaic Sequences: Acquisition, Processing and Use*. Amsterdam: John Benjamins.

Schmitt, N., Z. Dörnyei, S. Adolphs, and V. Durow. 2004. 'Knowledge and acquisition of formulaic sequences' in N. Schmitt (ed.), pp. 55–71.

Scribner, S. and M. Cole. 1981. *The Psychology of Literacy*. Cambridge, MA: Harvard University Press.

Searle, J. R. 1971. 'What is a speech act?' in J. R. Searle (ed.). *The Philosophy of Language*, (pp. 39–54). Oxford: Oxford University Press.

Segalowitz, N. and E. Gatbonton. 1995. 'Automaticity and lexical skills in second language fluency: Implications for computer assisted language learning'. *Computer Assisted Language Learning* 8/2–3: 129–49.

Seidlhofer, B. 2004. 'Research perspectives on teaching English as a lingua franca'. *Annual Review of Applied Linguistics* 24: 209–39.

Silberman, S. 2000. 'Talking to strangers'. *Wired* 8.05. http://www.wired.com/wired/ archive/8.05/translation.html. Accessed 12.05.08

Silk, M. 2004. *Homer: The Iliad*. (2nd edition). Cambridge: Cambridge University Press.

Sinclair, J. M. 1987. 'Collocation: A progress report' in R. Steele and T. Threadgold (eds.). *Language Topics: Essays in Honour of Michael Halliday*, (pp. 319–32). Amsterdam: John Benjamins.

Sinclair, J. M. 1991. *Corpus, Concordance, Collocation*. Oxford: Oxford University Press.

Sinclair, J. M. 2004. 'Preface' in B. Lewandowska-Tomaszczyk (ed.). *Practical Applications in Language and Computers*, (pp. 7–11). Frankfurt-am-Main: Peter Lang.

Skelton, J. R. 2005. 'Everything you were afraid to ask about communication skills'. *British Journal of General Practice* 55: 40–6.

Skelton, J. R. and F. D. R. Hobbs. 1999. 'Concordancing: Use of language-based research in medical communication'. *The Lancet* 353: 108–11.

Smith, K. 2006. 'The protolanguage debate: Bridging the gap?' in A. Cangelosi, A. Smith, and K. Smith (eds.). *The Evolution of Language: Proceedings of the 6th International Conference*, (pp. 315–22). London: World Scientific.

Smith, R. W. 2006. 'Natural language interface' in K. Brown (ed.). *Encyclopedia of Language and Linguistics* (2nd edition). Vol. 8, (pp. 496–503). Oxford: Elsevier.

Snowdon, D. 2001. *Aging with Grace*. London: Fourth Estate.

Snowdon, D. 2003. 'Healthy aging and dementia: Findings from the nun study'. *Annals of International Medicine* 139/5 (2): 450–54.

Snowdon, D., S. Kemper, J. A. Mortimer, L. H. Greiner, D. R. Wekstein, and W. R. Markesbery. 1996. 'Linguistic ability in early life and cognitive function and alzheimer's disease in late life. Findings from the nun study'. *Journal of the American Medical Association* 275/7: 528–32.

Sperber, D. and D. Wilson. 1995. *Relevance: Communication and Cognition* (2nd edition). Oxford: Blackwell.

Spöttl, C. and M. McCarthy. 2004. 'Comparing knowledge of formulaic sequences across L1, L2, L3 and L4' in N. Schmitt (ed.), pp. 191–225.

Sprenger, S. A. 2003. *Fixed Expressions and the Production of Idioms*. Nijmegen: Max Planck Institute.

Sprenger, S. A., W. J. M. Levelt, and G. Kempen. 2006. 'Lexical access during the production of idiomatic phrases'. *Journal of Memory and Language* 54: 161–84.

Stefanowitsch, A. and S. T. Gries. 2003. 'Collostructions: Investigating the interaction of words and constructions'. *International Journal of Corpus Linguistics* 8/2: 209–43.

Stevick, R. D. 1962. 'The oral-formulaic analyses of old English verse'. *Speculum* 37/3: 382–89.

Stubbs, M. 1993. 'British traditions in text analysis: From Firth to Sinclair' in M. Baker, G. Francis, and E. Tognini-Bonelli (eds.). *Text and Technology: In Honour of John Sinclair*, (pp. 1–33). Amsterdam: John Benjamins.

Stubbs, M. 2001. 'Computer-assisted text and corpus analysis: Lexical cohesion and communicative competence' in D. Schiffrin, D. Tannen, and H. E. Hamilton (eds.). *Handbook of Discourse Analysis*, (pp. 304–20). Oxford: Blackwell.

Stubbs, M. 2002. 'Two quantitative methods of studying phraseology in English'. *International Journal of Corpus Linguistics* 7/2: 215–44.

Stubbs, M. 2006. 'Technology and phraseology: With some notes on the history of corpus linguistics'. Paper presented at *Exploring the Lexis-Grammar Interface, University of Hanover*, 5–7 October.

Stubbs, M. 2007. 'On texts, corpora and models of language' in M. Hoey, M. Mahlberg, M. Stubbs, and W. Teubert (eds.). *Text, Discourse and Corpora*, (pp. 127–61). London: Continuum.

Tannen, D. 1984. *Conversational Style: Analysing Talk Among Friends*. Norwood, NJ: Ablex.

Tao, H. and C. Meyer. 2006. 'Gapped coordinations in English: Form, usage and implications for linguistic theory'. *Corpus Linguistics and Linguistic Theory* 2/2: 129–63.

Taylor, J. R. 2002. *Cognitive Grammar*. Oxford: Oxford University Press.

Thackeray, W. M. 1855/1964. *The Rose and the Ring*. London: Puffin.

Thurston, W. R. 1987. 'Processes of change in the languages of north-western New Britain'. *Pacific Linguistics B99*: Canberra: The Australian National University.

Thurston, W. R. 1989. 'How exoteric languages build a lexicon: Esoterogeny in west New Britain' in R. Harlow and R. Hooper (eds.). VICAL 1: *Oceanic Languages. Papers from the Fifth International Conference on Austronesian Linguistics, Auckland, New Zealand, January 1988*, (pp. 555–79.). Auckland: Linguistic Society of New Zealand.

Thurston, W. R. 1994. 'Renovation and innovation in the languages of north-western New Britain' in T. Dutton and D. T. Tryon (eds.). *Language Contact and Change in the Austronesian World*, (pp. 573–609). Berlin and New York: Mouton de Gruyter.

Tiersma, P. 1999. *Legal Language*. Chicago: Chicago University Press.

Todman, J., N. Alm, and L. Elder. 1994a. 'Computer-aided conversation: A prototype system for nonspeaking people with physical disabilities'. *Applied Psycholinguistics* 15: 45–73.

Todman, J., L. Elder, N. Alm, and P. File. 1994b. 'Sequential dependencies in computer-aided conversation'. *Journal of Pragmatics* 21: 141–69.

Todman, J., P. File, and S. Grant. 1997. 'TALK in different contexts'. *Communication Matters* 11/1: 17–19.

Todman, J. and E. Lewins. 1996. 'Conversation rate of a non-vocal person with motor neurone disease using the TALK system'. *International Journal of Rehabilitation Research* 19: 285–87.

Todman, J., E. Lewins, P. File, N. Alm, and L. Elder. 1995. 'Use of a communication aid (TALK) by a non-speaking person with cerebral palsy'. *Communication Matters* 9: 18–21.

Todman, J., D. Rankin, and P. File. 1999a. 'Enjoyment and perceived competence in computer-aided conversations with new and familiar partners'. *International Journal of Rehabilitation Research* 22: 153–54.

Todman, J., D. Rankin, and P. File. 1999b. 'The use of stored text in computer-aided conversation: A single-case experiment'. *Journal of Language and Social Psychology* 18/3: 320–42.

Tognini-Bonelli, E. 2001. *Corpus Linguistics at Work*. Amsterdam: John Benjamins.

Tomasello, M. 1998. 'Introduction: A cognitive-functional perspective on language structure' in M. Tomasello (ed.). *The New Psychology of Language*, (pp. vii–xxiii). Mahwah, NJ: Lawrence Erlbaum.

Tomasello, M. 2000. 'Do young children have adult syntactic competence?' *Cognition* 74: 209–53.

Tomasello, M. 2003. 'Introduction: Some surprises for psychologists' in M. Tomasello (ed.). *The New Psychology of Language, Vol.2*, (pp. 1–14). Mahwah, NJ: Lawrence Erlbaum.

Tomasello, M. 2005. 'Beyond formalities: The case of language acquisition'. *The Linguistic Review* 22: 183–97.

Tompkins, C. A., W. Fassbinder, M. T. Lehman-Blake, and A. Baumgaertner. 2002. ,The nature and implications of right hemisphere language disorders: Issues in search of answers' in A. E. Hillis (ed.). *The Handbook of Adult Language Disorders*, (pp. 429–48). New York: Psychology Press.

Toolan, M. 2006. 'Narrative: Linguistic and structural theories' in K. Brown (ed.) vol. 8, pp. 459–73.

Trudgill, P. 1989. 'Contact and isolation in linguistic change' in L. E. Breivik and E. H. Jahr (eds.). *Language Change: Contributions to the Study of its Causes*, (pp. 227–37). Berlin: Mouton de Gruyter.

Trudgill, P. 2002. 'Linguistic and social typology' in J. K. Chambers, P. Trudgill, and N. Schilling-Estes (eds.). *Handbook of Language Variation and Change*, (pp. 707–28). Oxford: Blackwell.

Tucker, G. 1996. 'So grammarians haven't the faintest idea: Reconciling lexis-oriented and grammar-oriented approaches to language' in R. Hasan, C. Cloran, and K. Butt (eds.). *Functional Descriptions: Theory in Practice*, (pp. 145–78). Amsterdam: John Benjamins.

Tucker, G. 2007. 'Between lexis and grammar: Towards a systemic functional account of phraseology' in R. Hasan and C. Matthiessen (eds.). *Continuing Discourse on Language: A Functional Perspective*, (pp. 951–75). London: Equinox.

Underwood, G., N. Schmitt, and A. Galpin. 2004. 'An eye-movement study into the processing of formulaic sequences' in N. Schmitt (ed.), pp. 153–72.

Universal Networking Language. *Specifications: Version 2005*. Available from http://www.undl.org/unlsys/unl/unl2005/. Accessed 10.02.08.

University of Redlands. 2001. 'Linguist promotes airline safety through language'. 27 September. http://redlandsapps.redlands.edu//news/archive/092701a.htm. Accessed 10.02.08.

Van Lancker, D. 1987. 'Nonpropositional speech: Neurolinguistic studies' in A. W. Ellis (ed.). *Progress in the Psychology of Language, Vol 3*, (pp. 49–118). Hillsdale, NJ: Lawrence Erlbaum.

Van Lancker, D., G. J. Canter, and D. Terbeek. 1981. ' Disambiguation of ditropic sentences: Acoustic and phonetic cues'. *Journal of Speech and Hearing Research* 24: 330–35.

Van Lancker Sidtis, D. 2002. 'Toward a dual processing model of language: Normal and neurologic studies'. *Language and Cognition Seminar Series 2002–3*. New York: Columbia University. http://www.columbia.edu/~remez/27apr03.pdf. Accessed 10.02.08.

Van Lancker Sidtis, D. 2004. 'When novel sentences spoken or heard for the first time in the history of the universe are not enough: Toward a dual-process model of language'. *International Journal of Communication Disorders* 39/1: 1–44.

Van Lancker Sidtis, D. and W. A. Postman. 2006. 'Formulaic expressions in spontaneous speech of left- and right-hemisphere damaged subjects'. *Aphasiology* 20/5: 411–26.

Van Lancker Sidtis, D. and G. Rallon. 2004. 'Tracking the incidence of formulaic expressions in everyday speech: Methods for classification and verification'. *Language & Communication* 24: 207–40.

Venneri, A., K. E. Forbes-McKay, and M. F. Shanks. 2005. 'Impoverishment of spontaneous language and the prediction of Alzheimer's disease'. *Brain* 128/4: E27.

Verhagen, A. 2003. 'The Dutch way' in A. Verhagen and J. van de Weijer (eds.). *Usage-based Approaches to Dutch*, (pp. 27–57). Utrecht: LOT.

Wagner, A. D., S. A. Bunge, and **D. Badre.** 2004. 'Cognitive control, semantic memory and priming: Contributions from the prefrontal cortex' in M. S. Gazzaniga (ed.). *The Cognitive Neurosciences III*, (pp. 709–25). Cambridge, MA: MIT Press.

Waibel, A. 1996. 'Interactive translation of conversational speech'. *Computer* 29/7: 41–8.

Walenski, M. and **M. T. Ullman.** 2005. 'The science of language'. *The Linguistic Review* 22: 327–46.

Wallace, M. and **A. Wray.** 2006. *Critical Reading and Writing for Postgraduates.* London: Sage.

Walmsley, J. B. 2006. 'Chomsky, Noam' in K. Brown (ed.) vol. 2, pp. 382–4.

Was, C. A. and **D. J. Woltz.** 2007. 'Reexamining the relationship between working memory and comprehension: The role of available long-term memory'. *Journal of Memory and Language* 56: 86–102.

Webb, S. 2007. 'The effects of repetition on vocabulary knowledge'. *Applied Linguistics* 28/1: 46–65.

Webster, J., S. Franklin, and **D. Howard.** 2007. 'An analysis of thematic and phrasal structure in people with aphasia: What more can we learn from the story of Cinderella?' *Journal of Neurolinguistics* 20: 363–94.

Weismer, S. E. 2004. 'Memory and processing capacity' in R. M. Kent (ed.). *MIT Encyclopedia of Communication Disorders*, (pp. 349–52). Cambridge, MA: MIT Press.

Wells, J. C. 2006. *English Intonation: An Introduction.* Cambridge: Cambridge University Press.

Whallon, W. 1969. *Formula, Character, and Context: Studies in Homeric, old English, and Old Testament Poetry.* Washington/Cambridge MA: Center for Hellenic Studies, Washington D.C., and Harvard University Press.

Whorf, B. L. 1956. *Language, Thought, and Reality: Selected Writings.* Edited by John B. Carroll. Cambridge, MA: MIT Press.

Wierzbicka, A. 1996. *Semantics: Primes and Universals.* Oxford: Oxford University Press.

Wiktorsson, M. 2003. *Learning Idiomaticity: A Corpus-based Study of Idiomatic Expressions in Learners' Written Production.* PhD thesis, Lund Studies in English. Vol 105. Lund: Lund University.

Williams, J. N. 1999. 'Memory, attention and inductive learning'. *Studies in Second Language Acquisition* 21: 1–48.

Wolfe, R. 1992. *Writing Comedy: A Guide to Scriptwriting for TV, Radio, Film and Stage.* London: Robert Hale.

Wong Fillmore, L. 1976. *The Second Time Around: Cognitive and Social Strategies in Second Language Acquisition.* PhD thesis, Stanford University.

Wong Fillmore, L. 1979. 'Individual differences in second language acquisition' in C. J. Fillmore, D. Kempler, and W. S.-Y. Wang (eds.). *Individual Differences in Language Ability and Language Behavior*, (pp. 203–28). New York: Academic Press.

Wray, A. 1992. *The Focusing Hypothesis: The Theory of Left-lateralised Language Reexamined.* Amsterdam: John Benjamins.

Wray, A. 1996. 'The occurrence of "occurance" and "alot" of other things "aswell"' in G. M. Blue and R. Mitchell (eds.). *Language and Education*, (pp. 94–106). Clevedon: Multilingual Matters.

Wray, A. 1998. 'Protolanguage as a holistic system for social interaction'. *Language & Communication* 18: 47–67.

Wray, A. 1999. 'Formulaic language in learners and native speakers'. *Language Teaching* 32/4: 213–31.

Wray, A. 2000a. 'Formulaic sequences in second language teaching: Principle and practice'. *Applied Linguistics* 21/4: 463–89.

Wray, A. 2000b. 'Holistic utterances in protolanguage: The link from primates to humans' in C. Knight, M. Studdert-Kennedy, and J. Hurford (eds.). *The Evolutionary Emergence of Language: Social Function and the Origins of Linguistic Form*, (pp. 285–302). New York: Cambridge University Press.

Wray, A. 2002a. 'Dual processing in protolanguage: Competence without performance' in
A. Wray (ed.). *The Transition to Language*, (pp. 113–37). Oxford: Oxford University Press.

Wray, A. 2002b. *Formulaic Language and the Lexicon*. Cambridge: Cambridge University
Press.

Wray, A. 2002c. 'Formulaic language in computer-supported communication: Theory meets
reality'. *Language Awareness* 11/2: 114–31.

Wray, A. 2004. '"Here's one I prepared earlier": Formulaic language learning on television' in
N. Schmitt (ed.), pp. 249–68.

Wray, A. 2008a. 'Formulaic sequences and language disorders' in M. Ball, M. Perkins,
N. Müller, and S. Howard (eds.). *Handbook of Clinical Linguistics*, (pp. 184–97). Oxford:
Blackwell.

Wray, A. 2008b. 'Genes and the conceptualisation of language knowledge'. *Genomics, Society
and Policy* 4/1: 58–72.

Wray, A. 2008c. 'The puzzle of language learning: From child's play to "linguaphobia"'.
Language Teaching 41/2: 255–73.

Wray, A., S. Cox, M. Lincoln, and J. Tryggvason. 2004. 'A formulaic approach to translation at
the post office: Reading the signs'. *Language & Communication* 24: 59–75.

Wray, A. and T. Fitzpatrick. 2008. 'Why can't you just leave it alone? Deviations from
memorized language as a gauge of nativelike competence' in F. Meunier and S. Granger
(eds.). *Phraseology in Language Learning and Teaching*, (pp. 123–48). Amsterdam: John
Benjamins.

Wray, A. and G. W. Grace. 2007. 'The consequences of talking to strangers: Sociocultural
influences on the lexical unit'. *Lingua* 117/3: 543–78.

Wray, A. and K. Namba. 2003. 'Formulaic language in a Japanese-English bilingual child: A
practical approach to data analysis'. *Japan Journal for Multilingualism and Multiculturalism*
9/1: 24–51.

Wray, A. and C. Pegg. (in press). 'The effect of memorized learning on the writing scores of
Chinese IELTS test takers'. In *IELTS Research Reports* 9.

Wray, A. and M. Perkins. 2000. 'The functions of formulaic language: An integrated model'.
Language & Communication 20/1: 1–28.

Wray, A. and J. J. Staczek. 2005. 'One word or two? Psycholinguistic and sociolinguistic
interpretations of meaning in a civil court case'. *International Journal of Speech, Language
and the Law* 12/1: 1–18.

Yorio, C. A. 1989. 'Idiomaticity as an indicator of second language proficiency' in K.
Hyltenstam and L. K. Obler (eds.). *Bilingualism across the Lifespan*, (pp. 55–72).
Cambridge: Cambridge University Press.

Zhanrong, L. 2002. 'Learning strategies of Chinese EFL learners: Review of studies in China'.
RTVU ELT Express: http://www1.openedu.com.cn/elt/2/4.htm. Accessed 10.2.08.

Index